Whole World on Fire

Whole World on Fire

*Organizations, Knowledge, and
Nuclear Weapons Devastation*

Lynn Eden

CORNELL UNIVERSITY PRESS ■ *Ithaca and London*

A volume in the series *Cornell Studies in Security Affairs,*
edited by Robert J. Art, Robert Jervis, and Stephen M. Walt

First published 2004 by Cornell University Press
Printed in the United States of America

Library of Congress Cataloging-in-Publication Data
Eden, Lynn.
    Whole world on fire : organizations, knowledge, and nuclear weapons devastation /
Lynn Eden.
        p. cm. — (Cornell studies in security affairs)
Includes bibliographical references and index.
    ISBN 0-8014-3578-1 (cloth : alk. paper)
    1. United States—Military policy—Decision making.   2. Nuclear warfare—Planning.
3. Nuclear mass fires.   4. Organizational behavior—United States—Case studies.
5. Science—Social aspects—United States—Case studies.   I. Title.   II. Series.
    UA23.E34 2003
    355.02′17′0973—dc21   2003012695

Cloth printing   10 9 8 7 6 5 4 3 2 1

Contents

Figures and Tables

Tables

Acknowledgments

It is a great pleasure to acknowledge those who have given me so much help and made *Whole World on Fire* possible. Ted Postol asked the question that led to this book, and over the years he has been unstintingly generous in helping me to answer it. With remarkable patience, he explained in layperson's terms the physics of mass fire and the rudiments of predicting nuclear blast and fire damage. Ted also collaborated with me on chapter 1.

The insight provided by a number of people in and out of government was essential. I want especially to thank Gilbert Binninger, Horatio Bond, Harold Brode, Vice Admiral Michael Colley (USN, ret.), Richard Grassy, William J. Hall, and Stanley Martin. For help and helpful conversations, I am also grateful to Jana Backovsky, General George Lee Butler (USAF, ret.), General Russell Dougherty (USAF, ret.), Irwin Fieldhouse, Tom Garwin, Major General Edward Giller (USAF, ret.), Fred Gross, John Haltiwanger, Major General Barry Horton (USAF, ret.) Carl Kaysen, Stanley Lawwill, Hugh Lehman, Major General Robert Linhard (USAF), Henry Nash, Bud Parsons, Eugene Sevin, Jerry Strope, and Merit White—not all of whom are alive as I write this. There are at least as many people I cannot thank by name because we spoke on a not-for-attribution basis; I am no less indebted to them. Of course, my acknowledgment in no way implies that those I have named, or not, would agree with what I have written.

I am grateful to archivists Ed Reese, Modern Military Records, National Archives, then located in Washington, D.C.; Tim Johnson in the Air Force Historical Center (now the Air Force Historical Research Agency) at Maxwell Air Force Base, Alabama; and Bill Heimdahl in the Air Force History Office (now the Air Force History Support Office), Bolling Air Force Base, Washington, D.C. I also thank historians of the Air Force Richard Kohn and Walter Poole. Sharon Theobald, of the U.S. Defense Threat Reduction Agency's Information and Analysis Center, provided government photographs of nuclear weapons tests. Vance O. Mitchell told me where to look in the National Archives, shared some documents, and helped me understand the organization of Air Force intelligence in the early post–World War II period. Tami Davis Biddle and David Alan Rosenberg very generously shared documents. Lorna Arnold made queries on the British side regarding documents, and I appreciate her effort.

Most of the documents I used, however, were not in the archives or were not easily found there. For his remarkable help with finding documents and with Freedom of Information Act requests, I thank William Burr, senior analyst at the National Security Archive, George Washington University, for great generosity. Jo Husbands and Daniel Barbiero provided some archival information on the National Academy of Science. Stan Norris and Matthew McKinzie provided information they have painstakingly synthesized on nuclear weapons. Finally, I cannot acknowledge by name those who gave me many of the most important documents I used—none of which are classified, but many of which I would have been unlikely to obtain otherwise. It would be incorrect to infer that the authors of these documents were the ones who provided them. Hal Brode, for example, provided me with only one of the many documents and briefings that he wrote or co-authored.

I have benefited enormously from hard questions and comments at talks I gave at the Peace Studies Program, Cornell University; Mershon Center Joint Series on Foreign Policy and Technology and Security in Post-Soviet Europe, Ohio State University; Seminar on Technology, Defense, and Arms Control, Massachusetts Institute of Technology; Adlai Stevenson Program on Global Security, University of California, Santa Cruz; International Relations Colloquium, Institute of International Studies, University of California, Berkeley; Triangle Universities Security Seminar, University of North Carolina at Chapel Hill; Program on International Politics, Economics, and Security (PIPES), University of Chicago; Olin Institute, Center for International Affairs, Harvard University; Thomas J. Watson Jr. Institute for International Studies, Brown University; and my home institution, the Center for International Security and Cooperation (CISAC), Institute for International Studies, Stanford University. I especially thank those who sent me comments or corresponded after reading talks, papers, or early versions of several chapters.

CISAC has provided great stimulation and support. I do not think I could have written this book anywhere else. I am especially grateful to Chip Blacker, David Holloway, and Scott Sagan for their insight, support, and friendship. I thank Michael May for his collegial counterarguments; I do not know if he will agree with the argument here, but it is stronger for his challenges. I am also grateful to Herb Abrams, George Bunn, Chris Chyba, Sid Drell, Ron Hassner, Deborah Gordon, Gail Lapidus, John W. Lewis, Mike McFaul, Alex Montgomery, William J. Perry, Paul Stares (now at the U.S. Institute of Peace in Washington, D.C.), Steve Stedman, Dean Wilkening, and other colleagues at CISAC for conversations and help. I thank the community of fellows from whom I have learned much over the years and who make CISAC such a pleasure for me. And I thank those at the Center with whom I have worked most closely: Analia Bond, Liz Gardner, Laura Parker, Lisa Saad, and Helen Sutton—and earlier, Gerry Bowman and Rosemary

Hamerton-Kelly. I have learned much from other Stanford colleagues; I want particularly to thank James G. March and W. Richard Scott. I appreciate Stephen Schneider's discussion with me about nuclear winter. I thank Julie Sweetkind-Singer for help with maps.

I thank the foundations that have supported my work at CISAC, the Carnegie Corporation of New York and the John D. and Catherine T. MacArthur Foundation. I am additionally grateful to the MacArthur Foundation for a Social Science Research Council–MacArthur Foundation fellowship in International Peace and Security that changed my life and led in a roundabout way to this book. I thank Ruth Adams for her personal interest and Kennette Benedict for help in thinking about organizations.

I have benefited from fine undergraduate research assistants. I especially thank Ben Valentino, Benjamin Olding, Dana Tennille Conley, Filip Stabrowski, and Rhead Enion. Several graduate students have provided indispensable help. I thank Nora Bensahel for her microfilm research, Alex Montgomery for his technical acumen, and the ever resourceful Ron Hassner for help with many aspects of research and photo research.

I have been fortunate to have superb readers throughout the process. David Dessler has read the manuscript at every stage and given me indispensable guidance. Early on he helped me untangle a serious problem; his solution allowed me to proceed with a much better argument. Martha Feldman and Paul Stockton read early and later versions of the manuscript and gave excellent advice (including to keep going). Throughout, Barry O'Neill provided powerful critique leavened with a ridiculous sense of humor. I am grateful to Ashley Ledbetter and Greg Grove for technical exposition of some material. I thank Lorna Arnold, Robert Axelrod, Tami Davis Biddle, Chip Blacker, Bill Burr, Neta Crawford, Bud Duvall, Paul Edwards, Colin Elman, Charlie Glaser, David Holloway, Ron Jepperson, Beth Kier, Donald MacKenzie, Eduard Mark, Rose McDermott, Matthew McKinzie, Steve Miller, Vance Mitchell, David Rosenberg, Scott Sagan, Graham Spinardi, and Chuck Tilly for careful readings of chapters of the manuscript. I thank Hal Brode, Itsie Hull, Alex Montgomery, and Ted Postol for reading the full manuscript.

I have benefited from superb editorial help. I thank Jack Snyder for encouragement and advice. I thank readers for Cornell University Press, Jon Mercer and Robert Jervis, for careful, stimulating, and constructive readings of the full manuscript. I thank an unnamed reader for the Press for thoughtful comments on early chapters. I thank Teresa Lawson and Katherine Goldgeier for exceptional conceptual and line editing at two different stages of the manuscript. I thank Cathi Reinfelder for excellent copy-editing. I thank Louise E. Robbins, at Cornell University Press, for top-notch production editing. I thank Roger Haydon, my editor at the Press—and possibly

the best editor in the universe—for his insight and editorial help throughout the process.

Despite the bounty of help I have received, no doubt errors remain and
my interpretations will annoy. I alone am responsible for what lies within.

Finally, I can hardly begin to express my gratitude to friends and family
who have over the years put up with me and this project. You know who you
are. Above all, I am grateful to Ruth Schoenbach for numerous readings, excellent diagrams on restaurant napkins, and for reminding me that there is
more to life than living with nuclear weapons.

LYNN EDEN

Stanford, California

Whole World on Fire

Introduction

Whole World on Fire is about a puzzle that is morbid, arcane, and consequential. Morbid, because it involves the devastation caused by nuclear weapons. Arcane, because it involves secret and obscure calculations by a government bureaucracy tucked away deep within U.S. military intelligence. And consequential, because it involves decisions at the highest level of government about using nuclear weapons.

The puzzle begins over a half century ago, in the years immediately following the end of World War II, and it continues to the present: How and why, for more than half a century, has the U.S. government seriously underestimated the damage that nuclear weapons would cause? How and why did the government, in devising its plans to fight strategic nuclear war shortly after World War II, develop detailed knowledge about the blast damage caused by nuclear weapons but fail to develop knowledge about an even more devastating effect? That effect was mass fire (popularly termed "firestorm"), such as the fire that burned down Hiroshima.

Knowledge of blast damage was codified into handbooks and computer programs used in war planning. Thus, military officers and others who were not highly technically trained could routinely predict damage to targeted structures and make choices of weapons and "designated ground zeros." However, no such handbooks or computer programs were developed to predict fire damage, and, as a result, no account of fire damage was taken in U.S. nuclear war plans.

The government's failure to predict fire damage in its plans to wage nuclear war has serious policy implications. War plans provide an important basis for procurement decisions. Because it has underestimated the damage caused by nuclear weapons, the United States has procured many more weapons than necessary to cause even the very high levels of damage demanded by the war plans. Before the major Cold War buildup of nuclear weapons, President Eisenhower's science adviser, George Kistiakowsky, wrote that because U.S. nuclear war planners "used blast effect as the only criterion of damage and neglected thermal radiation [and the] fires which will be caused by it . . . the question may be raised as to whether [it results] in overkill and will create unjustified additional 'force requirements.'" Looking back on the buildup that occurred during the Cold War, atomic scientist Hans Bethe said, "The numbers of weapons which were accumulated by both sides were absolutely absurd. Twenty thousand, thirty thousand—what do you do after the other country is already destroyed? . . . It makes absolutely no sense to have such numbers."[1]

War plans are the government's main means for envisioning what would happen were nuclear weapons used, and they deeply influence the views of the military officers and others who would act in a crisis. Because fire damage has been ignored for the past half century, high-level U.S. decision makers have been poorly informed, if informed at all, about the damage that nuclear weapons would cause. As a result, any U.S. decision to use nuclear weapons—for example, a political decision to employ a "limited" option to signal "restraint"—almost certainly would have been predicated on insufficient and misleading information. If nuclear weapons had been used, the physical, social, and political effects would have been far more devastating than anticipated.

In the post–Cold War period, the United States and Russia still have thousands of strategic nuclear weapons, and other countries also have substantial numbers, so these issues remain important. Any decision or threat to use nuclear weapons would in all likelihood be based on a severe underestimate of the damage that would result. Indeed, in the South Asian crisis of May 2002, the United States specifically sought to warn Indian and Pakistani leaders of the consequences of a nuclear exchange. However, a U.S. defense intelligence assessment prepared for that purpose was based on blast effects alone. The study estimated that twelve million people would be killed, but it did not include deaths from mass fire.[2] If it had, the estimate would have been much higher.

How could this systematic failure to assess nuclear fire damage have persisted for more than half a century?

The most common response is that fire damage from nuclear weapons is inherently less predictable than blast damage. In this view, no matter how severe fire damage might be at times, its probability and range vary so greatly that it cannot usefully be predicted for war planning purposes.

I claim otherwise. Nuclear fire damage is as predictable as blast damage: Mass fire and extensive fire damage would occur in almost every circumstance in which nuclear weapons were detonated in a suburban or urban area.[3] The circumstances in which mass fire damage would not occur—for example, during torrential rainstorms—are rare, and their probabilities would be calculable in advance. The uncertainties in the range at which mass fire would cause damage are no greater than the uncertainties associated with blast. Even more important, for the higher-yield nuclear weapons that have dominated the U.S. and Soviet/Russian arsenals for many decades, the range of severe damage from fire is likely to be significantly greater than the range of severe damage from blast. Under most circumstances, damage from mass fire would extend two to five times farther than blast damage.[4]

Establishing that fire damage is as predictable as blast damage and in many cases more consequential is an important part of this book, but it is not my goal to write a technical treatise. Others have done detailed analyses predicting the damage that mass fires would cause, and I draw on their work. Given that fire damage is as predictable as and generally more devastating than blast damage, my question is, Why did the government concentrate on developing predictions of damage from blast but largely ignore mass fire?

I approach this as a problem of the social construction of organizational knowledge in which the answer lies not in the physical world but in our history. I introduce two concepts: "knowledge-laden organizational routines" and "organizational frames." The process by which officers use handbooks or computer programs to predict damage to structures is a knowledge-laden *routine,* a mundane set of operations done repeatedly—the everyday stuff of organizational life. It is *knowledge-laden* because it carries within it very expensively acquired expert understandings and predictions. In this case, the everyday activities of organizational life involve developing plans to wage nuclear war, and the expert understandings are predictions of damage caused by nuclear weapons.

So why did the U.S. military develop organizational routines that predicted blast damage but not fire damage? Why has this system, much refined, endured to the present day?

Knowledge-laden routines are solutions to problems that those in organizations have decided to solve. I call the approaches to problem solving used by those in organizations—how problems are chosen and represented, how strategies are developed to solve them, and how constraints and requirements are placed on possible solutions—*organizational frames.*[5] Organizational frames encounter the present and look to the future. At the same time, they embody the past: foundational understandings of organizational mission, long-standing collective assumptions and knowledge about the world, and earlier patterns of attention to problems and solutions. All of this shapes how problems are later defined and how solutions are developed. Once solutions are established as knowledge-laden routines, they enable actors in organizations to carry out new actions, but they simultaneously constrain those new actions.

Whole World on Fire explains how such organizational frames shaped problem solving even in the face of new phenomena—here, the extraordinarily destructive atomic and hydrogen bombs. *How* this works is what I seek to explain. Always, my account is informed by the idea that organizations draw on past practices and ideas even as they innovate to solve new problems.

Whole World on Fire is about science, technology, organizations, and history. Predictions of blast damage coded in handbooks and later in computer software were simultaneously a result of *scientific* knowledge of the effects of nuclear weapons, a *technological* tool used to predict damage to targeted structures, and an *organizational routine* that shaped and was shaped by organizational conceptions of mission and of the outside world. They were also a result of complex *historical* processes.

Each aspect invites investigation. When I began my research in the early 1990s, I had two distinct historical investigations in mind, one focused on the decade of the 1980s, the other on the decade following World War II. First, I wanted to understand the outcome of an effort in the 1980s by a few scientists, doing exploratory studies for the Defense Nuclear Agency, to incorporate the damaging effects of mass fire into U.S. nuclear targeting routines. However, when I began this project, I did not know what the outcome would be. A decision on whether to incorporate fire damage had not yet been reached. Thus, my explanation would have to be able to explain *either* outcome. This forced me to take the idea of historical contingency very seriously; I could not escape understanding that whatever the outcome would be, it could have gone differently. (I learned in 1993 that the military decided in early 1992 to stop such work and to make no further effort to incorporate fire damage into nuclear war planning. I learned later that the issue was being revisited and, as far as I know, remains under consideration.)

Second, I knew that what was at stake could be explained only by examining the years soon after World War II, when knowledge about blast damage from nuclear weapons was first developed and codified and fire damage largely ignored. The newly formed U.S. Air Force was the organizational center of these activities. Those in targeting intelligence for the Air Force, particularly a small group concerned with the physical vulnerability of structures, began efforts to analyze and codify predictions of blast damage caused by nuclear weapons. This group played a significant role in shaping inquiry in postwar atmospheric nuclear weapons tests.

There were some historical mysteries in this period. The extensive use of incendiary weapons by the United States toward the end of World War II and the mass fire damage caused to both Hiroshima and Nagasaki by atomic bombs had led to the development of considerable expertise on the fire damage caused by bombing. However, those in Air Force Intelligence apparently did not use this knowledge in the early postwar period to develop damage predictions for atomic weapons. Why not? Further, an apparently contradictory pattern of continuity and change in bombing doctrine was puzzling. On the one hand, the basic categories that target intelligence analysts used throughout World War II and in the postwar period were consistent with "precision" bombing doctrine. On the other, by the end of the war, U.S. bombing operations had shifted to bombing large urban areas rather than "pinpoint," or specific, targets, and U.S. war plans in the late 1940s also targeted urban areas. Had there been a shift in doctrine or not? How was this to be understood?

As I grappled with issues of continuity and change, I was drawn back to the formative period of air force doctrine in the 1920s and 1930s. (Although my questions first ran backward in time, the historical analysis of this book proceeds in conventional chronological order.)

Lurking in these historical questions are broad organizational issues about how scientific knowledge is created by organizations and how that knowledge is ultimately encoded in technology and organizational routines. *Whole World on Fire* explores how organizations decide what they need to investigate in the physical world, and on what basis they design their investigations. It explains how organizations encode their understandings of the physical world in the technologies they use in their routines and in the technologies they produce.

Although the specific problem I discuss—predicting damage caused by nuclear weapons for use in nuclear war planning—is undeniably weird, the kind of organizational processes I examine, in which knowledge and assumptions about the physical and social world are encoded in documents, routines, and technologies, is pervasive in organizational life: aircraft pilots' checklists and procedures for takeoff, actuarial tables used to determine health and life insurance rates, routines used to navigate ships into harbor, hospital protocols for medical treatment, and the congeries of knowledge-laden routines and technologies required to build computers, aircraft, space shuttles, skyscrapers, and bridges.[6] Organizational routine builds technology, and technology builds organizational routine.

The potential for mishap is clear, not only because procedures may not be properly followed but because physical processes may be poorly understood or unanticipated, so their representation in documents, routines, and technologies may be inaccurate or incomplete. For example, the shipbuilding organization that built the *Titanic* did not understand just how brittle was the steel plate used in its construction; had this vulnerability been understood, the ship would in all likelihood have been designed differently (as was its sister ship after the *Titanic* sank).[7] In designing city buses, Grumman tested its models on streets that lacked New York City's potholes; the buses were destroyed when driven on real New York streets.[8] The builders of the World Trade Center designed it to withstand the impact of a Boeing 707, the largest jet airliner of the early 1960s, but not to withstand the fire that would be produced by many thousands of gallons of jet fuel burning inside the building.[9] I discuss these, and related cases, in the book's conclusion.

How do organizations build knowledge when they have little or no experience from which to learn? Untested plans, predictions, and technologies are not necessarily more vulnerable to mistakes, but they are more vulnerable to having those mistakes go undetected and uncorrected for long periods of time. In this case, the situation is exacerbated by conditions of secrecy that limit professional and public scrutiny. Because analysis and experimentation in the U.S. atmospheric nuclear weapons tests in the 1950s overwhelmingly focused on blast damage, Air Force Intelligence developed a strikingly incomplete representation of the physical world, in which the consequences of mass fire were not modeled. This incomplete representation became embodied in organizational routines and persisted for decades. Virtually all of the detailed predictions of damage were secret; what was not secret was so obscure that there has been no public oversight.

Another consideration is the form and content of the scientific and engineering knowledge that organizations use in problem solving. Goals shape what knowledge organizations seek and some of the requirements that solutions must meet. At the same time, the available expertise shapes the specific ways that organizations define problems and carry out investigations, and the available and valued forms of likely solution. Yet some of that expertise is not simply sought out by organizations but developed by them.

This enmeshing of organizational goals and disciplinary knowledge is particularly germane to understanding how those in Air Force Intelligence specified the form that damage prediction should take. For doctrinal reasons, they strongly preferred to predict damage to specific structures rather than to large areas. They also had more confidence in predictions that *looked* like those made by civil engineers rather than by fire protection engineers, who had less status. Although fire protection engineers had developed some ability to predict fire damage in World War II using nonquantitative visual analysis of maps, air force analysts characterized these predictions as imprecise, as "by gee and by gosh," because they did not conform to the standards of blast damage predictions made by civil engineers. Organizational goals shaped what knowledge was sought, but the experts who were consulted defined the standards used by the organization.

Writing about contemporary issues in science and technology has presented an uncommon problem in method and presentation. Scholars writing about the history and sociology of science and technology generally concentrate on controversies in which consensus, or "closure," has already been reached.[10] For example, there was controversy over whether inertial navigation technology could work until its success was proved shortly after World War II. There was debate about whether O-rings functioned properly in sealing space shuttles' booster rockets until investigation after the *Challenger* shuttle disaster determined that they had not.[11] In such cases, authors do not have to persuade the reader about the state of truth in the science or the workability of the technology under investigation.

This case does not offer the luxury of closure. The conventional wisdom among the scientists, civilians, and military officers who compose what is called the "nuclear weapons effects community" is that damage from blast is predictable but damage from mass fire is not. At the same time, the physicists who have most closely analyzed and investigated damage from mass fire—nuclear weapons effects expert Harold Brode and his colleagues at Pacific-Sierra Research Corporation, and Massachusetts Institute of Technology (MIT) professor Theodore Postol—have concluded that the conventional wisdom is wrong, and that damage from mass fire can be reasonably predicted. Their reports and published work have been met by skepticism but, so far as I know, by no published refutation. Because a controversy, or even potential controversy, has not been resolved does not mean that some understandings are not better than others. I therefore predicate my social historical questions on the physical understanding that damage from mass fire can indeed be predicted, and that it will very often be more extensive than damage from blast.

It is one thing to know that nuclear weapons are enormously destructive. It is another to have a detailed picture of the damage that would result from their use. Chapter 1 provides the empirical basis for my claim that the U.S. government has seriously underestimated damage from nuclear weapons. I compare the predictions of damage that would result from both blast and fire with the much lower levels of damage predicted when only blast is taken into account.

Chapter 2 presents and critiques alternative explanations for why organizational routines were developed to predict only blast damage. I also explain the idea of organizational frames; that is, the approaches used by those in organizations to define problems and seek solutions. I argue that earlier ways of knowing and doing in the Air Force shaped later inquiry. The process of problem solving produced organizational capacity in the form of expertise, specialized research programs, and knowledge-laden routines. The organizational capacity to predict blast damage but not fire damage resulted from the choices of actors, not from the physical world itself. It also shaped widely shared understandings of the reasons for organizational action.

The rest of *Whole World on Fire* develops my argument historically. Chapter 3 sketches the development of the air force doctrine of precision strategic bombing from the 1930s through World War II. From before World War II, air force officers understood the most important cause of damage to targets to be blast caused by high-explosive bombs. This shaped problem solving, and a "blast damage frame" became deeply instantiated in the organizational routines of the U.S. Air Force. By contrast, British doctrine and practice emphasized area bombing using incendiary weapons, leading to a "fire damage frame." With the all-out mobilization of World War II, the United States devoted some attention to fire damage, but far more attention and resources were put to predicting and optimizing blast damage.

The decade following the end of World War II proved critical to my story. In chapters 4 through 7 I show how organizational attention and resources were focused on solving problems related to the prediction of nuclear blast damage. I also show the lack of attention to predicting nuclear fire damage. Chapter 4 traces the great continuities between World War II and the early postwar period. Despite the unprecedented destructive power of the atomic bomb, those in Air Force Intelligence continued to hold the same conception of targets as during the war. Because of the historical association of pinpoint targets with damage from blast, as well as greater confidence in the predictability of blast damage, atomic blast was understood to be the relevant mechanism of destruction. In short, the "blast damage frame" carried over from World War II into the postwar period. The earliest schemes to predict damage from atomic bombs, devised in 1947 and 1948, focused only on blast.

But organizations do not simply solve problems. The process of problem solving shapes organizations. Chapter 5 shows how the early attempts to predict damage from atomic blast led in the early 1950s to an ambitious research agenda to acquire the specific knowledge necessary to make better predictions and to an expansion of organizational expertise. In this period, several outstanding professors of engineering were hired as consultants to help shape the research agenda, to interpret new data, and, above all, to develop the analytical basis for organizational routines that would enable better prediction of blast damage. No comparable research agenda was developed, and no comparable expertise mobilized, to predict damage from fire. By mid-1951, the "Vulnerability Number" system—an improved, if still preliminary, knowledge-laden routine for predicting blast damage—had been devised. This system set the basic form that organizational routines to predict blast damage have had ever since.

Chapter 6 shows how the research agenda that characterized the "blast damage frame" generated significant new knowledge in the U.S. nuclear weapons tests carried out in the early 1950s. Air Force Intelligence participated in these tests and verified and expanded the Vulnerability Number system. But Air Force Intelligence commissioned just a single study to predict mass fire damage. This effort, a reanalysis of the large area fires set during World War II, did not succeed in developing powerful predictions. Other government agencies concerned with civil defense and protection of military equipment did extensive experiments in the nuclear weapons tests on the effects of thermal radiation, but they did not study or predict damage from mass fire.

Chapter 7 returns to the development of organizational routines to predict blast damage. In the early 1950s, at the same time that the Vulnerability Number system was being refined, the hydrogen bomb was invented and tested. For expert engineers whom the government consulted, the increasing yield of nuclear weapons produced new problems in predicting blast damage having to do with the longer duration of the blast wave. By the mid-1950s, analysts had developed a method for calculating blast damage for higher-yield nuclear weapons, and by the late 1950s they had incorporated and simplified their method into a highly refined set of organizational routines. This set of knowledge-laden routines for predicting blast damage was called the VNTK system. (VN stood for Vulnerability Number; T and K denoted, respectively, type of structure and degree of sensitivity to the duration of the blast wave.) Although fire damage scaled up more quickly than blast damage from higher-yield weapons, no effort was made to predict such damage. By the early 1960s, there was a stark contrast between the ability to predict damage from blast and the inability to predict damage from fire.

Chapter 8 shows how a small "fire research community," funded by government agencies concerned with civil defense, reinforced war planners' understanding that mass fire damage was unpredictable. From the mid-1950s through the 1970s, this community of chemical engineers, fire protection engineers, foresters, and others researched many aspects of fire. They produced computer models of house fires, forest fires, and nuclear mass fires. However, their research on mass fires from nuclear weapons did not produce consistent and stable predictions of damage. Indeed, these researchers emphasized the great difficulty of developing such predictions, which buttressed the understanding of war planners that mass fire damage was unpredictable.

In the 1980s, however, something surprising began to happen. As chapter 9 details, the Defense Nuclear Agency, the government agency that directed research on nuclear weapons effects, began an effort, initiated by Harold Brode, to try to predict damage from mass fire for use in war planning. Brode had a decidedly different approach from that of the fire research community. By the early 1990s, Brode and his colleagues had developed a method for predicting both fire and blast damage, and the government came close to incorporating it into nuclear war planning.

Chapter 10 weaves another story into the same decade of the 1980s. Government funding for fire research benefited not only Brode and his colleagues but also researchers in the civil defense–funded fire research community. Throughout the decade, the fire research community claimed that damage from mass fire could not yet be predicted, Brode's work notwithstanding. This view was influential within the government. An ironic conjunction of historical circumstances at the end of the Cold War tipped the balance between these competing views on the predictability of mass fire damage and stopped the government's efforts to develop routines to predict fire damage from nuclear weapons. I then bring the history to the present, mindful of former Secretary of State George Shultz's admonition that "Nothing ever gets settled in this town."[12]

I conclude the book by examining the implications for our understanding of how organizations develop and use knowledge, and how organizations can change.

My historical investigations have drawn from a wide variety of sources, including secondary historical work, archival documents, unclassified but not widely available government reports, and interviews. For the early history, I relied primarily on secondary work, supplemented by some documentary sources and interviews.

For the early post–World War II period, I relied partly on archival sources, including declassified official histories that had been originally classified as confidential, secret, or top secret. I used archival records in the U.S. National Archives in Washington, D.C., and in the Air Force historical archives located at Maxwell Air Force Base, Montgomery, Alabama (many records of which are also available on microfilm at the office of the Air Force historian at Bolling Air Force Base just outside Washington, D.C.). This archival material often referred to classified material that was unavailable. "Pink slips" interleaved with the available documents indicated the specific classified documents that had been withdrawn from public view. In addition, some recently declassified documents pointed to material that was still classified; for example, a single volume of a declassified official history of a particular military organization indicated it was probably part of a chronological series of such histories. Using these clues, I made formal requests for the declassification of specific documents under the Freedom of Information Act. I eventually obtained some of them, and they have been invaluable.

For the period from the mid-1960s on, I used many conference proceedings and research reports written under government contract. Much of this material—known as "gray literature"—was printed by research organizations or government agencies but is not publicly catalogued or widely available. Almost all of it was given to me by individuals, sometimes in bits and pieces, sometimes in big cardboard boxes. Very few of these documents had been classified, although some were unclassified portions of secret reports.

For the early Cold War period and after, I was guided by interviews and correspondence with over sixty scientists, military officers, and civilians who had participated in the early atmospheric testing of nuclear weapons, analyzed nuclear weapons effects, or been involved in some aspect of predicting damage from nuclear weapons. The interviews ranged from telephone conversations to face-to-face discussions, the latter sometimes extending to many hours. I went to see people in Northern and Southern California; Omaha, Nebraska; northern Wisconsin; the Boston suburbs; and offices in the Pentagon and suburban Washington, D.C. In the Washington area, I got used to visiting offices that were locked or double-locked vaults. Once, there was so much rigmarole involved in getting into an interview (including difficulty in obtaining telephone listings for this government agency) that I felt that I must have penetrated into the hidden abode of the production of nuclear damage estimates. During phone conversations and in some interviews in person, I took notes. Almost all of the longer interviews were tape-recorded, some for attribution, some not.

Without these interviews, I could not have made my way: I would not have understood the problem, I could not have pieced together the broad chronology, I could not have found a number of important documents, I could not have made sense of the documents, and I could not have filled in what the documents do not say. Of course, I heard some contradictory and confusing accounts. I followed common sense. I triangulated evidence. I tried to understand what seemed confusing or inconsistent: Had I understood what someone meant? Why would someone have that perspective? Sometimes I changed my mind. Sometimes I discounted what did not fit. Although many explanations did not agree with my own, most of what I heard provided a surprisingly consistent historical picture.

In several of the chapters that follow, I rely on a few people as my co-narrators: They provide detailed accounts of what happened and how they and others were thinking. In what follows, I interweave these accounts with quotations from documents. I have often chosen to quote the informal language of those I interviewed rather than the less vivid bureaucratic language of documents, but I have done so only when the oral accounts were consistent with the documents.

Before looking closely at the history, let us first familiarize ourselves with some highly unpleasant aspects of nuclear weapons effects.

UNDERSTANDING NUCLEAR WEAPONS EFFECTS

Chapter

1

Complete Ruin

Dear Lynn: Fire can cause vastly more city damage and more complete damage to an urban area than blast, even from the largest of thermonuclear weapons. . . . Despite fifty years of blast research, the uncertainty encountered in blast damage variability in urban/industrial environments is actually very great—greater than the variability or uncertainty in fire damage. The fact is that fire tends to lead to complete destruction in this context . . . while blast damage remains partial and incomplete for many structures. The arguments that weather and climate variabilities make fire prediction highly uncertain are specious. Fire spread is the major factor, and that can be reliably predicted. . . . Because of the enhanced likelihood of spread in the event of a nuclear explosion in an urban center, fire damage is very likely to far exceed blast damage. For that reason alone, fire damage should be explicitly included in targeting considerations, even if it were more uncertain. But, even with the most extremes of weather, target susceptibility and operational circumstances, fire damage is not appreciably less predictable than that due to blast.

Harold Brode, letter to author, December 7, 1995

Imagine a powerful strategic nuclear weapon detonated above the Pentagon, a short distance from the center of Washington, D.C.[1] Let us assume a burst about 1,500 feet above (i.e., a "near-surface" burst), which is how a military planner might choose to wreak blast damage on a massive structure such as the Pentagon. Let us say that it's an ordinary clear day of 10 miles visibility and that the weapon's explosive power is 300 kilotons, the approximate yield of most modern strategic nuclear weapons. This explosive yield is equivalent to 300,000 tons, or 600 million pounds, of dynamite. It would be far more destructive than the 15-kiloton weapon detonated at Hiroshima and the 21-kiloton weapon detonated at Nagasaki,[2] and somewhat less destructive than the thousands of warheads in the megaton range formerly deployed in the U.S. and Soviet arsenals.[3]

I have picked Washington, D.C., because many readers are familiar with the city.[4] A single detonation on a capital city, however, does not depict a "realistic" scenario of destruction. When a former commander in chief of the U.S. Strategic Command read a draft of this chapter, he wanted to know why I put only one bomb on Washington. He said, "We must have targeted Moscow with 400 weapons." He explained the military logic of planning a nuclear attack on Washington: "You'd put one on the White House, one on the Capitol, several on the Pentagon, several on National Airport, one on the CIA, I can think of fifty to a hundred targets right off. . . . I would be comfortable saying that there would be several dozens of weapons aimed at D.C." Moreover, he said that even today, with fewer weapons, what makes sense in extremis would be a decapitating strike against those who command military forces. Today, he said, Washington is in no less danger than during the Cold War.[5]

What follows vastly understates the damage that would occur in a concerted nuclear attack, and not only because I describe the effects of a single weapon. I describe what would happen to human beings in the area, but I do not concentrate on injury, the tragedy of lives lost, or the unspeakable loss to the nation of its capital city. I omit these not because I think them unimportant but because I am concerned with how organizations estimate and underestimate nuclear weapons damage. Thus, I focus largely, as do they, on the physical environment and on physical damage to structures.

Keeping this in mind, let us examine some of the consequences of a nuclear weapon detonation, from the first fraction of a second to the utter destruction from blast and fire that would result within several hours. This will allow us to understand the magnitude of the damage from both effects, but particularly from fire, which is neither widely understood nor accounted for in damage prediction in U.S. nuclear war plans.

Zero Hour

The First Moments

Upon detonation of a 300-kiloton nuclear bomb, an extraordinary amount of energy would be released in an instant (about 300 trillion calories within about a millionth of a second). Initially, nearly all of this energy would be in the form of fast-recoiling nuclear matter that would be released into the surrounding environment. While a chemical explosion of comparable yield would release almost all its explosive power in the form of a powerful expanding shock wave, more than 95 percent of the energy initially released in a nuclear explosion is in the form of intense light. Since this intense light is of very short wavelength, in the soft X-ray range, it would be efficiently absorbed by the air immediately surrounding the weapon, superheating the air to very high temperatures and creating a ball of intense heat, commonly called a "fireball."

Because the early fireball would be so hot, it would expand rapidly. Almost all of the air that originally occupied the volume within and around the fireball would be compressed into a thin shell of superheated, glowing, high-pressure gas. This shell of gas would compress the surrounding air, forming a steeply fronted luminous shock wave of enormous extent and power. (In air, shock waves are generally referred to as "blast waves"; shock waves also occur in water and earth.)

By the time the fireball approached its maximum size, it would be more than a mile in diameter. It would very briefly produce temperatures at its center of over two hundred million degrees Fahrenheit (about one hundred million degrees Celsius), about four to five times the temperature at the center of the sun.

This enormous release of light and heat would create an environment of almost unimaginable lethality. Vast amounts of thermal energy would ignite extensive fires over urban and suburban areas. In addition, the extreme compression of air would quickly cause an intense blast wave and high-speed winds. The blast wave and the winds would crush many structures and tear them apart. The blast wave would also boost the incidence and rate of firespread by exposing ignitable surfaces, releasing flammable materials, and dispersing burning materials throughout the environment. Within minutes of a detonation, fire would be everywhere, as numerous fires and dispersed firebrands coalesced into a "large area fire," or "mass fire." (Physicists prefer these terms to the more common, but roughly synonymous, "firestorm.") This fire would cover a ground area of tens of square miles and begin to heat enormous volumes of air that would rise up while cool air from the periphery of the fire was pulled in to replace it. Within tens of minutes after the detonation, the pumping action from rising hot air would generate superheated ground winds of hurricane force in the fire zone, further intensifying the fire. Virtually no one within the area would survive (see Figure 1.1 and Measures of Destruction box).[6]

At Pentagon City, a shopping and office complex about 0.7 miles from ground zero at the Pentagon, light from the fireball would melt asphalt in the streets, burn paint off walls, and melt metal surfaces within a half second of the detonation. The interiors of vehicles and buildings in line of sight of the fireball would explode into flames. Roughly one second later, the shock wave and 750 miles per hour (mph) winds would arrive and toss burning and disintegrating vehicles into the air like leaves in a wind storm. Even

Figure 1.1. Aerial photo of parts of Washington, D.C., and northern Virginia, showing some of the area that would be engulfed in mass fire from a 300-kiloton nuclear bomb detonated 1,500 feet above the Pentagon. Mosaic based on U.S. Geological Survey Digital Orthophoto Quadrangles, 1.0 meter resolution: Washington West quadrangle, D.C., direction South East, version 1, and Alexandria quadrangle, Va., direction North East, version 1 (Washington, D.C.: Dept. of Interior, National Mapping Division, EROS Data Center, U.S. Geological Survey, 1988).

this far from the Pentagon, the blast wave and thermal radiation would be more powerful and destructive than they were at ground zero in Hiroshima. The overpressure would be roughly 36 pounds per square inch (psi), about equal to the overpressure at ground zero in Hiroshima. The duration of the blast wave, however, would be about two to three times longer, and the thermal radiation deposited by the fireball, 540 calories per square centimeter (cal/cm^2), would be roughly three times as great.

The compressed air and winds associated with the shock wave could cave in buildings and might even topple large office buildings. Although the massive concrete and steel office buildings at Pentagon City might not be knocked down, all nonsupporting interior walls and doors would be shattered and their fragments blown at high speed through the interior of the structure. The blast wave would also turn window frames and glass, heavy desks, tables and filing cabinets, chairs and other interior furnishings into missiles and shrapnel. The interiors of buildings that remained standing would, within minutes, be burning pyres of splintered walls, doors, and other combustibles. Seconds after the passage of the blast wave, suction effects created in part by the rising fireball at ground zero would reverse the winds, drawing them toward the detonation point at perhaps 50–70 mph. Tree stumps and any other objects that still stood could flip and be drawn toward the point of detonation.

Almost all of the Arlington National Cemetery, most of the Virginia Highlands and Addison Heights neighborhoods in south Arlington, and parts of Washington, D.C., reaching to the Lincoln and Jefferson memorials, are within 1.3 miles of the Pentagon (see Figure 1.2).

The fireball would, for a fraction of a second, shine more than 5,000 times brighter than a desert sun at noon. At this distance, about 166 cal/cm^2 of thermal energy from the fireball would radiate onto exposed surfaces in just seconds. This is more than fifteen times the thermal energy intensity at the edge of the mass fire that destroyed Hiroshima. Throughout the area— including, for example, at Arlington National Cemetery—grass, vegetation, and leaves on trees would explode into flames, and the surface of the ground would explode into superheated dust. Flames and black smoke would spew out from all combustible materials illuminated by the fireball. Any flammable material inside buildings (such as paper, curtains, and upholstery) that was directly exposed would burst into flame, at, for example, residences in Arlington and offices and shops in Pentagon City and Crystal City. The marble on the Lincoln and Jefferson memorials would crack, pop, and possibly evaporate. If the light from the fireball illuminated part of the bronze statue of Jefferson, the surface would melt. Trees and telephone poles would recoil from the flaming gases. Birds in flight would drop from the sky in flames. The air would be filled with dust, fire, and smoke. People visiting Arlington

MEASURES OF DESTRUCTION

Heat Energy

The tremendous amounts of light and heat—thermal radiation—released by a nuclear detonation are typically measured in terms of the thermal fluence, or energy, deposited onto exposed surfaces at a given range from the detonation. This deposition of energy is measured in units of calories per square centimeter (cal/cm^2). The amount of energy deposited decreases with range from the detonation point.

Ten cal/cm^2 is roughly equal to the amount of energy deposited 1.1 miles from ground zero by the 15-kiloton weapon that destroyed Hiroshima. Out to this range and slightly beyond, the intense heat initiated a nearly circular mass fire. The fire covered an area of roughly 4.4 square miles and burned with great intensity for more than six hours after the initial explosion (see Figure B.1). Between 70,000 and 130,000 people died immediately from the combined effects of the fire, blast, and nuclear radiation.[a]

The fire that resulted from the 21-kiloton atomic bomb detonated at Nagasaki is often characterized as not a true firestorm, but this is incorrect. The difference between the two fires was not in type but in the surrounding geography. Nagasaki was, in physicist Theodore Postol's words, "Hiroshima in a fireplace." Hiroshima sat on a flat plane surrounded by relatively distant mountains. Nagasaki was located in an upwardly sloping valley. The sides of the valley acted like the walls of a giant fireplace and the upward slope acted like a flue: The hot gases and fire-generated winds flowed, and fires spread, from low to high ground, up the flue. The area burned out by fire at Nagasaki was not circular as at Hiroshima, but the fire produced was a mass fire (see Figure B.2).

The experience at Hiroshima and Nagasaki suggests that 10 cal/cm^2 is a good first estimate of the range out to which a mass fire could be expected in a city attack. Analysts sometimes double the deposition of energy within which a mass fire could be expected, to 20 cal/cm^2, but the physical evidence suggests that this may be unnecessarily conservative.[b] Common fuels, such as dark paper, lightweight wood, dry leaves, etc., are ignitable at 3 cal/cm^2.

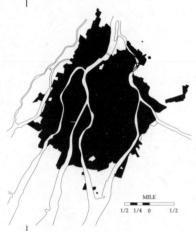

MILE

1/2 1/4 0 1/2

Figure B.1. Area destroyed by fire in Hiroshima, 1945. Redrawn from U.S. Strategic Bombing Survey, Physical Damage Division, *A Report on Physical Damage in Japan* (n.p., June 1947), fig. 32B.

Blast Pressure

The intensity of the blast wave is determined by the peak "overpressure" associated with it. The *overpressure* is defined as the air pressure above ambient air pressure at sea level. In the United States, air pressure is most often reported in units of pounds per square inch (psi). Normal air pressure at sea level is 14.7 psi; blast overpressure is the additional pressure. "The overpressure in the blast wave acts in all directions. . . . As a target is engulfed by the blast wave, overpressure acts to crush it. This crushing pressure lasts for a time duration which is dependent upon the weapon yield as well as the peak pressure level."[c]

Accompanying the blast front are very high winds. These winds also exert powerful forces on structures in the wake of the shock wave. Pressure due to the wind motion is often described as "drag pressure," or "dynamic pressure." Dynamic pressure is often more sensitive to time duration, and weapon yield, than is blast overpressure. The speed of the wind can be expressed in miles per hour (mph); the resulting forces can be measured as dynamic pressure or can be keyed to the associated peak overpressure. Hurricane force winds are about 75 or more miles per hour; wind speeds from nuclear detonations can be hundreds of miles per hour. The wind-drag forces on a targeted structure depend on the shape of the structure. As a structure changes shape and disintegrates under the action of overpressure and wind, a complex interaction between the wind and the disintegrating structure can result in greatly increased levels of damage.

Almost a mile and a half from ground zero, at a peak overpressure of 10 psi and accompanying winds of about 300 mph, the blast wave from a 300-kiloton nuclear weapon would overturn blast furnace superstructures, collapse and rupture gas mains in steel mills, and overturn cranes in shipbuilding yards. At about this overpressure, conservative measures of blast damage predict "severe damage" or "severe structural damage" to heavy industrial installations such as steel plants and chemical plants. For such plants, "severe damage" means "minimum repair time at least 6 months."[d] Hard military structures such as silos or underground bunkers that have been specifically designed to withstand nuclear effects are typically much more resistant to blast pressure. Overpressures of hundreds or thousands of pounds per square inch might be specified as necessary to inflict significant damage against these structures. A declassified document from the mid-1960s indicates that a 300-kiloton bomb would destroy a hard nuclear target at 7,200 psi.[e]

Figure B.2. Area destroyed by fire in Nagasaki, 1945. Redrawn from U.S. Strategic Bombing Survey, Physical Damage Division, *A Report on Physical Damage in Japan* (n.p., June 1947), fig. 32A.

[a] The estimates for immediate deaths at Nagasaki are 35,000–70,000. See Kenneth P. Werrell, *Blankets of Fire: U.S. Bombers over Japan during World War II* (Washington, D.C.: Smithsonian Institution Press, 1996), pp. 217, 218.

[b] Barbara G. Levi, Frank N. von Hippel, and William Daugherty, "Civilian Casualties from 'Limited' Nuclear Attacks on the Soviet Union," *International Security,* Vol. 12, No. 3 (Winter 1987/88), pp. 168–189, uses 20 cal/cm^2. Theodore A. Postol, "Possible Fatalities from Superfires following Nuclear Attacks in or near Urban Areas," in Fredric Solomon and Robert Q. Marston, eds., Institute of Medicine, National Academy of Sciences, *The Medical Implications of Nuclear War* (Washington, D.C.: National Academy Press, 1986), pp. 15–72, uses 10 cal/cm^2.

[c] Defense Intelligence Agency [DIA], *Physical Vulnerability Handbook—Nuclear Weapons* AP-550-1-2-69-INT (Washington, D.C.: DIA, 1 June 1969, with change 1 [1 September 1972] and change 2 [28 January 1974]), p. I-1.

[d] DIA, *Physical Vulnerability Handbook* (1969–1974), pp. I-3–I-12.

[e] The target category was nuclear storage (VN 51P6). Memorandum for the Chairman, Joint Chiefs of Staff, Subject: MRBM Requirements and Deployments, 10 March 1964, Enclosure 3, decimal file 471.94, Chairman's Files, Papers of Maxwell Taylor, Record Group 218, National Archives at College Park, Md. Document declassified through Freedom of Information Act request by National Security Archive, George Washington University.

National Cemetery or the Lincoln or Jefferson memorials who were directly exposed to the illumination of the fireball would be instantly killed. Others would not survive long.

It would take about four seconds after the detonation for the shock wave to arrive at the Lincoln and Jefferson memorials. They would collapse instantly. At this distance, 1.3 miles from the detonation, the leading edge of the blast wave would be compressed to an overpressure of approximately 12 psi. As the shock wave passed over, it would engulf all structures in high pressure and crush all but the strongest. It would generate ferocious 300–400 mph winds that would persist for about a second and a half. These winds, in combination with the crushing blast-wave overpressure, would tear many strong structures apart. Wood-frame and residential brick buildings would be completely destroyed. Other structures at this range, such as the Arlington Memorial Bridge and the George Mason Memorial Bridge, might not collapse, but anyone caught in the open or even sheltered behind these structures would be killed within seconds or minutes.

As structures broke up, the high winds would tear structural elements from attachments and cause them to disintegrate explosively into smaller pieces. Some of these pieces would then become destructive projectiles that could hit other objects, causing still further damage and creating yet more projectiles to be carried by the winds. The winds would also be laden with superheated dust and small fragments generated by the pulverizing action of the light flash and blast wave. The superheated, dust-laden winds would be strong enough to overturn heavy vehicles such as cars, trucks, and railroad cars. They would disperse flaming pieces of shattered structures that had already been ignited by the light from the fireball.

Just beyond this range, about 1.6 miles from the Pentagon, aircraft at Reagan National Airport would be exposed to a light flash from the fireball more than 3,000 times brighter than a desert sun at noon. The thermal fluence would be 108 cal/cm^2. The thermal radiation would melt and warp aluminum surfaces on aircraft. Interior sections of the aircraft illuminated by the fireball would burst into flames. The tires of the aircraft would catch fire, as would the tires and fuel hoses of any service vehicles near the aircraft.

The Capitol, the House and Senate office buildings, and the Library of Congress are all about 3 miles from the Pentagon, and just beyond is Union Station. The Mall and the White House are closer in (see Figure 1.2). The monumental structures on Capitol Hill are among the strongest civilian buildings in the world: They are reinforced concrete, two- to ten-story buildings of earthquake-resistant design. The surrounding neighborhood mostly comprises private two- to four-story dwellings with brick, load-bearing walls, surrounded by many trees. There are also a few industrial structures

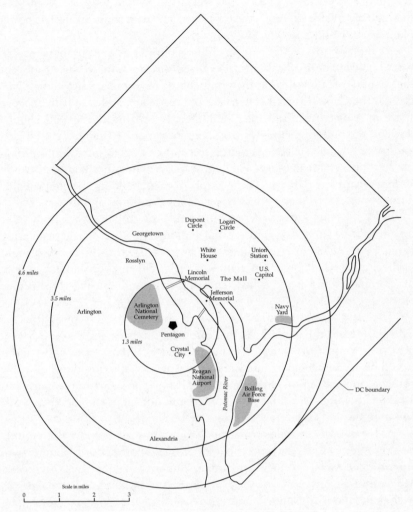

Figure 1.2. Map of Washington, D.C., area, showing radii of destruction at 1.3, 3.5, and 4.6 miles (assuming 300-kiloton nuclear weapon, near-surface burst, and 10 miles visibility). Values for thermal fluence at the three distances are 166, 20, and 10 cal/cm^2, respectively; values for overpressure are 12, 2.2, and 1.8 psi.

on Capitol Hill, for example, the First District Sub Station, an electric power plant at Sixth and E streets, SE.

At the Capitol, the fireball would be as bright as a thousand suns and would deliver about 28 cal/cm^2 to exposed surfaces, almost three times the thermal fluence deposited at the perimeter of mass fire at Hiroshima. Even though the Capitol is well constructed to resist fire, and stands in an open space at a distance from other buildings, light from the fireball shining through the building windows would ignite papers, curtains, light fabrics, and some furniture coverings. Large sections of the building would probably suffer heavy fire damage. The House and Senate office buildings would suffer even greater damage: The interiors of these buildings would probably burn. So would the area's adjacent residential buildings and trees.

Indeed, virtually everywhere within 3 miles of ground zero, innumerable fires would be ignited in and around buildings, and trees and vegetation would be set aflame. The clothing worn by people within direct line of sight of the fireball would burst into flames or melt, and areas of skin not covered by clothing would be scorched, charring flesh and causing third-degree burns.

The blast wave would travel 3 miles in about 12 to 14 seconds after the light flash from the fireball. At this distance, the blast wave would have a peak overpressure of 2.8 psi, it would persist for well over 2 seconds, and it would be accompanied by hurricane winds of 100 mph. Buildings of heavy construction on Capitol Hill would suffer little or no structural damage, but all exterior windows would be shattered and nonsupporting interior walls and doors would be severely damaged or blown down.

A distance of 3.5 miles from the detonation reaches more than a mile past the White House and encompasses the neighborhoods of Georgetown, Connecticut Avenue to the Taft Bridge, Dupont Circle, Logan Circle, and Mt. Vernon Square, most of the Navy Yard and Bolling Air Force Base, as well as northern Alexandria and much of Arlington, Virginia (see Figure 1.2).

At this distance, the light flash from the fireball would still be severe, delivering thermal fluence of about 20 cal/cm^2 to objects in line of sight, or double the fluence at the edge of the mass fire at Hiroshima. The light and heat to surfaces would approximate six hundred desert suns at noon. The tremendous rate of arrival of the flash of light and heat would cause black smoke to effuse from wood houses as paint burned off wood surfaces and would ignite furnishings within.

At Union Station, not quite 3.5 miles from the Pentagon, the majestic front facade of glass would be smashed into razor-sharp projectiles. Curtains, table cloths, and other combustibles would ignite on the upper decks. Blast damage would not be nearly as severe as it would be closer to the point of detonation, but streets would be blocked with fallen debris and burning material dispersed. The scouring effects of the high winds accompanying the shock wave would loft dust into the air. There would be fires everywhere. Dust and smoke would create a dense low-visibility foglike environment in the streets. The harsh environment would impede the ability of individuals and emergency response teams to move about.

At this and greater ranges from the detonation, fire ignitions would result from the tremendous release of thermal energy, which would deposit radiant light and heat on exposed surfaces, causing the simultaneous combustion of many surfaces and structures. Ignitions would also be caused by the breakup of structures from the blast wave and accompanying blast winds. Structural breakup would cause fires by releasing flammable materials (such as gas, chemicals, and other hazards as gas lines and industrial processes were disrupted), by exposing and shorting electrical lines and equipment, and by exposing additional ignitable surfaces. Such fires are called "blast disruption" fires. More ignitions would be caused by firespread from radiant heat and from the winds accompanying the blast wave, which would carry firebrands, burning material acting like torches.[7] In the immediate minutes after the detonation, innumerable fires would ignite out to 3.5 miles from the detonation. The area of ignition would be almost 40 square miles. In all probability, on a reasonably clear day, there would be a vast number of fires ignited by a fluence of 10 cal/cm^2, as at Hiroshima, to a distance of about 4.6 miles from the detonation. This area would be approximately 65 square miles (see Figure 1.2).

Mass Fire

Within tens of minutes after the cataclysmic events associated with the detonation, a mass of buoyantly rising fire-heated air would signal the start of a second and distinctly different event—the development of a mass fire of gigantic scale and ferocity. This fire would quickly increase in intensity. In a fraction of an hour it would generate ground winds of hurricane force with average air temperatures well above the boiling point of water (212°F, 100°C). This would produce a lethal environment over a vast contiguous area. The character of mass fire results from the simultaneous combustion of a large area containing a fuel load typical of a city or suburb.

The Pentagon is located near a relatively wide river, but fires would start simultaneously in large areas on both sides of the river. On the Washington side of the river opposite the Pentagon, an area of roughly 8 to 12 square miles contains combustible high fuel loading structures that would be consumed in a mass fire following the detonation. This fire alone would generate ferocious winds and air temperatures. The even larger area burning on the Pentagon side would also be consumed in a mass fire. The direction of fire winds in regions near the river would be modified by the water, but the overall wind pattern from these two huge and nearly contiguous fire zones would be similar to that of a single huge fire and will be treated as a single mass fire.

The first indicator of a mass fire would be strangely shifting ground winds of growing intensity in the targeted area. (These winds are entirely different from, and unrelated to, the earlier blast wave winds that exert "drag pressure" on structures.) These fire-winds would be caused by the inrush of air following the rise of a vast column of heated air from the fires within the many tens of square miles of the targeted area, much like a gigantic bonfire. As this heated air rose from the fire zone, its movement would create a low-pressure region below it near the ground. This would cause cooler air from surrounding ground regions to be drawn into the fire zone as ground winds. These winds would fan the fires, causing them to increase in intensity and spread, generating still higher volumes of hot rising air, which would in turn cause higher-speed ground winds of hurricane force.

Such inrushing winds would drive the flames from combusting buildings (usually near-vertical) horizontally toward the ground, filling city streets with hot flames and combusting firebrands, breaking in doors and windows, and causing the fire to jump hundreds of feet to engulf anything that was not yet combusting violently. These extraordinary winds, a physical consequence of the rise of heated air over vast areas of ground surface, would transform the targeted area into a huge hurricane of fire.

Within tens of minutes, the entire area, approximately 40 to 65 square miles—everything within 3.5 or 4.6 miles of the Pentagon—would be engulfed in a mass fire. The fire would extinguish all life and destroy almost everything else.

The Physics of Mass Fire

This description of the physics of mass fire is based on the work of a few scientists who have examined in detail the damaging effects of nuclear weapons. They include Theodore A. Postol, trained as a physicist and nuclear engineer at the Massachusetts Institute of Technology and now a professor there, and physicist Harold Brode and his colleagues at Pacific-Sierra Research Corporation in Santa Monica, California (now part of Veridian).

Postol is one of the country's leading non-government-funded technical experts on nuclear weapons, missiles, and arms control. He was the leading critic of the military's now-discredited claims that the U.S. Patriot missile successfully attacked Iraqi Scud missiles during the Gulf War. More recently, he has played a leading role in criticizing the Pentagon's antiballistic missile defense testing program. In 1990, Postol won the American Physical Society's Leo Szilard Award for Physics in the Public Interest "for his incisive technical analysis" of numerous national security issues. In 1995, he won the American Association for the Advancement of Science–Hilliard Roderick Prize for excellence in science, arms control, and international security.[8]

Brode's five-decade career has been devoted to the study of nuclear weapons effects. He received his Ph.D. in theoretical nuclear physics from Cornell University in 1951 and gained prominence at RAND (a prototypical defense consulting firm known as a think tank) in the 1950s working on blast effects. In this period, he first described the nuclear blast wave environment (later known as "Brode-fits"), a critical component for predicting blast damage. For most of 1961 to 1993, Brode served on the Scientific Advisory Group of the Defense Nuclear Agency (DNA), the government agency responsible for studying nuclear weapons effects; he was chair from 1980 to 1991. In February 1997, the Defense Special Weapons Agency, the successor to DNA, presented Brode with its Lifetime Achievement Award, the agency's "highest award for public service." It said that Brode had "achieved near legendary status as an expert in nuclear weapons effects."[9]

That mass fires have occurred, and that something like the mass fire described here *could* occur, is not in dispute. What is not widely accepted is that nuclear weapons detonated in urban or suburban areas would be virtually certain to set mass fires and that the resulting damage is as predictable as blast damage. The much more widely held view, described in chapter 2, is that the probability and range of mass fire depends on many unpredictable environmental variables, including rain, snow, humidity, temperature, time of year, visibility, and wind conditions.

However, the work of Postol, Brode, and Brode's collaborators shows that mass fire creates its own environment. Except in extreme cases, natural environmental factors do not affect the likelihood of mass fire. Although weather can affect the range at which fires will occur, this variation can be reasonably well predicted. For nuclear weapons of approximately 100 kilotons or more, the range of devastation from mass fire will generally be substantially greater than from blast. The extraordinarily high air temperatures and wind speeds characteristic of a mass fire are the inevitable physical consequence of many simultaneous ignitions occurring over a vast area. The vacuum created by buoyantly rising air follows from the basic physics of combustion and fluid flow (generally called hydro- or fluid dynamics). As the area of the fire increases, so does the volume of rising air over the fire zone, causing even more air to be sucked in from the periphery of the fire at increasingly higher speeds.

Only a few mass fires have occurred in human history: those created by British and American conventional incendiary weapons and the U.S. atomic bombs in World War II. These include the fires that destroyed Hamburg, Dresden, Tokyo, Hiroshima, and Nagasaki, as well as those that destroyed Kassel, Darmstadt, and Stuttgart, in Germany, and possibly others. The first mass fire in history was created by allied incendiary raids at Hamburg on the night of July 27–28, 1943. Within twenty minutes, two of three buildings within an area of 4.5 square miles were on fire. In three to six hours, this fire so completely burned out an area of more than 5 square miles that the area was referred to by damage analysts as the "Dead City." Well-documented accounts describe wind speeds of hurricane force within the city. Air temperatures were calculated to be between four and five hundred degrees Fahrenheit, hundreds of degrees above the temperature of boiling water. Between sixty and one hundred thousand people were killed in the attack.[10] A mass fire resulting from a modern nuclear weapon could be expected to burn out an urban or suburban area of a considerably larger size in a similarly brief time.

The unique features of the mass fire—the simultaneous combustion of many fires over a large area, which causes a great volume of air to heat, rise, and suck in large amounts of fresh air at hurricane speeds from the periphery—fundamentally distinguish it from other fires in history: the great urban fires that destroyed London (1666), Chicago (1871), and San Francisco (1906); the suburban fire that ravaged the Oakland, California, hills (1991); the vast forest fires that swept the logging regions of the Great Lakes states in the late nineteenth century, most famously at Peshtigo, Wisconsin (1871); and the largely rural Cerro Grande fire that destroyed about 48,000 acres— 75 square miles—near Los Alamos, New Mexico (1999).[11] These fires were terrifying and destructive. But they were large propagating *line fires,* not mass fires. They burned and spread for days and were not simultaneously set over very large areas. They generated high temperatures and winds, but not on the scale or with the intensity of mass fires.

Following the 1906 San Francisco earthquake, for example, a line fire destroyed just over 4 square miles (slightly less than the area destroyed at Hiroshima) during a three-day period. At the time, this fire was described as "the greatest fire in the history of the world."[12] However, like all large fires until Hamburg, only small fractions of a square mile burned at the same time. Since the area on fire at any one time was hundreds of times smaller than the mass fire described here, the fire did not generate the air temperatures and extraordinarily high winds characteristic of mass fires. In contrast to the mass fire at Hamburg, where the exceptional heat, inrushing winds, and flame-filled streets meant that "for most people there was no question of getting away,"[13] the San Francisco fire propagated slowly, making it possible for people to travel to the fire's perimeter and escape. (This is, of course, not to say that large line fires do not result in the tragic loss of life. At Peshtigo, Wisconsin, for example, more than a thousand people died.)[14]

The dynamics of mass fire are grounded in Newtonian laws of conservation of mass, momentum, and energy. These conservation laws were used more than one hundred years ago by the applied mathematician Horace Lamb in *A Treatise on the Motion of Fluids* (1879).[15] The results of Lamb's groundbreaking work are the classical hydrodynamic equations, which can be applied to mass fire. A nuclear detonation ignites material that releases energy into a fluid, the atmosphere. The region of atmosphere being heated can be approximated as a thin disk-shaped volume near the earth's surface. By solving the hydrodynamic equations, it is possible to calculate the flow of rising air from the heated fire zone and the lateral inflow of cool air near the ground from just outside the periphery of the fire zone. These equations model the behavior of mass fire. The detailed numerical calculations required to solve the partial differential equations that describe hydrodynamic processes are difficult. Brode and his colleagues solved the equations using computer codes. However, the equations can be roughly solved without elaborate calculation and can yield the same broad understanding. (Hydrodynamics also play an important role in the internal physics of nuclear weapons, beginning in World War II when "simpleminded brute force" calculations were done on IBM equipment to model the hydrodynamic implosion processes in the atomic bomb.)[16]

Fire environments created by mass fires are fundamentally more violent and destructive than fires of smaller scale, and they are far less affected by external weather conditions. Because their dynamics are dominated by the intense hydrodynamic flows generated by the vast releases of energy from combustion in an area of enormous size and the resulting rise of air over the fire zone, these fires are not substantially altered by seasonal and daily weather conditions.

There are, of course, uncertainties in the damage ranges associated with the initiation and spread of mass fires, and variations in environmental conditions could contribute to these uncertainties. For example, the location of the perimeter of mass fire following a nuclear attack cannot be predicted precisely; if the thermal energy intensity at the edge of a mass fire were approximately 10 cal/cm², as at Hiroshima, the area on fire would be larger than if the fire zone were demarcated by a thermal fluence of approximately 20 cal/cm². How the topography or the weather might affect the range of mass fire is also uncertain. However, the uncertainty in the range of damage associated with mass fire can be estimated and modeled, and is not greater than the uncertainty associated with blast damage. For blast damage, the range at which a 15 psi overpressure occurs is uncertain to plus or minus 15 percent.[17] The likelihood that a structure subjected to a specific blast overpressure would be damaged to the prescribed level will vary with construction details that are often unknown, orientation of the structure relative to the arriving blast wave, whether the structure is on the windward or leeward side of a hill, and whether the structure is in the pressure shadow of other structures. For fire damage, the range of uncertainty is comparable. For example, a 100 percent increase in visibility, from 5 to 10 miles, results in a change in the range at which 20 cal/cm² is deposited of about 16 percent.

Moreover, for higher-yield weapons (approximately 100 kilotons or more), under almost all conditions, fire will cause devastation far beyond the range of damage from blast. In addition, "fire may cause more complete and permanent damage. A structure only moderately damaged by blast may be gutted and rendered useless by fire. Similarly, building contents may survive the blast but be destroyed by the fires."[18]

What effect could the weather have on the probability and range of mass fire? Reduced visibility would not stop the initiation and development of a mass fire. For example, a reduction in visibility from 10 miles to 5, from the visibility of a relatively clear day to a misty rainy day, would reduce the thermal fluence at 3.5 miles from 20 cal/cm² to about 13 cal/cm², still enough to set many objects on fire. Thermal fluence of 20 cal/cm² would still occur 3 miles from the detonation, as far as the Capitol in the Pentagon example above, reducing the range of fire only about 14 percent, and still double the thermal fluence at the edge of mass fire at Hiroshima. If visibility were further reduced, to about 3 miles, thermal fluence at the Capitol would be about 10 cal/cm², the same as at the outer edge of mass fire at Hiroshima.

At close-in distances (1.5 to 2.0 miles), the flash from the fireball from a 300-kiloton detonation would set fires under virtually all weather conditions. Reductions in visibility because of rain, fog, haze, or smoke could absorb or scatter thermal radiation from the detonation and reduce, or attenuate, the amount that would reach exposed structures, equipment, and people. For example, with a reduction in visibility from 10 miles to 2 miles (from the elevated Metro station at Reagan National Airport, one could not see the Washington Monument, the Jefferson Memorial, or the Capitol), the thermal fluence on aircraft at National Airport, 1.6 miles from the detonation at the Pentagon, would be reduced from 108 cal/cm² to 52 cal/cm². Under these circumstances, the flash from the detonation would still be sufficient to destroy these aircraft by warping their metal surfaces and setting them on fire. (Even if the visibility were only about 1.5 miles, a devastating fluence of 36 cal/cm² would still be delivered to the aircraft.)[19] At 2 miles visibility, thermal energy of 20 cal/cm² would be deposited 2.2 miles from the detonation and 10 cal/cm² deposited at 2.6 miles.

Visibility in the Washington, D.C., area is 10 miles or greater about 64 percent of the time. Visibility is 5 miles or greater 90 percent of the time. And visibility is 3 miles or greater about 97 percent of the time.[20]

If the ground were snow-covered, vegetation covered by snow would not be ignited initially, but light and heat from the fireball would be reflected by the snow, roughly doubling the amount of light entering building windows. Further, during periods of cold weather when snow cover would be a factor, the warm interiors of buildings have very low relative humidities, greatly increasing the likelihood of ignitions. The mass fire set at Dresden in February 1945 by non-nuclear incendiary weapons occurred in "winter with snow on the ground. It was cold and wet and cloudy outside, but there was fuel inside where it was warm and dry." Similarly, in the first incendiary attack on Tokyo, in February 1945, the city "was covered by snow . . . but about one square mile was burned out."[21]

If a nuclear weapon were detonated below cloud cover, reflections off the clouds would increase the light shining into buildings by a factor of about two. When there is both snow and cloud cover, light reflected by both the snow cover and cloud bottoms could intensify the fire-initiating light flash from the fireball roughly by a factor of four.

Only if detonations occurred at altitudes above cloud cover or in periods of very intense rain or heavy ground fog would the size of the fire zone be as small as the zone of severe blast damage. Making very conservative assumptions that mass fire would require a high threshold to be set (20 cal/cm^2) and that severe blast damage would occur at a relatively low overpressure (5 psi), for a 300-kiloton weapon the range at which these values coincide—2.2 miles—occurs when visibility is only 2 miles. For visibility of 3 miles, the range of mass fire would be 2.5 miles, the area 135 percent of that covered by 5 psi. For visibility of 5 miles, the range of mass fire would be 3 miles, the area 185 percent of that covered by 5 psi, and for visibility of 10 miles, the range of mass fire would be 3.5 miles, the area 250 percent of that covered by 5 psi.

As we have seen, severe weather conditions in Washington, D.C., are rare and can be taken into account by military war planners. More generally, the likelihood of severe weather is known for many locations and time of year. In addition, real-time or near real-time weather data has been available on a global basis for decades. The U.S. military has maintained its own weather satellites "to forecast cloud cover . . . , predict the behavior of low-altitude weather systems . . . , [and] collect wind data."[22]

In sum, because of the great diversity of mechanisms leading to fire initiation and spread, it is reasonable to assume that a mass fire with a radius of 3.5 miles or more would ensue in all but the most extreme weather conditions and in spite of variability in the weather. Once this fire intensified, it would not be greatly affected by external weather conditions because the tens of millions of megawatts of power released by combustion would create a local environment on the ground so intense that it would be governed by the dynamics of the fire. The fire would generate its own extremely intense winds, air temperatures would be so high that wet surfaces would quickly dry, and the relative humidity within the fire zone would be very low. Such a fire, unlike those of smaller scale, would be only weakly influenced by details of the external weather conditions.

Damage from Blast vs. Damage from Blast and Fire

In the late 1970s, Brode and a team of scientists at Pacific-Sierra Research began to investigate the possibility of incorporating the effects of fire into damage prediction for nuclear targeting. This work was done under contract for the DNA. By the late 1980s, Brode and his colleagues thought they had developed an analytical basis for predicting the damage caused by fire from nuclear weapons. However, for reasons we will see in chapter 10, in early 1992, the federal funding for nuclear fire damage studies was canceled. Had the U.S. government accepted the work of Brode and his colleagues, this would have resulted in a major change in how the government calculated nuclear weapons damage.

We can see how great the changes would have been by comparing the differences in damage predicted in the above account of blast and fire damage from a 300-kiloton nuclear weapon detonated in a near-surface burst at the Pentagon, with the results of the method used by the U.S. government, which predicts damage only from blast. For many targets, although not all, the differences are great.

The government's method for predicting damage to structures, installations, and equipment is published by the U.S. Defense Intelligence Agency as the *Physical Vulnerability Handbook—Nuclear Weapons* (hereafter, the *Handbook*). It has been published in a number of editions, from 1954 to 1992.[23] The *Handbook* characterizes types of structures in terms of their physical vulnerability to blast effects using "physical vulnerability numbers," or "vulnerability numbers" (VNs) at specified damage levels (see Figure 1.3).[24] Physical vulnerability sounds like the opposite of the widely used term "target hardness," but for all practical purposes it is the same: A target is strong, or "hard," up to the point at which it is vulnerable, or fails. Physical vulnerability numbers correspond to blast overpressure in pounds per square inch (psi) for specified levels of damage. Physical vulnerability is always stated in terms of level, or kind, of damage that the structure would be expected to sustain at a given overpressure—for example, severe, moderate, or light damage. *Severe* structural damage requires "that degree of structural damage to a building which precludes further use of the building for the purpose intended without essentially complete reconstruction or replacement. A building sustaining severe structural damage requires extensive repair before it can be used for any purpose." *Moderate* structural dam-

TABLE I-3. (C) INDUSTRIAL INSTALLATIONS AND UTILITIES—Continued

Industry or Utility	Selected Element(s)[1]	Structure[1]	Predicted Damage	VN
Synthetic	Final processing buildings	SS/LSF	SSD	13Q7
		SS/RCLF	SSD	13Q7
	Fractionating towers	Cylindrical tower	Overturning	15Q7
...es (See Ordnance, Munitions, Heavy)				
...ding				
...ll Vessels and Submarines	Major shops (foundry, machine, etc.)	SS/SF (10–25TC)	MSD	12Q7
		SS/RC (10–25TC)	MSD	12Q6
	Assembly area—(locomotive and crawler cranes).	Cranes	Overturning cranes	15Q6
	Shipways and fitting-out areas	Cranes	Overturning light portal and tower cranes	11Q7
			Overturning gantry cranes	14Q9
			Distortion of runways of overhead cranes	15Q7
	Graving docks and dry docks (See Locks, Table I-6).			
...ge Vessels	Major shops (foundry, machine, etc.).	SS/SF (30–50TC)	MSD	13Q7
		SS/RC (30–50TC)	MSD	13Q6
	Assembly Area (Same as for Small Vessels above).			
	Shipways and fitting-out areas	Cranes	Overturning portal and tower cranes	13Q8
			Overturning gantry cranes	14Q9
			Distortion of runways of overhead cranes	15Q7
			Overturning hammerhead cranes	17Q9
	Graving Docks (Same as for Small Vessels above).			
...agrated Works	Entire plant	See Predicted Damage	Collapse and rupture of coke-chemical gas mains resulting in destruction of exhausters. Collapse of coke-chemical overhead piping. Overturning of blast furnace superstructure. Severe damage to control houses and controls of blooming and rolling mills. Collapse of gas and air system mains. (Minimum repair time at least 6 months.)	13Q6
...ke-Chemical	Coke ovens	See Predicted Damage	Collapse and rupture of gas mains resulting in destruction of exhausters. (Minimum repair time approximately 6 months).	12Q6
	Coke by-products—coolers, scrubbers, and fractionating towers.	See Predicted Damage	Overturning of vertical cylindrical steel columns.	15Q7
...Iron	Blast furnace	See Predicted Damage	Overturning of blast furnace superstructure. (Minimum repair time approximately 4 months).	13Q6

...otnotes at end of table.

Figure 1.3. A page from the Defense Intelligence Agency's *Physical Vulnerability Handbook—Nuclear Weapons* (1969–1974) characterizing structures in terms of type, predicted blast damage, and Vulnerability Number (VN). SS = single-story building; LSF = light steel-framed building; RCLF = concrete-framed building without crane or with crane of less than 10-ton capacity; 10–25 or 30–50TC = 10- to 25- or 30- to 50-ton crane, respectively; SSD = severe structural damage; MSD = moderate structural damage.

age is "that degree of structural damage to principal load-bearing members
. . . of a building which precludes effective use of the building for the purpose intended until major repairs are made."[25] The *Handbook* does not describe "light" damage for buildings, presumably because such damage
would not be severe enough to bother with in targeting calculations.

A large, heavy structure such as the U.S. Capitol might be expected to
sustain severe damage when subjected to blast overpressure of approximately 20 psi. Under the system used in the *Handbook*, the VN (i.e., VNTK)
code corresponding to overpressure for severe damage to this type of structure would be 18Q8. The same structure would be expected to sustain moderate damage when subjected to overpressure of approximately 15 psi; at this
level of damage, the same structure would be characterized as a 15Q5 target. (See chapter 7 for further explanation of the VNTK coding system.)

Despite the sophisticated understanding of blast waves and structural
response embedded in the VNTK system, for many types of targets the total damage that would occur in a nuclear attack is vastly understated because only blast damage is taken into account. For example, one type of
target of interest to military planners is the aircraft carrier. The *Handbook*
gives this class of target a VN of 11P0 for moderate damage. (In this code,
11 is a rating of target hardness that translates to blast pressure; P indicates
a type of target that responds mainly to overpressure, not drag pressure; 0
means the target is not sensitive to the duration of blast pressure.) At this
rating, according to the government's method of calculating damage, the
aircraft carrier would sustain "about half loss in ability to deliver weapons
effectively, because of damage to equipment or topside structure, or because
of personnel casualties." Target-acquisition and communication equipment, however, are predicted to be operative.[26] This code corresponds to
more than 8 psi, which in a 300-kiloton nuclear weapon attack on the Pentagon would occur about 1.6 miles from ground zero. For purposes of illus-
tration, such a target could be located in the Potomac River near Reagan
National Airport. At this range the thermal flash would be more than 4,000
times brighter than a desert sun at noon, and the winds would be over 250
mph. The light flash would ignite clothing, rubber, and exposed petroleum
products; seven seconds later, the blast wave and winds would overturn and
break up the fuel-laden aircraft. Under these conditions, the ship could become a floating inferno. It is highly unlikely that sailors on it would to be
able to deliver half of its weapons effectively.

Damage to aircraft on the carrier and a little farther away at Reagan National Airport is also underestimated. According to the *Handbook*, light
fighter and bomber aircraft located about 1.8 miles from a detonation and
oriented toward it ("nose-on") would sustain only "light damage," which it
describes as "structural failure of small control surfaces, bomb bay doors,

wheel doors, fuselage skin damage, and damage due to flying debris. Requires one to four hours repair but may permit limited flight."[27] At this distance, the blast wave would have a peak overpressure of a little less than 7 psi, sufficient to cause the complete collapse and disintegration of typical two-story wood-frame and brick buildings. The winds accompanying the blast would be a little less than 220 mph. Given that aircraft routinely fly nose-on into winds of several hundred miles per hour, we can see how the *Handbook* might arrive at such a prediction of damage.

However, when thermal radiation effects are considered, "light damage" seems understated. At a range of 1.8 miles, the light flash from the fireball would be thousands of times brighter than a noonday sun and the thermal fluence would be 85 cal/cm². This would cause the surfaces of the aircraft to warp and melt, and tires and other components to burst into flames, rendering the aircraft inoperable.

These targets would be deep within the perimeter of mass fire. Farther away from the detonation, all the built-up areas of Capitol Hill would be engulfed in a mass fire that would extinguish all life and destroy nearly all buildings and residences, large or small. Only the Capitol and some similarly monumental buildings on the Mall might be spared from complete destruction.

According to the methods used in the *Handbook,* for a 300-kiloton detonation, severe damage could only be expected against such massive buildings if they were within a range of 1 mile from the detonation (approximately 20 psi), and moderate damage only if they were within 1.2 miles (approximately 15 psi).[28]

What level of damage would the *Handbook* predict for the buildings on Capitol Hill, approximately 3 miles from the Pentagon? At this range, the blast overpressure would be about 2.8 psi, and would be accompanied by 100-mph winds, hurricane force. These forces would not meet the government's criteria for achieving severe or moderate damage. However, the thermal effects would cause damage that would be severe indeed.

Even if visibility were below 2 miles, which occurs only about 1.5 percent of the time in the Washington area, an area of 12 to 15 square miles would be destroyed. This is two to three times the area destroyed in the well-documented World War II incendiary attack on Hamburg on the night of July 27–28, 1943. If visibility were 5 miles or greater (90 percent of the time in the Washington area), an area of approximately 25 to 45 square miles would burn. When visibility is 10 miles or more (64 percent of the time in the Washington area), an area of about 40 to 65 square miles would burn.

Average air temperatures in the areas on fire after the attack would be well above the boiling point of water, winds generated by the fire would be hurricane force, and the fire would burn everywhere at this intensity for three to six hours. Even after the fire burned out, street pavement would be so hot that even tracked vehicles could not pass over it for days, and buried un-burned material from collapsed buildings could burst into flames if exposed to air even weeks after the fire.

Those who sought shelter in basements of strongly constructed build-ings could be poisoned by carbon monoxide seeping in or killed by the oven-like conditions. Those who sought to escape through the streets would be incinerated by the hurricane-force winds laden with firebrands and flames. Even those who could find shelter in lower-level subbasements of massive buildings would likely die of eventual heat prostration, poisoning from fire-generated gases, or lack of water. The fire would eliminate all life in the fire zone.

Organizational Frames

> Whether we like it or not, we can never sever our links with the past, complete with all its errors. It survives in accepted concepts, in the presentation of problems ... in everyday life, as well as in language and institutions. Concepts are not spontaneously created but are determined by their "ancestors."
>
> Ludwik Fleck, *Genesis and Development of a Scientific Fact* (1935)

Given the vast fire damage caused by nuclear weapons, and that such damage can be calculated with no less certainty than blast damage, why have the U.S. government's predictive routines in war planning calculated damage only from blast? The question is not academic: Calculations of damage have profound consequences for nuclear war planning, for weapons procurement, and for potential decisions to use nuclear weapons. What explains this astonishing omission?

Below, I explain how an organizational understanding developed in which blast damage seemed to be, and indeed became, more predictable than fire damage. My basic strategy is to show how earlier understandings and capacities shaped later inquiry and resulted in the development of knowledge-laden routines to predict blast damage but not fire damage. The development and application of knowledge follows not from "nature" itself but from organizational frames, approaches to defining and solving problems.

I first present plausible alternatives to my argument and explain why I do not use them. Some claim that mass fire damage has not been predicted in U.S. nuclear war planning because it is less predictable than blast damage, or less important, or that the evidentiary base from which to infer damage was weaker for fire than for blast, or that computer capabilities precluded fire damage prediction for many years. Others claim that fire damage has not been predicted because incendiary warfare is immoral or repellent. The last claim is that the U.S. Air Force had an organizational interest in not predicting fire damage. I then present my own argument about how organizations create knowledge and knowledge-laden routines. I elaborate the concept of organizational frames and sketch out how two specific organizational frames, the "blast damage frame" and "fire damage frame" operated historically. Finally, I explain how my argument relates to studies of science and technology and to scholarly work on organizations.

Possible Explanations for Why Fire Damage Not Predicted

This section considers seven possible explanations for why predictions of fire damage were not incorporated into knowledge-laden organizational routines developed by the U.S. government for use in nuclear war planning. The nuclear targeting and weapons effects communities provide four explanations for why blast damage, but not fire damage, has been incorporated into these routines. These explanations are grounded in the physical world, either in the nature of "nature" or in the limits of computer technology. Two alternative views—one based on morality, the other on psychology—are grounded not in physical phenomena but in human reactions to incendiary warfare.

The seventh explanation is different. The first six are all tailor-made in the sense that each was offered to me by participants in the process or by those trying to explain the puzzle as I presented it. The seventh is derived from an organizational interest approach widely used in the social sciences. Like the first argument that blast damage is more predictable than fire damage, this explanation presents a particularly important challenge to my claims.

Blast Damage More Predictable

In the view most widely held by those in the nuclear weapons effects and nuclear war planning communities, fire damage from nuclear weapons is simply too unpredictable to be meaningfully calculated. Most analysts and military officers do not disagree that under certain conditions, a nuclear weapon detonation could cause a mass fire. There is no disagreement that a mass fire occurred at Hiroshima and that it burned out an area of approximately 4.4 square miles. The immediate mechanisms by which a nuclear detonation could ignite fires are not disputed: the deposition of thermal energy on combustible materials; structures and containers breaking apart from blast; and the spread of fire from radiant heat, sparks, and firebrands.

But here agreement ends. In the dominant view, neither the probability of a mass fire following a detonation nor the magnitude of such a fire can be reliably modeled and predicted. This is because the conditions under which mass fire would occur are thought to be so complex, variable, and uncertain as to defy reliable prediction as to when such fires would occur and at what range such fires would burn. In other words, the physical processes are too complex and too variable to be predictable. Numerous environmental variables are thought to affect strongly whether a mass fire will occur: terrain, humidity, rainfall, temperature, time of year, and prevailing wind conditions. In addition, these interact with variables associated with targeted structures, particularly the amount of combustible material in structures and in building contents. Finally, the physical processes involved in igniting a mass fire are thought to be complex and little understood. Because of the complexity of the interactions among environmental variables, structures, and the processes of ignition, damage caused by fire is believed to be inherently less predictable than damage caused by blast.

This view has been held since World War II. To take but one historical example, in congressional testimony in 1961, Jerald Hill, from the physics department at RAND, explained that in estimating damage from blast, fallout, or fire due to nuclear weapons, assumptions always have to be made. However, fire estimation required many additional assumptions:

> Meteorological factors such as wind velocity, temperature, relative humidity, visibility, lapse of time since the last precipitation and presence or absence of inversion layers and cloud cover in the target area; fuel characteristics such as types of combustible materials, their surface density, uniformity of distribution and moisture content; topography, geometrical form and degree of builtupness in the target area; and, finally, numbers and distribution of sources of primary and secondary ignition from thermal and blast effects.[1]

A similar view regarding predictability was widely held throughout the 1990s by serving and retired military officers, from Air Force colonels to high-ranking generals and admirals; by civilians inside the government, including intelligence officials and civilian defense officials; by consultants outside the government; and within the academic community concerned with nuclear weapons policy.

This view is well captured in the words of an Air Force officer:

> There's great variation in trying to calculate [fire effects], variation in whether the windows are open or shut, whether the curtains are drawn or not, whether there's rain or snow, the time of year, the rainfall, humidity. Hiroshima and Nagasaki were largely paper cities. The fire effects

were tremendous. But there's great difficulty in calculating fire effects. . . . For large structures—large buildings like those on Penn Ave. or Constitution Ave., government buildings, like the Treasury Building—if the windows are closed and the curtains down, thermal may not do it.[2]

Similarly, according to a high-ranking nuclear war planner, Vice Admiral Michael Colley: "In Russia, or in other countries in that region, the time of year, the vegetation, the petroleum distribution system, the natural gas distribution system, all of those things have to be in a fire algorithm somehow, and there's no way to do it, in all honesty. . . . Time of year, day of the week, whether it rained yesterday or not, I mean it just [is] too cumbersome. . . . There are too many variables."[3]

In sum, in the dominant view, the unpredictability of mass fire from nuclear weapons explains its omission from damage prediction. This view is based on claims about the physical world and claims about the social processes by which scientific knowledge of nuclear weapons was discovered and applied. The implicit sociology is this: Those who developed the organizational capability to predict damage from blast (or, synonymously, the physical vulnerability of structures to blast), correctly perceived physical reality and acted rationally in response to the physical environment. There was "good reason" for what they did; that is, they reasoned and acted correctly. The underlying epistemology is one of rational action resulting from a correctly perceived environment. This is a "structural" explanation: to explain human action parsimoniously, we need only look to environmental determinants.[4]

Of all of the alternative explanations I present, this one poses the most important challenge to my argument. It provides a powerful alternative against which to test my claims that it was not the nature of "nature" that shaped scientific inquiry and subsequent knowledge of the physical world, but preexisting organizational purpose, knowledge, and routines.

Of course, it is not possible to test the validity of physical understandings in the social realm. Given a nuclear detonation, the actual effects of mass fire are independent of human understandings or investigations.[5] However, the issue of the *predictability* of mass fire is a social one; it depends on criteria regarding what is to be predicted, the required degree of certainty, and the required level of precision. Further, it is feasible to test the possible histories implied by each argument. Indeed, the following historical chapters are, in large part, structured by these possibilities. What do those possible histories look like?

The argument that mass fire damage was not incorporated into damage-predicting organizational routines because fire damage was far less predictable than blast damage implies that at some point those most concerned with predicting nuclear weapons damage would have made a thorough effort to predict both blast damage and fire damage—and failed to predict fire damage. What would such an effort look like? Basically, we would expect broad parity in organizational attention, in the form of high-level priorities, research programs, and so on; in commitment of financial resources; and in mobilization of expertise. Such investigation could have occurred before the invention of nuclear weapons. But even if it had been established with conventional incendiary weapons that the causes and consequences of mass fires were more difficult to predict than blast damage from high-explosive conventional bombs, we would still expect that in the postwar period considerable effort would have been made to understand and predict fire damage from nuclear weapons.

By contrast, my argument that earlier organizational ways of knowing and doing shaped later inquiry and resulting knowledge of the physical world implies a very different pattern of investigation. I would expect that greater attention, resources, and mobilization of experts would go toward measuring and predicting blast damage than fire damage during World War II, and that a similar pattern would hold after the war with nuclear weapons.

We will see that in fact this pattern of unequal attention and resources on the part of those organizations most concerned with damage prediction holds during World War II, immediately after, and in the postwar atmospheric nuclear weapons tests of the 1950s. This was a critical period, and it shaped much of what happened later.

Yet the history is quite complex. First, beginning in the early 1950s, organizations primarily concerned with civil defense, not war planning, carried out experiments and studies on ignition and large fires. The civil defense community mobilized considerable resources to study fire damage, although the program was not comparable to the effort made to predict blast damage after the war. The results contributed to the understanding by the larger community concerned with nuclear weapons effects—nuclear weapons scientists, civil defenders, and war planners—that nuclear fire damage could not be predicted. The sense of unpredictability was based not on successful experiments showing that fire damage was unpredictable but on a failure to consistently predict such damage.

Second, even though there was a great disparity in organizational attention during and after World War II, this disparity was not necessarily "locked in": Beginning in the late 1970s, some organizations that had earlier developed blast damage predictions started a concerted effort to predict fire damage and found that fire damage from nuclear weapons *could* be predicted. With sufficient attention, resources, and the mobilization of experts who cast the problem in a particular way, robust predictions of mass fire damage from nuclear weapons were developed. This raises the question of how such innovation was possible, but it is consistent with my claim that it was not "nature" per se that led to the understanding that fire damage was not predictable.

Blast More Important Cause of Damage

A second view widely held by those involved in, or familiar with, U.S. nuclear war planning is that although nuclear weapons may produce some damage from fire, in general, the damage caused by fire to targets of interest is less than the damage caused by blast.

The argument is commonly made that the targets of greatest interest in a U.S. "counterforce" nuclear strategy are relatively isolated or buried "hard" targets, especially missile silos and deep underground bunkers. For these targets, fire would probably not occur, or, if it did, it would not be the primary cause of destruction. In the words of one Air Force officer, thermal effects "don't matter for silos, deep underground structures. My nuclear weapons effects friends say if they try to do the same damage with thermal as with blast, you'll be within the radius of the blast anyway—against targets in which we're most interested."[6]

There is no dispute that this is true. Were nuclear targeting historically confined to missile silos and underground structures, this would indeed seem to be a satisfactory explanation for the disregard of fire damage. However, not only has the United States historically targeted a much wider range of structures, many in or near urban areas, but counterforce targeting of Soviet underground missile silos began more than a decade *after* the U.S. methodology for predicting blast damage to structures was developed. In other words, the targeting of hardened structures such as silos and underground bunkers cannot explain the emphasis on blast damage, which occurred well before such targeting began.

A more important argument dates back to the first years after World War II. It holds that blast is a more important cause of damage than fire to industrial and other urban structures, targets long considered important. According to the U.S. Strategic Bombing Survey (USSBS), at Hiroshima and Nagasaki the range of blast damage extended beyond the range of fire damage. Where fire occurred, it "merely" intensified the damage caused by blast.

> The structural damage to buildings in both cities was due to blast alone, blast and fire combined, and fire alone. Since the limits of structural blast damage to buildings extended beyond the burned-over areas, except for multistory, steel- and reinforced-concrete-frame buildings, it is believed that in most cases buildings which suffered mixed damage were structurally damaged by the initial blast, and subsequent fires merely intensified the damage.[7]

Another volume of the USSBS detailed the damage ranges at Hiroshima: "Structural blast damage to dwellings and other wood-frame buildings extended to 7,300 feet from ground zero, which was 1,050 feet beyond the fringe of fire damage."[8]

It is important to note two caveats in the Survey itself. First, structural blast damage did not extend beyond the burned-over areas to those buildings most likely to be deliberately targeted: multistory steel- and reinforced-concrete-frame buildings. These are the structures that contain heavy industry, government administrative offices, and military command centers, the most important targets in urban areas. Elsewhere, the Survey explicitly states that for these buildings the range of severe blast damage was less than the range of severe fire damage: "The heavy, strong, multistory, steel- and concrete-frame structures were damaged [by blast] only in an area relatively near the point of detonation and their burned-out, but otherwise undamaged, structural frames rose impressively from the ashes of the burned-over section."[9]

Second, beyond the fringe of fire damage, structural blast damage occurred only to dwellings and wood-frame buildings, which were not considered important targets, if targets at all. Given this, it is not clear why, on the basis of damage caused by the atomic bombs to Japan, blast was considered more important than fire in producing destruction. It is more judicious to say that, all in all, the damage radii from fire and blast were more or less equal.[10]

By 1950, the detailed descriptive statements of the USSBS became generalized in the forceful statement of the single most authoritative source in the open literature, Samuel Glasstone's *The Effects of Atomic Weapons:*

The shock wave produced by an air-burst atomic bomb is, from the point of view of . . . disruptive effect, the most important agent in producing destruction. . . . The other characteristics of an atomic bomb which can be employed in warfare, such as the presence of thermal and visible radiations, neutrons, gamma rays, and fission products, are, at present, not serious competitors in the production of damage by a bomb which is burst in the air. . . . A reason for the superiority of air blast as a producer of damage is found in the low air shock pressures . . . required to damage the majority of man-made structures.[11]

From my perspective, these early postwar understandings are important, but not as explanations. As with the argument that blast effects are more predictable than fire effects, these are understandings of actors *to be explained*. The task, then, is to explain why the dominant understanding was that blast was a more important cause of damage than fire.

Weaker Evidence of Fire Damage

Another explanation suggests that blast damage, but not fire damage, was taken into account in early targeting methodology because the remaining physical evidence—the evidentiary base from which to infer cause and predict effect on structures—was more intact for blast than for fire.[12] Physicist Harold Brode, who reanalyzed the U.S. Strategic Bombing Survey's data on Hiroshima and Nagasaki, said: "The evidence had disappeared. All they had were ashes. . . . When [the investigators from the Survey] went in there a month later, all they had to look at were buildings destroyed by blast or that were noncombustible. What was destroyed by fire was gone. They were not able to provide any useful information about particular structures destroyed by fire because there was nothing left, just ashes and mortar."[13]

Brode explained that damage analysts pay particular attention to "the incipient damage level . . . where damage [is] neither complete nor non-existent." This allows analysts to relate varying levels of damage to different distances from the detonation. Because something is usually left in buildings racked by blast, the incipient damage level and distance can often be determined. But, he said,

> It's very hard to look at a pile of ashes which has maybe already been cleaned up, or washed away, and decide you can learn much about what fire did and how it behaved in some structure. . . . In order to make a handbook of specific target response, they studied what they had. . . . It was easier with blast. The fire damage was by gee and by gosh, which was not satisfactory to engineers. . . . Nobody disputed that fire was a major damage mechanism but when it came to analyzing damage to specific targets, they felt more confident with blast damage.[14]

The importance of Brode's point lies not in the explanation regarding physical evidence, however, but in the insight it provides into how evidence, and lack of evidence, was construed. Brode makes clear the criteria for successful prediction of damage: the ability to analyze damage to specific targets via specific mechanisms of damage. Why was such a high premium placed on predicting damage to specific targets rather than, for example, to large areas that would be completely burned out? Why was the problem one of understanding how blast or fire "behaved in some structure"? As we will see in later chapters, the requirement for specificity in analyzing damage mechanisms in structures was demanding. However, this was not the only way that damage could have been analyzed. Estimates of the range of complete destruction of virtually all structures could have provided the basis for an alternative method for predicting vulnerability.

Another issue is just who considered fire damage to be unpredictable. We would expect that civil, or what were then commonly called structural, engineers employed by the government in World War II would feel more confident in predicting blast damage. But fire protection engineers (often employed by fire insurers and involved in devising fire safety codes) also worked for the government during the war and became quite proficient at interpreting and predicting fire damage from bombing raids. How were the latter regarded during the war? What happened to their expertise after the war? We will begin to see the answers in the next two chapters.

Limited Computer Capability

A fourth explanation is that limited computational capabilities precluded the prediction of fire damage in the 1950s. According to physicist Michael May, former director of the Lawrence Livermore National Laboratory, computers "were barely able to handle blast" in this period. May argues that computers did not have the power to carry out the myriad calculations required to model mass fire and predict damage: "You could not predict what would happen with the thermal loading that depends on varying weather conditions and a lot of other things." Further, according to May, it is incorrect to impute predictability backward in time. Brode developed "a sophisticated approach much later [but] I don't think he could have done [it] in the '50s. So in that sense there was a genuine unpredictability" due to the limits of computing.[15]

This argument raises interesting and difficult questions. How hard was it to predict blast damage in the 1950s? What was the nature of the accomplishment of such predictions? Did the prediction of fire damage require different or greater computer capabilities than the prediction of blast damage? We will see that May is correct in his claim that what was predicted later could not have been predicted earlier, specifically, that the computer codes developed in the 1980s to model the physics of mass fire were much more sophisticated than the earlier codes on which they were based. But the level of sophistication of blast damage prediction also became much greater over time. The question should be: With adequate resources, could predictions of fire damage have been developed in the 1950s that were comparable to blast damage predictions in the same period? We will see in chapter 9 that the answer is yes.

Incendiary Warfare Immoral

Some argue that incendiary weapons have never been widely developed or used in the United States because such weapons, which can easily result in widespread and indiscriminate killing of civilians, have been morally re-pugnant. Based on two moral injunctions articulated by St. Augustine—do not kill noncombatants and do not use unnecessary force—the injunction against the indiscriminate killing of civilians has long been incorporated into the international legal framework of war. This is taken seriously by the U.S. military and is an integral part of the training of U.S. military officers.[16] As a result, after World War II, U.S. war planners did not want to think of nuclear weapons as incendiary weapons and therefore did not attend to the problem of developing a methodology to predict fire damage from them.

I do not want to disregard the moral argument. The moral injunction against indiscriminate killing has been both a cause and a reinforcer of U.S. precision strategic bombing doctrine. Although it does not appear that moral considerations were paramount in the shaping of early doctrine, morality has served as an important justification for U.S. precision strategic bombing doctrine both before and after the advent of nuclear weapons. In addition, moral arguments were deployed during World War II (without great effect) by U.S. military officers opposed to the use of incendiary weapons. Finally, moral arguments have shaped the presentation by the U.S. military of its bombing strategy, in part by causing it to redefine what is a military target and who (if anyone) is a civilian.

Nevertheless, moral considerations did not stop the development and deployment of incendiary weapons during World War II. Moral views may have slowed the early development of incendiaries in World War II, but a more important cause was that the agency responsible for incendiary development was far more focused on a no less indiscriminate weapon, gas. Further, there is no evidence that after the war, moral disapproval of incendiary weapons caused war planners not to develop a methodology to predict fire damage from nuclear weapons. Rather, issues of predictability and mea-surement were the focus of attention. (In any case, while moral revulsion could lead to a refusal to predict the incendiary effects of nuclear weapons, one might as easily predict that moral sensitivity would lead to an insistence on such development, so that in war the United States would not inflict un-intended damage.)

Finally, without denying that U.S. military officers take seriously the in-junction that unnecessary killing of civilians should be avoided, one should not overestimate the sensitivity of officers to enemy casualties in the face of an imperative to win the war. In explaining the strategic bombing campaign against Japan in World War II, the officer who headed that campaign, Air Force General Curtis LeMay, said, "There are no innocent civilians. It is their government and you are fighting a people, you are not trying to fight an armed force anymore. So it doesn't bother me so much to be killing the so-called innocent bystanders."[17] And he wrote:

> We were going after military targets. No point in slaughtering civilians for the mere sake of slaughter. Of course there is a pretty thin veneer in Japan, but the veneer was there. It was their system of dispersal of industry. All you had to do was visit one of those targets after we'd roasted it, and see the ruins of a multitude of tiny houses, with a drill press sticking up through the wreckage of every home. The entire population got into the act and worked to make those airplanes or munitions [of] war . . . men, women, children.[18]

A more recent statement by a regular commentator on Air Force affairs has a similar tone: "The notion that vaporizing Japanese cities is unusually immoral is, rationally speaking, pretty silly. . . . What is the moral difference between frying a jillion people serially with lots of everyday explosives and frying them in parallel with an atomic bomb? . . . The Allies liquidated cities all the time. How many kids do you think burned to death in cities like Dresden, Germany? . . . Mass killing of civilians was everyday stuff."[19]

Incendiary Warfare Psychologically Repellent

A closely related argument is that the notion of dying, or inflicting death, by fire is psychologically repellent. Therefore, military officers and civilians shied away from using fire as an instrument of war. After the war, this repugnance caused U.S. war planners to not want to think about or predict fire damage from nuclear weapons.[20]

However, many aspects of military operations repellent to the public, and to academics as they sit around conference tables, are not beyond the ability of those responsible for carrying out war plans to consider and to implement. According to General LeMay: "We knew we were going to kill a lot of women and kids when we burned that town. Had to be done. . . . The whole purpose of strategic warfare is to destroy the enemy's potential to wage war. And this was the enemy's potential. It had to be erased. If we didn't obliterate it, we would dwell subservient to it. Just as simple as that. . . . There's nothing new about this massacre of civilian populations."[21]

As we shall see, neither moral considerations nor psychological sensitivity came into play in the scientific exploration of nuclear weapons effects after the war. Prediction of damage was understood in terms of military operations and the application of scientific knowledge. I found no evidence that psychological factors caused research in the postwar period to focus on blast rather than fire damage.

Air Force's Organizational Interest in Understating Damage

In this argument, the Air Force generated knowledge about blast damage but not fire damage because, by underestimating the effectiveness of nuclear weapons, the Air Force strengthened its claims that it required more. Because war is often much more difficult to fight than anticipated, because things go wrong in the process, because militaries often suffer weapons and other shortages, in order to gain adequate resources there are strong incentives to overestimate weapons requirements and to underestimate weapons effectiveness.[22]

Interest-based approaches work by explaining the actions or preferences of actors (whether individuals or groups) on the basis of those actors' notions of how to preserve or achieve an advantageous position in the future.[23] Corporations lie to the public to bolster market position or lie to investors to bolster stock price. Politicians will "kill their own grandmothers" to maintain or gain political power. Military organizations prefer offensive doctrines and offensive armaments because these will expand budgets, reduce uncertainty, protect autonomy, and preserve their "organizational essence."[24] Morton Halperin, who coined the term, defines *organizational essence* as "the view held by the dominant group in the organization of what the missions and capabilities should be." Military organizations seek to maintain capabilities such as aircraft and bombs in order to perform their missions effectively. Such capabilities require huge investments in research and production facilities and are by definition expensive.[25] One way to maintain or increase such capabilities is to understate the effectiveness of existing weapons.

The obvious argument that follows from this is that in the early post–World War II period, the U.S. Air Force had an organizational interest in understating nuclear weapons damage to bolster its claims for more.[26]

We can evaluate this argument in several ways. Do we find evidence in statements or in patterns of action that the Air Force understated the effectiveness of nuclear weapons to bolster its case for more? Is there evidence that an interest in understating weapons effectiveness played a role in shaping research about damage caused by nuclear weapons—specifically, that investigations that could have helped develop knowledge and predictions about fire damage from nuclear weapons were not undertaken because they might show "too much" damage, or that research on fire damage was manipulated to understate such damage, or that the results of research showing significant damage from fire were suppressed or ignored? If so, the argument that knowledge was not developed about damage from fire because of organizational interests in understating the effectiveness of nuclear weapons could be very strong.

Chapters 6 and 7 show instances in which Air Force officers interpreted nuclear weapons test results and advocated policies regarding damage from nuclear weapons that supported claims that many more nuclear weapons were needed. However, there is no evidence that these positions had much impact on the basic knowledge-generating processes within the Air Force. Indeed, chapter 7 shows that, in the early 1950s, the Air Force invested in research that indicated that blast damage was *greater* than had been previously predicted—in other words, that it would be possible to do the same level of damage with *fewer* nuclear weapons.

I am not arguing that interests do not exist or that they are not important. I accept that many actions are undertaken with cold calculation of future consequences. However, the kinds of general statements of interest that have been used deductively in security studies do not do the work that is required here, which is to explain how those in organizations come to want what they do, and how that shapes the knowledge they seek.

We need an approach in which conceptions of interest adhere closely to the historical context, allowing us to understand in specific terms how members of organizations think they can achieve their ends and, more broadly, how they choose their goals. Halperin's notion of organizational essence adds a cognitive dimension, allowing for somewhat greater specification of context. However, the very term is ahistorical. We need to understand the genesis of organizational purposes, assumptions, and understandings of problems and solutions in order to articulate context-specific understandings of interest. Once missions are articulated and commitments made, actors will likely try to perpetuate the organizational structures that allow them to carry out the actions to which they are committed. In other words, as organizational ways of knowing and doing are developed and maintained, interests emerge and coalesce around them. The key to explanation lies in understanding the goals and conceptions of problems and solutions. From this follows the efforts of actors to preserve and strengthen organizational interests. To argue otherwise is to put the cart before the horse.

Sociology of Organizational Knowledge

Organizational Frames

During the creation of organizations, and during periods of organizational redefinition or upheaval, actors articulate organizational goals and draw on and modify existing understandings, or knowledge, of the social and physical environment in which they must operate.[27] This creates frameworks for action that structure how actors in organizations identify problems and find solutions. I call the approaches to problem solving used by those in organizations "organizational frames."

Organizational frames include what counts as a problem, how problems are represented, the strategies to be used to solve those problems, and the constraints and requirements placed on possible solutions.[28] As those in organizations engage in problem solving, they allocate organizational attention and resources, develop and draw on expertise inside and outside the organization, and in general build organizational capacity to solve certain problems but not others. Ultimately, organizations are likely to create new knowledge and organizational routines that contain such knowledge. Once created, knowledge-laden routines enable actors in organizations to carry out new actions. At the same time, they constrain what those in organizations can do. One way knowledge-laden routines constrain is by appearing to be sensible or even inevitable. As the process of solving particular problems recedes into the past, organizational participants, who not only act but explain to themselves how their actions make sense, lose the understanding of choice and contingency inherent in organizational frames.[29]

I argue that organizational knowledge is not shaped directly by the physical world, but is socially constructed. By *knowledge* I mean representations of the world taken by actors as reliable information. I refer to both *explicit knowledge*—what actors think they know about the world—and *tacit knowledge*—what actors simply assume or take for granted about the world. By *organizational knowledge,* I mean representations of the world that are articulated or assumed at the organizational level. This is the knowledge that someone first coming into an organization must be cognizant of and appear to accept if he or she wants to be credible and effective within the organization. Individual actors need not accept, or fully accept, organizational knowledge for it to exert an overriding influence on organizational action.

I certainly do not deny a reality outside the social. However, our knowledge of that reality is always, and profoundly, mediated by the social: what actors already know, what they want to know, how they think they can go about learning more, and the criteria by which they judge and make new knowledge—all these are not found in nature but are socially determined. I accept the claim that "explanations for the genesis, acceptance, and rejection of knowledge claims . . . [must be] sought in the domain of the social world rather than in the natural world."[30]

Thus, what has appeared self-evident to many actors, that blast damage is more predictable than fire damage, is, for me, *the very thing to be explained.* Why, and how, did this particular set of beliefs come to be organi-

zational "common sense"? What was the origin of organizational understandings regarding the relative predictability of blast damage and fire damage? What level of specificity in prediction was thought to be necessary and
why? What impact did such understandings of the possibilities of, and requirements for, damage prediction have on how knowledge was developed
and incorporated into organizational routines? In sum, how did the organizational understanding develop in which damage caused by blast seemed,
and, in terms of the organizational routines developed, *became,* more predictable than damage caused by fire?

I emphasize interpretations of the environment, choices made by actors,
and contingent outcomes. I argue that past choices and actions structure future possibilities, both by shaping the understandings that actors bring to
new situations and by shaping the social environment in which decisions are
made and carried out. This follows the "institutionalist" approach in sociology and political science, which, in sociologist Walter Powell's words, is to
"show how choices made at one point in time create institutions that generate recognizable patterns of constraints and opportunities at a later point."
In this perspective, historical outcomes cannot be explained simply by "the
preferences of actors . . . but must be explained as the product of previous
choices, that were shaped by institutional conventions and capabilities."[31]

Institutional approaches do not assume rational, efficient, or adaptive
outcomes. In contrast to those who claim that changes in ideas and institutions are adaptive responses to changing environments, institutionalists attend to how older ways of understanding and acting persist vestigially "in
the presentation of problems . . . in everyday life . . . in language and institutions."[32]

Many institutional explanations emphasize the process by which, at critical junctures, certain courses of action are eliminated or made less viable
and others are made the basis of future action. These are often called "path-
dependent" arguments.[33] This is not to say that certain choices cannot be
revisited, but, in Margaret Levi's words, "the costs of reversal are very
high. . . . The entrenchments of certain institutional arrangements obstruct
an easy reversal of the initial choice."[34]

Why is this? The most powerful explanation is that path-dependent
processes are self-reinforcing (or, in the language of economists, subject to
"increasing returns"): "The *relative* benefits of the current activity compared with other possible options increase over time."[35] We have already
gotten a glimpse of the self-reinforcing nature of organizational frames and
knowledge-rich organizational routines. The literature on path dependence
draws our attention to four aspects. First, building organizational capacity
to solve problems entails considerable initial research and development
costs. Second, once particular approaches to problem solving are embedded

in organizational routines, they become part of larger coordinated organizational processes—in this case, part of the larger machinery of nuclear war planning. Third, use of these knowledge-laden routines leads to organizational learning, more refined routines, and greater capacity to solve problems. Finally, the increasing efficacy of the adopted routines provides a powerful rationale for continued use, and the approach taken seems more sensible than other potential approaches.[36] (Some explications of path dependence stress that highly "contingent," even chance, "events set into motion institutional patterns . . . that have deterministic properties" and become permanently "locked in."[37] However, neither chance nor lock-in seems to be the case here. We will see that the early development of blast damage prediction was deeply conditioned by the history preceding it. Further, the organizational inability to predict fire damage would have appeared to be locked in thirty-five years after the end of World War II, but appeared less so after. We will return to these issues in the book's conclusion.)

How were organizational frames embedded so deeply in organizational routines? How did they shape knowledge regarding the damage caused by nuclear weapons? To put some historical meat on the sociological bones of the argument, I sketch how military doctrine shaped the dominant organizational frame in the U.S. Air Force.

From its founding as a separate air service within the U.S. Army shortly after World War I, air force officers (then Army Air Service officers), defined the primary mission of their organization as the ability to destroy an enemy's crucial industrial and military assets through long-range strategic bombardment. By the 1930s, these officers had refined U.S. strategic air doctrine to one of "precision bombing of the critical points of specified [enemy] target systems"; this is generally called "precision strategic bombing doctrine."[38]

Barry Posen concisely defines *military doctrine* as the military means chosen to achieve political ends:

> Two questions are important: *What* means shall be employed? and *How* shall they be employed? . . . Military doctrine includes the preferred mode of a group of services, a single service, or a subservice for fighting wars. It reflects the judgments of professional military officers, and to a lesser but important extent civilian leaders, about what is and is not militarily possible and necessary. . . . Force posture, the inventory of weapons and military organization controls, can be used as evidence to discover military doctrine.[39]

Doctrine serves as a broad guide to organizational action. Doctrine articulates purposes and includes assumptions and knowledge about the world that are incorporated into organizational approaches to problem solving. Doctrine shapes and becomes part of specific organizational frames. Frames are doctrine-in-action.

In the case of the U.S. Air Force, implementing precision strategic bombing doctrine meant solving many problems; for example, designing, producing, and improving long-distance strategic bomber aircraft; designing bombs; training officers in flying, navigation, and bombing techniques; choosing the structures to be targeted in strategic bombing operations (including gathering intelligence; mapping economic, political, and military structures; and developing models of the effects that destroying specific types of targets would have on the economy and on the enemy's ability to prosecute war); and developing scientific understandings of the physical damage caused by bombs to targeted structures and applying those understandings to specific operations. It is the latter problem, and the processes by which understandings and organizational routines were carried over from conventional bombs to nuclear weapons, that I am concerned with in this book.

Because problems can be described at different levels of abstraction and because problem-solving activities can be described in many ways, how one analyzes frames in an organization depends on what one wants to know. In some cases, a functional analysis of the types of problems to be solved, a mapping out of how frames are structured within organizations, will be appropriate. In such an analysis, frames are likely to be hierarchically organized. Within higher-level frames (problem-solving activities related to broad programmatic issues) will be nested lower-level ones (activities related to highly specialized problems to be solved).[40] To the degree that key organizational goals and assumptions are not contested, there may be only a few functionally organized high-level frames shaping organizational activity. To the degree that key organizational goals and assumptions are contested, there may be considerable organizational strife and conflicting frames.

My main focus is two historical organizational frames that were developed around conventional weapons and which, to varying degrees, carried over into the nuclear realm. These frames were highly specialized and, to some extent, conflicted with each other. One was a widely held "blast damage frame" centering on damage from high-explosive conventional bombs. Historically, this frame was closely associated with precision strategic bombing doctrine. The other was a less widely held "fire damage frame" emphasizing damage from incendiary bombs. It was less closely associated with precision strategic bombing doctrine. Both frames were approaches to understanding and predicting damage, both existed in rudimentary form before World War II, and both were developed during the war. After the war, the approaches to problem solving associated with the blast damage frame carried over and were adapted to nuclear weapons, while the fire damage frame did not carry over.

In the blast damage frame, problems to be solved included understanding the physical phenomena of shock waves and the mechanisms by which they produce damage; predicting blast damage to types of structures or other kinds of relevant targets; transforming predictive methods developed by specialists into relatively easily used predictive organizational routines; and making specific predictions of damage for use in war and in war planning. Frequently involved were issues of accurate measurement and assessment of damage, whether in combat or in experimental situations.

As noted above, a strong historical association existed between precision strategic bombing doctrine and understanding, predicting, and optimizing blast damage. When U.S. bombing doctrine was first developed, the major weapons in the U.S. air arsenal were high-explosive bombs. Those developing bombing doctrine assumed blast weapons; those developing blast weapons assumed precision strategic bombing doctrine. Each was predicated on the other. Further, because blast damage from bombs was discrete and spatially limited, it appeared to be highly consistent with U.S. bombing doctrine. (Of course, to the extent that bombing operations were inaccurate, as they often were during World War II, blast weapons were not a very effective way to destroy "pinpoint" targets.)

The problem-solving activities associated with understanding, predicting, and optimizing damage from blast weapons were tightly interconnected with other organizational activities. This interconnectedness is one reason why organizational change is difficult. The blast damage frame tied many people and organizational activities together: research, development, and production of high-explosive bombs; target selection, and analysis and prediction of blast damage; aircraft design and aircraft crew training were all predicated on the assumption that the salient damage would be blast damage from high-explosive bombs. For example, the targets selected often appeared to be more vulnerable to high-explosive bombs than to incendiaries; aircraft were designed to carry high-explosive bombs, not incendiaries; and aircraft crews were trained to handle only high-explosive bombs.

By contrast, in the fire damage frame, the problems to be solved were related to developing incendiary bombs and gaining air force interest in using them; understanding the physical processes by which fires ignited and then spread; and assessing fire damage and making specific predictions of damage for use in incendiary bombing operations. Many fewer people were involved in these activities, and they often felt like a beleaguered minority.

Because, under certain circumstances, fire damage from incendiary weapons could spread far more widely than damage from conventional blast weapons, the fire damage frame fit less well with the assumptions and aspirations of precision strategic bombing doctrine. Indeed, those professionals most closely involved in assessing and predicting damage from incendiary weapons tended to operate within a different doctrinal understanding, in which "area" damage by fire, rather than "precision" damage by blast, was seen as a more effective way to degrade enemy capabilities and morale. As we will see in chapter 3, for U.S. political leaders and members of the U.S. military, area bombing was identified primarily with the British; American strategy was defined as different and dedicated to "precision." During the war, U.S. doctrinal understanding limited the influence of those advocating research on and development of incendiary weapons, including research to predict damage caused by fire.

A potential third organizational frame did begin to develop in the late 1970s: a "fire-blast damage frame" that combined predictions of damage from both nuclear fire and blast. This entailed developing the ability to predict mass fire damage and incorporating those predictions into the long-standing predictive machinery for blast damage. How this innovation came about after decades in which there was no organizational ability to predict fire damage, and the fate of the innovation, is explained in chapters 9 and 10.

How do we know a frame when we see one? This is an empirical question that can only be answered in the context of specific historical processes. What problems are actors trying to solve, and how do they conceive of solutions? What assumptions about the world and organizational purpose do they bring to problem solving? How do they explain why their actions are reasonable and sensible?

Frames can be seen, or "read," in knowledge-laden organizational routines. For example, knowledge gained from nuclear weapons tests resulted in predictions about the damaging effects of blast from nuclear weapons; these predictions were then put in the form of an algorithm that could be routinely used by organizational actors to solve specific problems involved in targeting nuclear weapons. These actors did not necessarily have a full understanding, or any understanding, of the physics involved (much like a sociologist might use statistical routines or "packages" on a computer without an in-depth understanding of the underlying mathematics). In other words, knowledge gained through problem solving was incorporated into organizational routines. These knowledge-laden routines are solutions we can analyze to see the problems that actors tried to solve, the knowledge base from which they worked, and the organizational goals they pursued.

But frames do more than shape organizational attention, knowledge, and action. The process of identifying problems and finding solutions shapes organizations themselves. As part of problem-solving activity, actors build organizational capacity to solve problems, and this, in turn, affects relatively enduring features of organizations: the expertise brought into or developed by organizations, specialized activity to carry out large-scale research, and routines developed within organizations, including knowledge-laden routines that embody and apply knowledge gained in research activities. Thus, frames can be discerned not only in organizational routines but in other enduring features of organizations: in organizational expertise and in specialized areas of activity.

This shaping of organizational capacity in the process of sustained problem-solving activities both enables and constrains. Available expertise, structured activities to carry out investigations, and knowledge-laden organizational routines all enable those in an organization to solve problems. At the same time, organizational capacity reinforces how actors in organizations define problems and search for solutions: certain expertise will not be brought to bear on problems, the organization will not be structured in certain ways to carry out investigations, and organizational routines will carry certain kinds of knowledge but not other kinds.

We have thus completed a circle: Understandings of problems and of possible solutions shape organizational actions, including routines; sustained problem-solving activities shape organizational capacities; organizational capacities (in the form of available expertise, structures to carry out investigations, and knowledge-laden organizational routines) shape organizational understandings of problems and possible solutions. Frames shape actions, which shape organizational capacities, which shape frames.

These self-reinforcing processes are sustained and deepened by three internal features of organizational activity. First, as organizations engage in problem-solving activities, they are likely to solve many problems. The competence and knowledge gained then contrasts all the more strongly with the lack of ability to solve other problems. Competence highlights incompetence. The problem-solving path taken becomes far more attractive than other potential options.

Second, actors in organizations do more than engage in problem-solving activities. They explain to themselves why their course of action makes sense, and why the chosen course of action makes more sense than other possible courses of action. In creating such accounts, past organizational choices become reified. In the enduring insight of James March and Herbert Simon, "The world tends to be perceived by the organization members in terms of the particular concepts that are reflected in the organization's vocabulary. The particular categories and schemes of classification [an organization] employs are reified, and become, for members of the organization, attributes of the world rather than mere conventions."[41] In this process, a sense of contingency is lost, and frames become taken for granted.

Third, as people engage in problem-solving activities over a period of time, building competence and believing in the correctness and importance of what they are doing, they develop vested interests: They want to ensure a continued flow of resources into their area of activity to ensure that they can continue what they are doing and what they believe in.

Organizational Change

How, then, do organizations change? The requirements for organizational change are daunting: Conceptions of problems and solutions must be changed, as well as organizational routines, capacities, accounts, and vested interests. Changing organizations means changing organizational frames.

If the impetus for far-reaching change comes from the top of an organization, changes in understandings of problems and solutions must penetrate throughout the organization. High-level directives will not be sufficient. If the impetus for far-reaching change comes from lower down in the organization, as it did in the development of predictions combining nuclear blast and fire damage in the late 1970s, these changes must then be embraced by those at the top (whether by persuasion or by replacement of personnel) and must penetrate throughout.

One persuasive account of change in organizations has it that powerful and well-connected actors within an organization redefine their external environment and the organization's goals, and then rebuild career paths within the organization to empower those holding this new vision.[42] In my terms, this suggests that powerful actors reconceive organizational frames and then build new organizational capacity to solve new problems and seek new solutions.

What would cause actors to rethink the environment in which an organization exists? Scholars generally posit some sort of external change or shock. The key, however, is not simply change in the environment itself, but how actors *interpret* that environment, including their understanding of the degree and significance of change.[43] Probably the most likely impetus to reinterpretation of the environment, or organizational mission within it, is when key actors believe that organizational survival is at stake. Another likely impetus for change is when key actors believe that environmental change provides great opportunity; for example, the changing knowledge- and technology-base in computing and biotechnology. Of course, a period of great opportunity may coincide with fears about organizational survival. Major change also occurs when one organization is taken over by another. In such a case, environmental change has swamped the targeted organization, and other actors, who had been outside, come inside and impose their interpretations of purpose on the organization.[44]

The prerequisites for organizational survival vary by types of organizational environments, and this has strong implications for understanding change. For example, corporations in market economies are far more vulnerable to external challenges that may threaten their very survival than are military organizations in peacetime. Military organizations compete for budget, prerogative, and some missions, but, once established, military services generally do not fear extinction. Peacetime military services are buffered from external shock in other ways as well. There is, for example, no electoral accountability for military officers. Many crucial military matters are shrouded in secrecy. The relative invulnerability to threats of organizational extinction and to some forms of external oversight mean that peacetime militaries should generally be resistant to changes in frames. On the other hand, more than many governmental organizations, whether at the local, state, or federal level, military organizations are sometimes subjected to tests, especially in war, that are severe, and severely judged. In such environments, particularly in the face of failure, militaries may be relatively open to changing mission and problem-solving orientations.

In this case, the actors who initiated changes in nuclear damage prediction in the late 1970s were not driven by issues of organizational survival in a greatly changing political environment; rather, they were being highly strategic in using both existing and new opportunities to pursue problems of which they had long been aware. Many organizational actors resisted radical changes in the existing blast damage frame, but a number did not. Whether major change would occur was highly contingent on changing historical circumstances, the coalitions of support that could be built at various levels within and across organizations, and, ultimately, the understandings of officers who rotated in and out of the military at the highest levels.

Science and Technology Studies; Organization Theory

I have fashioned my argument out of two distinct literatures: science and technology studies, and organization theory. Both are large multidisciplinary areas of inquiry. Science and technology studies comprise the history of science, the history of technology, the sociology of science and technology, the anthropology of science and technology, and, to some degree, the philosophy of science. Organization theory, often taught as organizational behavior in graduate schools of business, draws on the disciplines of sociology, economics, psychology, and political science, and ranges in method from economic analysis to ethnography—with much more emphasis on the former.

There are some deep affinities between these two. Both are concerned with collective cognitive representations of the world. Studies in science and technology are concerned with how communities of practitioners use representations of the physical and social world to produce scientific knowledge and technological artifacts, which then influence the social world—including dating puzzling rock strata; creating maps and carto-graphic technologies; inventing electric power; constructing knowledge in biology and physics; and building computers, nuclear weapons, missiles, and simulated worlds.[45] Organization theory is concerned with how actors in organizations use representations of the world as a basis for action—as premises controlling organizational behavior and problem solving; as classi-fication schemes that filter out ambiguous and inconsistent information, en-abling organizations to "absorb" uncertainty and turn it into "fact"; and, more recently, as part of the routines and processes by which organizations learn.[46]

In addition, both literatures are concerned with path-dependent proc-esses.[47] And both have developed or use explicit or implicit notions of frames.[48]

Yet, despite these affinities, until recently these fields have not built upon one another.[49] This may be due, in part, to deep differences in intellectual style between the two. On the one hand, the field of science and technology studies tends toward a style of theorized case studies (much like the disci-pline of anthropology), in which specific situations are understood as in-stances of some larger issue. Theoretical problems and claims are brought to bear in investigations of specific cases, and both the analysis of the case and the theoretical claims will be modified and elaborated in the course of inquiry. On the other hand, much organization theory, including some of the work I have found most valuable, tends toward the abstract, striving to achieve broad theoretical statements about the nature of organizations and about the proper agenda for organizational research, while it subordinates detailed case studies.[50] In practice, this has meant that relatively little at-tention has been paid to explaining the *processes* by which organizations de-velop knowledge and knowledge-rich routines.[51] If organization theory has drawn our attention to the salience of categories in shaping organizational life, it generally has not shown in a detailed way *how* categorical choices are contested, made, and modified.[52] This is, of course, the very thing at which studies in the history and sociology of science and technology excel.

But despite the strengths of science and technology studies, this litera-ture has not systematically studied organizations as the *locus* of the social shaping of technology and knowledge. The impact of organizations on the shaping of technology and the impact of technology on organizational life have been largely ignored.[53] This may be because much work in the sociol-ogy of technology focuses on late nineteenth and early twentieth century in-ventions ranging from artifacts, such as bicycles, Bakelite, and celluloid collars, to huge systems, such as the social and technological infrastructure involved in the generation, distribution, and consumption of electricity. Despite differences in scale, the locus of the social shaping and impact of technology is largely societal: the market, broadly conceived, where networks of inventors, scientists, engineers, entrepreneurs, and differentiated groups of potential consumers mutually shape artifacts and preferences. In this broad scheme, large-scale organizations are understood as producers of artifacts or as part of large-scale social and technological systems.[54] Internal organizational processes generally have not been the focus of attention.

Thus, the complementarity of these two literatures is clear. By expanding the concept of frames, which has been well-developed within the sociology of technology, to include cognition embedded in organizational routines, we can arrive at a deeper understanding of how knowledge is generated and sustained within organizations. Formative experiences in the histories of organizations near the time of founding or during turbulent periods of redefinition shape organizational frames that structure how actors in organizations identify problems and find solutions. Frames shape organizational routines and become institutionalized in them. Once routines are established, frames and the conceptions embedded in them are likely to persist, even as the environment changes.

Let us now examine how and why, for over half a century, fire damage from nuclear weapons was not incorporated into the U.S. military's organizational routines. We begin before World War II to gain perspective on the enduring understandings and institutional patterns that shaped later inquiry and knowledge.

CONSTRUCTING DESTRUCTION, 1940–1961

Chapter

Doctrine and Damage through World War II

The purpose of bombing is damage. The effort that underlies a bombing attack is gigantic: building airplane and bomb factories, development and production of the myriad accessories, training mechanics and crews, transporting shiploads of equipment and supplies—an effort that absorbed millions of American men and women. But the intended purpose of this stupendous effort can be summed up in the one ugly word: damage.

John E. Burchard, *Rockets, Guns and Targets* (1948)

O n the eve of its entry into World War II, the U.S. military had little knowledge about the physical processes by which bombs, whether high-explosive or incendiary, caused damage, and it had no ability to predict such damage. High-explosive bombs composed almost all of the U.S. stockpile, but, according to architectural engineer John Burchard, "When people worried at all about measuring what a bomb might do, they bored holes of different sizes into a plywood board, stretched paper of more-or-less uniform properties across the holes and evaluated the intensity of the blast from the diameter of the smallest hole over which the paper was broken."[1] The military also had virtually no understanding of explosive shock waves or of structural response to shock—both essential for predicting blast damage.

During the war, the U.S. government mobilized professors of civil engineering and others to understand, measure, assess, and predict damage from high-explosive bombs. These experts developed a great deal of knowledge about blast effects, devised methods to predict damage, and codified these predictions in a manual to aid those who selected bombs for bombing operations. By the end of the war, "it was possible to select, from experience and from the knowledge of what bombs would do, the probability of hitting near a target and, from the characteristics of the target, what sort of bomb load should be carried; for the paper and tube gauges there had been substituted sensitive electronic devices to measure the peak pressure as a function of milliseconds."[2]

By contrast, at the beginning of World War II, the U.S. military had virtually no incendiary weapons. During the war, the government developed some incendiary bomb capabilities and mobilized a handful of fire protection engineers to assess and predict fire damage. This mobilization was significantly different from the mobilization of engineers to predict blast damage. Fewer engineers were engaged to assess and predict fire damage, they were mobilized later in the war, their research base was in England, not in the United States, and they drew on different kinds of professional knowledge. Fire protection engineers, generally trained as chemical engineers and employed by fire insurance companies and fire departments, used a backward application of well-understood principles of fire insurance and fire codes to develop predictions of the "fire vulnerability," or "fire susceptibility," of buildings. These were, in the words of a prominent fire protection engineer, James McElroy, "fire protection plan[s], in reverse."[3] These engineers developed considerable ability to predict the damage caused by "ordinary" incendiary attacks but much less ability to understand, let alone predict, the damage caused by the unanticipated "firestorms" set during the war. Although the algorithms the fire protection engineers devised were, to a limited extent, incorporated into training programs and calculational aids to predict bomb damage, all in all, methods for predicting fire damage were neither as well developed nor as widely disseminated for use by the military as were methods for predicting blast damage.

How and why did this substantial disparity in organizational knowledge about damage caused by high explosives and incendiaries develop? During the war, why did the U.S. military pay far more attention to predicting blast damage than fire damage, and why, by the end, had the military routinized prediction of damage from blast far more than damage from fire?

Three kinds of processes were at work. First, the air force's doctrinal understandings of ends and means—the goals of strategic bombing and how those goals could be best achieved (what targets should be damaged and by what types of bombs)—along with organizational capabilities at the outset of the war, shaped the initial organizational focus in problem solving and the general approach taken to finding solutions. Specifically, the air force goal of destroying key nodes of an enemy's economy through precision bombing with high-explosive bombs led to an early emphasis on understanding, assessing, and predicting blast damage. This provided the template on which problems were elaborated, solutions were sought, and organizational capacity would be built during the war.

Second, the many surprises encountered in the experience of the war—including the great difficulty of implementing a strategy of precision bombing and, later, the surprisingly destructive efficacy of incendiary bombing—along with the vast resources available and the length of the war, led the U.S. military to broaden its approach to the problems considered and the solutions pursued. Despite this broadening, however, the underlying organizational goals and understandings of problems to be solved did not change: For the U.S. military, blast damage remained more important to understand and predict than did fire damage.

Third, military doctrine and the problems encountered in bombing operations shaped the government's mobilization of expertise and the knowledge developed to predict bomb damage. In large part because of military priorities for precision bombing of specific targets, greater resources were devoted to gaining the ability to predict blast damage from high-explosive bombs than fire damage from incendiary bombs.

British and U.S. Strategic Air Doctrine and Capabilities

Air warfare was a revolutionary development in the early twentieth century: The invention of the airplane was followed by the organizational development of national air forces and air doctrine, which prescribed the ends and means of air warfare. In strategic air doctrine, bomber-based air forces were envisioned as operating largely independently of naval and land forces to rain destruction behind enemy lines. These forces would primarily target war-supporting industries, including military production, and "civilian morale." U.S. Air Force General Curtis LeMay said it succinctly: "The whole purpose of strategic [air] warfare is to destroy the enemy's potential to wage war."[4] Not all air forces emphasized strategic air doctrine, but both the British and American did. (The Germans and Russians built their air forces largely as extensions of army artillery and emphasized tactical uses to support army actions on the battlefield. The French air force emphasized neither strategic nor tactical air doctrine but "agreed to fulfill every loosely defined mission available . . . and rejected any doctrine.")[5]

But what did it mean to destroy an enemy's potential to wage war? Relatively early in the development of strategic air doctrine, two different conceptions developed of what was to be damaged, how damage would destroy war potential, and how damage was to be inflicted. In one conception, civilian morale was targeted. In this view, if civilian morale could be shattered, then war-supporting production, support for an enemy government's policies, and overall political will to fight would all be greatly diminished. Aiming to destroy civilian morale was officially understood to mean targeting not civilians themselves but rather workers' houses ("dehousing" workers in the famous phrase of a British memorandum from World War II), factories essential for workers' livelihoods, and other centers of economic activity. In practice, this often entailed a policy of "area bombing" using incendiary bombs. In the other conception of strategic air doctrine, war-supporting industrial production was targeted. In this view, if specific critical points of production, such as aircraft factories and ball-bearing factories, could be destroyed, the ability to sustain a nation's war machine would collapse. In practice, this often meant trying to carry out a policy of precision bombing using high-explosive bombs.

These different emphases were not necessarily contradictory—indeed, both British and U.S. doctrine had elements of both—but they entailed different ideas about targets, implementation, and mechanisms of damage.

British Strategy: Aiming to Start a Conflagration

Historically, British air doctrine was mixed: It emphasized attacks on civilian morale but also sought the capability to carry out "selective attack" on industrial target systems. Nonetheless, undermining civilian morale—which was reflected in an area bombing strategy in World War II—was more deeply embedded in British doctrine than in American. British advocacy of the destruction of enemy morale by bombing dated back to the World War I era and appears to be part of the larger British (and continental) "cult of the offensive."[6] In 1919 Major General Hugh Trenchard, about to become chief of the air staff for the next decade, wrote, "the moral effect of bombing stands undoubtedly to the material effect in a proportion of 20 to 1." A contemporary letter from Secretary of War for Air Lord Weir to Trenchard links targeting morale and incendiary area bombing: "I would very much like if you could start up a really big fire in one of the German towns. . . . If I were you, I would not be too exacting as regards accuracy in bombing railway stations in the middle of towns. The German is susceptible to bloodiness, and I would not mind a few accidents due to inaccuracy."[7]

Before the outbreak of World War II, and for some time after the war began, the British Royal Air Force (RAF) aspired to selective, or precision, attacks. Major target systems included oil, aircraft production, aluminum plants, ports and shipping, communications, naval targets, and transport. The RAF largely adhered to a policy of selective bombing into the summer of 1941, but without much success. In historian Malcolm Smith's words, although civilian morale was rejected in the 1930s by the Air Staff "as a target in its own right, the speed with which it reappeared once war broke out implies that the importance of the supposed vulnerability of civilian morale remained a powerful underlying assumption in Air Staff minds."[8] In August and September 1940, in the Battle of Britain, and continuing after, the English were subjected to heavy urban area bombing attacks by the Germans. This resulted in direct pressure on the RAF from Prime Minister Winston Churchill for retribution bombing, an idea supported by the public. In September 1940, Sir Charles Portal, then commander in chief, Bomber Command, wrote: "We have not yet reached the stage of desiring to burn down a whole town, but when this stage is reached we shall do it by dropping a large quantity of incendiaries first and then a sustained attack with High Explosive to drive the firefighters underground and let the flames get a good hold." In October 1940 morale was added to the target list as an important "target" (although generally a secondary one).[9]

Over the course of the next year, British precision strategic bombing operations against Germany proved ineffective. At the same time, British analyses of the German area bombing of England (discussed below) showed that German incendiaries were more destructive than high-explosive bombs. These developments, coupled with the historical prominence of morale as a target, led the British Air Staff by September 1941 to formulate an ambitious new plan for the destruction of German towns and cities, which, in the words of historians Charles Webster and Noble Frankland, "naturally signalled the end of precision attack and the coming of area bombing."[10] In this strategy, "The destruction of residential and industrial centres and the spreading of the fear of death were tasks which called for a technique quite different from that needed for the destruction of a railway viaduct or even an oil plant. . . . Thus, instead of trying to blow up each building with high explosive, which was obviously an impossibly large task, the aim was to start a conflagration in the centre of each town, which, it might be hoped, would consume the whole."[11]

From before the beginning of war, the British had both high-explosive and incendiary bomb capabilities. Their main incendiary, first designed in 1934, was a 4-pound magnesium bomb. To solve operational problems of poor aim and inefficient stowage in aircraft, which limited the number of bombs that could be carried, incendiary bombs were clustered.[12] For the British Air Staff, the main problem of incendiaries was not aim but the insufficient weight of attack. In the words of Webster and Frankland, "Bomber Command wasn't dropping enough incendiaries or not within a short enough space of time to overwhelm German fire-fighting capacity. . . . In the light of these considerations, [in September 1941] the Air Staff now suggested that each Bomber Command attack should include a minimum of between 25,000 and 30,000 incendiary bombs . . . irrespective of the effect it might have upon the number of high-explosive bombs which could also be lifted." The air staff recommended that some high-explosive bombs be used in the opening phase of an attack, but the role was largely a secondary one "to force the fire-fighters off the streets and burst the water mains. This would give the incendiaries a better chance of doing their work."[13]

The British drew on, and developed, a number of organizations to gather and analyze information necessary to the air war effort. Among the more important were the Ministry of Economic Warfare, which developed information on industry for use in choosing air targets, and the RAF photointerpretation unit at Medmenham, which assessed damage and evaluated the effectiveness of British bombing attacks. British mapping and analysis developed to fit British air doctrine and operations, which were turning increasingly toward area bombing at night. Area bombing made "detailed maps of . . . target areas and accurate photographs of targets . . . unnecessary."[14] One description reads:

> In determining the aiming point for city attacks, Bomber Command prepared a zone map of the city based on aerial photographs. Administrative and residential areas between 70 and 100 per cent built-up were outlined in red. Similar areas between 40 and 70 per cent built-up were outlined in green. Major railroad facilities were outlined in buff and industrial areas in black. In most German cities the black areas lay largely on the perimeter. Area attacks on a previously unbombed city were aimed at the center of the red area, while subsequent attacks on the same city were usually directed against the center of the most heavily built-up areas which remained undestroyed.[15]

Many damage reports did not assess damage to specific structures. Early in the war, "the damage reports issued by the RAF interpretation unit at Medmenham were mostly area studies. . . . The damage was assessed according to the amount of the area damaged, and the industrial plants affected were placed in general classes depending on the percentage of the plant damaged."[16]

One British organization, however, analyzed bomb damage to specific structures, and it became an important organizational connection between the British and Americans.[17] In the fall of 1940, after the German bombing of Britain, the Ministry of Home Security set up a research unit known as RE 8 (Research and Experiment Department, Section 8), under Reginald Stradling at Princes Risborough, to catalogue and analyze the damage. Some photointerpretation units in England did "first phase" analysis within twenty-four hours or "second phase" analysis within forty-eight hours; RE 8 did "third phase target analysis"—the most detailed assessment possible.[18] Stradling's group studied every bombing incident they could, recorded the damage, identified the type and size of enemy bombs, and analyzed the

varying effects of German high-explosive bombs and incendiaries on different types of buildings. In July 1942, RE 8 began to analyze the vulnerability
of German industrial targets. They also compared German bombs and
British bombs, analyzed which British bombs would be required to achieve
specific damage against Germany, and assessed Allied bomb damage to German towns. The group analyzed the effects of incendiaries and high-explosive bombs on various structures and in varying urban configurations and
estimated total economic loss as well.[19] As we shall see below, U.S. scientists,
engineers, and others visited and worked in RE 8.

American Strategy: "Right in the Pickle Barrel"

American strategic air doctrine during and immediately after World War
I was also mixed. An early strategic bombing plan drawn up during the war,
known as the Gorrell plan, noted that "the manufacture of [German] shells
and bombs is dependent upon the output of a few specific, well-known factories turning out the chemicals for them. . . . If the chemical factories can
be blown up, the shell and bomb output will cease."[20] But in the same period air power advocate William (Billy) Mitchell variously emphasized targeting enemy air forces, "vital centers," and morale. It is probably fair to say
that in the early years, U.S. strategic notions were broad, sharing with British
doctrine the basic notion that "long-range attacks against the enemy's vital
centers would be decisive," and consistent mainly in advocating an independent air force.[21]

In the 1920s and 1930s, an elite group of officers at the U.S. Army's Air
Corps Tactical School began to refine U.S. air doctrine and to differentiate
it from British doctrine. As early as the mid-1920s, one text, in the words of
historian Stephen McFarland, advocated "strike[s] at specific points, including individual buildings, warehouses, offices, water plants, power
plants, and aircraft."[22] During the 1930s, the Tactical School "invented its
own special concept of industrial attack—precision bombing of the critical
points of specified target systems."[23] Thus, air officers moved away from notions of destroying vital centers and became committed to a doctrine of
strategic precision bombing, in which specific key "nodes," or "bottleneck"
targets, such as ball bearings and machine tools, would be destroyed. This
was also called an "industrial web theory."[24] Major General Haywood S.
Hansell, Jr., who was deeply involved in the development of precision bombing doctrine in this period, provided this example:

We discovered one day that we were taking delivery on new airplanes
. . . [and] the delivery of controllable pitch propellers had fallen down.
Inquiries showed . . . it was a relatively simple but highly specialized

spring that was lacking, and we found that all the springs made for all the controllable pitch propellers of that variety in the United States came from one plant and that that plant in Pittsburgh had suffered from a flood. There was a perfect and classic example. To all intents and purposes a very large portion of the entire aircraft industry in the United States had been nullified just as effectively as if a great many airplanes had been individually shot up, or a considerable number of factories had been hit. That practical example set the pattern for the ideal selection of precision targets.[25]

Precision doctrine was extremely ambitious—or, in the understanding of those developing it, "visionary"—and placed great demands on analytical, informational, technological, and operational capabilities. To be effective, this doctrine required the ability to understand which target systems were indeed vital, to locate crucial enemy structures within that target system, and to deliver the proper weapons accurately to small targets. Yet all of these capabilities were weak before and during World War II. For example, the problem of target selection was, according to Hansell, "essentially a problem for industrial economists, but no economists were available and no money was available to hire them" before World War II, and the air force developed its ideas on its own.[26]

Historians have pointed to several reasons for the development of such a demanding precision doctrine by the U.S. Army Air Corps. First, high-level political and general public opposition to mass civilian bombings may have been a factor. In contrast to the high-level British official's statement in 1918 that he would "not be too exacting as regards accuracy," the U.S. secretary of war, Newton Baker, stated in the same period his opposition to "promiscuous bombing upon industry, commerce or population."[27] Second, cultural currents of Taylorism and industrial efficiency, and the later experience of the Great Depression, likely contributed to the military's awareness of the importance of industry and the interdependence and fragility of modern economies.[28] Third, in the early and mid-1930s, agreements and legislation assigned to the air force the responsibility of coastal defense and limited the organization's mission to defensive purposes.[29] Historians have argued that "the need to hit a ship at sea put a premium on 'precision' capability" and that "airmen presented their ideas of strategic bombardment in the guise of plans for defense, specifically the defense of America's coast, which stressed the reinforcement of Hawaii and Panama. Coastal defense became the airmen's Trojan horse," for the purchase of long-range bombers.[30] Fourth, the Army's own tradition of precision marksmanship may well have carried over into the development of the Army Air Corps doctrinal development.[31]

The air war plan that was developed on the eve of U.S. entry into World

War II was mixed: It emphasized precision strategic bombing doctrine, but also incorporated the possibility of weakening enemy morale later in the war. The four officers who drafted the war plan, called AWPD-1 (Air War Plans Division-1), in early August 1941 were all "stalwart disciples" of the strategic bombing theory developed at the Air Corps Tactical School; three of the four had taught there. AWPD-1 targeted three main components of the German economy: electric power, transportation, and oil. Planners thought that destroying 124 "vital targets" would destroy German war-making capability. According to a vivid account of the planning process, the planning group "noted that civilians might also be attacked directly once their morale had weakened due to sustained suffering and a lack of faith in Germany's ability to win the war. 'However, if these conditions do not exist,' the planners cautioned, 'then area bombing of cities may actually stiffen the resistance of the population.'"[32]

On the eve of U.S. entry into the war, air doctrine was largely a set of statements about actions and consequences that had no historical precedent: large-scale "precision" bombing of specific key nodes would disrupt the highly interdependent modern economies necessary for fighting modern wars. The air force (since the summer of 1941, the U.S. Army Air Forces) had untested weapons, virtually no operational experience, and a rudimentary state of knowledge regarding potential targets, the damage that would result from bombing those targets, and the political results that could reasonably be expected from such bombing.

Nevertheless, precision bombing doctrine was deeply embedded in the air force—in planned operations, training, and equipment. As I noted in chapter 2, those who developed precision strategic bombing doctrine assumed blast weapons; those who developed blast weapons assumed precision strategic bombing doctrine. Thus, before and during the first years of the war, doctrine and bomb capabilities developed at the same time and reinforced each other. This close association was evident on the eve of World War II: The U.S. bomb arsenal was predominantly high-explosive blast weapons. In the fall of 1941 (in the same period when British strategy and operations were moving toward area bombing), the U.S. Army Ordnance Department, working within the assumption of precision strategic bombing doctrine, standardized 250-, 500-, 1,000-, and 2,000-pound high-explosive bombs in its arsenal.[33] U.S. aircraft were equipped with bomb racks configured only to hold high-explosive bombs, and the air force trained its men only in the use of high-explosive bombs.[34]

Other capabilities, most notably the precision aim made possible by the Norden bombsight, were also closely associated with precision strategic bombing doctrine. The Norden bombsight, in theory if not always in wartime operations, greatly improved the ability to aim bombs. This bombsight was first available in the late 1920s and early 1930s and lent credibility to the idea of precision bombing. It did not, however, precede doctrine: "The Norden bombsight was not available until after the doctrine based on accurate bombing was well on the way to formulation."[35] It was in connection with the bombsight that the phrase "pickle barrel" was coined and later used to describe, with great exaggeration, U.S. bombing "accuracy" in World War II—as in U.S. Air Force General Henry "Hap" Arnold's phrase, "tossing it right in the pickle barrel."[36] (Still, U.S. bombing accuracy in World War II left something to be desired. On U.S. radar bombing missions, for example, only 5 percent of bombs fell within a mile of the aim point.)[37]

We see the inverse relationship as well. Before the war, military officers associated incendiary methods primarily with area bombing. This association was also made by advocates of incendiary bombs. In the words of an early champion, the chemist J. E. Zanetti: "All-out warfare is here and must be faced. It is elementary that the achievement of conflagrations should be the aim of users of incendiary bombs when attacking combustible areas of large cities."[38] It is hardly surprising, then, that the air force, oriented toward precision bombing, did not develop incendiary weapons, delivery capabilities, or training in their use.

Reflecting doctrine and resulting low organizational priority, incendiary weapon development in the interwar period had been divided between two agencies within the U.S. Army, neither of them strongly committed to the development of incendiary weapons. The Chemical Warfare Service, nominally in charge, was principally concerned with developing poison gas, not incendiaries. The Ordnance Department was responsible for incendiary bomb casings, but concentrated on developing high-explosive bombs.[39] From the perspective of a leading fire protection engineer, Horatio Bond, the Chemical Warfare Service's "preoccupation" with gas warfare and the U.S. Army Air Forces' commitment to high-explosive bombs "explain[s] why fire attacks did not have the place they deserved in the early war plans, quite apart from the unfamiliarity of airmen with fire possibilities."[40]

In September 1941, the United States had one type of incendiary bomb standardized in its arsenal, the 4-pound AN-M50, but it had a high dud rate.[41] In addition, chemical development work was just beginning on solving the critical problem of how to thicken gasoline for "jellied" incendiary bomb fillings.[42] According to a historian of U.S. incendiary weapons, John Mountcastle, the United States was "incapable of employing incendiary weapons of any type at the beginning of its active involvement in World War II."[43]

Bond argued that organizational experience, expertise, and technological and operational capabilities were all connected in a single system in which organizational assumptions and capabilities regarding blast weapons were linked to precision bombing doctrine: "The air force planners might be expected, because of experience and training, to evaluate the air factors, but how fires are started or spread on the ground was completely outside their field of experience. Probably most important, the U.S. air forces at the start of the war were geared to the use of high explosive bombs. *Planes, bombs, bombsights, training, were all tied together to produce blast damage to 'precision' targets.*"[44]

Although precision bombing doctrine and the closely tied blast damage frame were dominant, some effort was put into developing incendiary weapons as part of the vast mobilization for war. Authority for weapons development was consolidated in the Chemical Warfare Service in the fall of 1941. While still concerned primarily with gas warfare, the Chemical Warfare Service began to develop new and improved incendiary weapons in conjunction with the National Defense Research Committee (NDRC; discussed below), chemistry professor Louis Fieser of Harvard University, and Standard Oil and other chemical companies.[45] By mid- to late 1943, almost two years after the United States had entered the war, "aimable" clusters of incendiaries began to be available for use in bombing operations. Numerous problems had been solved regarding aiming, safety, and reliability, including the reduction of damage to weapons during shipping. In addition, bomb racks on aircraft began to be reconfigured and training procedures modified. In early 1944, the mass production of reliable incendiary weapons was undertaken.[46] It would not, however, be easy to assimilate these weapons into target intelligence and bombing operations.

Air Target Intelligence and Bombing Operations

Air Target Intelligence in Europe

Doctrinal assumptions and organizational capabilities at the outset of the war shaped the acquisition of knowledge regarding what was to be bombed, how, and with what effect. An authoritative history of U.S. air intelligence during World War II put it succinctly:

American daylight precision bombing depended upon a determination of the critical systems within the enemy's industrial and military structure, evaluation of specific targets within these broad categories, and the ability to destroy these precise targets most effectively and efficiently. This required detailed information and analyses not only pinpointing the critical targets within broad industries but also addressing the vulnerabilities of specific targets such that operational planners could focus on the most critical elements of any given target.[47]

Closely related to choice of targets were choice of weapons and "feed-back on the effects of an attack," or damage assessment. *Damage assessment* included evaluating the physical damage to a target and, more broadly, the impact of physical damage on the economic output or military capacity of the target and the impact of reduced output or capacity on the enemy's total war-making ability.[48] This complex of activities went under the rubric of "air intelligence," or "air target intelligence." Air target intelligence activities were far flung, taking place in multiple organizations and sites in the European and Pacific theaters, and in Washington. Those in air intelligence generally provided recommendations to operational commands, which then made final choices regarding specific aim points, weapons selection, bomb routes, tactics, and so on.

In Europe, the central figure in air target intelligence was Army Air Force Colonel Richard Hughes, a former British army officer who had become a U.S. resident in 1929. Beginning with the formal establishment of the U.S. Eighth Air Force Headquarters in England in June 1942, Hughes worked in U.S. target intelligence.[49] At first Hughes worked for the assistant chief of staff for intelligence (A-2). His responsibilities included "refining target priorities, target analysis and tactical planning, . . . preparing target maps and objective folders, coordinating with American and British economic warfare units, and operational analysis." To provide smoother coordination with operational planning, in December 1942 Hughes moved his target branch over to the assistant chief of staff for plans (A-5), but he continued to do similar work.[50]

Hughes lacked the trained personnel in his target branch to do the required analysis. To remedy this, he helped establish a new organization composed of highly trained economists who could do both broad economic analysis and detailed analysis of specific targets. The organization, established in September 1942, was called the Enemy Objectives Unit (EOU). EOU was headed by Chandler Morse and included, among others, Harold Barnett, Carl Kaysen, Charles Kindleberger, Walt W. Rostow, and William Salant.[51] It operated out of the Economic Warfare Division of the American Embassy in London and reported directly to Hughes. In September, immediately after its formal establishment, Hughes directed EOU "to provide detailed analyses of designated targets," including the "importance of [a particular] plant within [an] industry, functions of buildings, vulnerability of processes, probable rate of recovery after successful attack, and the sections of the target which should constitute the proper objective of attack."[52]

The EOU developed "aiming point" reports, which were very different from the British zone maps in which the bombers aimed first at the center of the most built-up areas of a city. The aiming point reports provided "a way to think about the precision bombardment of specific targets."[53]

Hughes and EOU worked closely with those in other organizations, for example, operational analysts in the air force, who, like the economists, were highly trained and systematic thinkers. One organization with which EOU and Hughes had a contentious relationship was the Committee of Operational Analysts (COA), which, despite the name, was not composed of operations analysts. COA was founded in December 1942 to advise General Arnold, commander of the U.S. Army Air Forces, on targeting for strategic bombing. Both COA and EOU agreed on precision bombing doctrine, but they disagreed about what should be targeted. Certainly those in EOU thought COA's analyses poor. According to a former EOU economist, "We referred to them as the flying colonels" (many of the military representatives on COA were colonels), "and we thought they were full of shit." This economist derided two of COA's favorite "target systems": grinding wheels and ball bearings. COA thought that destruction of these industrial elements would effectively hinder enemy war mobilization, but EOU's economists thought there were substitutes for them in production and use. Grinding wheel production could be shifted to hundreds of ceramic factories. And, because engineers overdesigned on ball bearings, the Germans could conserve, go without, or use inferior ball bearings. "The point was that neither target system met one of EOU's tests: 'What doesn't have a good substitute?'" Other tests included the physical vulnerability of structures and how long it would take for destruction of the target system to affect the battlefield. EOU's preferred target system was oil.[54]

EOU worked closely, if sometimes contentiously, with the British. For example, much of the data EOU analyzed was provided by the British Ministry of Economic Warfare. From an American point of view, the "information compiled by the British Ministry of Economic Warfare . . . and Air Ministry Air Intelligence tended to address the enemy's economic and industrial capabilities from a perspective devoid of technical detail."[55] The British, on the other hand, "viewed the Americans' preoccupation with specific buildings and bridge spans as evidence of 'undue optimism and even faint morbidity.'"[56]

EOU also worked closely with RE 8, which collected data and assessed the physical damage from German bombs dropped on England. In the spring of 1943, RE 8 became an Allied agency, with both British and Americans assigned to it.[57]

Although some consideration was given to incendiary bombs toward the end of 1943, EOU, COA, and air force officers in the field predicated most of their analyses on the use of high-explosive bombs. According to Mountcastle, "In spite of the British enthusiasm for incendiaries . . . the majority of the newly arrived U.S. air commanders [in the Eighth Air Force] were determined to rely on High Explosive (H.E.) bombs with which they had trained in the United States." Similarly, another historian writes, "At first the crews and even the operations officers at headquarters opposed the use of incendiaries. They believed that the best way to destroy a target was with heavy explosive bombs."[58]

Fire Protection Engineers as Interlopers

The lack of organizational interest in a strategy of area bombing resulted in a late start in developing incendiary bombs and in mobilizing experts on fire damage. In contrast to a sizable arsenal of high-explosive bombs, the U.S. military had virtually no incendiary weapons capability at the beginning of World War II, nor did it have an ongoing research program to measure the effectiveness of incendiary weapons or to understand the means by which fire caused damage to various kinds of structures. During the war, chemists from universities and industry developed effective incendiary bombs and studied the relative effectiveness of various types of incendiaries in experimental settings.

Fire protection engineers were the professionals mobilized to assess and predict damage from incendiary weapons. Fire protection developed as a practical discipline in the United States shortly after the Civil War as architects and engineers analyzed the failure of so-called "fireproof" buildings constructed with cast iron columns. The Great Chicago Fire of 1871, which "leveled a huge portion of the city," gave the profession a boost as "architects examined the ruins to understand why the fireproof buildings failed and how they could be improved."[59] In 1896, fire protection engineers, fire insurance companies, and manufacturers founded the National Fire Protection Association to develop technical standards for fire safety.[60]

Fire protection engineers first became formally involved in the war effort when the British invited Horatio Bond, the chief engineer for the National Fire Protection Association, to visit RE 8 at Princes Risborough in the winter of 1942. Bond was an "MIT man," who had graduated in 1923 with a degree in engineering administration. During the war, he worked in the U.S. Office of Civil Defense.[61]

According to James McElroy, a fire protection engineer who was recruited into war work by Bond the next year, the British had invited Bond over "to find out if there wasn't some way that American fire prevention experience could be useful from a destructive point of view."[62] Bond went to England in December 1942 and returned to the United States in April 1943, where he resumed his work at the Office of Civil Defense and began to recruit American fire protection engineers to work with the British. He had some difficulty finding engineers willing and able "to turn their interests around. . . . The trouble is, they're made to try to prevent fires. . . . Fortunately, there were two or three men" who were interested. Bond enlisted two colleagues, McElroy and U.S. Army Major Forrest Sanborn, to work in RE 8 on bomb damage assessment and damage prediction.[63] Both McElroy and Sanborn worked in fire insurance before the war. Referring to himself and Sanborn, McElroy wrote, "We two, for a whole year (June 1943 to June 1944), were the only men with fire prevention experience actively in the air warfare business."[64]

Drawing on principles of fire insurance—in which fire breaks (such as parapeted walls or distance between buildings) and the combustibility of contents and structures were of critical importance—and knowledge used in fire fighting about the causes of fire ignition and fire spread, McElroy and Sanborn developed predictions of the vulnerability of structures to fire damage during the war.[65] According to Bond, "The destruction of cities . . . was not hit-or-miss. The amount of destruction to both cities and industries could be calculated in advance."[66]

But fire protection engineers felt beleaguered, ignored, and professionally unappreciated, particularly in the early years of the war. McElroy wrote:

> In the early days the U.S. air forces (and the civilian scientific advisers of it) didn't want fire engineers mixing in their business. You may think that is a little startling but, as a matter of fact, it was true. There were physicists and chemists and statisticians and every other imaginable professional background in on this matter of the effectiveness of air force operations, but fire engineers were looked upon as interlopers. We really got to England because the British were anxious to obtain the professional fire experience they did not have in their own country.[67]

Similarly, many years later, Bond said, "The average fellow in the Air Force didn't have the foggiest idea about these incendiaries that a few novices on the outside were puttering and sputtering about, like me."[68]

Moreover, just as the U.S. military equated effective damage against specific targets with high-explosive bombs, fire protection engineers equated effective damage from incendiary weapons with the area bombing strategy of their British counterparts. Bond, for example, thought that the British "decision to carry out area attacks on cities was a logical and practical one." Indeed, he thought, given the effectiveness of incendiary bombing and the ineffectiveness of bombing with high explosives, the British strategy was more sensible than the American one. He noted that Americans "were inclined to put a low estimate on the total or cumulative effects of widespread fire destruction in cities. We had to deal with this point of view throughout the war."[69] In the spring of 1943 Bond wrote, "We may be overlooking an important weapon if we do not take full advantage of damage to the enemy that can be caused by fire. . . . It seems to me, therefore, that a very definite policy should be developed for looking into the use of fire as a weapon. We need to use fire bombs like those being employed by the British with such promising results." (In the same month that Bond wrote his memo, Commanding General Hap Arnold was informed in a staff memo that "We have absolutely no incendiary bombs that will meet the Air Force requirements and standards for precision bombing of specific continental targets.")[70]

However, before the unprecedented incendiary attack on Hamburg in the summer of 1943, fire protection engineers made relatively restricted claims regarding the types of targets that could be destroyed in fire attacks. These targets fell outside those of interest to U.S. target planners. For example, in the spring of 1943, Bond prepared notes for the EOU on the "fire vulnerability of various occupancies." According to Bond and McElroy,

> The notes suggested that good incendiary targets were such things as lumber yards, . . . warehouses, and dwellings. However, such occupancies were of no interest. The economists wanted to know about the fire vulnerability of airframe assembly and airplane engine plants, electrical appliance manufacturing, machine shops, synthetic rubber and synthetic oil plants, plants manufacturing airplane and submarine components, power houses and like occupancies. These occupancies were unpromising as incendiary targets . . . unless the roof structure was combustible.[71]

Expectations of the magnitude of damage that could be caused by incendiary bombing changed with the horrifying demonstration of effectiveness in the second of three British air attacks on Hamburg in late July 1943. Serious fire damage had been inflicted before—for example, at Lübeck, Rostock, and Cologne in the spring of the previous year. The first incendiary attack on Hamburg, on the night of July 24–25, 1943, burned about 1.5 square miles (see Figure 3.1).[72]

The second incendiary attack, on the night of July 27–28, resulted in something previously unknown: the world's first mass fire (then called a "fire storm"). Fires were set in an area of more than 17 square miles. One area of more than 5 square miles was completely destroyed by fire; it was referred to by fire protection engineers as the "Dead City."[73] Between fifty and sixty thousand people in the fire zone were killed.[74]

Irrefutably included in the area of destruction were the industrial targets of primary interest in U.S. air force "precision" doctrine. According to Mountcastle, the British attacks caused "massive damage to all major industrial sites in the city," including, for example, huge cranes in shipyards made unusable from warping in the heat of the firestorm. Hamburg demonstrated that incendiaries were far more powerful than even advocates had

Figure 3.1. Hamburg's city center, burned in the fire attack of July 24–25, 1943. View from a church tower in August 1943. Source: H. Brunswig/Bildarchiv Preussischer Kulturbesitz.

TABLE 3.1.
TONS OF U.S. BOMBS DROPPED IN THE EUROPEAN THEATER OF OPERATIONS,
JANUARY 1944 THROUGH APRIL 1945, MONTHLY AVERAGE

Time period	High explosive	Incendiary
Jan.–June 1944	37,000	3,600
July–Dec. 1944	52,000	6,100
Jan.–April 1945	72,000	8,500

Source: Richard G. Davis, *Carl A. Spaatz and the Air War in Europe* (Washington, D.C.: Smithsonian Institution Press, 1992), appendix 20.

tended to argue previously and made the possibility of incendiary attacks more attractive to U.S. military officers.[75]

The firestorm at Hamburg, and the disastrous U.S. losses in the August 1943 "precision" air attacks against Regensburg and Schweinfurt, led to some increases in U.S. incendiary operations and to policy changes over the next year: the first attack against a city center, Münster, in the fall of 1943; a directive from General Arnold in November that when daytime precision bombing could not be undertaken, radar-aided area attacks against the German air force should be; and area attacks on the center of Berlin in the winter and spring of 1944.[76]

The increasing use of incendiary bombs by the U.S. air force is reflected in monthly averages of weight of bombs dropped. Once incendiary bombing began in mid-1943, it increased steadily from a monthly average of 3,600 tons for the first six months of 1944 to an average of 8,500 tons by the end of the war in Europe. Even with this considerable increase, incendiary bombing was an order of magnitude less than high-explosive bombing in the same period. High explosives dropped averaged 37,000 tons per month for the first six months of 1944 and increased to 72,000 tons per month by the beginning of May 1945 (see Table 3.1). Overall, the strategy remained one of precision bombing, in aspiration if not in fact, and the bomb loads were overwhelmingly high explosive. Of a total of almost a million tons of U.S. bombs dropped in the European theater of operations, from August 1942 through April 1945, nearly nine-tenths were high explosive (see Table 3.2).

By contrast, the British, committed by 1942 to area destruction using incendiaries in combination with high explosives, typically employed incendiary bomb loads of 50 percent or more by weight. For example, in attacks on Hamburg in the summer of 1943, incendiaries composed 46 percent of the total weight of bombs dropped; in attacks on Cologne (May 1942), and in firestorm attacks on Kassel (October 1943) and Darmstadt (September 1944), incendiaries composed 60 percent of the bomb weight.[77]

TABLE 3.2.
TONS OF U.S. BOMBS DROPPED IN THE EUROPEAN THEATER OF OPERATIONS,
AUGUST 1942 THROUGH APRIL 1945

Year	High explosive	Incendiary	Total
1942	1,700	—	1,700
1943	49,000	7,000	56,000
1944	534,000	58,000	592,000
1945	288,000	34,000	322,000
TOTAL	873,000	99,000	972,000

Source: Richard G. Davis, *Carl A. Spaatz and the Air War in Europe* (Washington, D.C.: Smithsonian Institution Press, 1992), appendix 20.

Air Target Intelligence against Japan

Planning for the air war against Japan began later than air war planning in Europe. In the underlying emphasis on precision bombing doctrine and in tying physical vulnerability analysis to economic effects, air target analysis against Japan was organized similarly to analysis in the European theater. There were, however, conceptual and organizational differences.

Long before potential Japanese targets were systematically analyzed, there was wide awareness of the extensive fire damage caused by the major earthquake in Tokyo in 1923.[78] Air advocate Billy Mitchell publicly stressed the vulnerability of Japanese cities to firebombing. In the early 1930s, Mitchell wrote, "These towns are built largely of wood and paper to resist the devastations of earthquakes and form the greatest aerial targets the world has ever seen. . . . Incendiary projectiles would burn the cities to the ground in short order."[79] And in 1940, in correspondence with General Arnold, retired General Claire Chennault advocated the efficacy of incendiary bombing against Japanese cities, writing that U.S. bombers could "burn out the industrial heart of the Empire with fire-bomb attacks on the teeming bamboo ant heaps of Honshu and Kyushu." (In the same correspondence, Arnold had written that the United States was committed to precision bombing and that the "use of incendiaries against cities was contrary to our national policy of attacking military objectives.")[80]

It is against this backdrop of a widespread sense of the special vulnerability of Japanese structures to incendiary attack that the first wartime target studies began. Unlike in Europe, where the study of potential targets resided mainly with the Eighth Air Force, in the Far East the lead was taken by air force intelligence in Washington (officially, the Air Intelligence Service of the Army Air Forces).[81] Their first target study, of Japan, Korea, and Manchuria, was completed in March 1943. Reflecting precision bombing doctrine, it focused primarily on industry. It listed eight leading target systems—aircraft production, nonferrous metals, naval bases and shipyards, iron and steel, petroleum, chemicals, automotive assembly, and rubber processing—and recommended fifty-seven key targets from that list. According to Ronald Schaffer, a leading historian of air operations in World War II, the study "did not describe the cities per se as primary target systems."[82]

Just after this report was submitted, General Arnold also tasked his advisory group, COA, to study bombing objectives in Japan. COA began the study that spring and developed a mixed strategy of precision and area bombing. In November, COA recommended several specific industrial target systems and also added urban areas to be bombed. According to Schaffer, COA reported that "the most important targets appeared to be merchant shipping, aircraft plants, steel, and urban industrial areas. The committee believed that a series of massive firebomb attacks on urban areas would produce a major disaster for Japan."[83] In February, April, and June of 1944, studies by COA and by the Joint Chiefs of Staff continued to emphasize specific industrial targets—and to include urban areas as well. In June, COA established a subcommittee on incendiaries. By the fall of 1944, COA was still recommending a mix of point targets (now shipping and aircraft) and urban areas, but the emphasis on urban areas was greater than the year before.[84] In September, the subcommittee on incendiaries reported to COA that fire raids would be more effective in Japan than in Germany, but subcommittee members emphasized that many unknowns made estimates of the weight of attack and specific weapons recommendations highly uncertain.[85]

Meanwhile, early in 1944 the work of gathering information and preparing target folders for the air campaign in the Far East had been delegated to a joint ad hoc intelligence committee mainly composed of officers from Air Force, Army, and Navy intelligence. In September, a more formal multiservice organization, the Joint Target Group, was established to develop air intelligence against Japan. According to historian John Kreis, the Joint Target Group's "mission [was] integrating and coordinating preattack and postattack intelligence analyses of air targets in the war against Japan." Its two primary activities were to prepare target folders and to assess the results of past bombing missions.[86]

Army Air Force Brigadier General John Samford headed the group; the deputy was Naval Commander Francis Bitter, who had headed the Navy's primary target group, the Air Technical Analysis Division (ATAD). Like ATAD, the Joint Target Group was a "combined military and civilian organization and the major part of the personnel gathered for Bitter's project were transferred to this new and more comprehensive group." The Joint Target Group consisted of four major sections: Economic Vulnerability, Physical Vulnerability, Production, and Evaluation. Within Physical Vulnerability were sections on statistical analysis, structural analysis, high explosives, and incendiary bombs. "The overall purposes of this Section were to study the physical characteristics of Japanese targets, recommend proper weapons for their destruction, estimate the quantity of those weapons required, and check results of the attacks against the preattack estimates."[87] As we will see in chapter 4, the Joint Target Group prefigured the organization and problem-solving focus of air target intelligence in the postwar U.S. Air Force.

The Joint Target Group incorporated analysis of the damage caused by incendiary bombing more fully than had been done previously in the war by any U.S. target intelligence organization. The group employed a few fire protection engineers, for example. However, the primary methodology of the organization was built around precision bombing. According to a British member of the Joint Target Group, mathematician Jacob Bronowski, most of the group's output comprised "more than a dozen volumes" describing Japanese industries "and the targets offered by them."

> In general, each volume begins with an overall appreciation of an industry, its place in the Japanese economy, its importance in the war situation at the time of writing, and its vulnerability. The rest of the volume is then devoted to individual plants, with photographs and descriptions, and with a detailed analysis from photo interpretation of the construction and physical vulnerability of the main buildings. On the basis of this analysis, certain weapons (high-explosive and incendiary) and methods of attack are recommended and others are not recommended. . . . All this material seems to us of the greatest value, admirably set out, pleasant to handle and easy to follow.[88]

Despite General Arnold's interest in experimenting with incendiaries (while continuing with precision bombing operations),[89] pressure for incendiary use from his headquarters in Washington was unavailing until 1945. General Hayward Hansell, who headed the Twenty-first Bomber Command, doggedly stuck to precision bombing despite its ineffectiveness due to fierce winds and heavy cloud cover. Hansell told Arnold that he had "'with great difficulty implanted the principle that our mission is the destruction of primary targets by . . . precision bombing methods,' which he would not abandon just when he was 'beginning to get results.'"[90] His bosses were not so pleased with his results, and Hansell was replaced at the beginning of 1945 by the operationally innovative General LeMay. The weather also foiled LeMay's attempts at precision bombing. He then undertook ferocious incendiary attacks against Tokyo and other Japanese and Japanese-occupied Asian cities, culminating in the atomic bombings of Hiroshima and Nagasaki.[91]

Scientists and Engineers at War

In the United States, science was mobilized for war on an unprecedented scale. The central organization to harness science for the war effort was the National Defense Research Committee (NDRC), a government body founded in June 1940 as part of the larger mobilization of the state for war. NDRC members represented the War and Navy departments and major research universities. Vannevar Bush, the president of the Carnegie Institution, was appointed chair. A year later, in June 1941, President Roosevelt established an office of wider scope, the Office of Scientific Research and Development (OSRD), with Bush as director. The OSRD directed the now-subordinate NDRC and a new committee on medical research; in October 1943, a third major subdivision of OSRD was established, the Office of Field Service, to train scientists to work directly in military theaters of operation. NDRC surveyed military research requirements; shaped a wide-ranging research agenda; negotiated contracts with academic research teams assembled under Committee auspices and with industrial contractors; and provided liaison between university researchers, contractors, the military, and other government organizations. In December 1942, the original four divisions of NDRC were reorganized into nineteen divisions working on a vast multitude of projects.[92] Divisions were composed of staffs, members who provided advice and direction, and consultants, many of whom did research under contract. Researchers under contract with NDRC worked with close colleagues in the same discipline and/or institution; scientists or engineers from other disciplines and NDRC divisions; researchers working directly under military auspices in government laboratories and military operational units; employees in other government agencies; and British colleagues.

The greater centrality of blast weapons and the assessment of blast damage, and the relative marginality of incendiary weapons and fire damage analysis, was written into the organization of NDRC. Those working on problems related to blast weapons were associated with Division 2, Structural Defense and Offense, which studied, among other things, the effects of conventional high-explosive bombs on targets, and Division 8, Explosives, which worked on developing and improving high-explosive bombs and was closely affiliated with Division 2. (Part of Division 8 was later absorbed into Division 2.)[93] In addition, those working in and with the Office of Field Service were generally more oriented toward high-explosive bombs than toward incendiaries. Indeed, John Burchard, a professor of architectural engineering at the Massachusetts Institute of Technology (MIT), headed Division 2 before becoming the head of the OFS.

Within NDRC, those working on problems of incendiary warfare were associated with the Fire Warfare section of Division 11, Chemical Engineering. Division 11 was broadly parallel to Division 8; both were based on the science of chemistry and performed in-depth research to improve U.S. bombs. There was, however, no equivalent to Division 2 to study the effects of incendiary weapons on targets, and this surely reflected the lower priority placed on incendiary warfare. The main work in the assessment and prediction of fire damage to targets was done by American fire protection engineers, working first under the auspices of RE 8 in England and by mid-1945 with the Joint Target Group in the United States.

Understanding and Predicting Blast Damage

At the outset of the war, the physical processes that caused blast damage were not well understood. The theoretical basis for understanding shock waves had been developed in the nineteenth century by Pierre-Henri Hugoniot and later expanded by David Leonard Chapman and Emile Jouguet to describe the very high-pressure explosions known as detonations. However, before World War II, most applied work had been done on relatively weak shock waves. The chemist George Kistiakowsky, who did important work during the war on the theory of detonations, explained that at the beginning of the war, "the theory of the effects of explosives on the surroundings was dormant. Indeed, conversations with technical personnel engaged in work on military explosives in 1940–41 showed a rather general prevalence of the [incorrect] idea that the shock waves were not responsible for the damaging effects of explosives. Rather, there was thought to exist a separate phenomenon of the 'blast,' following the shock some distance behind and responsible for the damage."[94]

Division 8, Explosives, sponsored research on air-blast gauges and other instruments, the optimum height of air burst for high-explosive charges, numerous other experiments with high-explosive charges, and abstract mathematical work on the theory of the interaction of shock waves. Some of the theoretical work later was sponsored by Division 2.[95]

According to Burchard, unlike many other divisions of NDRC concerned with the development of weapons, Division 2 was a knowledge and information division, largely concerned with "the pursuit and application of new knowledge to military operations."[96] The primary interest of the division lay in understanding the effects of high-explosive bombs on targets and on the effects of projectiles (bullets) on materials, especially concrete and armor.

Division 2 pursued knowledge based on the intensive collection and analysis of data regarding bomb damage effects and on fundamental research. In the early fall of 1941, more than a year before Bond went to England to investigate the analysis of damage from incendiary weapons,

Burchard and a member of Division 2, H. P. Robertson, professor of mathematical physics at Princeton, went to England to consult with Sir Reginald Stradling, then chief scientific adviser, Ministry of Home Security, and others. They brought back British gauges for the measurement of blast and a substantial quantity of the bomb damage reports developed by RE 8. They also developed a keen interest in the effects of German bombing on individual building types and in British work on operational research.[97]

At the same time, Division 2 contracted out research projects to a number of U.S. institutions, among them the California Institute of Technology, the University of Illinois, MIT, and Princeton University, where the division established an institutional presence, the Princeton University Station. These contracts were to develop instruments to measure blast and to gain in-depth understanding of the characteristics of shock waves in air, earth, and water.[98]

It was under these contracts that knowledge was developed about how shock waves cause structural deformation and damage. This knowledge was developed in a relatively new area of engineering called *dynamic analysis,* in which the *duration* of forces acting on structures is key. Dynamic analysis is used to calculate structural response to the forces generated by high explosives or earthquakes. (In contrast is "static" analysis in which forces such as gravity or those resulting from snowfall are treated as unchanging.) Research had been done in dynamic analysis in the 1930s, and a classic text on it by Theodor von Karman and Maurice Anthony Biot was published in 1940. Research undertaken during the war drew on and developed this body of engineering analysis.[99] Among those involved were several academic civil engineers: Robert J. Hansen, from MIT; Nathan Newmark, from the University of Illinois; and Merit P. White, from the University of Massachusetts. As we will see in later chapters, after the war these three would consult closely with Air Force Intelligence on predicting blast damage from atomic weapons.

Division 2 not only developed knowledge but disseminated it widely within the military. In late 1942, through the Princeton University Station, Division 2 agreed to train groups of technically able "young engineers and architects" to serve air force bomber commands as operations analysts specializing in weapon selection and damage assessment.[100] The training courses were held at Princeton; each course lasted six to eight weeks. The courses ran from the spring of 1943 through the summer of 1945. The training emphasized the analysis of blast effects on targets, but personnel from Division 11 also lectured on the properties and effects of incendiary weapons.[101] One analyst in the Navy's Air Technical Analysis Division, Richard Grassy, completed the training program at Princeton in the spring of 1944. After the war Grassy became the highest-level civilian in the physical vulnerability section in Air Force Intelligence.[102] We will hear directly from Grassy in chapter 4.

Through the Princeton University Station, Division 2 also developed a field manual to aid those directly involved in military operation to predict damage from high-explosive bombs and to select bombs and fuses. The manual, a loose-leaf book of data sheets called *Effects of Impact and Explosion,* was part of an effort sponsored by Division 2 to collect, analyze, and, where necessary, extrapolate information regarding the behavior of blast weapons upon reaching their targets. By 1944 analysts for the Joint Target Group used the manual to determine the physical vulnerability of specific types of targets, such as airfields, oil storage tanks, and bridges. Although Division 2 itself was concerned only with analyzing blast damage, once it began work on the manual, it cooperated with Division 11 to include some effects of incendiary weapons. Again, reflecting the lower priority placed on the prediction of fire damage, "several sheets dealing with incendiaries were included, but the conclusion of the war cut short this extension of the book's scope."[103]

By the end of the war, Division 2 had developed the theoretical underpinnings for the dynamic analysis of structural response to blast and had trained military officers to analyze and predict damage from high-explosive conventional bombs. We will see later how this effort influenced postwar predictions of blast damage from atomic weapons.

Understanding and Predicting Fire Damage

Within NDRC, there was no group comparable to Division 2 to analyze damage from incendiary weapons. The few fire protection engineers working in England were not under NDRC auspices. The Fire Warfare section of Division 11, was, however, broadly comparable to at least part of Division 8. This section was instrumental in improving various incendiary weapons and in testing and evaluating their relative effectiveness. Some of this testing was done in large-scale simulations of model towns. These tests are particularly interesting because such large-scale experiments on the fire damage caused by nuclear weapons would not be conducted in U.S. nuclear weapons tests after the war.

In the summer of 1942, incendiary tests under NDRC auspices began on condemned farm buildings at Jefferson Proving Ground, Indiana. In June 1943, in an effort to improve incendiary weapons and understand the damage caused by them, including fire spread, the Chemical Warfare Service, in conjunction with Division 11, the Army Air Forces, and Standard Oil, began to build models of buildings and towns at several U.S. test sites. During the war, these buildings were burned down by incendiary bombs, rebuilt, and burned again.[104]

Industrial-type buildings were constructed and bombed at Edgewood Arsenal, Maryland. At Eglin Field, Florida, Japanese villages, called "little Tokyos," were constructed by NDRC and the Army Air Forces "to enable experts to evaluate fire spread in groups of buildings and to estimate the most destructive ratio of high explosives to incendiary bombs." The most extensive field tests on the relative effectiveness of various incendiary bombs were conducted at Dugway Proving Ground, Utah.[105]

Beginning in late March 1943, construction was started at Dugway on full-scale model German and Japanese villages. Architects who had practiced in Germany and Japan designed the structures and attended to details of design, materials, and construction. According to an air force observer:

> The effort that went into the construction of the mock towns was enormous. At Dugway, for example, buildings designed by the architects covered a five square mile area. Constructed of brick, wood, and tile at an estimated cost of $575,000, the German structures were authentic even in their furnishings. Heavy German furniture, bedspreads, rugs, and draperies were installed. . . . To describe the target as a series of "typical" enemy structures would be a gross understatement and an injustice to the talent which was employed in making these buildings as truly authentic as humanly possible down to the last detail. They were "typical" even insofar as the curtains, children's toys, and clothing hanging in closets were concerned. Nothing was overlooked. Those houses represent the type in which 80% of the industrial population of Germany is housed.[106]

For the Japanese structures at Dugway, an official from Standard Oil "undertook a 25,000 mile search of the West Coast and Hawaiian Islands to collect an adequate supply of the Japanese straw floor mats known as 'tatami' used in the dwellings. . . . The wood used in the structures. . . . Russian spruce, was located on the West Coast, shipped across the continent to New Jersey for milling, and finally reshipped to Utah as finished structural members. This wood was used in the Japanese dwellings to simulate 'hinoki,' which is used extensively in Japanese construction."[107]

Extensive tests were held from May to September 1943.[108] In mid-December, Army Private Jack Couffer observed:

> The sterile towns stood several miles apart on the otherwise empty Utah plain, like abandoned movie sets picturing the aftermath of a devastating plague. . . . As I strolled through the deserted lanes and looked into empty windows, I visualized with awful clarity this place peopled. . . . Crowded with life, the narrow aisles between buildings would be bustling with . . . people coming and going to the factories, hawkers, shop-

pers, kids playing games. Casting aside that mental picture it was easy to imagine without emotional involvement the torching of this sterile village. . . . When again I saw in my mind's eye the town as it really would be, my flesh crawled. I was very glad I was seeing it in this way, without people.[109]

Investigators found that while there was a higher probability of quickly starting fires in the Japanese structures, more than a third of the most destructive fires—those that fire departments could not control—occurred in the German structures. According to one historical account, "The potentialities of incendiary warfare in a country of crowded cities were further emphasized by near-conflagration conditions which occurred several times throughout the tests."[110] Investigators, however, were more concerned with understanding how test results varied with different conditions of humidity and dampness of wood than with developing models of large-scale fire behavior.

The resources allocated during the war to evaluating damage from incendiary weapons through simulations were quite substantial. Although less than those devoted to research high-explosive bombs, they were greater than those devoted after the war to evaluating fire damage in atomic weapons tests.

The most important knowledge about the phenomenon of mass fire and the damage it caused came not from these incendiary weapons tests but from the extensive and careful observations by fire protection engineers in their work with RE 8, the Joint Target Group, and the U.S. Strategic Bombing Survey in the European and Pacific theaters. Horatio Bond headed fire damage studies for the U.S. Strategic Bombing Survey in Europe, organized in the fall of 1944. The findings of the European survey were used by the Joint Target Group in planning the air war against Japan. Forrest Sanborn headed the fire damage studies for the Survey in the Pacific.[111]

The knowledge developed in assessing and predicting damage from incendiary attacks was largely based on the practical knowledge of engineers experienced in observing fire behavior. Until the summer of 1943, all large-scale fires—whether forest, urban, or deliberately set in wartime attacks—were large "line" fires that had one or several points of origin but were not begun by the simultaneous ignition of very large areas. The phenomenon of mass fire, first set at Hamburg in July 1943, was unknown at the beginning of World War II.

In the Bombing Survey, fire protection engineers carefully described the first "great fire" set at Hamburg in July 1943, including the exceptional damage it caused. They understood Hamburg and other firestorms in Europe as marked by the rapidity with which they were ignited:

The development stages of the fire storms in Hamburg, Kassel and Darmstadt had one common feature. That is the relatively short time in which primary individual fires were started within an extensive built-up city area. It has been estimated that within 20 minutes after the first attack wave had dropped their bombs on Hamburg, two out of three structural units within an estimated 4.5 square mile area were afire. . . . Unlike the usual conflagration, the fire had not progressed by easy stages from one small start. Conflagrations in the past have usually developed over a period of hours. It is this time factor that makes what happened at Hamburg, Kassel, Darmstadt and elsewhere phenomenal.[112]

Fire protection engineers hypothesized several necessary conditions for such fires. First, they thought that they depended on the availability of a certain amount of combustible fuel. They measured this in terms of the "builtupness" of areas (i.e., the ratio of roof area to ground area) and the combustibility of buildings.[113] Over the decades, the understanding that a minimal fuel load is a precondition for a mass fire has held up.[114]

Second, they thought that variable and unpredictable aspects of natural weather conditions were an important determinant of whether a large area fire would occur. Bond thought that weather conditions "were perhaps more a factor in helping the incendiaries to start fires than in any other way. This part of the problem of air attack has been inadequately explored, but in the greatest raids on Hamburg, weather conditions were relatively favorable for the starting of fires. There had been a month of unusually dry weather," which he characterized as an "abnormal drying-out process" caused by "abnormally low" humidities and high temperatures. "Dry weather, too, was said to precede successful attacks at Kassel, Wuppertal and Darmstadt."[115]

At the same time, fire protection engineers were aware that Dresden had been blanketed in winter snow when Allied bombing destroyed it in a firestorm in the winter of 1945, and that some successful incendiary attacks against Japan had been made in snow and rain. Indeed, the analysis of fire damage in Japan was self-contradictory. Robert Nathans, a fire protection engineer who helped plan incendiary attacks on Japan, wrote: "Snow at the time of the first Tokyo attacks [in February 1945] may have limited the extent of that damage," but precipitation and moisture absorption by building material "did not offer the serious handicaps that had been supposed. Successful attacks were made even during light rains and often within a matter of hours after heavier rainfall. The mission against [an area near Kobe and Osaka] was run when the moisture content of wood and other porous materials should have been a decided deterrent. Within the previous 48 hours, there had been continuous heavy rain yet 37 percent of this large area was destroyed in that one attack." Sanborn generalized that when incendiary "attacks were carried out during rain storms, the damage averaged 20 per cent less than normal."[116] These statements were not consistent with claims that low moisture and humidity were significant preconditions for firestorms.

The air war against Japan also convinced fire protection engineers that unpredictable ambient wind conditions played an important role in the character of large area fires. In describing the large area fires in Europe, fire protection engineers had referred to "fire storms," which they distinguished from "conflagrations in the past." They did not use the term "mass fire." In the analysis of fire damage against Japan, including damage from atomic bombs, fire protection engineers used somewhat different terminology. In the most detailed contemporary account, the U.S. Strategic Bombing Survey, Sanborn referred to the large area fires set in Japan as "mass fires." *Mass fires* referred to either "fire storms" or "conflagrations." The difference between them lay in the prevailing natural wind conditions. Low-speed winds permitted firestorms to develop; high-speed winds caused conflagrations. Sanborn wrote: "In the attacks against Japan, the interacting fire winds set up by many individual incendiary fires, together with the contributing effects of radiation over intervening spaces, often tended to merge the aggregate blazes into one inferno, with its own pillar and fire wind. Under the influence of certain ground and meteorological conditions, the mass fire sometimes took the form of either a fire storm or a conflagration."[117]

Fire protection engineers (and others) defined a *fire storm* as consisting of "a wind which blew toward the burning area of [a] city from all directions."[118] The engineers wrote that a fire storm was characterized by an "inrushing fire wind [that] usually developed in from 15 minutes to an hour and reached high velocities. Japanese firemen . . . reported winds of near-cyclone force which uprooted trees, blew over automobiles, tore clothing from persons' bodies, and sent roof tiles, boards, sheet iron and other debris spiralling into the air. . . . The area of fire spread was small and nearly uniform in all directions around the perimeter."[119] Although causing almost total destruction within the burning area, the inward-blowing fire storm was considered to be "a decisive factor in *limiting* the spread of the fire beyond the initial ignited area."[120]

By contrast, a *conflagration* resulted when naturally occurring high-speed winds caused the fire to spread in the direction in which the wind was blowing:

In a conflagration, the pillar of a mass fire, once it had been established, slanted appreciably to leeward [the direction in which the wind was blowing] and the hot burning gases contributed much to the ignition of combustible materials on the ground. The chief characteristic of the conflagration was the presence of a fire front, an extended wall of fire moving to leeward preceded by a turbid mass of pre-heated vapors. The progress and destructive features of the conflagration were therefore much greater than those of the fire storm, for in the conflagration the fire continued to spread until it could reach no more combustible material.[121]

This distinction survived among fire experts and the broader public for many decades, but physicists now consider it a false distinction. They prefer the term "mass fire" and do not consider "fire storms" and "conflagrations" to be distinct phenomena. Although high ambient winds could spread parts of a mass fire outward, physicists consider this to be a detail. What is crucial is that mass fires create their own fierce inward-blowing winds. These fire-generated winds are not dependent on ambient wind conditions.

The professional training of many fire protection engineers in chemical engineering also shaped their understandings of mass fire. Sanborn, for example, thought that mass fires were driven by the same chemical processes that drove smaller fires. Further, his understanding of these chemical processes was a functional one in which an oxygen "deficiency" caused an influx of new air to supply the missing oxygen.[122]

Although the chemical account of mass fire also survived for many years among fire experts, it too is not accepted by physicists as an accurate depiction of mass fire, which is driven not by the disappearance of oxygen—there is no reason to think that oxygen "seeks" to replenish itself—but by the rising heated air of many ignitions causing violent inward winds and utter devastation within a large area.

The understanding of fire protection engineers would have ramifications in the postwar period. Fire protection engineers were aware of the vast damage caused by incendiary weapons, but they had not developed a framework at the end of the war that enabled prediction of mass fires. In their view, variable humidity, wind, and other meteorological conditions made the probability and range of mass fire impossible to predict. The expert opinion of fire protection engineers undoubtedly contributed to the widespread postwar understanding that mass fire from atomic bombs was unpredictable. But more important than an unsolved problem is the determination to solve it. Critically important in shaping the organizational focus on blast damage from atomic bombs was the general adherence by those involved in damage prediction to air force doctrine favoring precision bombing, and the association they made between precision bombing and blast damage.

Early Postwar Atomic Planning

Hit the right targets, at the right time, in the right way, at the right places, and with enough of the right weapons. This is the dream of every bomber crew and of every officer who plans a[n] . . . air strike.

Lincoln R. Thiesmeyer, *Combat Scientists* (1947)

The end of World War II was a period of intense organizational redefinition and expansion for the air force. Given the prestige gained by the U.S. Army Air Forces during the war, wartime understandings that the organization would gain independence from the Army after the war, and American political leaders' vastly expanded sense of U.S. interests and responsibilities in the international arena, the postwar period presented a great opportunity for the air force: to become a separate service equal in both statute and stature to the Army and Navy. This would enable it to gain the resources and organizational capacity to carry out a considerably expanded mission in the postwar period.[1] The U.S. Air Force was formally established by the National Security Act of 1947.

In this context of expanded national security concerns and a domestic political environment of competitive plenty, how was the atomic bomb to be understood? For what military purposes could atomic bombs be employed? What physical effects were expected to be the main cause of destruction? How was this new technology to be conceived in the context of wartime understandings that the fundamental strategic mission of the air force was one of "precision bombing"?

The assumptions most deeply ingrained in the air force during the war—that specific industrial and other installations as parts of critical target systems were to be destroyed by the blast effects of air-dropped *conventional* weapons—carried over to the understanding of *atomic* weapons in the immediate postwar period: Specific installations were to be targeted, and the relevant mechanism of destruction would be blast. The association of precision bombing and blast damage was a historical one. Because of the early priority of precision bombing in World War II, greater knowledge had been developed about blast damage than fire damage, making blast damage more predictable by the end of the war. These understandings of what would be targeted and what would be the means of destruction served as the basis for the organizational capabilities developed, the knowledge acquired, and the routines invented regarding prediction of damage in the postwar period.

On the face of it, a conception of employing *atomic* weapons to carry out *precision* bombing doctrine may seem absurd. These are weapons of mass destruction. What's precise about them? With this new, immensely destructive technology, how could there *not* have been a change from the wartime understandings of mission and means? Why was there not a decided shift to an area conception of targets and the incorporation of fire as a major cause of damage?

The answer lies in the organizational continuity from World War II to the immediate postwar period. The legacy of World War II carried over in personnel, organizational goals, knowledge, and an inherited sense of the problems to be addressed and the solutions to be sought. Those involved in war planning and damage prediction were aware of the immense destructive power of the atomic bomb, but rather than embark on philosophical speculation about the changing nature of warfare—not an activity bureaucracies are well equipped to undertake—in the absence of higher-level directives to do things in a radically different way, they incorporated the atomic bomb into their inherited sense of organizational goals, knowledge, and problems to be solved: How were specific installations to be destroyed by blast?

We will see that the history did not unfold quite as neatly as my argument would suggest. For some at Air Force Headquarters involved in broad conceptual war planning and for those at the Strategic Air Command involved in detailed operational planning in the early postwar period, conceptions of targeting *did* change, from an emphasis on precision attacks of selected target systems to plans for concurrent and concentrated atomic attacks on targets within large urban areas—in short, to a somewhat greater emphasis on area targeting.

However, atomic war planning involved more than broad conceptual planning and operational planning in the field. Critical to the war planning process was the selection of targets and prediction of damage to those targets by analysts in Air Force Intelligence. Here, precision bombing doctrine largely shaped how targets would be understood and damage assessed. Many of those responsible for postwar target intelligence in the Air Force had done similar work during World War II, and they carried into the postwar era the precision bombing concepts they had used during the war. Postwar target intelligence included determining the economic, political, and military function and the vulnerability of targeted systems; specifying the function and location of specific installations within those systems; and predicting the damage that would result from atomic attack to specific installations.

Such continuities can be seen in the first major postwar project of those in target intelligence: the *Bombing Encyclopedia of the World,* a global compendium of potential targets. The goal of precision bombing established during World War II, in conjunction with the understanding at the end of the war that blast damage was more predictable than fire damage, also shaped the earliest postwar studies in 1947 and 1948 designed to predict atomic blast damage. The 1947 study does not at first glance appear to conform to my expectations: It predicted blast damage, but it did so on an *area* basis. However, the study was largely an accommodation to information shortfalls. Within a year, better target information became available, and planners for the first time predicted atomic blast damage to specific installations. Planners were consistent about what they wanted to accomplish: As soon as they could delineate specific installations for war planning purposes, they did.

Atomic War Planning

The U.S. planning process for atomic war was complex.[2] (*Atomic war* refers to war that would be carried out with atomic bombs. With the invention of the hydrogen bomb, the term was changed to *nuclear war* in the mid-1950s.) In principle, atomic war planning occurred at three levels: (1) *high policy,* where the National Security Council, with the president's approval, articulated presidential policy guidance; (2) *strategic planning,* where military planners, both on the working staff of the Joint Chiefs of Staff and on the staffs of the services (particularly war planners on the Air Staff at Air Force Headquarters), articulated strategic concepts, wartime goals, relevant target sets, and scenarios; and (3) *operational planning,* where intelligence analysts on the Air Staff and operations researchers and others at the Strategic Air Command provided extremely detailed specifications that turned strategic planning into fully elaborated plans for the employment of atomic weapons in war.[3] Operational planning specified target installations within designated target sets, predicted damage to those installations, determined exactly where atomic bombs should be detonated, determined the most efficient choice of weapons and delivery systems to achieve damage, devised routes to and from targets, and specified the exact timing of detonations over targets.

In principle, the decisions made at the presidential level governed the decisions made by strategic planners, and these in turn provided the framework for operational planning. In theory, a single understanding of purpose, problems to be solved, and range of acceptable solutions governed atomic war planning in a highly articulated and hierarchical planning structure.

In practice, something quite different occurred. The first president with responsibilities for atomic war planning, Harry S. Truman, appreciated that such weapons were extraordinarily powerful (though he did not have a detailed understanding of just how destructive) and was reluctant to provide explicit directives for atomic war planning—or to become involved in operational details at all. Truman's reluctance stemmed from his desire to be able to threaten the use of atomic weapons for diplomatic purposes, for which no detailed planning was necessary, and his lack of desire to think about actually using them. In historian David Rosenberg's words, Truman was unwilling, or unable, "to conceive of the atomic bomb as anything other than an apocalyptic terror weapon, a weapon of last resort."[4] Further, he understood that the more explicit political directives were, the more resources and authority the military would ask for to carry them out. Thus, there were significant differences in organizational understandings of what was desirable and possible, and gaps in specification from the political to the planning levels. Finally, those at the political level depended on the knowledge and routines that resided at the operational level. Thus, the ways of knowing and doing embedded at the operational level exerted an independent influence on war planning.

Strategic War Planning

Without explicit political guidance, planners on the staff of the Joint Chiefs and on the Air Staff devised mobilization and war planning studies that, by the summer of 1947, assumed that the Soviet Union was the enemy and that atomic weapons would be used.[5] These war plans were devised in the context of the military's collective efforts to define the strategic environment and claim a share of the federal budget; interservice struggles to define missions, priorities, prerogatives, and budget shares; and mundane planning for the next fiscal year.

These planners engaged in some relatively creative, if alarming, thinking about the atomic bomb. The perceived scarcity of atomic weapons (given the extraordinary levels of destruction planners believed were required), in conjunction with the vast destructive power of atomic weapons, led Air Force planners to emphasize concentrated attacks on urban areas. Reflecting ideas developed in the preceding year that atomic weapons could "kill a nation," in the fall of 1948, Colonel Dale O. Smith advocated "concurrently attacking every critical element of an enemy's economy *at the same time*. . . . If all the critical industrial systems could be destroyed in one blow . . . a nation would die. . . . The targets should be the most vital enemy urban areas. Here all major industry is located."[6]

The secondary literature emphasizes similar ideas. "When nuclear war planning began in earnest," Rosenberg writes, the focus on target systems such as transportation, the petroleum industry, and electric power was "diluted, reflecting scarce resources, poor intelligence, and operational difficulties. . . . From 1947 through 1949, the separate target systems within the Soviet Union grew less important, while governmental control centers and 'urban industrial concentrations' became primary objectives."[7] This amalgamation of target systems and concentration on urban areas indicates that it was not at the level of strategic planning that notions of precision bombing carried over from the wartime period.

Strategic Air Command

We see something similar when we turn to the Strategic Air Command (SAC), which, according to Rosenberg, "had primary responsibility for operational planning."[8] It is probably more accurate to say that SAC had the last word on operational planning. As we will see, it did not have the first. After General Curtis LeMay became commander in the fall of 1948, SAC gained unprecedented influence. Indeed, at the level of popular culture, SAC became an icon—from the 1955 movie *Strategic Air Command,* starring Jimmy Stewart, to Stanley Kubrick's 1964 black comedy, *Dr. Strangelove or: How I Learned to Stop Worrying and Love the Bomb.*

SAC was responsible for developing the final operational war plan, including logistical and tactical planning. In the words of Stanley Lawwill, a high-level operations analyst at SAC during this period: "SAC war planners selected the specific targets, weapons, DGZs [designated ground zero, the position on the ground under the detonation], bombardment units, defense suppression weapons tactics, etc."[9] SAC was also responsible for final assembly and distribution of air target folders, which embodied the war plan and contained detailed map and target information. These folders were used in training by SAC air crews and would have been used by them in the event of atomic war. (The reader may recall *Dr. Strangelove*'s Major Kong receiving an order to attack the Soviet Union and opening his air target material, which described targets to be destroyed by the plane's nuclear weapons.)

SAC took recommendations from Air Staff officers working in target intelligence (Targets or Targeting) at Air Force Headquarters in Washington and reworked them in the light of operational considerations. According to Lawwill, those in Targets did studies, developed theory, and recommended targets. "We [analysts at SAC] either used [Air Staff recommendations] or not as we saw fit." The Air Staff "didn't tell us what to do. It was the other way around. . . . We levied requests on the Air Staff. They didn't direct us to do anything. In turn, we briefed our warplans to the JCS [Joint Chiefs of Staff]. . . . I remember no time when CINCSAC [Commander in Chief, Strategic Air Command] was over-ruled."[10]

SAC's authority stemmed from its special knowledge of military operations. According to Lawwill,

> I . . . was very sensitive to the many operational problems that seemed routinely to be ignored by Air Staff planners and their advisors. You may rest assured that Gen. LeMay knew operational problems in minute detail and could be very persuasive in laying them out for folks who hadn't really sweated out war planning and peace-time training exercises.[11] . . . We had many visitors at SAC Headquarters who came with prepared presentations on all sorts of matters they thought would be of interest to SAC. In particular, we had regular visits with personnel of HQ USAF Intelligence (primarily, Targeting) with results of their most recent studies in target selection and recommended tactics. The latter [recommended tactics] were frequently laughed off by the SAC staff; the former [studies in target selection] were also, on occasion.[12]

Lawwill "remembered one visit well." Among the visitors from Targeting was a mathematician, Hal Germond, whom we will encounter again. According to Lawwill, Germond had "devised a (then) very sophisticated program for Intelligence's new state-of-the-art computer. That program selected from among all the known targets of an approved 'vertical' target system (say, electric power generation)—those that would have the greatest pay-off for n assigned weapons." SAC saw numerous problems with Germond's program, including that the calculations were misleadingly precise. "All calculations were carried out to *six* decimal places! When the presentation was over Gen. LeMay turned to Zim [Carroll Zimmerman, LeMay's chief operations analyst] and asked 'Shall I insult them or do you want to do it?' Zim said, 'Let's let Stan.' So I did. I told them they had built a skyscraper on a pile of loose sand. . . . General LeMay closed the meeting by asking the HQ USAF Targets people, 'Didn't any one of you ever fly a combat mission?'"[13]

SAC's view of targeting was far closer to the idea of "killing a nation" than to precision bombing. SAC analysts referred to early postwar planning as their "city-busting phase" in which they understood their orders to be: "Extreme damage to designated targets. Level Moscow if you can."[14] According to Lawwill, when there were only about twenty-five to thirty atomic weapons in the stockpile, "We were just dropping them on city centers,

I mean planning to drop them on city centers." Cities were understood as a "horizontal target system. . . . We didn't care if we were shooting at churches, industry, government centers, we wanted to level the town."[15]

By the late 1940s, city busting gave way to *vertical target systems*—differentiated industrial target systems, such as petroleum and electric power, and other specified systems such as government control centers, port facilities, and transportation networks.[16] Lawwill said that "vertical target systems really got a rush . . . as soon as we had enough [atomic] weapons. . . . As soon as we had enough weapons . . . we started applying them." He said that going to a vertical system was "in mind from the very beginning," that there were two to three dozen vertical systems analyzed and ready.[17]

By August 1950, target systems were categorized into three major types: (1) *industrial targets,* now called Delta targets for *d*estruction of the industrial base; (2) *strategic military targets,* called Bravo targets because, when destroyed, they would *b*lunt the ability of the Soviet Union to deliver atomic weapons; and (3) *conventional military targets,* such as depots, called Romeo targets because, when destroyed, they would *r*etard the ability of the Soviet Union to attack conventionally.[18] Although these target categories were put into targeting directives in the summer of 1950, Bravo and Romeo targets were added to actual plans later, and SAC continued its earlier emphasis on the need "to deliver the entire stockpile of atomic bombs . . . in a single massive attack."[19]

This emphasis continued. Referring to a nuclear war plan presented by SAC in 1954, Rosenberg writes, "The most significant aspect of the SAC [war] plan is the way in which operational considerations blurred the distinctions between different types of targets." According to the Navy captain who heard the briefing of the war plan, "The final impression was that virtually all of Russia would be nothing but a smoking, radiating ruin at the end of two hours."[20]

Given the emphasis on urban area targets ("killing a nation" and "city busting") and a blurring of distinctions between target types, it is clear that SAC was not the source of organizational continuity in precision bombing doctrine. The picture changes, however, when we look to the Air Force target intelligence analysts who prepared the target lists, made recommendations to SAC, and, as it turns out, did much more.

Target Intelligence

The analysts who worked in target intelligence have been virtually invisible in the historiography.[21] But it is precisely at this "shirt sleeve level" of target intelligence that we will see the crucial continuities in conceptions of precision bombing.[22]

As mentioned, target intelligence was the responsibility of analysts working at Air Force Headquarters in Washington. In the first five years after the war, target intelligence was done by the Strategic Vulnerability Branch within the Air Force's Air Intelligence Division. In 1950, the Strategic Vulnerability Branch became the Air Targets Division, then the Deputy Directorate for Targets, and, by the late 1950s, the Directorate for Targets. In all cases, Targets, or target intelligence, reported to the head of Intelligence in the Air Force (see Figure 4.1).

Those in target intelligence had wide-ranging responsibilities for gathering information on potential targets; this included enumerating specific installations as parts of larger target systems, systematizing that information into encyclopedic compendia and recommended target lists, and coordinating the detailed target and mapping information that composed the air target folders used by SAC air crews. As important, analysts in target intelligence provided recommendations to SAC regarding choice of targets, choice of weapons, exact locations where weapons should be detonated, and analyses of the damage that would result.

Despite the broad target systems articulated by war planners, those in target intelligence overwhelmingly operated within the assumptions of precision bombing doctrine. Consistent with this doctrine, they assessed and predicted blast damage, but not fire damage, from atomic weapons. In other words, this small group deep within the Air Force intelligence bureaucracy carried ways of knowing and doing associated with precision bombing doctrine and the blast damage frame. Its categorical understandings of targets in large part determined the organizational knowledge that would be acquired (indeed, required) regarding target characteristics and atomic weapons effects. This knowledge then provided the basis for the development of organizational routines to calculate blast damage to targets.

But could SAC not override their target recommendations in actual war plans? SAC could, and did, override recommendations, but it nonetheless depended on target intelligence for knowledge of targets—including location and economic and physical classifications—and for methods of predicting damage. SAC's analytical capabilities were limited. Referring to SAC's Strategic Analysis Division, one Washington-based target intelligence analyst told me: "Really, they didn't have much of an organization out there. If so, it was very small. We met with them occasionally. They had nowhere near the same analytical capabilities that we had."[23]

Those at SAC understood their dependence on target intelligence. Although Stan Lawwill told me that the Air Force "didn't tell SAC what to do, it was the other way around," in the next sentence he said that "we at SAC only used what they [Targets] passed down. We used [blast] overpressure" in predicting damage. Further, according to Lawwill, "Once there were

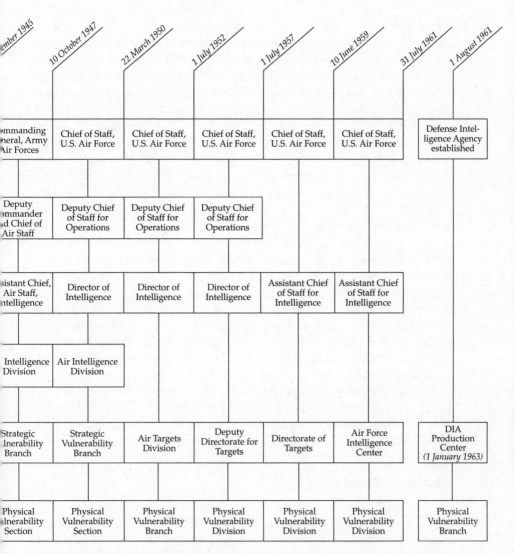

Figure 4.1. The role of Physical Vulnerability in Air Force Intelligence, 1945–1961. Redrawn from USAF Historical Division, Research Studies Institute, Air University, *Organization of the Army Air Arm, 1935–1945* (Maxwell Air Force Base, Ala.: Air University, July 1956); Herman S. Wolk, *Planning and Organizing the Postwar Air Force, 1943–1947* (Washington, D.C.: Office of Air Force History, U.S. Air Force, 1984); *Organizational Charts, Headquarters USAF 1947–1984*, AFP 210–215 (Washington, D.C.: Office of Air Force History, U.S. Air Force, 1984); Directorate of Intelligence, Air Targets Division, "History of the Air Targets Division, January 1950 thru 30 June 1950"; "United States Department of the Air Force Organization and Functions," May 1951–December 1960, on file in Air Force History Office, Bolling Air Force Base, Washington, D.C.

enough atomic weapons in [the] stockpile to get past the city-busting phase
. . . we (I) carefully planned each DGZ as a function of weapon yield, height
of burst, target hardness, and target location."[24] By definition, *target hardness* is a measure of physical vulnerability to particular effects, and it incorporated the methodology for predicting blast damage to specific targets
developed by those in target intelligence. Thus, Lawwill, the SAC analyst
responsible for planning where each atomic weapon would detonate, depended on target intelligence in Washington for his knowledge of both target location and target hardness. Although, as we have seen, SAC's
conception of bombing operations was broader than precision bombing,
SAC's methods for assessing atomic damage came from an organization
working within that doctrine: Damage was predicted to specific installations, and the damage predicted was blast.

Building on knowledge developed during World War II, those in target
intelligence began to systematize, refine, and extend basic and practical
knowledge relevant to choosing targets and to predicting damage. Their project was to standardize the categorical assumptions, calculational routines,
and predictions necessary to develop plans to deliver atomic weapons capable of achieving very high levels of damage against designated targets. These
early conceptions and routines were foundational. Without them, large-scale
atomic targeting could not proceed. Once established, they became the basis
of further elaborations of targeting procedures; at the same time, they significantly constrained and channeled future development. To understand this
process, it is necessary first to understand who did what in Air Force Intelligence and the close organizational proximity of those who determined what
was to be targeted to those who predicted damage to those targets.

Organization of Intelligence

Air Intelligence was part of the headquarters organization of the U.S.
Army Air Forces and, after October 10, 1947, of the newly independent U.S.
Air Force. In the decade following the end of World War II, Air Force Intelligence was reorganized many times (see Figure 4.1).[25] Rather than giving
a detailed account of these reorganizations, my concern is to explain the
major activities within Intelligence during this period. Building on wartime
organization, Air Force Intelligence was involved in a wide range of knowledge-generating activities.

In the early postwar period, Air Force Intelligence was composed of
three divisions: (1) the Executive Division, responsible for policy and procedures, including counterintelligence; (2) the Air Information Division, responsible for collection and research (this division had five branches:
Collection, Library, Air Attaché, Photographic, and Publications); and (3)

the Air Intelligence Division, responsible for studies and analysis. The Air Intelligence Division had five branches: Offensive Air, Defensive Air (which studied the defensive arrangements of other countries), Air Facilities, Air Estimates, and, of particular interest to us, Strategic Vulnerability.[26]

By mid-1952, Air Force Intelligence had been reorganized into three areas of activity (in addition to administration and policy functions): (1) the Deputy Director for Collection and Dissemination collected intelligence regarding allied and potential adversary air capabilities; (2) on the basis of intelligence collected, the Deputy Director for Estimates provided finished intelligence estimates of potential enemy and allied capabilities regarding air warfare; and (3) the Deputy Director for Targets developed intelligence on air targets. This last area included identifying the functions of specific installations as part of larger target systems, locating installations and representing them on maps and charts, predicting damage that could be done to them with atomic weapons, and estimating the number of atomic weapons required to achieve certain specified levels of damage. Let us look at target intelligence in more detail.

Strategic Vulnerability Branch

Immediately after the war, target analysis was done by a small, newly formed group in the Pentagon called the Strategic Vulnerability Branch (SVB). As noted above, this was one of the branches within the Air Intelligence Division. SVB was a sort of successor to the Joint Target Group, discussed in chapter 3, and was set up to "continue this type of work."[27] Like the Joint Target Group, SVB was a multiservice command, composed of officers and enlisted men from the Air Force, Army, and Navy; civilians were also involved. The mission of air analysts in World War II had been to "Hit the right targets, at the right time, in the right way, at the right places, and with enough of the right weapons."[28] The mission of SVB reflected this understanding. As stated succinctly, if somewhat formally, by its director of research, James T. Lowe, who himself had worked in the Joint Target Group during the war, SVB's mission was "to ensure that the right bombs may be delivered to the right targets concomitant with the decision to wage war."[29]

SVB had eight sections. Six were geographical; they did the kind of analysis that the Enemy Objectives Unit and some in the Joint Target Group had done during World War II.[30] According to Richard Grassy, an analyst hired into SVB shortly after the end of the war:

The principal membership of the geographic sections were principally economists. . . . [They] stud[ied] the economies of the target countries and would determine whether these particular systems were the ones that would do the most damage to the [enemy's] war effort. And they considered many systems. They might consider electric power, they might consider petroleum, they might consider aircraft, whatever, transportation, whatever. And on the basis of their study of the intelligence available, they would then arrive at a conclusion that a particular system would have a major effect, if it was eliminated.[31]

In addition to studies of target systems, the geographic sections systematically compiled and analyzed data on specific individual installations.[32]

Within SVB was the Physical Vulnerability Section (PV). This section "was charged with the responsibility for the continual research, development, and review of the susceptibility of targets to damage on any given target." At first, PV was billeted only six people (out of a total ninety-one positions in SVB). The first two positions filled were head of section, a naval officer, John S. Patton, and a secretary, Helen Astin. Both had worked for the Physical Vulnerability Section of the Joint Target Group during the war. In early 1946, Grassy was hired as a structural analyst, the first civilian professional in PV. Grassy had been trained as a geological engineer. As an air target analyst for the Navy during the war, he had completed the Princeton University training course set up by Division 2 of the National Defense Research Committee and had then done air targeting in the Pacific.[33] After the war, he became the longest-serving and highest-ranking civilian in PV; he was there from 1946 until he retired in 1972. For many years, he held the position of deputy chief, the highest rank a civilian could hold. (The position of chief was reserved for military officers.) In June 1946 a second civilian professional was hired: Carl F. Kossack, a Ph.D. in mathematics who had also worked for the Joint Target Group.[34]

After the economists had picked potential target systems and targets, according to Grassy,

> Then it would be up to us in PV to tell them how much this would cost in terms of weapons—not monetary, but how many weapons would be required to do the job on this—and then what level [of damage] would be accomplished. That was, I would say, the basic philosophy, certainly in the beginning. Because you must remember that first there was this great history of strategic bombing in World War II. And second, there was a limited number of atomic weapons available in the beginning. There weren't hundreds of them . . . So it was a problem of how you could do the most with what you had.[35]

How did those choosing target systems and those determining weapons requirements and predicting levels of damage know which problems to solve and the kinds of solutions to seek? Despite distinctive new challenges—a not well-understood technology, the atomic bomb, and an international political situation in which the United States had unprecedented power—the basic understanding of mission, the kinds of problems to be solved, and the broad nature of solutions sought were all built on the template of World War II experience. According to Grassy,

> There was no doubt about what we [in PV] were supposed to be doing. How to accomplish that, though, had to be worked out, especially with regard to nuclear weapons. We had a very definite mission and we retained that mission throughout our history and that was to estimate weapon requirements and predict damage. . . . And it was very specific right from the beginning. And that would be, at least initially, sort of a continuation of what had been going on in World War II.[36]

Organizational mission was formally approved by senior military officers,[37] but the details of which problems were to be solved and how to go about solving them were worked out at lower levels: "We [in PV] sort of said we were in charge of estimating weapon requirements and predicting damage levels. That was our job. . . . [When] we started working, we had a clear idea of . . . what we were supposed to do. But there were many echelons [above] that didn't really know how we did it or what was involved in doing it."[38]

In April 1949, most of the Strategic Vulnerability Branch moved from the Pentagon to a building called "Tempo U" (for "Temporary Building U") in Washington, D.C.[39] Tempo U was located where the Smithsonian's National Museum of American History now stands on the Mall, facing Constitution Avenue and running between Twelfth and Fourteenth Streets. Like other temporary structures put up on the Mall during the war, Tempo U was "a gray, creaking two-story temporary barracks-like building,"[40] a "firetrap" with "no air conditioning." At first, said Grassy, it had ceiling lights with metal reflectors and "tremendous 1,000 watt bulbs . . . throw[ing] out a lot of heat. . . . Geez, it was terrible."[41] The building was compartmentalized by access to sources of information. One analyst said he knew who analyzed atomic power "only when they were pointed out at coffee break. . . . At night all the stuff was cleared and went into safes or burn bags."[42]

Targets

Air Force Intelligence was reorganized in March 1950. The Strategic Vulnerability Branch became the Air Targets Division, with similar functions and more personnel.[43] In Grassy's understanding, by the early 1950s, those working in the Air Targets Division had three principal concerns: "What are the targets, how many [weapons] do you need for them, and how do you get there?"[44] Reflecting this understanding, by mid-1952, Targets—now formally the Deputy Directorate for Targets—was organized into three divisions: Target Analysis, Physical Vulnerability, and Target Materials. Together, the three divisions performed the same basic functions as had the original eight sections of SVB. The Target Analysis Division developed information on targets, a task originally lodged in SVB's geographic sections. According to an organization chart from the period, this division analyzed military, political, and economic resources "world-wide from an air targeting point of view." It also published and maintained the *Bombing Encyclopedia,* discussed below. The Physical Vulnerability Division (PV) determined "the physical vulnerability of particular targets," estimated "weapon requirements to obtain desired degrees of damage," and predicted "the effects of specific weapons on targets." The Target Materials Division oversaw the development and distribution of air target materials.[45] These tasks remained stable throughout the 1950s. There were large organizational changes in Air Force Intelligence toward the end of the decade, but the activities of those involved in target intelligence remained largely the same.

In late 1958, the renamed Directorate of Targets left Tempo U, which was torn down shortly after, and relocated to Arlington Hall, a former private girls' preparatory school in Arlington, Virginia. It was a "beautiful location," with a "campus and attractive brick Victorian buildings [with] lots of trees and flowers." It had been commandeered by the government during the war for code-breaking operations, and the military had built on the campus two-story buildings that were very similar, "frankly, probably identical" to Tempo U.[46] The move signaled more than an improvement in landscape. The Directorate of Targets now became the nucleus of a new organization called the Air Force Intelligence Center (AFIC). As successor to the Directorate of Targets, AFIC continued as a "joint" organization with Air Force, Army, and Navy participation. Those who had been involved in Targets continued, with one significant change: The division lost its entire mathematical analysis branch and, with it, the branch's advanced computing capability.[47]

AFIC was short-lived. The Defense Intelligence Agency (DIA) was established in the fall of 1961, and, by 1963, AFIC, including those in PV, became absorbed into DIA's Production Center. The functions of the Production Center remained at Arlington Hall until 1984 when most of DIA was consolidated at Bolling Air Force Base.[48] This, however, gets us ahead of our story.

Despite the changes in organization, there were significant continuities in the evolution of target intelligence from the immediate postwar period through at least the 1960s: in mission, in the focus of those in PV, and in the close organizational ties of those involved in picking targets and those involved in predicting damage to them. Let us now turn to see how the categories of precision bombing doctrine carried over from World War II.

The *Bombing Encyclopedia*

The first major postwar project of SVB was an extensive compendium of potential targets known as the *Bombing Encyclopedia of the World,* or *Bombing Encyclopedia,* or *B.E.*[49] The encyclopedia was a veritable census of potential destruction and indicates that wartime doctrine carried over into postwar analysis.

The underlying logic of the *Bombing Encyclopedia* was that of precision bombing, which necessitated the systematic collection of information on many individual installations. In 1946, SVB began compiling lists of installations.[50] The ultimate goal was to have information on every potential target in every country.[51]

Preliminary work on Soviet installations began in January 1946. By mid-July, according to the Daily Activity Report for SVB, "5,594 target numbers [had] been assigned and 4,715 IBM cards punched for the *Bombing Encyclopedia.*"[52] By June 1947, 4,000 industrial targets in the Soviet Union alone were listed in the *B.E.*[53]

According to Henry Nash, a civilian who worked in the section on Soviet government control centers, "We were filled with a kind of enthusiasm, thinking we were working on something that was just beginning to get formulated." The work had the feel of a scholarly enterprise. "We were really 'about' getting a target into the *Bombing Encyclopedia.* We never really knew why we got one in. It made it perplexing and euphoric. It took a long time. We'd submit lists, they'd be sent out of the office. . . . Six months later, a party headquarters I had identified at Kharkov, for example, would appear on the list. My superior would bring it. Others would gather round." Nash's whole group was able to get "maybe 15 to 20 a year" into the *Encyclopedia.* Then they would go out to lunch to celebrate. "It was taken very seriously."[54]

By the early 1950s, the scope of the *Bombing Encyclopedia* had become global. There is only one known extant copy in Air Force archives of an early edition. According to the unclassified table of contents, by 1952 the *Bombing Encyclopedia* was published in three volumes.[55] The first volume listed specific installations alphabetically within cities. In the words of the *B.E.,* the volume was "an alphabetical arrangement of potential targets arranged by cities within countries." The *B.E.* listed installations in ninety-six countries, zones, or political regions, including virtually all of Europe, Africa, and the Middle East and most of Asia. The most extensive coverage was of the Soviet Union. About 350 of over 1,000 pages listed potential targets in the Soviet Union—on the order of 10,000 potential targets. The two German zones were about 100 pages, and France was some 50 pages.[56] This extensive catalogue served as the master list of potential targets, strategic and tactical, for both conventional and nuclear bombing.[57] (By 1960, the *B.E.* contained more than 80,000 potential targets and provided the basis for the target list known as the National Strategic Target List [NSTL], which was used in the first multiservice U.S. strategic nuclear war plan, the Single Integrated Operational Plan [SIOP].)[58]

The alphabetical arrangement implied that installations could be added and removed at will. It implied precision bombing in which certain installations would be targeted for destruction and others would not. This categorical understanding of targets came directly out of the extensive targeting experience of World War II and embodied a logic that continued for decades—and in all likelihood, continues to the present.

The *Bombing Encyclopedia* required detailed knowledge of economic, political, or military functions of installations and the exact geographical location of those installations. The 1952 *B.E.* provided the following remarkably detailed set of categories of information for every installation listed:

- the functional name of the installation (e.g., aircraft engine plant);
- any distinguishing descriptive term, such as an area of a city;
- if the installation were located underground;
- distinguishing names;
- plant number;
- a census-like seven-digit category and product number that indicated in detail the functional category of the installation (e.g., raw material production; basic processing; basic services such as electric power; civilian end products' military end products such as aircraft, ammunition, and ships; "urban areas and installations peculiar thereto" such as "government"; and air, other military, and naval installations);
- coordinates of latitude and longitude;
- elevation above sea level;
- an eight-digit identifier known as the B.E. number that uniquely identified the installation and allowed the user to locate it on the master air mapping system used by the Air Force, the World Aeronautical Chart.[59]

According to front matter in the first volume, the other two volumes presented much of the same information but arranged differently. Volume 3 listed installations alphabetically within target systems. It was a "categorical arrangement of the potential targets. . . . Each category is listed separately and the potential targets arranged alphabetically therein." Volume 2 cross-referenced volumes 1 and 3; it was "arranged by installation numbers within World Aeronautical Charts and without regard to countries."[60]

The logic of the *Bombing Encyclopedia* can perhaps be seen most clearly when contrasted with the wartime British publication, the *Bomber's Baedeker: Guide to the Economic Importance of German Towns, Cities, and Industries*. Even the names attest to a different logic: *encyclopedia* connoting an encompassing collection of individual items; *Baedeker*—a sick joke on the well-known German travel guides put out by Baedeker—connoting a focus on cities. The *Bomber's Baedeker* explicated the goals of area bombing: "Destruction and damage to dwellings and de-housing of population . . . destruction and damage to factories and commercial property and the interruption of public utility services and communications . . . loss of working time due to general dislocation of economic life . . . expenditure of manpower and materials in rehabilitation measures."[61]

Not surprisingly, the categorical arrangement of the *Bomber's Baedeker* was different from that of the *Bombing Encyclopedia*. The *Bomber's Baedeker* rated over a hundred cities according to their economic importance, and also rated the concentration of economic activity.[62] About two-thirds of the *Baedeker* consisted of tables of cities and towns in which the number, but not the location, of important industrial sectors were tallied. For example, Berlin had four transportation targets of first priority, sixteen of the second, four of the third, and so on for public utility services, solid fuels, liquid fuels and substitutes, iron, steel, and ferro-alloys, through shipbuilding, rubber and tires, leather, and foodstuffs.

In the *Bomber's Baedeker*, targets were urban areas; the precise location of specific installations was not germane. Urban areas were treated as a whole. The *Bombing Encyclopedia* listed individual installations, chosen as part of larger target systems. The function and exact location of individual installations was paramount; that the destruction of any one installation would inevitably mean vast damage to a large area surrounding it was not important. This framework would be significant for the development of a methodology to predict damage from atomic weapons.

The First Study to Predict Damage From Atomic Bombs

The strong analytical focus in U.S. target intelligence on the enumeration of thousands of specific installations was consistent with a doctrine of precision bombing. But how was damage from atomic bombs to be understood and predicted? Damage to what? What damage was considered relevant and why?

Of course, some innovation in damage prediction was likely. The atomic bomb was a remarkable new weapon. Its unprecedented destructive power had been horrifically demonstrated over Japan, but at the end of the war scientists and others had no *detailed* professional understanding of its phenomenology and effects. (Grassy referred to this lack of knowledge: While the mission of those in PV was clear, "how to accomplish that, though, had to be worked out, especially with regard to nuclear weapons.")

At the same time, the historical association in World War II between precision bombing and blast damage had led to a significant capability to predict blast damage and the assumption that the relevant mechanism of damage was blast. According to Grassy, fire effects "really hadn't come to anybody's attention" right after the war. "It was not an aspect of atomic weapons that was of interest or that anyone knew much about. It was completely overshadowed by the obvious blast effects. We saw these as blast weapons."[63]

Predictions of blast damage to specific installations were carried out by 1948. However, the first postwar study of damage from atomic weapons, done in 1947, does not conform to this pattern. Rather, it uses an area concept. But there is a straightforward explanation: At the time, analysts could not locate specific Soviet installations. Given the emphasis on specific installations in the *Bombing Encyclopedia*, we would expect that as target information became available, blast damage to specific installations would be estimated. By 1948, this is what was happening.

The first efforts to predict damage from atomic bombs occurred in the early summer of 1947. The damage calculation was done by Richard Grassy, the structural analyst at PV. According to Grassy, the Physical Vulnerability Section of SVB "was requested to do a limited target study of the atomic bomb damage to certain industrial cities in the USSR. . . . These cities had been selected because they contained installations considered important to the war effort. . . . We didn't have any idea of where these installations were located. And the idea was to put enough weapons on [them] to achieve sufficient damage."[64]

In all likelihood, PV's damage study was done in support of an Air Staff study of the requirements for an atomic bomb attack on the Soviet Union. It assumed that a decision had been made "on or prior to D-Day, to launch at the earliest possible time an all-out air offensive, using atomic weapons to the maximum extent of U.S. capabilities." The Air Intelligence Division of the Air Staff "prepared a list of industrial cities in Eurasia on which the U.S.S.R. is or would be dependent for production of military supplies and equipment. . . . The requirement for atomic bomb stocks is determined, basically, by the number of atomic bombs necessary to destroy the industrial areas of the cities on this list." Calculations were "performed for the 49 most important U.S.S.R. targets." The study found that to destroy these targets required "100 atomic bombs burst on target." Given operational loss factors of about 50 percent, "approximately 200 atomic weapons would have to be delivered from stockpile for this purpose." For this study, PV estimated

> the number of bomb hits needed for a military decision. . . . The target system on which the calculation is based comprises the major urban areas which may be expected to be in Russian hands . . . plus certain isolated industrial targets. For each of these targets, the area was obtained from intelligence sources, and the number of hits required to eliminate the target was computed from this factor alone. . . . Once the area of a target had been found or estimated, the number of bombs needed to destroy its effectiveness was calculated by finding the number of bombs needed to destroy half the built-up area on the assumptions that the radius of destruction of the bomb was approximately 1 mile and that the ground-zero of the bomb is about equally likely to occur anywhere within the target area.[65]

A list of cities targeted in the Air Staff study is not available. However, we can get a sense of what such a list looked like from a description of the mobilization plan being prepared at about the same time for the Joint Chiefs of Staff. According to a careful reading by historian Stephen Ross, the Chiefs' mobilization plan "called for dropping thirty-four atomic bombs on twenty-four Soviet cities. Moscow would be hit with seven bombs, Leningrad with three and Karkov [Kharkov] and Stalingrad with two each. Baku, Gorki, Dnepropetrovsk, Prosny, Zaporoshye, Omsk, Chelyabinsk, Molotov, Ufa, Stalinsk, Nizhny Tagil, Stalino, Sverdlovsk, Novosibirsk, Kazan, Kuibyshev, Saratov, Magnitogorsk, and Chkalov would receive one bomb each."[66] We cannot tell exactly how many cities were targeted in the Air Staff plan, but we can see from the Chiefs' mobilization plan that large cities were often targeted with more than one weapon.[67]

According to Grassy, who did the damage calculation: "In this study, the number of nuclear weapons (nominal, 20 kt [kiloton]) sufficient to achieve structural damage to . . . the light steel-frame structures in each of the target cities was determined. Light steel-frame structures were chosen as being representative of many industrial installations."[68]

How did Grassy estimate damage to light steel-frame structures if he did not know where those installations were located?

> We didn't deal with any individual installations because we didn't have that information. The people who ran the study ascertained that x city had so many steel installations or other kinds of installations. . . . We knew the outline of the area, we knew all installations were inside that area. We did separate weapons requirements for each city, depending on

the area they gave you. We assumed everything was in the urban area.[69]
. . . We considered these cities as area targets, because, well, in the first
place, we didn't have anything like the detailed intelligence to conduct
a more detailed study, so we considered them as area targets and we estimated the amount of damage there would be for . . . industrial structures. . . . And I did this in a very crude fashion.[70]

It would appear that although, by the summer of 1947, the *Bombing Encyclopedia* listed 4,000 industrial targets in the Soviet Union, the information was insufficient for the purposes of this Air Staff damage study. It is
likely that the data linking function of installation and exact location were
fragmentary or not compiled for all the cities targeted in the study. Further,
at the time of the study, Grassy and his colleagues had very limited access to
information on atomic damage.[71] Although the analysts at PV were responsible for calculating damage caused by atomic weapons, they did not
have the Restricted Data clearances needed to see information about atomic
weapons! Thus, Grassy performed all damage calculations using non-Re-
stricted Data. According to him, "Lack of clearance to receive Restricted
Data–Atomic Energy Information was a major factor in limiting the early
effectiveness of PV."[72] In fact, the only data on atomic damage available to
PV analysts were measures of damage "as given in the summary USSBS [U.S.
Strategic Bombing Survey; pronounced "us bus"] report, with no detail at
all."[73] Grassy is referring here to the unclassified report by the Chairman's
Office, U.S. Strategic Bombing Survey, entitled *The Effects of Atomic Bombs
on Hiroshima and Japan,* published in June 1946.[74] The forty-three-page report had only one page of relevant information (listed in Table 4.1). The report presented damage from blast effects, but no comparable listing for fire
damage.

The Effects of Atomic Bombs listed the areas within which virtually all
structures of particular types had been destroyed by blast. For example, at
Nagasaki, virtually all light steel-frame buildings were destroyed within an
area 3.3 square miles from the detonation; that is, within a radius of 5,400
feet, or just over a mile. Damage to similar structures at Hiroshima was almost identical. (For the 1947 study, Grassy used only the data for light steel-
frame buildings. For the 1948 study, he used most of the building types
listed.)[75] The estimated level of blast damage was called either "structural"
or "severe," and the terms meant the same thing: in plain English, the building had been destroyed.

Technically, the areas of damage were arrived at by calculating a "mean
area of effectiveness" (discussed below). Although *The Effects of Atomic
Bombs* referred to the "area within which buildings were damaged," PV analysts understood that "mean area of effectiveness" was the actual technical

TABLE 4.1.
BLAST DAMAGE FROM ATOMIC BOMBS: INFORMATION AVAILABLE TO ANALYSTS IN PHYSICAL VULNERABILITY, 1947

Type of building	Type of damage	Area within which buildings were damaged (square miles)[a]	Radius of damage (feet)[b]
Reinforced concrete (earthquake and non-earthquake resistant)	Structural		
Hiroshima		0.05	700
Nagasaki		0.43	2,000
Heavy steel frame	Structural		
Nagasaki		1.8	4,000
One-story light steel frame	Severe		
Hiroshima		3.4	5,500
Nagasaki		3.3	5,400
Multistory, load-bearing brick-wall	Severe		
Hiroshima		3.6	5,700
One-story load-bearing brick-wall	Severe		
Hiroshima		6.0	7,300
Nagasaki		8.1	8,500
Wood-frame domestic	Severe		
Hiroshima		6.0	7,300
Nagasaki		7.5	8,200
Wood-frame industrial and commercial	Severe		
Hiroshima		8.5	8,700
Nagasaki		9.9	9,400

Source: Unless otherwise noted, information compiled from United States Strategic Bombing Survey [USSBS], Chairman's Office, *The Effects of Atomic Bombs on Hiroshima and Nagasaki* (Washington, D.C.: GPO, 30 June 1946), p. 30.

[a]Called "mean area of effectiveness" in USSBS, Physical Damage Division, *A Report on Physical Damage in Japan* (n.p., June 1947), originally classified Restricted, table 37, p. 176, and figures 33–37, pp. 178–182.

[b]Easily calculated from the area; figures later presented in USSBS, Physical Damage Division, *Report on Physical Damage in Japan,* table 37, p. 176; see also figures 33–37, pp. 178–182.

measure used.[76] The summary report did not provide the radius of damage, but this was easily calculated from the area.

We now have a clearer picture of how Grassy estimated weapons requirements. As noted, at Nagasaki, almost all light steel-frame buildings within a mile of detonation were severely damaged by blast. Assuming that industrial buildings were light steel frame, and that all industrial installations were inside the delimited area for each city targeted in his study, Grassy then developed an estimate of what percentage of industrial structures in each Soviet urban area would be destroyed by one weapon, or, the same thing, how many weapons would be required to destroy all the industrial structures in a given area.[77] Of course, the weapons estimate depended on the size of the city. If the city were less than 3.3 square miles, one weapon would be required to severely damage all of its industrial structures. If it were larger, more would be required.

Grassy used a mathematical concept called mean area of effectiveness (MAE), which was developed early in the war by British analysts and later used by the Joint Target Group and the U.S. Strategic Bombing Survey. Calculations based on MAE provided estimates of damage against some basic types of industrial structures. There were several methods for calculating MAEs, but the essential idea was that it provided a summary measure, in the words of the Strategic Bombing Survey, of "the area within which all existing target units of a prescribed class will, on the average, be damaged to a prescribed degree by a prescribed weapon." The specific way that "average" was calculated need not concern us here.[78]

In sum, the first postwar study of damage from atomic bombs was based on calculating damage to installations within urban *areas*. This was not because of a doctrinal shift to area bombing. The goal of damaging specific installations, and predicting damage to them, had carried over into the postwar period, but in 1947 Grassy did not have information on specific installations, their locations, and their structural type. At the same time, the 1947 study calculated damage from blast, not from fire. This reflected the wartime priority accorded to the prediction of damage from blast, resulting in greater knowledge about blast damage than fire damage. The Strategic Bombing Survey report of 1946 had published blast damage data only.

But is this too neat? When Dick Grassy first told me that he had done a study in which he had calculated damage to areas, not to specific structures, I was surprised. At the time, I wondered if there had been a shift in organizational common sense that I would have to confront. I asked Grassy if considering cities as area targets seemed unsatisfactory at the time. He replied:

Oh, yeah, sure. It was unsatisfactory for everybody. In the first place, the people who were interested in the strategic aspects, many were not interested particularly in gross assessments of the level of what percentage of a structure of a certain type that you were taking out in a city. They wanted to know what was going to happen to specific targets. See, the Strategic Vulnerability Branch came into existence after the experience of World War II where strategic bombing, as far the U.S. was concerned, was concentrated on *specific* target systems. And that philosophy was carried over into this, and the desire was to be able to select certain strategic systems, as they had done in the case of conventional bombings, and take those out with nuclear weapons. *So they wanted to be able to say specifically this target installation will have this probability of this specific damage. . . . Never was the Strategic Vulnerability Branch interested in just doing massive damage. That wasn't the purpose.* So that's the philosophy they carried over, and this area approach just didn't answer their questions. They couldn't say this is how we would affect a particular industry that was strategically important. So, the task was to try to develop a way to do that.[79]

Altogether, then, there is clear evidence that precision bombing doctrine, and the assumption that blast damage was both the most appropriate and most predictable form of damage against specific installations, continued to exert an important influence in the postwar period, even in the earliest study of atomic damage in which the location of specific installations simply was not available. Given this, it is not surprising that by 1948, analysts calculated damage against specific installations, and the damage calculated was from blast.

The "Cookie Cutter" Model

In the spring of 1948, with the intensification of the Cold War, the Air Force initiated "a crash program to produce detailed target and damage information to substantiate [and elaborate] the early 1947 atomic target study."[80] Using newly available information, Grassy started to answer the questions he and others were interested in. What blast damage would *specific* installations sustain in an atomic attack? Again, we cannot be certain of the exact study Grassy worked on, but most likely it was related to annex HARROW, prepared by the Air Staff, in support of the Joint Chiefs of Staff emergency war plan called BROILER–FROLIC–HALFMOON. (Despite its name, BROILER, like all nuclear war plans since, was premised on blast damage. Work on BROILER began in the late summer of 1947 and was approved for planning purposes in March 1948. It was revised shortly after, as FROLIC, and, following consultation with British and Canadian military officers, revised as HALFMOON and approved in May 1948.)[81]

Grassy and others in Physical Vulnerability now had significant new information. First, they had much better information on the location of various types of installations in the Soviet Union.[82] Second, far more detailed Bombing Survey reports on the effects of the atomic bombs had been published. These reports provided the data and calculations on which the summary unclassified 1946 USSBS report had been based and included charts detailing the correspondence between probability of damage to various types of structures and distances from ground zero. Third, in February 1948, the military chief of PV and Grassy had received their Q-clearances for Restricted Data. This gave them access to reports from the government's atomic weapons laboratory, Los Alamos, and to files from a multiservice organization concerned with atomic weapons, the Armed Forces Special Weapons Project (AFSWP).[83] Access to Los Alamos reports allowed PV analysts to study an important report by the British physicist William Penney on blast overpressure. (In 1947, Penney became the head of the British nuclear weapons program.)[84]

Immediately after the war, Penney had observed the damage at Hiroshima and Nagasaki. Despite the somewhat experimental cast to the bombings of Hiroshima and Nagasaki (the Bombing Survey stated that "Hiroshima was an excellent test target for the atomic bomb"), only very rough measures of the effects of the bomb had been taken during the attacks themselves.[85] Afterward, Allied observers estimated bomb effects from the physical evidence. Penney's study estimated blast overpressure at various distances from the detonations. By measuring the displacement of simple objects, such as tombstones, Penney calculated the overpressure required to move them the observed distances. These calculations were then published in a Los Alamos report, classified Restricted Data. As soon as he got access to Penney's work, Grassy systematically "plotted [these data] for each of the bursts" at Hiroshima and Nagasaki. From that he "established a distance–overpressure relationship."[86] In other words, Grassy was now able to associate any distance from ground zero with a corresponding overpressure, and vice versa. And, using the Bombing Survey data, Grassy was able to associate any distance from ground zero or overpressure at that distance with probability of damage to each type of structure described in the Survey.

This new information allowed PV analysts to overcome a problem inherent in the measure of damage they had used earlier, the mean area of effectiveness. The main problem with the measure was that it was descriptive, calculable only *after* the fact: measures of MAE "relate[d] only to one particular bomb detonating at one particular height."[87] Measures of MAE could not be used to predict damage to types of structures when yield and height of burst varied. For planning purposes, PV analysts wanted to develop a general method by which to predict damage to specific installations.

Such a method could be developed if they could correlate levels of damage to structures with a mechanism of destruction that varied systematically with yield, height of burst, and distance from the detonation. And that is what Penney's study of blast overpressure enabled.

For PV, correlating damage to types of structures with blast overpressure from an atomic detonation was the solution to developing a general method of damage prediction. According to Grassy, "What I had to do—my problem—was to relate the damage for each of these [structural] categories to overpressure. . . . We knew the distances from GZ [ground zero] to the various structures. . . . If we were going to try to interpolate to other weapons or to other burst heights, we had to have some parameter to tie it to, and the obvious one was overpressure."[88] In other words, if they could generally describe the relationship between overpressure and damage to types of installations, this would serve as the basis for prediction. For various types of structures, the closer to ground zero, the greater the overpressure and resulting damage. Similarly, as bomb yield increased, overpressure and resulting damage should predictably increase. Finally, as height of burst decreased, and the point of detonation was brought closer to structures, overpressure and resulting damage should predictably increase.

In order to implement this solution, simple in theory, several problems had to be solved, and this is the significance of the new information available by the spring of 1948. This new information provided detailed data on the distribution of damaged structures at various distances from ground zero at Hiroshima and Nagasaki and also estimates of overpressure at varying distances from the detonation. Once Grassy gained access to these data, he could combine them and devise a general method for predicting blast damage to various types of structures.

For his study, Grassy constructed curves for each of the five types of structures categorized in the USSBS: reinforced concrete, heavy steel frame, light steel frame, brick load-bearing walls, and wood-frame industrial and commercial buildings. For each curve—that is, building type—Grassy correlated the probability of damage with overpressure (see Figure 4.2b for Grassy's sketch of typical curves). In these diagrams, the horizontal axis represents the overpressure, and the vertical axis the probability of structural damage. Thus, a given type of structure exposed to a high overpressure had a very high probability of sustaining structural damage and exposed to a low overpressure had a low probability of sustaining such damage. One other point: because Grassy had already related overpressure to distance from ground zero, the horizontal axis could be understood not only as measuring overpressure but as measuring distance from ground zero.

Grassy and his colleagues understood that at higher overpressures (or at lesser distances), the probability of damage to specific structures would be

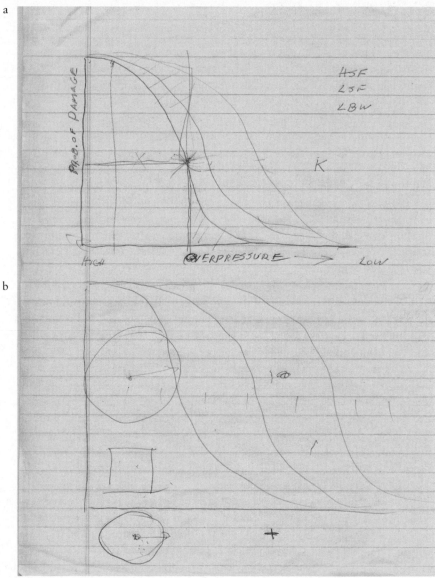

Figure 4.2. a. Richard Grassy's sketch of the "cookie cutter model." In this model, a structure with a probability of damage of less than 50 percent, indicated by the double horizontal line, survives (to the right of the double vertical line); the same structure with a probability of damage greater than 50 percent (to the left of the vertical line) does not. (Initials refer to other aspects of damage prediction which are not relevant to explication of the cookie cutter model.) b. Grassy's sketch of probability of damage curves for three typical building types. As overpressure decreases (x-axis from left to right), probability of damage (y-axis) decreases. Different curves represent different building types.

higher. However, it was one thing to sketch out the relationship and another to provide a routine method for calculating the probability of damage. For calculation, the analysts used what they called a "cookie cutter" model. That is, for each type of structure, they designated an overpressure at which they estimated the probability of structural damage to be approximately 50 percent and simply said that if a structure were subjected to that overpressure or higher, it would be assumed to be damaged, and if it were subjected to less overpressure, it would be assumed to be undamaged.[89] (See Figure 4.2a.)

Grassy, interpreting the horizontal axis in terms of distance, explained, "If the weapon landed here [pointing to the left of the vertical line in Figure 4.2a], we would say anything within [this distance from ground zero] would be considered damaged. That's the original, that was the cookie cutter."[90] Of course, PV analysts understood that some structures subjected to more than the designated overpressure would not be damaged and that some structures subjected to less than the designated overpressure would be damaged. The "cookie cutter" could not take this variation into account, but it was a good first estimate.

In order to predict damage to specific Soviet targets and to recommend the optimum location for detonating weapons and the number of weapons required, PV analysts required detailed knowledge about the location of Soviet installations. They gained this knowledge by the spring of 1948.

The simple "cookie cutter" model became widely used by those in Air Force targeting. According to Stan Lawwill, the operations analyst at SAC, "At first, our information on target hardness from HQ USAF Intelligence was purely psi [pounds per square inch]—a single number for each target . . . called 'cookie cutter.'"[91]

PV analysts had gained a great deal of predictive ability over the earlier measure of MAE. Using Penney's estimates of overpressure, they could now roughly calculate how overpressure would vary with yield, height of burst, and distance from detonation. Given this, for a type of structure located at a designated distance from the detonation, they could now predict whether the structure would be destroyed. This is an important moment in the development of a methodology for predicting the damaging effects of atomic weapons. Although the analysis was still simple and organizational capacity was limited, the *focus* of inquiry had been set: to predict damage from blast for specific installations.[92]

Why No Concerted Effort to Predict Fire Damage?

We have seen that the earliest postwar estimates of damage were based on blast. Although the U.S. Strategic Bombing Survey contained estimates of blast damage, fire damage, and combined blast and fire damage, Grassy's first postwar estimates relied on measures of blast damage only: the USSBS mean area of effectiveness for structural damage from blast. Grassy's next estimates built on the parameter of blast overpressure.

In theory, other means of destruction could have been used. PV analysts could have estimated the *thermal fluence,* that is, calories per square centimeter (cal/cm^2), as it varied with yield, height of burst, and distance from the detonation. At Hiroshima, the perimeter of mass fire within which virtually everything was destroyed (and which was, therefore, a good measure of severe damage), occurred about one mile from the detonation, approximately the same radius as severe damage for light steel-frame buildings; at this distance, the thermal fluence deposited was estimated at 10 cal/cm^2. This was published in the first edition of Glasstone's unclassified *Effects of Atomic Weapons* in 1950 and was based on data from the Strategic Bombing Survey.[93] There is no obvious reason why the relationship of thermal fluence and range could not have been calculated by the spring of 1948.

The deposition of thermal fluence of 10 cal/cm^2 is the basic measure used in much of Theodore Postol's published work on fire damage from nuclear weapons. Why was it not used in developing damage predictions in the late 1940s? Because those in target intelligence did not try to predict fire damage and focused instead on blast damage.

Predicting blast damage carried over from World War II in at least three ways. First, many of those in target intelligence in Washington had been involved in predicting blast damage in World War II. Second, for those in target intelligence, the doctrine of precision bombing also carried over. In Grassy's words, the goal "was focused entirely on, almost entirely on specific installations. . . . The goal was to assess the impact on the nation's economy or war economy and you had to get at that with specific targets. At least, most people thought so."[94] As we saw in chapter 3, specific targets were historically associated with blast damage, not fire damage.

Third, the assumption that fire damage was inherently less predictable than blast damage continued. When I asked Grassy if there had been discussion in the early postwar years about incorporating fire into damage calculations, he answered:

> I don't think we ever got into any discussions about it, really. I suppose that was because we were instinctively convinced that while [fire] might add to the effect, you couldn't predict how much it would add to it, and you couldn't predict with what certainty it might occur. I think that's roughly the feel. . . . We knew that the damage from blast was quite certain. And it appeared that it could be reasonably predicted, although we

didn't have very good tools in the beginning for it. And that while fire could supplement this, it was not the major source of interest.[95]

Because fire damage seemed less inherently predictable, those in PV could not see a way to develop a methodology for prediction. According to Grassy:

> We had no way to put a handle on the possibility of fire in connection with atomic weapons. There were so many factors that involved pure chance. We could see no practical approach. So many things were involved: the general condition of the target, not just the construction, but litter or rubbish that could serve as points of ignition. Plus the proximity to material that's flammable. Plus the probability that it will sustain. If it does sustain, will it spread throughout the building? If so, will it spread to other buildings? All of these events were subject to chance, and it just seemed to us—well, we had no way to introduce so many factors.[96]

Grassy's recollection is consistent with that of fire protection engineer Horatio Bond, who had returned to private life after the war. When asked if the Air Force had been interested in what he had to say about the effects of atomic weapons, Bond replied that he had "no knowledge that they were particularly concerned. I don't remember hearing from any of them."[97]

In sum, by the late spring of 1948, analysts in the Physical Vulnerability Section in Air Force Intelligence had developed a preliminary system to predict blast damage to individual installations and had applied it to targets in the Soviet Union. This simple system was based on analysis of the available data on atomic bomb damage at Hiroshima and Nagasaki and on information on the location of specific Soviet installations. It was also based on a preliminary understanding of the behavior and effects of blast waves from atomic weapons that PV analysts shared with a larger community of scientists and engineers. The next several years would see a significant increase in analysts' ability to predict blast damage.

5

New Inquiry about Blast

In view of its great importance to the national security, the problem of atomic blast damage has been under continuous study from the first bomb. . . . Fortunately for the present knowledge of the field of atomic blast damage, there is the Japanese experience to draw on as well as a substantial amount of experimental information developed in bomb tests since the War.

Memorandum: The Implication of the BUSTER–JANGLE
Blast Measurements, 29 January 1952

From 1948 to 1951, analysts in Physical Vulnerability (PV) of Air Force Intelligence greatly refined their ability to predict damage from atomic blast. Based on what they knew and needed to know, PV analysts drew up an ambitious research agenda to acquire additional knowledge regarding blast forces and resulting damage to structures. Some of the investigations they proposed were to take place in forthcoming atomic weapons tests. Analysts also reexamined data from Hiroshima and Nagasaki and developed a way to predict blast damage that superseded the "cookie cutter" model they had developed in 1948 (see chapter 4). This new solution—the Vulnerability Number, or VN, system—became the enduring basis of blast damage prediction for use in U.S. war planning.

PV analysts worked within a defined set of problems that focused organizational attention; they refined their search for solutions and improved the solution they had developed earlier. But they did not simply solve problems of atomic blast damage prediction; they also built knowledge and organizational capacity in the form of mathematical and engineering expertise, specialized research, and increasingly fine-grained predictive routines. They hired additional employees, outside consulting engineers, and contractors who designed, built, and instrumented structures to carry out specialized experiments on structures in atomic weapons tests. Results from the tests, combined with extensive analytical work done by consultants and contractors, would later enable those in PV to revise the VN system into the VNTK system, a set of highly refined, knowledge-laden routines to predict blast damage to structures (see chapter 7).

None of this precluded predicting damage from mass fire. Had prediction of blast and fire damage been similar—drawing on similar physical models, for example—the increased capability to solve one might have led to the solution of the other. But the problems of prediction were not similar.

The overwhelming attention to predicting blast damage had two consequences. First, it led to a great disparity in organizational capabilities. By the mid-1950s, nuclear weapons analysts better understood blast phenomena and could make refined predictions of damage from blast. They did not explore mass fire phenomena and could not predict fire damage. Second, PV analysts thought their ability to predict blast damage and inability to predict fire damage came not from choices about which problems to tackle, but from an inherently greater predictability of blast damage. Their own achievement reinforced their belief that blast damage was more predictable. They understood the differences in organizational capability to predict blast damage and fire damage as "attributes of the world" rather than as the result of their own actions.[1]

To understand how analysts developed knowledge about one aspect of atomic weapons damage but not another, and the ramifications of this focus on later problem solving, we must first examine what was known about blast shortly after World War II.

State of Knowledge about Blast

By mid-1948, knowledge of atomic weapons was based on the detonations at Hiroshima and Nagasaki, and on early postwar atomic weapons tests in the Marshall Islands, which sit about halfway between the Hawaiian Islands and northern Australia. The first test series, Operation CROSSROADS, was held in the summer of 1946 at Bikini Atoll, a coral reef surrounding a lagoon of more than 200 square miles. Operation CROSSROADS involved two detonations, Shot ABLE and Shot BAKER. (Each series of tests was named as an operation; each test, or detonation, was named as a shot. This nomenclature was used throughout the postwar testing program.) For each shot, a fleet of about seventy target ships was arrayed in the lagoon. The second shot, BAKER, was the first underwater explosion of an atomic weapon, and it was spectacular. A column of water almost a half mile in diameter shot more than a mile into the air, collapsed heavily into the lagoon, and caused "a tidal wave of spray and steam" to rise and "smother the fleet."[2] This "moving blanket of radioactive mist" severely contaminated numerous ships and caused a planned third shot to be canceled.[3]

The second test series, Operation SANDSTONE, was held in the spring of 1948 at the neighboring atoll of Eniwetok and consisted of three shots, X-RAY, YOKE, and ZEBRA.

At this time, analysts had a broad understanding of what happened to the blast wave as it formed at the time of detonation and then propagated into the environment; this was called the "phenomenology" of the blast wave. They had some understanding of the blast pressure forces on structures; these forces were called "loads." And they had a preliminary understanding of the deflection, or distortion, of structures in response to these forces; this distortion was called structural "response." If the distortion from blast were great enough, it would result in damage.[4] Damage was not a category of nature. It depended on whether the distortion met certain agreed-on definitions, called "damage criteria." These criteria included "structural damage," "severe damage," and "collapse"—and, less severely, "moderate damage" and "light damage." To develop a good predictive model of blast damage required an intricate understanding of force loadings and structural response.

Those in the atomic weapons effects community understood that the tremendous release of energy from an atomic detonation caused nearby air to compress into a superheated high-pressure shell, or wave, of air that expanded rapidly outward. This was called the *blast wave*, or sometimes, the *shock wave*. The outside edge of the blast wave formed what was called the blast, or shock, *front*. The first major unclassified technical discussion of atomic weapons effects, the 1950 edition of *The Effects of Atomic Weapons*, said "The essential features of a shock wave are an abrupt rise in pressure, followed by a gradually decreasing pressure, lasting for about a second." Blowing in the same direction behind the front was an accompanying "intense wind which persist[ed] but with diminishing velocity, throughout the pressure phase."[5]

The blast wave delivered "a giant blow due to the sudden onset of pressure, followed by a more or less steady force on the structure, directed away from the source of blast, which lasts until the blast wave envelopes the building," according to *The Effects of Atomic Weapons*. The forces associated with the initial "giant blow" and the envelopment of the building were measured as "overpressure." As the blast front passed by the structure, pressure from the wind, called *drag pressure*, or *dynamic pressure*, continued: "The effect of these winds . . . is to produce a force on the structure for a relatively long time after the shock front has enveloped it and passed by." In sum, "Two factors operate to destroy the structure: the crushing effect of the [over]pressures developed on the structure as it becomes surrounded by the shock wave, and the aerodynamic drag of the air mass or wind motion behind the shock front. It is apparent, therefore, that a properly anchored weak structure may be crushed without being displaced bodily, or, if it is weakly anchored a strong structure may move without being crushed."[6]

Early analyses based on observations at Hiroshima differentiated between structural response to overpressure and to drag pressure. For example, the British counterpart to the U.S. Strategic Bombing Survey, the British Mission Survey, estimated the yield of the atomic bomb dropped on Hiroshima by using both blast overpressure effects and blast wind effects. And in 1946, those studying air blast during Operation CROSSROADS "capitalized on information gleaned from the blast damage surveys on Hiroshima and Nagasaki, where a permanent record of the blast winds (dynamic pressures) were recorded in the bent flagpoles, lightning rods, etc."[7]

By 1945 scientists and engineers understood that all structures responded to both overpressure and dynamic pressure, but that different structures responded differently: Some structures were more vulnerable to the intense crushing overpressure from the blast wave, which was of relatively short duration, while others were more vulnerable to the less intense but longer-lasting dynamic pressure from the blast wind. For example, multistory, reinforced concrete–frame buildings close to the explosion at Hiroshima and Nagasaki were primarily damaged by being crushed by the blast wave: "Heavy damage [was] caused by the downward force exerted on the roof. Depending upon its strength, the roof was pushed down and left sagging or failed completely." Other structures were more sensitive to drag, or dynamic, forces. These included slender structures that the shock wave passed by very quickly, such as telephone poles that "snapped off at ground level carrying the wires down with them" and smokestacks and bridges. Also sensitive to drag forces were those structures that, in effect, tore themselves apart. These buildings included shed-type steel buildings used for manufacturing with "roofs and siding . . . of corrugated sheet metal. . . . The first effect of blast was to strip off the siding and roof material." Because the siding did not tear off easily, it transferred substantial force to the steel frame and produced considerable structural damage. This led to several types of failure. "Close to the explosion the buildings were pushed over bodily," and at greater distances buildings were left leaning away from ground zero "as though struck by a hurricane of stupendous proportions."[8]

Despite the voluminous data collected on the atomic bombings of Hiroshima and Nagasaki and the broad understanding of structural sensitivities to overpressure and drag pressure, the data on blast phenomenology, force loadings, and structural response provided a weak basis for developing a quantitative model to predict damage. The estimates of blast over-pressure were imprecise. During the war, physicist Wolfgang Panofsky had invented a gauge to obtain pressure-time data. These gauges were mounted in parachute-retarded canisters. Such canisters were used at Hiroshima and Nagasaki to measure blast pressure. Although these measurements were highly accurate, there was "an uncertainty in the canister positions relative to the nuclear burst point, the altitude of the canisters at the time of shock arrival, and a definition of the air properties between the burst point and the canister positions." This led to uncertainties as great as 100 percent.[9] In addition, although the Strategic Bombing Survey described atomic damage to structures, the information was insufficiently detailed to provide a basis for analyzing structural response.

The first postwar atomic weapons tests began to address these problems. At Operation CROSSROADS in 1946, a large effort was made to improve the instruments to measure blast overpressure and wind pressure, and to study the effects of atomic weapons on ships, equipment, and material.[10] However, the radioactive contamination of ships at the second shot, BAKER, caused early termination of the operation. At Operation SANDSTONE in the spring of 1948, some experiments were held at the first two shots, X-RAY and YOKE, "to determine blast damage to a variety of structural shapes," including cubes, prisms, and cylinders, "made of concrete, steel, and wood." About a hundred shapes were exposed at each shot.[11]

The data were still insufficient: "The drag on various structural shapes due to the wind caused by the explosion is not readily available. . . . However, it is believed that the interest in aerodynamic effects may result in such information being developed."[12] This deliberately vague passage in *The Effects of Atomic Weapons* refers to experiments then being planned for the 1951 GREENHOUSE EASY shot.

It is worth noting how problems of damage prediction were *not* conceived at this point. PV analysts did not consider their lack of knowledge about the physical processes that caused and sustained the mass fires set in World War II as a set of problems to be solved. They did not try to determine how they could develop a better physical understanding of the phenomenology of mass fire, what data they would need to develop such an understanding, or how they could develop predictive models of mass fire damage.

Nor did they weigh the relative importance of atomic blast versus fire in damaging structures. Without carefully reanalyzing data from Hiroshima and Nagasaki or planning controlled experiments in nuclear weapons tests, analysts believed they already knew the answer. The consensus was that "the shock wave produced by an air-burst atomic bomb is, from the point of view of . . . disruptive effect, the most important agent in producing destruction."[13] This understanding was based on wartime understandings rather than focused postwar inquiry. Indeed, it guided postwar inquiry.

Shaping the Research Agenda

After the war, PV analysts began to develop crude methods for predicting blast damage. At first they had access only to a brief published summary of atomic weapons effects at Hiroshima and Nagasaki; by 1948 they had gained access to highly classified reports that allowed them to relate structural damage to estimated overpressure.

However, the process of gaining such information was highly bureaucratic. In the immediate postwar years, PV analysts had requested information that would allow them to better predict damage to structures. According to Richard Grassy, PV would "state its requirements" for information on "weapons effects, forward these through proper channels, and trust that the needed data would be supplied in due time." In 1946, the analysts' request for weapons effects research was forwarded by the Air Force chief of staff, General Carl Spaatz, to the Department of Defense's Research and Development Board, but "with no result." In late 1947, PV compiled more specific requirements for information on atomic weapons effects, which were sent to a technical liaison committee at Kirtland Air Force Base, New Mexico. PV received a response to this request in March 1948, but, according to Grassy, the study, though highly classified, "added little, if any, information. The suspicion began to grow that such information did not exist."[14]

The obvious source of new information in the immediate postwar period was the U.S. atomic weapons testing program. Grassy said that in the early postwar period "it was not felt necessary by the policy makers to get target personnel involved" in the development of atomic weapons effects tests or the analysis of test results. According to Grassy, the two early postwar test series, Operations CROSSROADS and SANDSTONE, "came and went without any participation by PV personnel in the formulation of the test programs." Except for some information gained at Operation CROSSROADS on the vulnerability of ships, "no information suitable for physical vulnerability analysis of targets had been obtained."[15] In fact, the tests in CROSSROADS had been narrowly conceived, driven by service interests; they were first proposed by the Air Force to test the vulnerability of naval vessels,[16] and they were not carefully executed. Although numerous structural shapes were exposed to blast at Operation SANDSTONE, PV analysts were not consulted about these experiments and did not find the results useful.

In the late spring of 1948, after the cookie cutter model had been developed and the SANDSTONE tests concluded, PV analysts began a more aggressive interorganizational effort to gain information. They arranged to brief high-level Atomic Energy Commission (AEC) officials on their approach to predicting blast damage and on their requirements for detailed information on blast effects on structures. Joining AEC officials at the briefing were five prominent scientists closely associated with the atomic weapons testing program: Norris E. Bradbury, Edward Teller, George Gamow, Isidore I. Rabi, and John von Neumann. After the presentations, Bradbury, the director of the Los Alamos national laboratory, explained that the information PV sought was simply not available; the recently concluded Operation SANDSTONE had been mainly about weapons development and "shed no light on the problem." According to Grassy, Bradbury thought "a military oriented test was needed to develop the required data." Planning then began by the AEC and PV to "develop the information required to predict blast damage to targets."[17]

It is worth noting here that most atomic testing was designed to help develop weapons, not to study their effects. Experiments focused on atomic weapons development were controlled by the Atomic Energy Commission and its weapons laboratory, Los Alamos. Projects focused on atomic weapons effects had much lower priority and were generally directed by the military. These research proposals were developed by groups within each service in conjunction with the Armed Forces Special Weapons Project (AFSWP), a multiservice organization that provided liaison between the military and the Atomic Energy Commission. The military's proposed experiments ultimately had to be approved by the Department of Defense's Research and Development Board, the highest level civilian organization overseeing military applications of science and engineering research.[18]

In February 1949, the Research and Development Board's Committee on Atomic Energy formed an ad hoc panel to investigate the optimum height of burst for atomic weapons (optimum, that is, from the perspective of causing damage to targets).[19] Some of the same people who had participated in the earlier meetings between PV and the AEC served on this panel. Von Neumann chaired and Grassy served as secretary.[20] Also on the panel were Fred Reines, from Los Alamos Laboratory; Paul C. Fine, of the Military Applications Division of AEC; Curtis Lampson, technical director of the Army's Ballistic Research Laboratory in Aberdeen, Maryland; Greg Hartmann, senior civilian at the Naval Ordnance Laboratory; and Harry L. Bowman, who taught civil engineering at Drexel Institute and had been the director of the Physical Vulnerability Division of the U.S. Strategic Bombing Survey.[21]

At the first meeting of the panel, in late February 1949, von Neumann asked about the state of knowledge regarding blast effects and what additional information was needed "to be able to predict the effects of blast on targets." In response, Grassy reviewed the methodology used by PV for arriving at probability of target damage (i.e., the "cookie cutter" model). He also "called attention to the deficiencies in knowledge" about damage prediction and argued for greater information on the overpressures required to damage targets, the radius at which the required overpressures were produced, and the optimum height of burst for achieving the required overpressures—that is, on "virtually everything."[22] He suggested several kinds of investigations, which were incorporated into the panel's final report to the Committee on Atomic Energy in the summer of 1949. They included partial and full-scale experiments on structures in future atomic tests and also nonatomic studies of the deflection of shock waves around structures.[23]

The panel's recommendations, approved by the Research and Development Board's Committee on Atomic Energy in late September, "had a profound influence on subsequent atomic tests and provided the necessary stimulus for a broad research program on atomic blast effects."[24] The recommendations "served as a basis for formulating the program of tests and contracts for developing the information we needed" and "supported our needs . . . for full-scale tests and experiments, scale experiments, and so on."[25] The approved recommendations were more than an imprimatur of PV's program; they represented the shared understandings of the atomic weapons effects community spanning several organizations.

The panel's meetings occurred in the context of more specific planning for atomic weapons tests, and by the time the panel submitted its final report, planning for the next series of atomic tests was already well underway. This test series, Operation GREENHOUSE, was to be held at Eniwetok Atoll in the spring of 1951. Modeled along the same organizational lines as SANDSTONE, GREENHOUSE was headed by a Joint Task Force commander, under whom was a small high-level group called the Joint Proof Test Committee.[26]

Like SANDSTONE, Operation GREENHOUSE would mainly test new weapons designs. In fact, the two series of tests were closely related; planning for the weapons development tests in Operation GREENHOUSE began immediately after the completion of SANDSTONE. However, the military pressed for more emphasis on weapons effects tests in GREENHOUSE. In the words of physicist Frank Shelton, a participant and historian of U.S. nuclear weapons tests, "having sat out SANDSTONE, the military services pressured for an extensive program of nuclear weapon effects experiments."[27] The military received the go-ahead to design such experiments, but they remained "ancillary experiments" that were not to interfere with tests for new weapon designs. Working with AFSWP, the Army, Navy, and Air Force proposed experiments to test, in the words of historian Barton Hacker, "the effects of atomic weapons on people, structures, and equipment."[28] (Weapons effects on people were not directly tested, but a large biomedical program included often lethal exposure for pigs and mice.)

The military's proposed experiments were extensive. Many sought to understand the physical vulnerability of structures and equipment that would be used by U.S. forces and to develop protective measures. Only the Air Force experiments were for offensive purposes, "designed to test atomic bombs on enemy targets."[29] Not surprisingly, the Physical Vulnerability Branch originated and planned the Air Force program for structure tests. The goal was "to obtain basic data on blast loading of structures and response of structural models and prototype structures in an effort to develop improved techniques for making physical vulnerability analyses of atomic bomb targets."[30]

GREENHOUSE's Joint Proof Test Committee was responsible for recommending the military's experiments to the Joint Chiefs of Staff, who would then consider the proposals and pass them on the Department of Defense's Research and Development Board for final approval. Because of the complexity of the program, a separate structures panel was set up under the Joint Proof Test Committee to vet service proposals and provide advice to the committee.[31]

In late 1949, the Joint Proof Test Committee proposed structures experiments to the Joint Chiefs of Staff. The list of proposed Air Force structures (see Table 5.1) gives a vivid sense of the investigations that PV analysts had in mind. These proposed experiments confirm the investigators' overriding interest in understanding blast: With the sole exception of the "five log cabins to test incendiary effects," all of the experiments were to examine blast effects on structures. The structural types were based on categories developed during World War II, with the one exception again of the log cabins. Clearly, log cabins could not support an enemy's war-making capability and thus were not targets of military interest; in fact, PV's understanding of incendiary effects was so rudimentary they chose structures whose main virtue was that they would burn easily.

By early December, the Joint Proof Test Committee had approved these proposed experiments and sent them to the Joint Chiefs of Staff, who forwarded them to the Research and Development Board for final approval.[32] In late December, von Neumann and Robert Oppenheimer, who were vetting the military's proposals for the Research and Development Board, held up approval of most of the Air Force list, largely for reasons of expense. However, Grassy went to Princeton immediately after Christmas to brief them, and was able to get most of the Air Force structures projects reinstated.[33]

Thus, in early 1950—11 months after it was first proposed—PV's research agenda for investigating blast effects and structural response was set to proceed as part of Operation GREENHOUSE in the spring of 1951. The process had been one of persuasion in an interorganizational context; to

TABLE 5.1.
STRUCTURES PROJECTS PROPOSED BY AIR FORCE FOR GREENHOUSE

Project Number	Type of Structure
3.3.1	Key industrial type building
3.3.2	Industrial building with light crane
3.3.3	Industrial building with long spans
3.3.4	Industrial building with short spans
3.3.5	Load-bearing wall
3.3.6	Fractionating column to test key components in oil-refining target complex
3.3.7	Five log cabins to test incendiary effects
3.3.8	Single-story industrial structures
3.3.9	Girders and bridges
3.3.10	Transformers and switchyards

Source: Frank H. Shelton, *Reflections of a Nuclear Weaponeer* (Colorado Springs, Colo.: Shelton Enterprise, 1988), table 4-2, p. 4-8.

gain approval, PV analysts had to persuade key scientists, engineers, and military officers of the merit and practicality of their plans. Had there not been widespread agreement that it made sense to carry out research within the blast frame, PV's research agenda would not have won approval. But broad consensus did not necessarily guarantee inclusion in Operation GREENHOUSE. Von Neumann proved to be the critical figure in the process: He attended the initial meeting between PV and the AEC in the spring of 1948; he chaired the ad hoc panel of the Research and Development Board's Committee on Atomic Energy; and he, along with Oppenheimer, had final say, on behalf of the Research and Development Board, on the military's specific proposals for structures experiments to be held in GREENHOUSE.

Gaining Organizational Expertise

In this same period, from 1948 to 1950, PV substantially expanded its professional staff. The organization added several engineers who worked at the Strategic Air Command in Washington but did not want to move to the Omaha area when SAC was relocated there in 1948. These included Sargant White, who had a bachelor's degree in civil engineering from Catholic University; Marlin Shure, who had a bachelor's degree in civil engineering from Penn State University; Eustaquio ("Ponce") DeLeon, who had a master's degree in civil engineering from Cornell; and Charles Walker, who had a bachelor's degree in mechanical engineering from Worcester Tech. During the war, Walker had worked in the Joint Target Group as a fire protection engineer. However, like the other engineers at PV, he worked on blast, not fire, effects. PV also hired Walter Hiner, who had a bachelor's degree in civil engineering from the University of Minnesota, and whom Grassy said "was probably the best of the whole lot as far as technical ability. He was the strongest theoretically." According to Grassy, whose own training was in geological engineering from the University of Cincinnati, the engineers at PV were competent, they "had years of experience . . . a lot of experience," although "we didn't have many advanced degrees."[34] The engineers were joined by mathematicians Herbert Solomon, who had trained at Columbia University and worked in Air Force Operations Analysis, and Hallett ("Hal") Germond, who had a Ph.D. from the University of Wisconsin and was hired from RAND. The group also included Frank Genevese, who had a doctorate in physics from Cornell and was hired from the Central Intelligence Agency.[35]

In 1950, PV hired three prominent professors of civil engineering as consultants to provide intellectual guidance in structural analysis: Robert J. Hansen, at the Massachusetts Institute of Technology, Nathan M. Newmark, at the University of Illinois, and Merit P. White, at the University of Massachusetts.[36] The three knew each other from their "Division 2 days during the war," when they studied the effects of high-explosive bombs, including structural response and bomb damage. White described the three as "very good friends."[37]

All three were trained as civil engineers, with backgrounds in the analysis of earthquakes and other dynamic processes such as shock in water. They were part of a small community who had become expert in predicting structural response to conventional high-explosive bomb blast effects during World War II. There was a connection between their backgrounds in dynamic analysis and their work on blast effects.

A key concern of civil engineering is the analysis and calculation of forces, called loads, on structures. In *static analysis,* the forces analyzed are treated as unchanging (e.g., the weight, or "dead load," of a building structure itself) or as very slowly applied (e.g., the weight, or "live load," of people moving in and out of a building or of accumulating snow). By contrast, in *dynamic analysis,* the onset and duration of force is key.[38] Newmark said it simply: "The behavior of a structure under so-called 'static' loads, or under very slowly applied loads, is quite different from the behavior of the same structure under rapidly applied loads such as those which arise from wind gusts, earthquake, impact, or blasts from explosion of a bomb."[39]

The key insight of dynamic analysis is that when an external force is applied very rapidly to a structure, it is modified by the structure. Analysis of the behavior of the structure is carried out in a step-by-step procedure in which the motion of the structure is calculated in small increments of time so that the ongoing modifications of force can be calculated.

By the late 1940s the basic concepts of dynamic analysis were fairly well understood by academic specialists, but not yet by many well-trained civil engineers. In Grassy's words, "See, this was an entirely new field . . . that the practical run-of-the-mill engineer hadn't encountered."[40] Calculating dynamic loads using the standard tools of static analysis, such as "equivalent static loading," could lead to highly misleading results.[41]

Merit White's background in dynamic analysis was not untypical of PV's consulting professors. As a graduate student, White had specialized in the effects of earthquakes on structures. In 1942, as a young assistant professor at the Illinois Institute of Technology, he joined the staff of Division 2 of the NDRC. According to White, Division 2 comprised "mainly structural engineers and physicists all working on damage and weapons characteristics. . . . The physicists showed great adaptability, more than the engineers. They could do engineering work. . . . We got along very well." In the last half-year of the war White worked for the Joint Target Group and after the war for the U.S. Strategic Bombing Survey doing blast damage assessment in Europe.[42]

Grassy, the chief civilian analyst in PV, had met Hansen, Newmark, and White in the spring of 1944 at a training course at Princeton on bomb damage prediction. It was Grassy who recommended hiring the three, although it was unusual in the early postwar years for government bureaucracies to hire consultants for ongoing analytical work.[43]

Nathan Newmark would become the key figure in refining understandings of structural response to atomic blast effects and in developing the computational methodology used by PV to predict damage. By the mid-1950s, Newmark's elegant and powerful methods for calculating structural response became the foundation of PV's organizational routines for damage prediction. Newmark was an outstanding engineer. Merit White described him as "one of the most capable people I've ever known. Fantastic. He had both an intuition and an analytical capability." Another engineer who worked closely with Newmark described him as having "prodigious energy."[44] Newmark built the University of Illinois, long a center of engineering excellence, into a major training center for military officers studying for advanced degrees in structural engineering. Many of those officers then participated in the nuclear weapons effects tests. Newmark "led it all, he was the head of the mafia" that "examined the vulnerability of structures to air blast and developed the methodology for quantification . . . [of] air blast and structural response. . . . They were *it*."[45]

In late 1949 Newmark wrote his first report for PV. It is evident from the report that he had already developed powerful methods for calculating dynamic structural response. Based on studies he had done in the preceding decade, he wrote that his computational "procedures are applicable to loadings caused by wind, earthquake, or impact, as well as blast," but that "the analyses require certain assumptions, some of which are still subject to uncertainties. However there is enough of a background of experimental and empirical verification of the general principles to warrant the feeling that the procedures will certainly lead to qualitatively correct results, and that quantitatively the errors are probably no larger than those due to the inherently variable factors associated with the detonation of any type of explosive substance."[46]

Newmark enumerated key areas of research needed to make his method applicable to the prediction of nuclear blast damage. He first described deficits in knowledge about blast forces (which were similar to those described by Grassy in early 1949): "In the analyses described herein it has been assumed that the blast pressures are known, and that the behavior of structural materials is predictable under dynamic loads of rapid application. Basic data are necessary to furnish the information required to apply the methods. In short we must learn how blast pressures act on structures of different external shapes, and how the blast forces are diffracted around and behind structures before we can apply the procedures with confidence." Newmark also said more research was required to better understand dynamic structural response: "We must learn further how the failure of component parts of a structure affect the forces transmitted to it. Such matters as the effect of failure of window glass, sheet metal siding, roofing, curtain walls, all have an effect on the resistance of the entire structure, and little is known about these problems." He argued that although some information could be gained using models, full-scale tests would be required to study "the mechanics of structural resistance."[47]

The expertise of these structural engineers added enormously to the intellectual horsepower at PV. When asked to compare these consultants' expertise to that of the engineers at PV, Grassy replied that "they had much more research and theoretical background. We hired them as authorities in their field. . . . [They] had experience in damage to structures during World War II—in studying it from the standpoint of making predictions from conventional weapons."

What could they do that the PV staff could not? Grassy said, "Ordinarily, engineering doesn't deal with [dynamic loading] at all. . . . This was a brand-new area."[48]

From Merit White's perspective, the analysts and officers at PV were "nice people in general and interested, but of course didn't have any background or knowledge. . . . They had bachelor's degrees at most. Some were perhaps not even engineers." He rated their technical abilities as "not very high . . . They didn't have the ability to make good judgments about what they were trying to do. I felt they were perhaps second rate people, to be perfectly frank, compared to me. And Newmark was perhaps two steps above them. . . . They were nice people, I liked them, they were doing their best."[49]

White generally analyzed specific targets for PV; "for example, a protective structure for a weapon or a shelter. Analysis would go from weapon and distance and what was known about the target—could be imaginary or based on intelligence from Russia—and there'd be a mathematical analysis of the behavior of the structure.[Their analyses were] very unreliable. I'd tell them how I'd do it and they'd do it with me."[50]

(Thinking back on his experience, Merit White observed that damage prediction could be understood in "sociological and humanistic" terms or in technical terms. "The way the people I worked with understood this, we were dealing with a technical problem. . . . It was interesting. It was fun to see results after predictions. I had no particular political attitude. Like most engineers I wasn't concerned with the politics and the rights and wrongs of humanity. . . . It was a matter of doing something useful.")[51]

Merit White helped in the early design of structures for Operation GREENHOUSE, and he consulted with Armour Research Foundation of the Illinois Institute of Technology, the contractors who built the structures and instrumentation. Hansen did the initial plan for instrumentation at GREEN-HOUSE and also advised on structures.[52]

These consultants were important in helping PV develop its research agenda, and their expertise greatly increased the organization's potential to predict damage from blast. However, Hansen, Newmark, and White did not have the training in physics that would have provided insight into how to predict damage from fire, and they did not try to make such predictions. Even many years later, reflecting widely held understandings, White said: "The fire contribution was much more unpredictable than high explosives [during World War II]. It was true then and I think it continues to be true with nuclear weapons. . . . What you'd really like to predict is the borderline . . . structures on the edge of [destruction]. I have no idea what the contribution of fire is at that point. . . . If you have ordinary structures, my feeling is the effect of thermal radiation would be less, much less, at that point."[53]

In short, the preexisting problem focus and search for solutions led to an increase in organizational capacity to solve certain kinds of problems but not others. Both the problem focus and the enhanced capacity in the form of added expertise guided the kinds of investigations that would be carried out, the problems that would be solved, and the explanation for why some problems were solved and others were not.

No fire experts were hired to predict the vulnerability of structures to the fire effects of atomic bombs. Aside from the experiment on five log cabins, and one interesting exception that I discuss in chapter 6, virtually no effort was made in PV to predict mass fire damage from atomic weapons, and no outside expertise was added to enable such prediction.

Inventing the VN Scale

By 1950, Physical Vulnerability had a strategy in place for acquiring knowledge over the next half decade or so. It had gained interorganizational approval of an ambitious research agenda for acquiring new knowledge about blast loading and structural response; this research was to be carried out in nuclear weapons tests and also in some non-nuclear experiments. PV had expanded its personnel and hired as consultants three professors of engineering who would help develop the research agenda and assist in understanding and calculating blast damage; most important, Newmark and his associates would devise powerful computational routines for predicting structural response to blast. The first nuclear weapons test data from PV's research agenda would be generated at Operation GREENHOUSE in the spring of 1951.

At the same time, PV analysts were also concerned that the "cookie cutter" model they had developed in 1948 to predict blast damage to individual installations was inadequate in at least two respects. First, in this model, the relationship between overpressure and blast damage was all or nothing: At a designated overpressure, either a target was destroyed or it was not. But PV analysts recognized, in Grassy's words, "that it wasn't a matter of all of them being damaged within" the area subjected to a given overpressure and none "of them being damaged without."[54] Even among apparently identical structures, and certainly among the broader structural categories delineated in the USSBS reports, there would be "differences in design, materials, workmanship, orientation, [and] shielding," which meant there would be variation in the overpressure at which similar structures would sustain a given level of damage. But how great was the variation, and how could it be incorporated into predictions of blast damage?[55]

Closely related was a problem of calculation. Part of the job of PV analysts was to estimate the number of weapons that would be required to achieve structural damage to given targets. This was a matter of efficient placement and allocation: Where should each weapon be placed to maximize damage, and how many weapons would that require? The cookie cutter model could not answer these questions because it could not predict, for example, high probabilities of damage that were less than 100 percent.

By the late spring of 1951, one of the mathematicians at PV had invented a damage prediction model that superseded the cookie cutter; it was called the Vulnerability Number, or VN, system. The elementary framework was published internally on March 2, 1951, before the GREENHOUSE tests took

place, as Physical Vulnerability Technical Memorandum-4, "A Classification of Structures Based on Vulnerability to Blast from Atomic Bombs
(U)."[56] Subsequently revised to incorporate information from nuclear
weapons tests and expanded to include many more targets, the VN system
was published in June 1954 as the Air Force's first physical vulnerability
handbook, *Target Analysis for Atomic Weapons*.[57] The VN system employed a simple format for representing the relationship of blast overpressure to blast damage and enabled those in PV to make calculations they
could not previously make. Later, Newmark's more sophisticated predictions of blast damage would modify this format (see chapter 7). The modified format has endured to the present day.

The First VN Scale

In 1950, PV analysts began with a short-term, in-house effort to reana-
lyze blast damage data from Hiroshima and Nagasaki. This project took advantage of the additional personnel hired and the increasing availability of
a wide range of relevant classified material. It was an empirical study of the
"variation of the critical overpressure[s] associated with damage" to various
types of structures at Hiroshima and Nagasaki. "The object of this study
was to determine the magnitude of this variation and to develop a practical
means for introducing this variation into damage probability and calculations."[58] The analysts based their study on the USSBS physical damage reports on Hiroshima and Nagasaki and also used "reports by the Manhattan
Engineering District and the Navy Bureau of Yards and Docks as sources of
information on structural details of buildings, type and extent of damage,
and range and orientation of buildings with respect to GZ [ground zero]."
Because direct measurement of blast overpressures on the ground in Japan
had not been made, the analysts relied on height-of-burst curves provided in
a 1949 Los Alamos report from which they "interpolated or extrapolated"
overpressure values on the ground.[59]

In the first phase of the study, buildings were classified according to the
structural categories used in the USSBS (reinforced concrete, heavy steel
frame, light steel frame, brick load-bearing walls, and wood-frame industrial
and commercial buildings).[60] According to Grassy, "For each building, distance from GZ, percent of floor space suffering structural damage, and the
overpressure corresponding to range from GZ were determined. This basic
portion of the investigation was accomplished under the direction of Walker,
with White, Hiner, [and] DeLeon."[61] This detailed empirical analysis—"by
far the most thorough evaluation of existing data," in the words of a contemporary RAND study—refined the basic overpressure–damage curves and
corresponding distance–damage curves first drawn by Grassy in 1948.[62]

The second phase of the study "involved the mathematical analysis of the structural and blast data [that] had been assembled." This part of the study was conducted by the mathematician Hal Germond. Germond's analysis "confirmed that there was no truly lethal overpressure above which all structures of a specific category suffered structural damage and below which the structures would escape damage. Instead, the probability of damage varied with the overpressure to which it was exposed."[63]

After studying the assembled data, Germond came into Grassy's office late one day—"he'd wait until just shortly before normal quitting time, then he'd come in and sit down, go over any thoughts or problems he had"—and proposed what became the Vulnerability Scale. Grassy recalled, "I thought it was a heck of a good idea. . . . We had objectives in mind of what we wanted to be able to do . . . but Germond deserves all the credit for the actual scale."[64]

Instead of determining an overpressure at or above which a target would be predicted to sustain structural, or severe, damage (i.e., the target would be "killed"), and below which it would be predicted to sustain no damage at all (i.e., "not killed"), the Vulnerability Scale captured uncertainties of structural response by assigning to structural types probabilities of sustaining a designated level of damage that varied with different overpressures. These varying probabilities were coded into each Vulnerability Number; the Vulnerability Numbers together comprised the Vulnerability Scale (soon to be called the Vulnerability Number [VN] system).[65] In other words, instead of the cookie cutter model's assumption that a structure was either destroyed or survived (see Figure 4.2a), the Vulnerability Scale allowed analysts to assign a probability of damage that varied with the overpressure. In Grassy's words, "When we went to the [VN] scale, we took into account the whole probability relationship. . . . We used the whole curve which associated overpressure, or range, with the probability of damage."[66]

The Vulnerability Scale is easiest to understand when the vulnerability of a given type of structure is represented as a curve in an overpressure–damage function in which the x-axis represents overpressure and the y-axis represents probability of damage (see Figure 5.1). Each curve had a designated VN and represented the probability of achieving a specified type or level of damage (such as structural or severe) as a function of overpressure. Because, for a given yield and height of burst, overpressure corresponded to a given distance from ground zero, the relationship between probability of damage and overpressure could also be represented on a distance plot, a distance–damage function, in which more vulnerable structures, with lower VNs, were represented by curves farther to the right (see Figure 5.2).[67]

Grassy provided a notional example of how PV analysts used the overpressure–damage relationship to calculate damage. For a given target, the

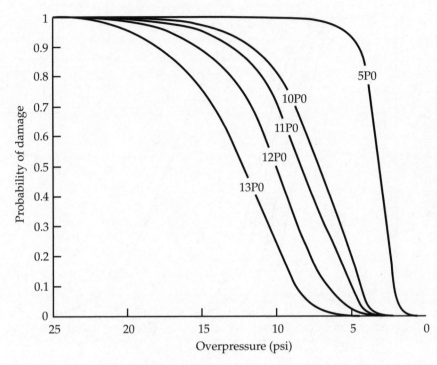

Figure 5.1. Overpressure–damage function for structures at Hiroshima. Curves show relationships for structures characterized by different Vulnerability Numbers. Source: courtesy of Theodore Postol.

greater the overpressure, the higher the probability of damage: "If you had
a particular target at 10 psi [pounds per square inch], the probability of
damage might be 10 percent. If you had the same target at [15] psi, the probability of damage might be 50 percent. If you had the same target at [20] psi,
the probability of damage might be 90 percent."[68]
    Let us take a specific example: heavy storage tanks used in chemical
manufacturing plants might well have been assigned a VN of 13. At a peak
overpressure of 12 psi, such structures would be considered to have a 50 percent probability of sustaining at least structural damage—in this case, rup-
turing[69] (see Figure 5.1). Assuming a weapon yield comparable to that at
Hiroshima, the tanks would be exposed to 12 psi if they were located approximately 3,150 feet from ground zero (see Figures 5.1 and 5.2). If the
tanks were located closer in, at approximately 3,000 feet from ground zero,
corresponding to a peak overpressure of about 13 psi, they would have a 60
percent probability of sustaining structural damage. Farther away, at approximately 3,350 feet from ground zero, corresponding to a peak over-

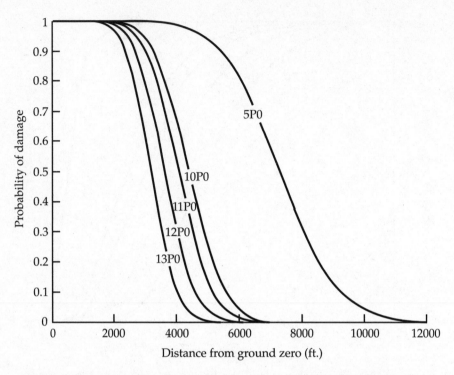

Figure 5.2. Distance–damage function for structures at Hiroshima. Curves show relationships for different Vulnerability Numbers. Source: courtesy of Theodore Postol.

pressure of 11 psi, the tanks would have a 40 percent probability of ruptur-
ing.

Suppose that some types of storage tanks were considered slightly more
vulnerable to blast damage and were assigned a lower VN of 12. Such structures would be more vulnerable, and less blast pressure would be required
to damage them. Structures assigned a VN of 12 would be considered to
have a 50 percent probability of sustaining structural damage when subjected to a peak overpressure of 10 (not 12) psi, and would be located at a
distance of approximately 3,600 feet (not 3,150 feet) from ground zero. If
the same structures were located 250 feet closer, at about 3,350 feet, and thus
subjected to an overpressure of 11 psi, the probability of damage would be
60 percent. If they were yet closer in, at about 3,150 feet, and subjected to
an overpressure of about 12 psi, the assigned probability of damage would
be 70 percent.

We can see from these examples the values in Germond's Vulnerability
Scale. Each VN had a median overpressure value for structural damage with
a standard deviation of plus or minus 20 percent—for "a bin of 40 percent

uncertainty." The median value represented the overpressure and the corresponding range from ground zero at which a given type of structure was expected to have a 50 percent probability of sustaining structural damage.[70]
This median value corresponded to the designated overpressure in the
cookie cutter model at or above which a structure was expected to fail. But
unlike in the cookie cutter model, in the Vulnerability Scale, the probability
of damage varied with overpressure.

This early VN system had two strengths. First, the system well represented the uncertainty and inexactness of knowledge regarding the relationship between overpressure and blast damage. Structures could be
classified only as whole numbers on the VN scale. For example, a structure
could be classified as a VN 13, having a 50 percent probability of sustaining
at least structural damage when exposed to 12 psi, or as a VN 12, having the
same damage probability when exposed to 10 psi, but there was no intervening category for such a damage probability at 11 psi. Because of uncertainties in structural response, it was sensible not to make more fine-grained
estimates. In physicist Harold Brode's words, those in PV had "invented a
sensible but crude categorization that acknowledged uncertainties in structures and at what levels of blast they'd fall down. . . . The system . . . was
crude but adequate. . . . It was understood that targeting is an imprecise
art."[71]

Second, the scale enabled PV analysts to *do* something they could not do
before: calculate varying probabilities of damage as the location of a given
type of structure changed relative to ground zero. Grassy said the VN system "eliminated the cookie cutter approach. And it facilitated the computation of target damage. . . . [It] had an important effect on operational
planning."[72]

Although it would later be refined considerably, the initial Vulnerability
Scale, as first published in the spring of 1951, became the basis of the blast
damage prediction system used from 1951 to the present day.

By 1951, PV analysts had shaped an agenda for research to be carried out
in laboratory studies and in forthcoming atomic weapons tests, expanded
the expertise they could use to predict blast damage, and devised a foundational predictive routine. The basis of that routine, the VN system, was
grounded in an extensive reanalysis of blast damage inflicted at Hiroshima
and Nagasaki. We turn now to the U.S. nuclear weapons testing program of
the early 1950s and the added knowledge it generated.

Chapter

6

Nuclear Weapons Tests

> In the 1953 [nuclear weapons] test [ANNIE], two essentially identical houses,
> of a type that is common in the United States, were employed at different
> locations. They were of typical wood-frame construction, with two stories,
> basement, and a brick chimney. . . . Since the tests were intended for study-
> ing the effects of blast, precautions were taken to prevent the houses from
> burning. The exteriors were consequently painted white. . . . The windows
> facing the explosion were equipped with metal venetian blinds having an
> aluminum finish. . . . The houses were roofed with light gray shingles . . . of
> asbestos cement [or] asphalt shingles. . . . There were no [gas or electrical]
> utilities of any kind.
>
> Samuel Glasstone, ed., *The Effects of Nuclear Weapons* (1957)

In the first half of the 1950s, the U.S. government developed the hydrogen
bomb and stepped up its atmospheric testing of nuclear weapons. (With
the H-bomb's invention, both fission-based atomic bombs and fusion-
based hydrogen bombs became known as nuclear weapons.) The main goal
in the testing program was to increase the destructive power and efficiency
of nuclear weapons. This involved experiments to test new designs and to
gain a better understanding of the internal workings, the physics, of the
weapons themselves.[1] The U.S. nuclear weapons laboratories, Los Alamos
national laboratory and the new Lawrence Livermore national laboratory,
directed the weapons development tests.

In many of the same weapons tests, though with lower priority, the Department of Defense investigated the damaging effects of nuclear weapons
on targets, military equipment, and plant and animal life. Some of these experiments were designed to help plan and prepare for offensive nuclear war
and some to help defend against nuclear attack. The Armed Forces Special

Weapons Project (AFSWP) led the military effort; Air Force Intelligence's Physical Vulnerability Division (PV) and other service groups participated in these tests. Civilian agencies such as the Forest Service and the Federal Civil Defense Administration also participated.

As the yields of nuclear weapons increased to hundreds of kilotons in this period, the destructive effects of thermal radiation, including the distance at which mass fire could occur, became relatively greater than the destruction caused by blast. Nonetheless, there continued to be a much greater focus on the investigation of air blast phenomena and blast damage.

Some knowledge was gained about damage caused by thermal radiation from nuclear detonations—for example, the threshold conditions under which various materials would ignite—but no knowledge was gained about the phenomenon of mass fire. Indeed, a single analytical effort by the fire protection engineer John Wolverton to retroactively predict fire spread and damage from the large area fires of World War II failed. Thus, as blast damage became even more predictable—calculations were made with greater confidence and predictive routines applied to a wider range of structures—mass fire damage remained unpredictable, and no calculational routines were developed.

The period of intense experimentation and research in the early 1950s provides a rich source of historical data with which to explore the question of why predictions of damage from mass fire were not developed. We will see that part of the answer lies in how unequal resources—organizational attention, budget, and personnel—were applied to blast and fire damage investigations.

"The Whole World Was on Fire"

From 1946 through 1956, fourteen series of atmospheric weapons tests were held at two test sites—in the Marshall Islands in the western Pacific Ocean at the Pacific Test Range and in Nevada, about 65 miles northwest of Las Vegas, at the Nevada Test Site (see Table 6.1). Each operation was composed of from two to seventeen detonations, for a total of eighty-four nuclear weapons shots, bearing names such as Dog, Easy, George, Mike, Annie, Encore, Harry, Grable, Bravo, Met, Apple-2, and Cherokee.[2] Occasionally, operations were combined, as in Operation Upshot–Knothole, held in the spring of 1953.

In the early 1950s, the development of the thermonuclear, or hydrogen, bomb led to much higher-yield weapons. It was clear to observers at the time that "with the advent of thermonuclear weapons . . . yields would increase a thousandfold."[3] In the eleven test shots before the spring of 1951, atomic weapon yields had ranged from 1 to 49 kilotons; the average yield was 19 kilotons—about the yield of the bomb that devastated Nagasaki.[4] Opera-

TABLE 6.1.
U.S. NUCLEAR WEAPONS TESTS, 1945–1956

Operation and Shot	Location	Yield (kilotons)[a]	Date[b]
TRINITY	Alamogordo, N. Mex.	21	July 16, 1945
CROSSROADS	Bikini Island		
ABLE		21	June 30, 1946
BAKER		21	July 24, 1946
SANDSTONE	Eniwetok		
X-RAY		37	April 14, 1948
YOKE		49	April 30, 1948
ZEBRA		18	May 14, 1948
RANGER	Nevada Test Site		
ABLE		1	January 27, 1951
BAKER		8	January 28, 1951
EASY		1	February 1, 1951
BAKER-2		8	February 2, 1951
FOX		22	February 6, 1951
GREENHOUSE	Eniwetok		
DOG		81	April 7, 1951
EASY		47	April 20, 1951
GEORGE		225	May 8, 1951
ITEM		45.5	May 24, 1951
BUSTER	Nevada Test Site		
ABLE		< 0.1	October 22, 1951
BAKER		3.5	October 28, 1951
CHARLIE		14	October 30, 1951
DOG		21	November 1, 1951
EASY		31	November 5, 1951
JANGLE	Nevada Test Site		
SUGAR		1.2	November 19, 1951
UNCLE		1.2	November 29, 1951
TUMBLER-SNAPPER	Nevada Test Site		
ABLE		1	April 1, 1952
BAKER		1	April 15, 1952
CHARLIE		31	April 22, 1952
DOG		19	May 1, 1952
EASY		12	May 7, 1952
FOX		11	May 25, 1952
GEORGE		15	June 1, 1952
HOW		14	June 5, 1952
IVY	Eniwetok		
MIKE		10,400	October 31, 1952
KING		500	November 15, 1952
UPSHOT-KNOTHOLE	Nevada Test Site		
ANNIE		16	March 17, 1953

(*continued*)

TABLE 6.1. (continued)

Operation and Shot	Location	Yield (kilotons)[a]	Date[b]
UPSHOT-KNOTHOLE	Nevada Test Site		
NANCY		24	March 24, 1953
RUTH		0.2	March 31, 1953
DIXIE		11	April 6, 1953
RAY		0.2	April 11, 1953
BADGER		23	April 18, 1953
SIMON		43	April 25, 1953
ENCORE		27	May 8, 1953
HARRY		32	May 19, 1953
GRABLE		15	May 25, 1953
CLIMAX		61	June 4, 1953
CASTLE			
BRAVO	Bikini Island	15,000	February 28, 1954
ROMEO	Bikini Island	11,000	March 26, 1954
KOON	Bikini Island	110	April 26, 1954
UNION	Bikini Island	6,900	April 25, 1954
YANKEE	Bikini Island	13,500	May 4, 1954
NECTAR	Eniwetok	1,690	May 13, 1954
TEAPOT	Nevada Test Site		
WASP		1	February 18, 1955
MOTH		2	February 22, 1955
TESLA		7	March 1, 1955
TURK		43	March 7, 1955
HORNET		4	March 12, 1955
BEE		8	March 22, 1955
ESS		1	March 23, 1955
APPLE-1		14	March 29, 1955
WASP PRIME		3	April 4, 1955
HA		3	April 6, 1955
POST		2	April 9, 1955
MET		22	April 15, 1955
APPLE-2		29	May 5, 1955
ZUCCHINI		28	May 15, 1955
WIGWAM	Pacific		
WIGWAM		30	May 14, 1955
PROJECT 56	Nevada Test Site		
PROJECT 56 #1		0	November 1, 1955
PROJECT 56 #2		0	November 3, 1955
PROJECT 56 #3		no yield	November 5, 1955
PROJECT 56 #4		very slight	January 18, 1956
REDWING			
LACROSSE	Eniwetok	40	May 4, 1956
CHEROKEE	Bikini Island	3,800	May 20, 1956
ZUNI	Bikini Island	3,500	May 27, 1956

TABLE 6.1. (continued)

Operation and Shot	Location	Yield (kilotons)[a]	Date[b]
REDWING			
YUMA	Eniwetok	0.19	May 27, 1956
ERIE	Eniwetok	14.9	May 30, 1956
SEMINOLE	Eniwetok	13.7	June 6, 1956
FLATHEAD	Bikini Island	365	June 11, 1956
BLACKFOOT	Eniwetok	8	June 11, 1956
KICKAPOO	Eniwetok	1.49	June 13, 1956
OSAGE	Eniwetok	1.7	June 16, 1956
INCA	Eniwetok	15.2	June 21, 1956
DAKOTA	Bikini Island	1,100	June 25, 1956
MOHAWK	Eniwetok	360	July 2, 1956
APACHE	Eniwetok	1,850	July 8, 1956
NAVAJO	Bikini Island	4,500	July 10, 1956
TEWA	Bikini Island	5,000	July 20, 1956
HURON	Eniwetok	250	July 21, 1956

Source: U.S. Department of Energy, *United States Nuclear Tests, July 1945 through September 1992*.
DOE/NV—209-REV 15 (U.S. Department of Energy, December 2000), pp. 2–9.
[a]One thousand kilotons = one megaton.
[b]Greenwich Mean Time.

tion GREENHOUSE, Shot GEORGE, held at Eniwetok Atoll in the Marshall Islands on May 9, 1951, was the first nuclear yield of more than 100 kilotons. Physicist Herbert F. York wrote: "For the first time ever a tiny thermonuclear flame burned on the surface of the earth."[5] Edward Teller, who was at Shot GEORGE, remarked that "Eniwetok won't be big enough for the next thermonuclear detonation."[6]

A little more than a year later, on November 1, 1952, the first "true" thermonuclear device was tested, at Eniwetok. This was Operation IVY, Shot MIKE, and it produced an extraordinary yield of more than 10 *megatons;* that is, the explosive equivalent of more than ten million tons of dynamite. This was almost seven hundred times greater than the yield of the atomic bomb that destroyed Hiroshima. Tests of very high-yield bombs continued. At Operation CASTLE, held in the Pacific in the spring of 1954, five of the six shots were 1.5 megatons or more; three were larger than the MIKE shot, and ranged from 11 to 15 megatons.

As yields increased, the effects of nuclear weapons changed. The pursuit of organizational knowledge in the 1950s and later must be understood in this context. It was obvious that higher overpressures, and hence, increased blast damage, were produced at greater distances from the detonation; these overpressures and corresponding damage would have to be measured, understood, and predicted. In addition, in the early 1950s, PV's consulting engineers realized something less obvious: As the yield of nuclear weapons increased, so did the duration of the blast wave (most important, the duration of the dynamic pressure of the winds associated with the blast wave, or "drag"). This greater duration would increase damage to structures sensitive to wind pressure—those susceptible to being torn apart. For example, on structures from which siding could be torn loose, the siding would then act like sails in a hurricane, ripping apart the rest of the structure. That meant that for certain kinds of structures, as weapon yields increased, less overpressure was required to achieve specified levels of damage, or, synonymously, the same overpressure produced more damage, that is, a damage "bonus." By the mid-1950s, analysts involved in predicting blast damage to structures would incorporate the effects of higher-yield weapons into their analytical routines to predict damage (see chapter 7).

Observers at nuclear weapons tests were also aware of the tremendous light and heat—that is, thermal radiation—generated by the first high-yield nuclear weapons tested. The task force commander at Operation GREEN-HOUSE, General "Pete" Quesada, described Shot GEORGE's unprecedented yield of 225 kilotons as "the greatest spectacle within recorded history . . . the brilliant light radiating from Eberiru [islet in the Eniwetok Atoll] . . . boiling and seething as it . . . catapulted upward to an altitude of 70,000 feet or more."[7]

Shot MIKE's yield of 10.4 megatons, on November 1, 1952, was even more dramatic. The fireball at Hiroshima had measured about one-tenth of a mile across; Shot MIKE "expanded in seconds to a blinding white fireball more than three miles across."[8] According to historian Barton Hacker, "MIKE surprised the experts and awed observers. One shipboard witness found the shot 'not easily described.' First 'a brilliant light' and 'the heat . . . felt immediately' 35 miles away. 'The shock wave and sound arrived . . . two and one-half minutes after the detonation.'" Other observers described the shot as "A flash many times brighter than the sun," heat that felt like the "momentary touch of a hot iron," and "You would swear that the whole world was on fire."[9] According to the report of a survey team, fish 3 miles away had been seared by the heat as though "dropped in[to] a hot pan"; 14 miles away on a small island, trees and brush were "scorched and wilted," and birds "were sick, some grounded and reluctant to fly and some with singed feathers."[10] (The damage from Shot MIKE also "made it apparent that . . . civil defense planning had to be revised . . . from a policy of duck and cover to one of evacuation, where time permits.")[11]

Scientists and engineers understood at the time that in higher-yield weapons, thermal radiation "scaled up" more rapidly than did blast pressure. The rapid increase in the deposition of thermal energy was evident not only in observation but in the assiduous measurements of thermal fluence taken at many nuclear weapons tests. Moreover, it was a matter of simple physics that, other things being equal, the range at which a given peak over-pressure occurred scaled as the cube root of the yield, but the range at which a given amount of thermal energy per unit area was deposited varied as the square root of the yield. By increasing weapon yield 50 times, for example, from 20 kilotons to 1 megaton, blast overpressure at a given range would in-crease approximately 3.7 times, but thermal energy at the same range would increase approximately 7 times. As significant as were increased overpres-sure and duration effects in higher yield weapons, the increase in thermal ra-diation was greater.[12]

The rapid scale-up of thermal radiation has strong implications for damage prediction. Because thermal radiation increases more rapidly than does blast overpressure, in higher-yield weapons mass fire ignition and result-ing damage would occur to a distance beyond that of significant blast dam-age. For nuclear weapons of approximately 100 kilotons or more, fire damage would occur far beyond the perimeter of the blast damage; blast damage would be engulfed by the effects of mass fire.

However, the devastation from mass fire that would occur to a range be-yond that of significant blast damage was not a subject of sustained investi-gation in the early 1950s. There was no concerted effort to use observations, measurements, or physical understandings of the increased intensity of thermal radiation at higher yields to try to predict fire damage—nor, fol-lowing from this, was a capability to predict damage from mass fire devel-oped. In Ted Postol's words: "All these fucking things have burned down and these guys are worried about whether a nail came out of a wall or not."[13] (In fact, the government did study the "holding power" of nails.)

With this in mind, let us turn to the investigations of nuclear blast dam-age to structures for which PV had extensively prepared.

Blast Tests on Structures

Less than two months after the publication of the Vulnerability Scale, the first major experiments of nuclear weapons effects on structures and equipment were held at the Eniwetok Atoll in Operation GREENHOUSE, Shot EASY, on April 20, 1951. The yield was 47 kilotons, about three times the yield of the bomb dropped on Hiroshima. The GREENHOUSE EASY structures program investigated nuclear blast effects on twenty-seven civil-ian and military structures—"full-sized and scaled-down structures built at various ranges from the shot tower." The program also examined the effects of air blast on aircraft.[14] The Air Force structures were those proposed ear-lier by PV; they were the only structures built to gain information for offen-sive purposes.[15] According to a contemporary official history of PV, "The efforts of the Physical Vulnerability Branch over a period of more than two years bore fruit during April 1951 with the detonation of an atomic bomb at the Eniwetok Proving Grounds. The testing . . . showed promise of yielding considerable valuable data useful in predicting damage. . . . All structures were carefully instrumented in order to determine structural response and blast loading. Total cost of this Air Force Structures Program was of the order of 2 1/2 million dollars."[16]

Nathan Newmark's 1949 study for PV had called for basic data on blast forces and for the necessity of learning "how the failure of component parts of a structure affect the forces transmitted to it." Such "mechanics of structural resistance" could only be studied in full-scale nuclear weapons tests.[17] GREENHOUSE EASY was the first opportunity to test and refine Newmark's calculations of structural response. According to Richard Grassy, "Develop[ing] the analytical means for calculating the response of the structure to the blast loading . . . was the essential knowledge that we were seeking. See, up to that point we had no way to verify the response of structures to this type of loading. Then we developed methods that would apply to other structures."[18]

Three engineers from PV, Grassy, Walter Hiner, and Sargant White, were at the GREENHOUSE EASY shot, along with all three consulting engineers, Robert Hansen, Nathan Newmark, and Merit White. Before the detonation, Hansen, Newmark, and White predicted the damage that would be sustained by various structures and "sealed them" until after. According to White, "The predictions were pretty good."[19]

The structures experiments at GREENHOUSE also provided new information on drag force damage. At GREENHOUSE, "we were groping" with duration and drag, said Grassy. "After the tests, it was certainly evident that drag and duration were important. Just looking at the results of the damage, it looked like a big windstorm."[20]

PV next participated in nuclear weapons effects testing at Operation JANGLE, Shot UNCLE, at the Nevada Test Site on November 29, 1951. JANGLE UNCLE was an underground detonation in which the military studied the response of structures to ground shock. Again, PV developed the structural proposals for the Air Force.[21] The Air Force tested eleven different structures, including reinforced-concrete retaining walls and circular concrete walls.[22] Some additional studies of blast effects were carried out at the Nevada Test Site in the late spring of 1952 at the combined Operation TUMBLER–SNAPPER—for example, on land mines, trees, and aircraft—but it does not appear that PV participated.[23]

At about the same time as JANGLE, planning for more important tests began. In the fall of 1951, the chief of AFSWP recommended to the Joint Chiefs of Staff a large-scale weapons effects testing program to be conducted in the spring of 1953. The proposed operation was code-named

KNOTHOLE. Planning for KNOTHOLE was combined with weapons development tests planned for Operation UPSHOT to be held at the Nevada Test Site.[24] The structures tests were held at Operation UPSHOT–KNOTHOLE—at Shot ENCORE, on May 8, and at Shot GRABLE, on May 25—and were "designed to yield data for target analysis purposes."[25] According to Grassy, "Again, the structural proposals originated with PV. . . . The KNOTHOLE structures largely were items cut from the original GREENHOUSE program to reduce costs."[26] The structures tests (officially, "Program 3: Structures, Material, and Equipment") were extensive. Program 3, which consisted of twenty-eight projects, "involved more projects at UPSHOT–KNOTHOLE than did any other program conducted during the series." These included tests of blast damage on buildings, bridges, railroad equipment, underground shelters, field fortifications, navy structures, mines, stands of coniferous trees, military equipment and weapons, and field medical equipment.[27]

At GRABLE, scientists observed "massive equipment and structural damage" from blast winds. The next year, physicist Frank Shelton, who worked for AFSWP, used the measurements and studies of drag pressure at UPSHOT–KNOTHOLE to produce the first detailed analysis of the distance–drag pressure relationship.[28] Drag pressure was not reflected immediately in the VN scale, but it did come into play later.

In the same period, PV and AFSWP contracted with research organizations such as RAND and the Armour Research Foundation of the Illinois Institute of Technology to carry out additional studies of blast pressure and blast damage. Some of the studies analyzed results from the nuclear weapons tests; others undertook additional empirical or analytical studies. According to Grassy, "a lot of studies were done by Armour. After GREENHOUSE, I approached them to see if they'd analyze a couple of specific industries based on GREENHOUSE. . . . One was a power plant, the Calumet Power Plant [owned by Chicago Commonwealth Edison]. The other was an oil refinery in Gary, Indiana. They did very well [evaluating and predicting damage produced by atomic air blast], and this led to further studies. They worked on at least a half dozen contracts."[29]

After these studies, PV contracted with Armour to establish "a more complete vulnerability scale which would delineate into classes, according to their susceptibility to structural damage, a multitude of structural types (buildings and equipment) which are of military interest." Armour applied the basic methods developed by Newmark "to a wide variety of structures and equipment to establish their position in the vulnerability scale." Armour also assembled tables and graphs and prepared "a manual giving the analytical methods in such form as to permit their ready application to other structures of interest as may rise."[30]

The engineers in PV used these vulnerability ratings to develop their own sample target complex that ran "the scale of vulnerability numbers usually found in industrial complexes." The hypothetical complex provided "information upon which to base an analysis of warhead deployment required for reduction of strategic targets." The complex included "an airfield, an aircraft plant, a motor vehicle plant and associated buildings, a machine equipment plant and associated buildings, a steel plant and associated buildings, a petroleum refinery, a shipyard, and a built-up area. . . . DGZs [designated ground zeros] were placed to cover important single targets, groups of targets, combination of groups, and the entire complex."[31]

In this same period, RAND analysts also examined the overpressure required to damage parked aircraft, the physical vulnerability of steel mills, the response of a drag-type structure to blast, and the destruction of structures by blast wind.[32]

The tests of blast damage to structures, particularly those at GREENHOUSE EASY, UPSHOT–KNOTHOLE ENCORE, and UPSHOT–KNOTHOLE GRABLE, in concert with numerous additional empirical and analytical studies done by PV or contracting organizations, led to the verification, refinement, and expansion of the VN system. In June 1954, PV published the first physical vulnerability handbook for nuclear weapons, *Target Analysis for Atomic Weapons*.[33] The manual was based on Newmark's calculational methods, transposed into the VN system. Damage to a large number of types of structures from blast overpressure could now be easily and routinely predicted by PV analysts. Analysts at the Strategic Air Command and elsewhere also used the system.

Solving the Puzzle of Air Blast Pressure

As analysts developed the VN system, scientists struggled to understand the behavior of nuclear blast waves. Early in the atomic weapons testing program, observers noted a troubling discrepancy between predicted and measured blast overpressure. In 1948 at Operation SANDSTONE and in 1951 at Operation GREENHOUSE, air blast pressure measurements on the ground were somewhat lower than had been predicted.[34] According to Shelton:

It did not take me very long to learn . . . that some strange things can happen to the blast waves produced by nuclear explosions. You wouldn't say the blast wave on shot EASY of GREENHOUSE was all screwed up, but it sure wasn't what all the theoreticians had predicted and used in order to predict the blast loading and response of the various military structures on the test.[35]

The measurement and prediction of blast overpressure and other nuclear weapons phenomena fell outside PV's bailiwick. According to Grassy, "It was not part of our program. We didn't study the blast wave in our program. We measured parameters of the blast wave at our structures, but we did nothing on the general characteristics of the blast wave."[36] Nonetheless, the behavior of the blast wave had great implications for PV's damage prediction: If the blast wave was not understood and could not be reliably predicted, the overpressure–damage relationship on which PV based its damage predictions would be suspect.

The first question observers asked was this: Was the blast wave acting in an unexpected way or were the observations incorrect? The government laboratory Sandia was responsible for measurement of blast pressure, structural accelerations, and displacement strains. In Shelton's words, "Immediately after the [EASY] shot, Sandia . . . personnel were under pressure to be absolutely certain that the 'funny looking' blast records were real, and not some glitch in the instruments or recording system." However, blast measurements taken by others corroborated Sandia's results.[37] The discrepancies were not due to incorrect observations.

If the discrepancies were clear, their significance, causes, and implications for operational planning were not. It was possible that the discrepancies were not significant. The shots at SANDSTONE and GREENHOUSE had been tower shots, with heights of burst lower than expected for actual operations. Air bursts, like those at Hiroshima and Nagasaki, caused blast damage over wider areas than did ground bursts. In this period, before the development of hardened silos and underground structures, air bursts "optimized" blast damage to targets of interest to military planners. If the discrepancies occurred only in very-low-altitude detonations, they might be of only minor theoretical interest. If, however, the pressure predictions for higher-altitude detonations from air-dropped weapons were inaccurate—if much of the standard "height of burst curves" relating the height of burst to the ground range of blast pressure were incorrect—then the entire analytical basis of damage prediction for war planning could be in question.

Thus, the military made a concerted effort to measure blast pressure on the four air-dropped shots of Operation BUSTER in the fall of 1951. (These were Shots BAKER, CHARLIE, DOG, and EASY, with heights of burst ranging from approximately 1,100 feet to 1,400 feet.)[38] However, "contrary to expectations, the peak air pressures on Operation BUSTER were very much lower than predicted. . . . The discrepancies between the measured and predicted pressures were as much as a factor of 3 . . . The shape of the blast wave was extremely irregular."[39]

Did the lower-than-predicted blast pressure mean that the resulting damage would be lower and that the effectiveness of the existing stockpile was less than had been understood?[40] Some officers in the Air Force thought so. According to a staff memorandum to Air Force Chief of Staff Hoyt Vandenberg in late 1951, "The Drastic Implications of BUSTER Air Blast Measurements," Operation BUSTER "revealed that measurements of earlier nuclear explosions had exaggerated blast effects by as much as one-half to two-thirds, indicating that weapons requirements had been underestimated in all previous war plans."[41]

Such understandings had a direct impact on the work of PV. In February 1952, PV was ordered to stop production of Special Data Sheets, the documents that tied together blast pressure, nuclear weapons, and predicted damage for use in war planning.[42]

The military's logic was straightforward. Because blast pressure was lower than previously calculated, and blast pressure caused blast damage, blast damage must be lower than previously predicted and weapons requirements greater than previously understood. In other words, "the inference was immediately drawn that the damage to be expected over an actual target was significantly lower than had been thought prior to BUSTER."[43]

However, according to scientists at Los Alamos and Sandia (one of whom, Fred Reines, later won a Nobel Prize for discovering the neutrino), this inference was incorrect. What was uncertain was not the level of damage that would occur, but the blast pressure required to cause that level of damage. Because the original characterization of the relationship of height of burst and damage was based on the *actual damage* inflicted on Japan, and because of uncertainties in the original measurements of blast pressure over Japan, the discrepancies in predicted overpressures did not imply that less damage would occur than previously understood. As the analysts dryly noted, "It is self-evident that no experience gained at BUSTER can change the atomic damage actually inflicted on Hiroshima and Nagasaki." These analysts drew an opposite conclusion from that of the Air Force: "In fact, the BUSTER curves have shown that the pressures required to damage buildings are somewhat lower than those previously assigned." They were confident that "the BUSTER data do not indicate the need for a drastic revision of the damage potential of our present stockpile." However, this "should not in any sense imply that the blast problem is as well understood as it should be. On the contrary, it can be argued that the lowering of the peak pressures . . . is indicative of a hitherto unsuspected phenomenon peculiar to atomic explosions," the interaction of thermal radiation and the blast wave. The authors considered this of theoretical interest, worth pursuing in future weapons tests.[44]

The military considered the discrepancies between the predicted and actual ground-level overpressures to be of more than theoretical interest. Not only was PV ordered to halt the production of Special Data Sheets in early

1952, but at about the same time, the Joint Chiefs of Staff, acting on a recommendation from AFSWP, asked the Atomic Energy Commission to add
nuclear weapons tests to measure overpressure. The test series was referred
to as the "quickie" operation. Formally named Operation TUMBLER, it was
combined with Operation SNAPPER, already scheduled for the spring of
1952 at the Nevada Test Site.[45] The first three shots, ABLE, BAKER, and
CHARLIE, produced normal blast pressure waves, but the fourth shot, DOG,
at a lower scaled height of burst, did not. As in four of the shots in the earlier Operation BUSTER, the measured pressures at DOG were "as much as a
factor of 3 less" than predicted from height of burst curves.[46]

By the late summer of 1952, test participants had analyzed the results of
TUMBLER in preparation for a blast review meeting sponsored by AFSWP.
According to Shelton, who attended the meeting as an observer, "all the blast
'gurus' and radiation people attended."[47] By this time, a general understanding had emerged among the blast gurus about why the pressure on the
ground was so much lower than had been predicted in these shots.

The predictions had been based on the reasonable assumption that the
ground was a "nearly ideal" surface; that is, a flat surface that reflects, and
does not absorb, the energy—both thermal and blast—that strikes it. In the
shots where blast pressure was less than predicted, the detonations raised
clouds of dust and caused the ground to absorb significant amounts of heat
energy. These thermal interactions with the ground surface ahead of the
blast wave caused a lower pressure "precursor" blast wave to slip ahead of
the regular blast wave, like a "toe," or cat's paw. This precursor wave de-
formed the shape of the main blast wave from that predicted on an ideal surface and reduced the main wave's pressure on the ground.[48]

Considerable research on precursor blast waves would continue over the
next several years,[49] but by the summer of 1952, analysts broadly understood the physical processes that had led to the anomalous results. This enabled them to put their earlier findings in perspective. Although blast waves
behaved differently on nonideal surfaces, analysts understood that in "many
situations" relevant to nuclear targeting, "especially in urban areas, nearly
ideal blast wave conditions would prevail."[50] Hence, the established analytical basis for predicting damage was sound and concerns about the effectiveness of the nuclear weapons stockpile were groundless; weapons
requirements had not been underestimated. PV resumed its production of
Special Data Sheets in the summer of 1952.[51]

It is not surprising that an applied scientific community would undertake
focused investigation of anomalous findings that bore on nuclear weapons
effectiveness and war planning. But this investigation stands in sharp contrast to the lack of organizational curiosity about the uncertainties involved
in predicting damage from mass fire produced by nuclear weapons.

The Failure to Predict Mass Fire: The Wolverton Report

Only a single effort was made by analysts in PV to understand and predict damage from mass fire.[52] PV's failure to predict fire spread in large urban areas reinforced the organizational understanding that blast damage
was predictable and that fire damage was not.

PV first proposed to study the spread of urban area fires in early 1951,
but, according to the official history, the study was delayed "due to inability
of securing a suitable contractor."[53] The history does not indicate what
caused this difficulty, but the problem itself is revealing. Presumably, PV
could have looked for a scientist in an organization like RAND or an expert
in fire protection to do the study, but the difficulty suggests a less strong professional research base for the analysis of incendiary damage than blast
damage. Unlike civil engineering, fire protection engineering was not a well-
recognized research discipline in universities. Unlike the civil engineers
Hansen, Newmark, and White, who had Ph.D.s and were research professors, the fire protection engineers Bond, McElroy, and Sanborn had undergraduate engineering degrees and worked in the fire insurance industry in
standard setting, applied research, and inspection.

In late 1952 a "suitable contractor" was found: the fire protection engineer John Wolverton, who had previously analyzed fire damage in Japan for
the U.S. Strategic Bombing Survey.[54] Wolverton, the chief of fire protection
for the U.S. Army Corps of Engineers in the 1950s,[55] was probably as qualified as anyone with similar war experience to undertake the study. With a
team of four, Wolverton conducted archival research in the Air Research Division of the Library of Congress and produced a text with hand-drawn
graphs summarizing his results. The study was published by PV in September 1955.[56]

Wolverton analyzed data from World War II "to evaluate the principal
parameters affecting the spread of fire in urban areas so that the vulnerability of such areas to fires resulting from bombings can be estimated." By
fire spread, Wolverton referred to fire whose reach or radiation spreads
"from building to building across streets or other open spaces from the area
of origin, and which is of magnitude beyond the control of available fire-
fighting facilities." Wolverton understood such fire spread to characterize
"conflagrations or area fires."[57]

Wolverton drew on the methods of fire protection engineering for his
analysis. These methods were based primarily on fire insurance practices
that used aerial photographs to construct fire insurance maps. Firebreaks
and the combustibility of structures and contents were coded to enable prediction of fire ignition, fire spread, and ultimate fire damage. The fire protection engineers' understanding of conventional fire spread worked well to

predict fire spread and much of the "ordinary" damage caused by incendiary bombs during World War II—for example, in Berlin—but it worked less well for the mass fires caused by incendiaries and atomic bombs.[58]

Using a variety of photographic and other sources, Wolverton analyzed fire spread in six German cities and four Japanese cities that had suffered large area fires from a single bombing attack. The best-known were Hamburg, Hiroshima, and Nagasaki; he also included the German cities of Essen, Darmstadt, Kassel, Barmen, and Elberfeld (the last two were townships of Wuppertal, analyzed in the U.S. Strategic Bombing Survey), and the Japanese cities of Kure and Sakai.[59]

Working within the standard understanding of fire protection engineers, Wolverton distinguished three kinds of large area fires: (1) peacetime conflagrations, (2) wartime conflagrations, and (3) firestorms. This categorization is important in understanding Wolverton's failure to predict fire spread. Although peacetime conflagrations often spread from a single point of ignition and wartime conflagrations resulted from bombing attacks that caused "a large number of ignitions in a relatively short period of time," the standard understanding was that each occurred when ambient winds— those caused by meteorological conditions—were high. Because of this, Wolverton thought that "in either case the mechanics of fire spread from building to building are similar."[60] Wolverton thought ambient winds might either fan a fire and take "complete control of fire direction and . . . intensity of the heat," as in the great fires of Baltimore, San Francisco, and Tokyo, or retard fire spread by blowing flames and heat away from some buildings.[61] In his view, conflagrations, whether wartime or peacetime, did not result in fire-induced inward-rushing winds. Crucial to Wolverton's analysis was the categorization of wartime and peacetime conflagrations as similar phenomena because both occurred when high ambient winds were present. But the emphasis on wind conditions was misplaced.

Wolverton also distinguished a special kind of wartime conflagration called a firestorm (spelled as two words, fire storm, at that time), which, he said, would occur only in the "absence of a strong, natural ground wind." In this circumstance, "a fire storm is likely to develop in any large, combustible, densely built-up area in which hundreds or thousands of fires are initiated almost simultaneously." According to Wolverton, the term was "coined in Germany in World War II to describe a conflagration characterized principally by a great inrush of air across the entire perimeter of the burning area. This fire wind which was caused by the great volume of hot gases rising from the mass fire area, tended to restrict outwardly the spread of fire but made spread almost certain inside the burning area. The most famous fire storm is the great Hamburg fire, in which the fire-wind velocity possibly exceeded 100 miles per hour."[62]

Although Wolverton conceived of firestorms as a special kind of conflagration, he examined them as part of the broader phenomena of wartime conflagrations rather than as a separate phenomenon. "No attempt is made in this study to analyze separately the conflagrations in which fire storms were reported to have occurred."[63] Wolverton recognized that much of the data on the fires he was examining would not be available to him, including data about naturally occurring winds.[64] Given data limitations, Wolverton attempted to isolate other factors that he thought affected the spread of fire in large area fires.

Wolverton tested five predictors of fire spread in his study. First, was there greater fire spread and greater damage in areas of higher, rather than lower, building density? (*Density* is the percentage of ground covered by buildings.) Second, could distance between buildings be correlated with fire spread? In other words, did greater space between buildings retard or stop the spread of fire, and was this relationship consistent across cities? Third, what was the effect of building density on the distance between buildings required to stop the spread of fire? Did areas of greater building density require greater distances to stop the spread of fire? Fourth, what was the effect of *building volume*—that is, density times height of buildings—on the distance between buildings required to stop the spread of fire? Fifth, because similar building volumes are possible with different heights of buildings (a spread-out two-story building can have the same volume as a tall building with a small footprint), was there a consistent relationship among various combinations of building densities and heights and the distance between buildings required to stop the spread of fire?

All but one of Wolverton's tests failed to show relationships between the variables he examined and fire spread. Only the second, the relationship of distance between buildings and fire spread, showed weak results.[65] A sense of Wolverton's findings can be gained from his conclusions about his third and fourth tests: "The density-distance evaluation in Test III failed to establish any consistent relationship between building density and the distances which stopped fire in either German or Japanese cities. . . . Unfortunately, the volume-distance evaluation in Test IV failed to establish any consistent correlation between building volume and the distances which stopped fire in either German or Japanese cities."[66]

Wolverton's results stand in stark contrast to the results of the reanalysis of blast damage at Hiroshima and Nagasaki undertaken by PV analysts. That study introduced the VN scale, the most refined prediction of damage to structures of different types to that date (see chapter 5). Wolverton's study, published four and a half years later, proved unable to predict fire spread in urban area fires. He failed to find the relationships he had expected regarding fire spread, and he did not attempt a more ambitious quantitative

formulation: "It is evident . . . that, even if it could be developed, a mathematical formula containing all of the variables necessary to account for
wind, moisture content, size and contents loading of buildings, terrain, etc.,
would be very complex. Also, there would be doubt as to the value of such
a formula for use in predicting fire spread in a potential target city for which
only limited information on physical characteristics are available."[67] It
seems likely that Wolverton's failure caused PV to cancel a project in the
same period called "Mathematical Technique for Prediction of Fire Damage in Target Complexes."[68]

Why did Wolverton fail? In his terms, there was too much variation and
too little information, particularly meteorological information, to allow
prediction of fire spread: "Wind, temperature, rain, humidity, terrain, building construction and contents loading, building areas and heights, building
density, building contiguity, and firefighting activity are the principal variables which affect fire spread. . . . Unfortunately, lack of definitive information about meteorological conditions preceding and during the wartime
conflagrations studied made it infeasible to evaluate the effects of wind, temperature, rain, and humidity on fire spread."[69]

From the perspective of later physicists, Wolverton failed not because
there were too many variables affecting fire spread and too little information
about them but because Wolverton had misspecified the problem. He had
classified wartime and peacetime conflagrations together because he
thought they occurred in high ambient winds and were spread outward by
them. By contrast, he thought firestorms occurred in low ambient winds and
spread inward. However, what Wolverton and other fire protection engineers
understood as separate phenomena—firestorms and wartime conflagrations—were actually a single phenomenon, "mass fire."

Mass fires are characterized by numerous near-simultaneous ignitions
that cause a significant heating of air, which rises and pumps large masses
of cooler air out and down. This cooler air is then drawn at high speeds into
the fire zone at ground level. Mass fires thus generate significant winds that
spread the fire violently inward, as in a huge bonfire. "The fire creates its own
fire machine."[70] Mass fires can occur in high or low ambient winds. Some
mass fires can be affected by independent wind conditions, but not critically
so. For example, preexisting wind conditions could change the shape of the
perimeter of a mass fire, but they would not account for the dynamics of fire
spread, which are generated by the fire itself. (The physics of mass fire is discussed in more detail in chapter 1.)

Peacetime conflagrations are significantly different. These are "line fires"
with different physical dynamics. *Line fires* are distinguished from mass fires
by the magnitude of initial ignitions: Mass fires are started by many initial
ignitions; line fires may be started by a single ignition or a few ignitions.

Some line fires, like the great urban fires in London, Chicago, or San Francisco, can be very large indeed, but they are not mass fires. The spread of large line fires can be strongly affected by independent ambient wind conditions. And some large line fires do generate winds, but not on the scale of a large simultaneously combusting area.

What Wolverton and other fire protection engineers understood as firestorms and conflagrations in World War II were mass fires, but they analyzed them as though they were large line fires. In so doing, they misconstrued fire spread in mass fires to be determined by independent wind and numerous other meteorological variables. This understanding, which is not confirmed by physics, has persisted to this day among many who are considered experts on fire effects.

Wolverton recognized that firestorms generated their own intense winds that spread fires inward, but he did not analyze the physical dynamics by which they did so. Instead, in treating mass fires as though they were large line fires, he looked for outward spread caused by ambient wind and other weather conditions. Not surprisingly, he found no strong relationship between the variables he examined at the periphery of the fire (e.g., density and height) and mass fire spread—which, after all, does not depend on such variables but is determined by the physical heating of the air that causes an inrush of fire-generated winds. The key to analysis is the wind generated by mass fire, which then controls the dynamics of that fire. Wolverton did not examine this.

Inattention to Mass Fire: Experiments on Thermal Radiation Effects

At the same time that Wolverton and his team were ensconced in the Air Research Division of the Library of Congress reviewing the history of fire spread during World War II, various military organizations, the U.S. Forest Service, the Federal Civil Defense Administration, and other nongovernmental contractors carried out experiments on thermal radiation as part of the U.S. nuclear weapons testing program. These experiments, or projects, measured thermal radiation and investigated the damaging effects of thermal exposure on military equipment, animals, materials, and structures. They were quite extensive (although less extensive than the experiments on blast). As with studies on blast effects, AFSWP coordinated the military's proposals on thermal radiation effects and helped win the Atomic Energy Commission's approval to proceed.[71]

As a member of AFSWP and its Panel on Thermal Radiation in the early 1950s,[72] then Air Force Lieutenant Colonel Ed Giller was familiar with the entire range of nuclear weapons effects tests, including effects of blast, thermal radiation, gamma radiation, neutron radiation, and fallout. According to Giller, there were "all kinds of thermal tests, from the ridiculous to the sublime." These tests attempted to "study the shape of the thermal pulse, how fast it went, and how hot [it got] . . . what would happen under various conditions. Suppose you were in a foxhole or a forest?" Although only a few nuclear tests were specifically designated as effects tests, "we used *every* shot as a weapons effects test. *Some* were specially marked. But we took data on damn near every test."[73] The experiments began as early as Operation CROSSROADS in 1946; the main projects were carried out in Nevada from Operation BUSTER–JANGLE in the fall of 1951 through Operation TEAPOT in the spring of 1955. (Giller's "foxhole" refers to the Army's Desert Rock exercises, designed to train troops and to test military tactics for the nuclear battlefield. The exercises were first held at BUSTER–JANGLE; they continued through Operation PLUMBOB in 1957.)[74]

These experiments were larger-scale, more visible, and involved many more people than did Wolverton's retrospective study of fire damage from strategic bombing. The focus of the experiments was also different from Wolverton's. With few exceptions, they did not concentrate on fire spread so much as on immediate ignition or other effects of thermal radiation. They took a disaggregated approach that examined the effects of the deposition of thermal energy on a variety of materials, from pine needles to aircraft surfaces.

The Effects of Atomic Weapons, published in 1950, implicitly lays out the style of research and the research program that would be pursued:

> The most important physical effects of the high temperatures due to the absorption of thermal radiation are, of course, ignition or charring of combustible materials and the burning of skin. The ignition of materials involves a large number of factors, and it is, in general, very difficult to establish definite conditions under which such burning will or will not occur. Somewhat similar considerations apply to skin burns.[75]

This passage, and the associated research program, argues against the notion (discussed in chapter 2) that it was morally or psychologically repugnant to the U.S. military to plan, or even to think about, destruction and death caused by fire. Within the experimental context of the U.S. testing program, nuclear weapons effects of all sorts, including ignition, charring, and skin burns, were objects of scientific inquiry. In this context, there is no reason to think that the effects of mass fire would not have been understood similarly.

Like Wolverton's study, the experiments on thermal radiation effects added little to the knowledge about the likelihood and dynamics of mass fires or the ability to predict damage to structures of military interest for use in war planning. But, unlike Wolverton's study—which tried, but failed, to predict the conditions under which fire spread would occur—these experiments did not attempt to predict when ignitions would coalesce into mass fire. Rather, by focusing on the effects of thermal radiation on materials, these experiments, like the work on blast, examined the effects of nuclear weapons *as though* no mass fire would ensue.

The sponsoring organizations were primarily interested in developing defensive measures to protect military equipment, soldiers, civilian structures, and the civilian population from the direct effects of exposure to thermal radiation. However, some of these studies could have been relevant to predicting fire damage from nuclear weapons for use in war planning. Measuring thermal fluence at various ranges, the flammability of materials, and the intensity of ignition points could have provided a useful basis for understanding the ranges from ground zero at which mass fires might be expected to occur, but only if measured in conjunction with an understanding of the physical dynamics—the large-scale heating, rising, and pumping of air—that characterize mass fire. As in the Wolverton report, these dynamics were not studied. And as was the case with the Wolverton report, not developing such knowledge reinforced the belief that mass fire was unpredictable. The history of thermal experiments undertaken in the nuclear weapons tests tells us not that mass fire was unpredictable, or was found to be unpredictable, but that in this period no one tried very hard to predict it.

With the exception of the log cabin experiment discussed in chapter 5, PV analysts did not try to predict damage caused by ignition or by mass fire in the nuclear weapons testing program. In contrast to their direct involvement in experiments on blast damage to structures, PV analysts were not involved in experiments to understand or predict fire damage to structures.

Giller said military planners were not interested in mass fire "in any mathematical or quantitative way."

> Of course, people muttered about it. . . . But thermal was so dependent on things you had no control over. . . . Suppose it rained? It was wet? You had high humidity? You wouldn't get a fire. That was one reason we couldn't use it in VNs. What if it was wet or dry? Night or day? . . . The military needs to know: What does it take to destroy a target, put it out of business? The military is very conservative. If they think it might be 8 psi, they'll plan on 10 psi. Blast lent itself to that. . . . The question was, was it just shock or also drag forces?[76]

Although the military did not try to predict the likelihood or range of mass fire, some military organizations and contractors did conduct research on the effects of thermal radiation and develop defensive measures against those effects, including "hardening" equipment and designing protective clothing. Summarizing the kinds of experiments that were sponsored by AFSWP, Giller said, "We put out airplanes, tanks, locomotives that were running, pigs dressed in uniforms. . . . We built what we called the Yucca National Forest," a stand of sawed-off pine trees planted in concrete.[77]

Pigs dressed in uniforms?

Giller explained that the Army was interested in the protection offered by military uniforms. Because pig skin is similar to that of humans, the Army Quartermaster cut uniform fabric and put it on the pigs. "We were pretty much Edisonian in approach—very pragmatic," Giller said. "We'd try this and try that, whatever worked. We measured everything."[78]

Giller was referring to projects in which military organizations, including Army signal, engineer, and quartermaster units, Navy bureaus of ships and aeronautics, and Air Force groups such as the Wright Air Development Center, subjected aircraft, trucks, tanks, radar, tactical communications, ammunition, field stoves, medical equipment, water tanks, and railroad equipment to blast, thermal, and other effects.[79]

Giller was also referring to biomedical studies of blast, thermal, and radiation effects on the "living animal tissues" of dogs, pigs, and rats.[80] (These investigations included the excruciating scenes of burnt pigs seen in the documentary film *The Atomic Cafe*.) These projects were carried out by organizations such as the Naval Medical Research Institute, the Medical College of Virginia, the Office of the Surgeon General, the Naval Radiological Defense Laboratory, and the Air Force School of Aviation Medicine.[81]

Not atypical was an experiment carried out at Operation BUSTER – JANGLE by the Medical College of Virginia and the Office of the Surgeon General in which they exposed dogs to thermal radiation: "The primary objective was to determine the biological relationship between burns produced on dogs in the laboratory and those caused by a nuclear detonation. The secondary objective was to determine the protection afforded against burns by military fabrics."[82]

Pigs were also dressed in uniforms in Operation UPSHOT – KNOTHOLE, shots ENCORE and GRABLE, as "Project 8.5, Thermal Radiation Protection Afforded Test Animals by Fabric Assemblies."

> The purpose . . . was to evaluate the protection against skin burns afforded by service and experimental clothing. Six hours before the shot, 15 project personnel spent about three hours transporting 56 pigs to the shot area. They anesthetized the animals and placed them in field exposure holders. Forty-two pigs were clothed with fabric ensembles and exposed at eight stations. Twelve animals were placed at three stations in cylindrical aluminum containers with fabric-covered portholes. The

remaining two were covered with protective cream. The animals were placed at locations 660 to 2,090 meters from ground zero.[83]

AFSWP also sponsored research by the U.S. Forest Service. Given its historical mission to control forest and wildland fires, some of them very large, the Forest Service was probably the government organization most interested in the incendiary effects of nuclear weapons. The Forest Service concentrated on thermally induced ignition of materials and, to a lesser extent, ignition of residential structures. It did not study the physics of mass fire.

The Forest Service first became involved in national defense during World War II when military authorities enlisted it in civil defense efforts against the threat of incendiary attack, including incendiary balloon attack on the western United States by Japan. (A thousand fire balloons reached North America during the war.) Indeed, Smokey Bear developed from wartime fire prevention efforts. Some in the Forest Service saw the postwar period as an opportunity to develop the research capacity of the Service, which, historically, had been based more on "personal and empirical" knowledge than on scientific investigation; in 1948, the Forest Service organized its first Division of Forest Fire Research.[84]

In the postwar nuclear weapons tests, the Forest Service undertook projects on thermal and blast effects on forest fuels, trees, and small structures. The Service carried out its first experiments at Operation BUSTER–JANGLE in the fall of 1951, examining the effects of thermal radiation and blast effects on forest fuels, such as pine needles, hardwood leaves, and grass, arranged at six stations at various ranges from ground zero.[85]

In a meeting held in late January, 1952, the Forest Service's director of fire research, A. A. Brown, referred to the BUSTER–JANGLE experiments and to upcoming projects at Operation TUMBLER–SNAPPER, to be held in the spring of 1952. According to Stephen J. Pyne, author of the monumental history *Fire in America,* Brown reported that "we have been given a classified military project of broad scope," the significance of which "is that it enables us to do a lot of highly technical work we need for our own programs, though nothing can be published on it until declassified. One of its primary objectives is to measure the thermal and blast effects of A bombs in a natural environment. This project has already gained a great deal of prestige for the Forest Service and is regarded as highly successful by the Military." Brown also noted that the project helped "to gain recognition by both civilian defense and military authorities of the importance of forest, brush, and grass fires in any air war."[86]

At Operation TUMBLER–SNAPPER, the Forest Service tried to determine the minimum thermal energies required to ignite common forest fuels. The studies also sought to provide information "for possible offensive and defensive military operations in woodland areas."[87] In the same tests, the Forest Service conducted experiments on the incendiary effects of atomic bombs on building sections to "determine the probability of primary fires resulting from a nuclear detonation in urban areas." Four types of sections were tested: a cubicle room, a right-angle corner between walls, a right-angle corner with a cornice, and a roof section. According to a government report, they were "constructed and mounted to resist demolition by the blast so that only the incendiary effects of the nuclear detonation would be shown."[88]

In "Project 3.3, Blast Damage to Trees—Isolated Conifers," Operation TUMBLER – SNAPPER, the Forest Service tried to predict blast damage to isolated trees. Before each shot, personnel placed four trees and instruments at each of four stations at varying distances from ground zero. The trees were approximately 50 feet high and anchored in concrete (the "Yucca National Forest" described by Giller).[89] The Naval Radiological Defense Laboratory, the Naval Material Laboratory, the Naval Electronic Laboratory, and the Department of Engineering, University of California, Los Angeles, also conducted thermal effects projects at TUMBLER – SNAPPER.[90]

The most ambitious experiments were carried out by the Forest Service at Operation UPSHOT – KNOTHOLE in the spring of 1953. This was the same operation at which PV carried out major tests to study the effects of blast on structures. At shots ENCORE and GRABLE, the Forest Service studied the ignition of interior and exterior kindling fuels.[91]

Most important, at ENCORE, the Forest Service studied the "vulnerability of urban structures" to fires ignited by thermal radiation.[92] One project was known as "the house in the middle": three small wood-frame houses with materials outside, such as newspapers, weeds, and rags.[93] Giller recalled: "We put up houses, with new paint, with old paint, with trash in the yard."[94] According to *The Effects of Nuclear Weapons*, the three "miniature [6 by 6 foot] wooden houses," each with a yard enclosed by a wooden fence, "were exposed to 12 calories per square centimeter of thermal radiation." The house on one side had weathered and decayed siding, and the yard was littered with trash. The house on the other side also had weathered and decayed siding, but the yard was free of trash. The house in the middle had well-maintained and well-painted siding, and the yard was free of trash. The first house with a yard full of trash quickly burst into flame and burned to the ground. The house on the other side with an unlittered yard sustained some ignitions and, after 15 minutes, burst into flame and burned down. The middle, well-maintained house with a clean yard "suffered scorching only." *The Effects of Nuclear Weapons* said the project demonstrated "the fact that the accumulations of ignitable trash close to a wooden structure represented a real fire hazard."[95]

At ENCORE, the Forest Service also studied two small wood houses, each shaped like a block, with different furnishings inside. The block houses were sturdily constructed, each a 10-by-12-foot single-room structure with a 4-by-6-foot window facing the detonation. These houses were closer to ground zero than the three miniature houses, and each of these was exposed to thermal radiation of 17 calories per square centimeter (cal/cm^2). One house contained rayon drapery and cotton rugs and clothing: "It burst into flame immediately after the explosion and burned completely." The other house contained vinyl drapery and woolen rugs and clothing: Although ignitions occurred, "a recovery party entering an hour after the explosion was able to extinguish [the] fires." According to *The Effects of Nuclear Weapons,* this project demonstrated "the value of fire-resistive furnishings in decreasing the number of ignition points."[96]

The immediate engulfing in flame ("flashover") of one of the block houses surprised the Forest Service, which had expected a slower fire buildup in such heavy, if combustible, materials. Researchers considered the flashover to be anomalous and did not try to explain it until almost thirty years later (see "Encore Effect" section in chapter 10).[97]

Projects demonstrating the hazards of ignitable trash and the virtues of plastic drapery in decreasing ignition points were of limited scope, but they contributed to a general understanding of direct ignition by thermal radiation. Such experiments demonstrated the importance of the density of ignition points (the number of ignitions in a given area) as a factor in thermal ignition and that exterior combustible materials, such as "paper, trash, window curtains, awnings, excelsior, dry grass, and leaves . . . might be expected to ignite when exposed to from 3 to 5 calories per square centimeter of radiant energy."[98]

As part of an effort to typify fuel loads and to estimate the probability of ignition and immediate fire spread, such projects could have been relevant to developing knowledge about ignitions leading to mass fire. But the military was not intent on predicting damage from fire. Even the Forest Service's limited studies of fire behavior were not of interest to the military; by 1956, AFSWP had stopped sponsoring such research by the Forest Service. In the words of the official history of AFSWP, "Because of the lack of military requirements for fire behavior data and fire growth studies, the AFSWP no longer continued to sponsor research in this field by the Forest Service, Department of Agriculture. Although the Services were not currently interested in fire growth studies, there was a scattered interest in fire prevention."[99]

One other civilian agency was concerned with the fire effects of nuclear weapons: the Federal Civil Defense Administration (FCDA), which developed out of civil defense activities in World War II and began operations in

January 1951 as an independent agency.[100] The FCDA carried out large-scale and highly publicized projects in the nuclear weapons testing program. Given the size of the FCDA's projects, the agency could have developed significant knowledge about the dynamics of mass fire had it, for example, built sufficient numbers of structures and examined the heating and motion of air resulting from ignition of those structures. The FCDA, however, was even less interested in the incendiary effects of nuclear weapons than was the Forest Service. Its goal was to gain knowledge to allow meaningful protection of civil society in the event of nuclear attack. The interest in protecting society against such attack lends a bizarre quality to accounts of civil defense projects. Sociologist Lee Clarke explains why: Like other symbolic plans to "tame" disaster, civil defense plans for recovery from nuclear war are "fantasy documents" that enable organizations to "lay claim to mastery and thoughtfulness" about "problems for which there are no solutions."[101] Whether those involved in civil defense planning thought their solutions unrealistic, however, is an open question.

Like the Forest Service, the FCDA first participated in nuclear weapons tests at Operation BUSTER–JANGLE in the fall of 1951. At shots BAKER, CHARLIE, and DOG, the FCDA tried to evaluate "the effects of nuclear blasts on small shelters for family use." However, "since the project was a late addition to the test program, there was not time to instrument the structures completely. Improvised methods . . . were used."[102]

By Operation UPSHOT–KNOTHOLE, at the nationally televised 16-kiloton Shot ANNIE, held on March 17, 1953, the FCDA was working on a larger scale. The FCDA called its projects "Operation DOORSTEP"; the idea was "to show the people of America what might be expected if an atomic burst took place over the doorsteps of our major cities."[103] At Shot ANNIE, according to the official history of the Atomic Energy Commission, two wood-frame houses, eight backyard shelters, and "fifty automobiles of various types, colors, and operating conditions" were subjected to the effects of a 16-kiloton nuclear weapon. The automobiles were exposed to "indicate whether the family car would provide any effective protection against the radiation, heat, and blast of a nuclear bomb." In the words of the history, the FCDA found that "the family automobile would be relatively safe outside a ten-block radius for a small weapon of this type, provided that some windows were left open to prevent the roof from caving in on the passengers. Most heavily damaged cars that did not burn and were not radioactive could be driven away soon after the shot."[104]

The FCDA experiments on two wood-frame houses at Shot ANNIE were among the most widely reported in the postwar nuclear weapons testing program; in these projects, thermal effects were deliberately *suppressed* so that the response of residential structures to blast could be better understood. The houses were painted white, the windows equipped with venetian blinds, the roofs were asbestos, and there were no gas or electrical utilities of any kind. "House No. 1" was built 3,500 feet from ground zero and subjected to peak blast overpressure of about 5 pounds per square inch (psi). It was exposed to thermal fluence of about 25 cal/cm^2, sufficient to cause it to burn in the absence of heroic measures. (See Figure 6.1.) Given the measures taken to prevent it from burning, it was expected to be almost completely destroyed by blast. "Indeed it was," according to *The Effects of Nuclear Weapons*, "but the chief purpose was to see what protection might be obtained by persons in the basement." "House No. 2" was built 7,500 feet from ground zero and subjected to peak blast overpressure of 1.7 psi. It was exposed to thermal fluence of about 10 cal/cm^2, about the same as the outer perimeter of the area that completely burned in Hiroshima. It was correctly predicted that the house would sustain damage but would remain intact. Even though exposed to the lesser fluence, the house "was badly charred but did not ignite."[105]

The FCDA carried out similar experiments at Operation TEAPOT, Shot APPLE-2, held on May 5, 1955.[106] At this 29-kiloton shot, also widely publicized, the FCDA constructed ten buildings "representing a typical American community, complete with houses, utility stations, automobiles, furniture, appliances, food, and mannequins dressed as family members."[107] In addition to evaluating "the effects of a nuclear detonation on a civil community," the FCDA planned to "test the capabilities of local Civil Defense organizations to respond to such an emergency with prompt rescue and recovery operations."[108]

Among the structures were two wood-frame houses similar to those at Shot ANNIE, but with significantly stronger construction to provide greater protection against blast effects (e.g., "superior nailing of all the framing members and sheathing, siding, subflooring, flooring, etc. using special grooved nails with greater holding power").[109] The FCDA placed these structures where the overpressures would be 4 psi and about 2.6 psi.

The FCDA also built four other pairs of houses at Shot APPLE-2 and placed them where the overpressures were the same as at the 1953 test, about 5 psi and 1.7 psi. Given the higher yield, all the structures were exposed to thermal fluences greater than that at comparable overpressures in Shot ANNIE—at least 10 cal/cm^2. It appears that all the residential structures at Shot APPLE-2 were either made fireproof, as at Shot ANNIE, or were made of fire-resistant materials such as concrete, brick, or masonry.[110]

Were the objectives in the tests on residential structures only "to determine the elements most susceptible to blast damage and consequently to devise methods for strengthening structures of various types," it would have been methodologically sound to control for effects such as fire. The tests, however, were more ambitious: "to provide information concerning the

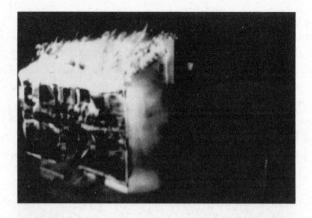

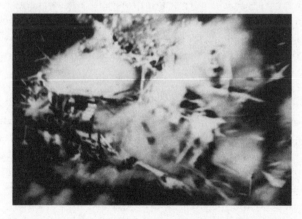

Figure 6.1. House No. 1 at UPSHOT–KNOTHOLE, ANNIE, smoking and splintering in just over 2 seconds. From civil defense experiments on blast effects of a 16-kiloton nuclear weapon on two wood-frame houses. Deliberate precautions were taken to prevent the houses from burning. Source: U.S. Defense Threat Reduction Agency photographs, Kirtland Air Force Base, New Mexico.

amount of damage to residences that might be expected as a result of a nuclear explosion and to what extent these structures could be subsequently
rendered habitable without major repairs," and "to determine how persons
remaining in their houses during a nuclear attack might be protected from
the effects of blast and radiations."[111] Given the low likelihood that many
structures in the United States would, or could, be made so fireproof (e.g.,
"no utilities of any kind"), and the virtual certainty that in a nuclear attack
many such structures would be engulfed in a mass fire, such experiments
could not provide reliable information on damage to structures or persons.
(In the best-of-all-possible-worlds style of logic employed by the FCDA,
American houses could be made fireproof by the time of the big one. According to the first edition of *Home Protection Exercises,* published by the
FCDA in the same year as Shot ANNIE, 1953, it was essential that the home
be subjected to a systematic regime of "fireproof housekeeping"—and, in
case there were some fires, that home owners be self-sufficient: "Fighting
fires in your home or neighborhood will be up to you.")[112] The FCDA's experiments at Shot APPLE-2 were the last major civil defense projects in the
U.S. nuclear weapons testing program.

     In the projects carried out by military organizations, the Forest Service,
the FCDA, and others, much was learned about the effects of thermal radiation on military equipment, animals, isolated parts of structures, a small
number of structures with ignitable material nearby, civilian artifacts, and
materials.[113] However, the most important physical effects of the high temperatures resulting from the absorption of thermal radiation were not examined—not the burning, scorching, charring, and ignition of materials,
but the collective result of multiple ignitions: the large-scale heating and rising of air that would cause cooler air at the periphery to be sucked in and
numerous ignitions to be fanned irresistibly inward into a mass fire.

     The projects of the postwar nuclear weapons tests stand in stark con-
trast to the experiments carried out in the United States during World War
II, in which simulated cities were built and subjected to incendiary attack (as
discussed in chapter 3). Given the experimental precedent in World War II
and the enormous resources available in the postwar period to develop and
test nuclear weapons, it seems possible that the nuclear weapons testing program could have mounted experiments on the dynamics and effects of mass
fire. According to physicist Harold Brode, such a program would have been
feasible. The government already had in place "elaborate instrumentation
and test beds," and an experimental fire program "would not have been more
costly or extensive than that mounted to explore blast phenomena." The
program would also have required a supporting theoretical effort to develop
"models of mass fires and the accompanying atmospherics," but at a "small
fraction" of the cost of field tests.[114]

Of course, those devising the experiments would have needed a strong interest in mass fire dynamics and damage, either to plan nuclear war or to plan defensive measures. They would also have needed to build scientific expertise in the physics and effects of mass fire—which did not exist in the early postwar period. Fire protection engineers understood important aspects of incendiary warfare, but they did not have the expertise to model the air and temperature flows characterizing mass fire. However, had the nuclear testing decision-makers been interested in mass fire, they could have turned to physicists who were capable of such modeling, some of whom were already involved in understanding the physics of other aspects of nuclear weapons.

Instead, the studies of thermal radiation were limited in scope and did not provide knowledge that could be applied to nuclear targeting. A small number of structures were built, such as the miniature wood-frame houses and furnished block houses, but these were not targets of interest to nuclear war planners. More structures were built to develop knowledge about blast effects for use in war planning; as we have seen, some of them were made fire resistant. Because, all in all, only a few structures were built on the desert, there were few objects to burn.

Yet, even in the desert, without a program to simulate urban or suburban structures, enormous heat was produced that would have ignited numerous structures had they been there. According to a press release from the 23-kiloton yield Shot Badger, Operation Upshot–Knothole, held in the spring of 1953: "The entire desert seemed to erupt. . . . The intense heat wave ignited hundreds of Joshua trees and as the strong winds carried the dust away the whole desert was aglow with these flaming torches."[115]

7

The Hydrogen Bomb
and Damage Codes

In all this targeting business, they tend to be very conservative. They want to be *damn* sure they got it sort of thing. And that's why when they go after a big steel mill, they're not content with knocking down the rolling mill buildings, and turning over a few of the machines. They want to take it apart, brick by brick, those big furnaces.

Civilian involved in nuclear targeting, 1989

In the early 1950s, the Air Force's Vulnerability Number (VN) system coded the vulnerability of structures to blast damage at varying overpressures. This codification made nuclear war planning much easier: Knowing the overpressures required to destroy target types, an officer could then determine the probability of damage to a particular target at a given overpressure and distance. (In the VN system, nuclear weapons were assumed to have a yield of 20 kilotons, approximately that of the bombs that destroyed Hiroshima and Nagasaki.)

At the same time, development of the hydrogen bomb resulted in a thousandfold increase in the yield of nuclear weapons, from the equivalent of thousands of tons of dynamite to millions of tons. By November 1952, the U.S. government had tested a hydrogen bomb of more than 10 megatons.

As the yield of nuclear weapons increased, the duration of the blast wave and, in particular, the duration of the winds associated with the blast wave, became longer. The Physical Vulnerability Division's (PV) consulting engineers quickly realized this had serious implications for damage predictions. In a higher-yield weapon, the force from wind drag pressure would be applied to structures for a longer time, increasing damage to structures that were sensitive to wind pressure—for example, long shedlike structures with frangible siding that would be pulled off in high winds. The longer duration of the blast wave meant that, for some structures, a higher-yield weapon produced more damage *at the same overpressure* than a lower-yield weapon.[1] These engineers began to adjust the VN system to take account of increased damage to some structures from higher-yield weapons.

By the mid-1950s, PV had created a more elaborate method to predict blast damage: the VNTK system. This system allowed nuclear war planners to take into account the greater wind damage from higher-yield weapons on certain kinds of structures. The VNTK system was first published in 1958 in the first edition of *Nuclear Weapons Employment Handbook,* which became the standard handbook for predicting damage to targets from nuclear weapons.[2] The same system, with further refinements, is still used today.

The increasing refinement of knowledge-laden routines to predict blast damage occurred at the same time that another damage-producing phenomenon in higher-yield weapons was becoming even more pronounced: thermal fluence from thermal radiation was observed to increase with yield more rapidly than blast pressure. Thus, other things being equal, in higher-yield weapons, the range of damage from mass fire would increase more rapidly than would blast damage. So, why were PV analysts focused on the additional effects of duration on blast damage and not on the possibility of much greater damage from mass fire?

The answer lies in organizational capabilities and selective attention. PV's consultants were intellectually equipped to explore and understand blast effects but not at all equipped to explore mass fire effects. One could hardly have expected the civil engineers Nathan Newmark, Robert Hansen, or Merit White to focus their attention outside their professional expertise, which was in understanding and predicting structural response to dynamic forces.

A close examination of the processes of organizational problem solving shows how matters might have taken a different turn, and why they did not. The most obvious impetus for a change of focus would have been strong direction from high-level Air Force leadership. Placing greater emphasis on area bombing, for example, could have prompted greater interest in predicting mass fire damage, which historically had been associated with such bombing. Even without a change in mission, high-level leadership could have directed PV analysts to develop predictions of mass fire damage. This would have required considerable financial resources; the hiring of additional consultants, such as physicists from universities or from RAND; and a research program to understand mass fire phenomena and develop damage predictions.

Although it did not happen, it could have. Had Curtis LeMay, the head of the Strategic Air Command (SAC) from the late 1940s to the late 1950s, decided that predicting damage from mass fire was a high priority, it seems likely that such predictions would have been developed. (This is not as hypothetical as it may seem. LeMay was well aware of fire damage. He had, in his own words, "roasted" targets in World War II. In the event of mobilization for nuclear war, he planned to requisition eight target analysts from PV to SAC Headquarters, one of whom would be a "fire specialist."[3] LeMay did not, however, try to develop an organizational capacity to predict fire damage before war mobilization.)

In the absence of strong direction from high-level leadership either to change organizational mission or to be especially attentive to damage caused by mass fire, what happened is what we would expect: Research priorities were defined by those already engaged in research. In exploring the new phenomena associated with higher-yield weapons, the same organizational actors worked with the same experts to solve new but not entirely novel problems; not surprisingly, both the problems and solutions were those that lay within the consultants' areas of expertise.

The organizational processes examined here take us further in our understanding of organizational frames. In the early postwar years, organizational goals shaped the problems to be solved. To build organizational capacity to solve these problems, PV brought in experts to help predict blast damage—the problems determined the experts.

With the introduction of the hydrogen bomb, the experts now determined the problems to be solved. These were new problems resulting from higher-yield weapons—but they were problems of a certain kind. The organizational capacity built to solve the initial problems now formed the structure within which new problems would be defined and solved. In the absence of these experts, these new problems would not have been apprehended and would not have been solved when they were. But their considerable achievement must be understood as resulting from, and reinforcing, the highly selective organizational attention of the blast damage frame.

The development of the VNTK system also bears on the issue of organizational interest (discussed in chapter 2). *Organizational interest* explains actions or preferences on the basis of actors' notions of how to preserve or achieve future advantage. For instance, in the early postwar period, the Air Force sought to increase its military capabilities in anticipation of fighting a future war. One way to increase capabilities was to very conservatively estimate the effectiveness of weapons: the less damage each one caused, the greater the number of weapons required to carry out the Air Force's mission of destruction. Thus, the argument goes, the Air Force had an organizational interest in understating damage from nuclear weapons in order to bolster its claims that more weapons were needed. Developing knowledge about blast damage and ignoring mass fire damage would have been consistent with that strategy.

Indeed, the development of the early VN system at first appears consistent with an organizational interest in understating damage to gain more weapons. However, I found no evidence that the attention to blast damage and neglect of fire damage was motivated by an Air Force interest in new weapons. The only hint I found was a memo to the Air Force chief of staff in late 1951 (described in chapter 6), which said that air blast measurements taken during Operation BUSTER indicated that blast damage up to then had been seriously overestimated and that this had "drastic implications" for nuclear weapons requirements: Many more would be needed than previously estimated. However, this line of argument was criticized as incorrect, was not pursued, and did not seem to drive the development of knowledge of nuclear weapons effects.

Similarly, organizational interests did not determine procedures for building knowledge-laden routines. In a meeting held in late 1954, PV briefed the Strategic Air Command on the main elements of the VNTK system. SAC officers were reluctant to accept the system, which by predicting *additional* damage from the longer duration of the blast wave in higher-yield weapons, shaved weapons requirements. But there is no evidence that SAC tried to manipulate the process by which PV's analysis would be judged or adopted. On the contrary, SAC urged only that the VNTK system not be adopted until the damage predictions be verified in already scheduled nuclear weapons tests. Until that was done, the older VN system was to remain in place. SAC's conservatism delayed the adoption of the VNTK system, but SAC accepted that the new method for predicting damage would be evaluated in established and highly visible (if classified) scientific testing procedures that it could not control. Its position was not driven by deliberate calculations of consequence.

The Effects of Higher-Yield Weapons

K Factor

At the same time that the simpler VN system was being verified and expanded in the early 1950s, Newmark and his colleagues were at work refining the same system.

In late January 1950, President Truman announced that he had "directed the Atomic Energy Commission to continue its work on all forms of atomic weapons, including the so-called hydrogen or superbomb."[4] By the time Truman made his announcement, the engineers consulting to PV would have already understood that much-higher-yield weapons were a distinct possibility. Their whole orientation toward understanding and predicting damage, in which damage was related to the duration of pressure, prepared them to understand that the longer duration of the blast wave at higher yields could cause significantly greater damage to certain kinds of structures.[5] Professor William Hall, a close colleague of Newmark's at the University of Illinois, said that the understanding of the effects of duration at higher yields would have "come very directly out of Newmark's work. . . . It simply would not have been a surprise."[6] Given their basic knowledge, the analysis was straightforward. According to Merit White, in his consulting with PV, "We generally made our calculations in a step-by-step process but there was nothing difficult about it."[7]

It was one thing for Newmark, Hansen, and White to accommodate an increased duration of blast pressure through detailed dynamic analyses of particular structures. It was another, however, to simplify calculations so that those who were not professors of engineering could explicitly take the effects of yield and duration into account. The VN system of 1951 had been a first step in embedding sophisticated engineering knowledge of structural response into organizational routines. The VNTK system was a further development of such knowledge. The T in VNTK characterized types of structures and equipment by whether they mainly responded to overpressure (P-type targets) or to drag pressure (Q-type targets). The K in VNTK characterized structures and equipment by their degree of sensitivity to yield and to the duration of blast pressure on a scale from 0 (not sensitive) to 9 (very sensitive).

Newmark did critical work on both aspects, the T and the K. Although I have not been able to locate the work Newmark did for the government in this period, certain things are clear. First, Newmark did not do the initial analysis on the effects of duration of the blast wave on blast damage for PV. Second, an unclassified published article by Newmark makes it clear that by the fall of 1953, he had quantitatively characterized structures by the main types of pressure to which they responded (the T in VNTK) and had developed the calculational basis for characterizing structural sensitivity to yield, the K factor. The article, "An Engineering Approach to Blast Resistant Design," provides insight into the classified work Newmark undertook in this period.[8]

In his classified research, Newmark focused on understanding and predicting varying levels of damage to structures, or "the deflection at which a target is damaged to the extent desired." Newmark's work was "extremely useful for damage prediction" and for "determin[ing] the peak pressure for damage."[9] In the published article, by contrast, Newmark focused on preventing structural collapse.[10] In fact, the physical model that predicted the forces required to cause damage or collapse was the same as the one needed to design new structures that could withstand those forces. Uncertainties aside, a structure that would collapse when subjected to air blast pressure of 5 pounds per square inch (psi) would not collapse if subjected to slightly less. Thus, through his article on blast-resistant design, we can trace the classified research that Newmark did for the government on the blast pressures required to cause structures to collapse.

The close connection between classified and unclassified research suggests the symbiotic relationship between the government and scholars in the production of knowledge in the post–World War II period. The government funded Newmark to develop knowledge for nuclear war planning purposes. However interesting or important Newmark may have thought it to develop methods to predict blast damage from nuclear weapons, such funding contributed to the support of a large research group in diverse structural dynamics at the University of Illinois. According to Hall, who arrived as a graduate student at Illinois in 1949, it was "exciting" to work with "a highly talented and active group." By 1951 "at the latest" Newmark "had a large number of graduate students working on the blast and shock problem. . . . An immense amount of research work was undertaken in . . . numerical analysis as well as laboratory and field experiments." The research was in "areas ranging from properties and fracture of metals (related to the ships breaking in half in the N. Atlantic and N. Pacific), to blast and shock for military structures and facilities."[11] Underlying these explorations was the development of a "very simple . . . very powerful computational tool" that became known as the Newmark Beta method, a method of wide application for calculating dynamic structural response. Developing the method "took an immense amount of labor." There were a "jillion students over about ten years" who produced dissertations on it.[12]

In the early 1950s, it was understood that two forces operated to destroy structures: "the crushing effect of the pressure developed on the structure as it becomes surrounded by the shock wave, and the aerodynamic drag of the air mass or wind motion behind the shock front."[13] It was also understood that structures were differentially sensitive to these types of pressures. Although it had been observed after the bombings of Japan and in the early atomic weapons tests that some structures were more sensitive than others to drag pressure from winds, the insight regarding differential structural response had not been systematically incorporated into categories used in simplified engineering calculations of building response. By 1953, Newmark had gone beyond illustrative examples of structural types and had mathematically typified blast pressure on overpressure-sensitive, or P-type, structures, and on drag-sensitive, or Q-type, structures.[14]

At the same time, Newmark began to develop a relatively simple computation that characterized structures by their sensitivity to the duration of blast pressure, particularly the duration of blast winds, which varied with yield; this characterization, embodying a sophisticated physical understanding, allowed an adjustment in predicted damage to be made. The more sensitive the structure to duration, the relatively greater the damage at higher yields. This characterization of the sensitivity of structures to duration and yield was called the K factor by 1954.

According to Hall, Newmark did the "spadework" for the K factor "in the 1950 to 1953 time period."[15] In his 1953 article on blast-resistant design, Newmark published the conceptual basis of the *K factor*, a constant that characterized the sensitivity of a given structure type to the duration of blast pressure.[16] More specifically, he developed a generalized mathematical equation applicable to blast pressure durations ranging from very short to very long. The equation related peak force loading required to cause the collapse of a structure at a particular yield (p_{max}) and structural yield point (q_e) to the natural period of vibration of the structure (T), the duration of the blast pressure (t_1), and brittleness, or ductility, of the structure (μ).[17] The published equation was not itself the K factor, but it provided the conceptual underpinning. Only a few steps were required to get from the equation to the K factor.

In a classified study for the government completed at about the same time that his article was published, in the fall of 1953 or shortly after, Newmark developed the K factor by slightly simplifying the published equation and putting it into a ratio: the numerator was the simplified equation for any chosen yield; the denominator was the simplified equation for a 20-kiloton yield. This standardized a chosen yield against a 20-kiloton yield. Canceling out parameters that appeared in both the numerator and denominator, Newmark arrived at the K factor, which characterized the sensitivity of structures to the duration of the blast pressure, which depended on yield. Newmark then refined his computational methods for PV under a multiyear contract to develop "a simplified system for the rapid analysis and solution of structural vulnerability problems."[18]

PVTM-13

Newmark's classified study on the K factor was probably done under the auspices of the Armed Forces Special Weapons Project (AFSWP). In any case, PV analysts were aware of it and "snatched it up as soon as it was available."[19] Newmark's study had "noted that for many structures the probability of damage was more closely related to the dynamic pressure of the blast wave rather than the overpressure. . . . Newmark's paper showed that when you got into yields of megatons—larger yields—then the duration associated with these large yields has a great effect on the response of these structures. With lower yields, duration might be on the order of a second. With higher yields, duration would be on the order of several seconds." For those structures vulnerable to drag forces (e.g., "a steel framed building with corrugated sides"), the blast wave acts "like a wind on the structures."[20]

As soon as Richard Grassy, the head civilian at PV, got Newmark's study, he assigned Frank Genevese to see "how we could apply it." The first result was a classified technical memorandum published internally by PV: PVTM-13, *Influence of the Duration of the Longer Positive Phase on Weapon Radii*, dated 27 May 1954. PVTM-13 was an exploratory memo in which for the first time an analyst within PV applied the K factor to the kinds of targets that had already been incorporated into the VN system—the same building types characterized in the U.S. Strategic Bombing Survey of World War II.

According to Grassy, in this study, "Frank [Genevese] developed [probability of damage] curves for certain basic structural categories, a few of them, a few basic structural categories. . . . They were the same specific structures we used [in 1951.]" But now, Genevese took into account the effects of duration on certain types of structures by means of Newmark's K factor.[21]

Just as Hal Germond had earlier taken PV's work on specific structural types and created a more generalized VN scale (see chapter 5), so now Germond incorporated Genevese's probability of damage curves for specific structural types into what would become the VNTK system. Drawing on Newmark's work on P-type and Q-type structures, and his own earlier VN scale, Germond, working with Genevese, now "devised two vulnerability scales, one for overpressure sensitive targets ('P' targets) and the other for dynamic pressure sensitive targets ('Q' targets)." Both scales allowed an adjustment for duration, the K factor, but this was much more important for Q-type targets than for P-type targets. This uniform system for the two kinds of structures was the VNTK system.[22]

From the perspective of a nuclear targeteer, the VNTK system allowed an adjustment in calculations of damage as weapon yield varied. For an Air Force officer, the system consisted of a set of organizational routines in which the officer, in planning the destruction of a specific target or set of targets, looked up the specific target in the *Bombing Encyclopedia* (see chapter 4). Among other information, the *B.E.* entry gave specific map coordinates and the VNTK code. The VNTK code provided the officer with three kinds of information: (1) a rating for target hardness—the VN number that translated into psi; (2) the target type, P or Q; and (3) a K factor from 0 to 9 that rated the sensitivity of the structure to yield. Taking this information, plus the yield of the weapon with which he planned to destroy the target, the officer then read a chart (there were separate charts for P- and Q-type structures) to determine the required overpressure or drag pressure to cause a designated level of damage. In effect, the chart allowed a targeteer to "adjust" a structure from one VN to another. For example, a mill building with a high K factor, let's say a VNTK coding of 13Q7, if subjected to a several-hundred-kiloton weapon could become recoded as equivalent to a less hard target, say, an 11Q0 target.

For nuclear war planners, the VNTK system simplified a complex set of calculations into a set of organizational routines that even those who were not highly technically trained could use. According to Hugh Lehman, who worked in PV in the late 1950s, the VNTK system is "a method that takes care of all that kind of stuff. Most people [involved in targeting] to this day don't [understand the details of damage calculation]. You got lawyers, MBAs. With the VN or computer or slide rule, he can take account of all that and do a better job."[23]

The "better job," however, did not include the damage caused by the deposition of thermal energy on all exposed surfaces that would warp and melt metals and cause many materials to ignite instantly, and by the mass fire that would engulf the entire area within minutes.

"You Got to Show Me"

Despite PV's quick adoption of Newmark's method and its incorporation into the developing VNTK system, there was considerable controversy in late 1954 and early 1955 when the Strategic Air Command raised objections to PV's methodology. It is fortunate for my analysis that there was such controversy, and that there are detailed records of it: It allows us to examine closely the issue of organizational interests. From an organizational interest perspective, it is not surprising that an organization with a goal of being able to win a nuclear war by inflicting maximum damage would want to ensure that it had adequate means to do so. Lower predictions of damage would strengthen claims for buying more weapons. The VNTK system did the opposite: It predicted more, not less, damage, which, by getting more "bang for the buck," decreased weapons requirements.

The first intimation in the documents that the predictability of additional damage at higher yields was an issue can be seen in the spring 1952 RAND study, *A Re-examination of Hiroshima-Nagasaki Damage Data*, briefly discussed in chapter 5. The RAND study noted that for higher-yield weapons "some correction for the effect of the increased duration of the blast is in order. . . . Theoretically, the duration of blast loads is expected to affect significantly the response" of structures. However, the authors, Marc Peters and Andrew Marshall, were most impressed with the difficulty of predicting increased damage. "At what point in the scale of yields an adjustment in the expected damage curves is justified is not known at present. . . .

Any allowance for the longer blast duration associated with these yields should suggest a bonus in the intensity of damage, particularly for heavier structures, rather than an increase in the critical damage radii."[24] In other words, rather than modifying procedures for estimating damage, the authors posited an uncalculated "bonus" effect. As with fire damage, *bonus* meant damage that would not be calculated.

Organizational interests came into high relief in a meeting held between the Strategic Air Command and the Physical Vulnerability Division of Air Force Intelligence on November 17, 1954.[25] There were two main issues at the meeting. How much damage against designated targets was enough? And, could the damaging effects of the longer duration of the blast wave in higher-yield weapons be calculated with confidence? On both issues, there was sharp disagreement. Several people from PV attended the meeting, including Grassy and Germond.

SAC took issue with the treatment of damage criteria (how much damage was enough) in the first physical vulnerability handbook for nuclear weapons, *Target Analysis for Atomic Weapons,* just published in June 1954 by PV.[26] This publication used the VN system (revised and expanded since 1951), and SAC objected to the basis of the VN system itself. The VN scale assigned to each type of structure probabilities of damage that varied with overpressure on the structure. Thus, an analyst could calculate the overpressure at which a structure had a 50 percent probability of being severely damaged, as well as the overpressure at which a structure had a 90 percent probability of being severely damaged.

SAC, however, only wanted to know when severe damage, or collapse, would occur with a 90 percent probability. According to one SAC representative, "Damage of a lesser degree, even though sufficient enough to render an installation inoperative for a period of time, is not sufficient for planning purposes."[27] This was the bureaucratic rendition of SAC's damage goals: "Extreme damage to designated targets. Level Moscow if you can."[28]

From PV's perspective, SAC was proposing to turn back the analytical clock to the late 1940s. But SAC was proposing not the older "cookie cutter" model of damage prediction, which by convention was predicated on a 50 percent probability of damage, but a cookie cutter in which severe damage, or collapse, would occur with a 90 percent probability. According to Grassy, "They were making this a cookie cutter. It didn't look realistic. They were using the 90 percent range, and that's all."[29] In the meeting, PV argued that "acceptance of a single, rigid, damage objective, such as collapse, was not compatible with the nature of its work. Rather damage objectives must be set up in the light of the overall objectives of a definitive study."[30] The official history of PV dryly noted that "a difference of philosophy with respect to damage levels to be sought in target studies was . . . apparent."[31]

Another issue raised at the meeting concerned SAC's lack of confidence in Newmark's calculations of additional damage caused by the longer duration of the blast wave in higher-yield weapons. While SAC agreed that the long duration of the positive blast pulse associated with large-yield weapons "did exist" and would result in enhancement of the damage, "it was SAC's opinion that assessment of the magnitude of the effect, even though based upon the analyses of competent structural engineers, could not be considered valid and therefore should not be used until specifically verified by full scale nuclear tests."[32] More than forty years later, Grassy recalled: "[SAC's] attitude was: 'I'm from Missouri . . . you got to show me.' . . . I guess I was a little exasperated, but nothing serious. We [in PV] thought *we* were conservative." SAC, he said, was "overconservative."[33]

Some PV analysts were also "overconservative." Grassy, Genevese, and Germond had all worked closely with the consulting engineers on developing the VNTK system and were convinced of its merits, but not everyone in PV was convinced. According to retired Air Force Colonel Fred Gross, who worked in PV in this period (and who edited the 1958 *Nuclear Weapons Employment Handbook*), in early 1955, "we had big arguments over whether or not dynamic pressure was more effective on certain kinds of structures than others. . . . It was the kind of thing engineers always argue about." Two civilians in PV were "just very conservative in their calculations" and did not accept that longer duration implied an adjustment for higher-yield weapons for certain kinds of targets.[34]

By the time of the meeting between PV and SAC in mid-November 1954, detailed planning had begun for paired experiments in Operation TEAPOT, to be held in the spring of 1955 and in Operation REDWING, to be held a year later. The experiments at TEAPOT would measure damage to several simple drag-type structures from a nuclear weapon in the kiloton range. The experiments at REDWING would measure damage to identical structures from a weapon in the megaton range.[35] If, at the same overpressure, the structures in the second test were more damaged than the structures in the first test, then the VNTK system would be considered validated. These were the crucial "proof of concept" tests of predicted damage from the effects of longer duration in higher-yield weapons.[36] SAC was willing to abide by the results.

TEAPOT MET and REDWING CHEROKEE

The first experiments were held in Nevada at Operation TEAPOT, Shot MET, on April 15, 1955 (three weeks before the widely publicized experiments at Shot APPLE-2 on the effects of a nuclear weapon on a "typical American community"; see chapter 6); the second experiments were held at

Eniwetok Atoll in the Pacific at Operation REDWING, Shot CHEROKEE, on May 20, 1956.

The yield at TEAPOT MET was 22 kilotons.[37] The positive phase duration of the blast wave was 0.9 second. At this shot, a steel-frame shed with frangible siding and roofing was subjected to a peak overpressure of 6.5 psi and a dynamic pressure of 1.1 psi.[38] Substantial damage resulted: The shed's side panels and roof were blown off. The shed was distorted by the blast, but remained standing (see Figures 7.1 and 7.2).

The yield at REDWING CHEROKEE was many times greater, 3.8 megatons.[39] In this test, an identical steel-frame shed was subjected to a peak overpressure of 6.1 psi and a dynamic pressure of 0.6 psi, but the positive phase lasted several seconds. In this case, not only were the roof and side panels blown away but the frame collapsed and the shed was flattened (see Figure 7.3). Nothing remained standing. *The Effects of Nuclear Weapons* concluded that "damage to drag-sensitive structures can be enhanced, for a given peak overpressure value, if the duration of the positive phase of the blast wave is increased."[40]

REDWING CHEROKEE provided the empirical validation of what PV's consulting engineers had long before calculated. It settled the issue of the predictability of the damage caused by the longer duration of the blast wave in higher-yield weapons. Gross recalled that the issue was "resolved in late 1955 or early 1956. . . . The evidence from . . . the tests became overwhelming. The [arguments of the] diehards just went away."[41]

Even before the experiments at REDWING CHEROKEE proved that there was a calculable damage "bonus," from the longer duration of higher-yield weapons, PV was moving ahead with the VNTK system.[42] Shortly after REDWING CHEROKEE, Newmark spent over a week briefing members of PV on the results of the two tests and explaining how to calculate vulnerability using what he called his "Rapid Methods" technique to take into account the duration effects of drag pressure. In this same period, PV began a vast revision of the 1954 *Target Analysis for Atomic Weapons*.[43] By the end of 1957, PV was preparing the final draft of its successor, the *Nuclear Weapons Employment Handbook*, published in 1958.[44]

What were the differences between the 1954 and 1958 physical vulnerability handbooks? The 1958 handbook was "much more extensive" and was printed in two versions: "a looseleaf for professionals to use [and] a bound version for senior people to put in their bookshelves." For the first time, the physical vulnerability handbook categorized targets as P-type or Q-type, and included target type and the K factor (i.e., the duration effects of drag pressure) in calculations of physical vulnerability.[45]

Revisions to the VNTK system continued. The K factor was significantly revised in 1961.[46] Later, P- and Q-type targets were distinguished into an al-

Figure 7.1. Steel-frame shed before nuclear weapons tests at TEAPOT and REDWING. Source: Samuel Glasstone and Philip J. Dolan, eds., *The Effects of Nuclear Weapons,* 3d ed. (Washington, D.C.: GPO, 1977), p. 173, fig. 5.48a; U.S. Defense Threat Reduction Agency photograph.

Figure 7.2. Steel-frame shed after TEAPOT MET, 6.5 psi peak overpressure. Source: Glasstone and Dolan, *The Effects of Nuclear Weapons,* p. 174, fig. 5.49; U.S. Defense Threat Reduction Agency photograph.

Figure 7.3. Steel-frame shed after REDWING CHEROKEE, 6.1 psi peak overpressure. Source: Glasstone and Dolan, *The Effects of Nuclear Weapons,* p. 176, fig. 5.51a; U.S. Defense Threat Reduction Agency photograph.

phabet soup that included L, M, N, O, and more target types.[47] The empirical estimates in the handbook have been updated, and there have been numerous revisions.[48] The algorithms that used to include the tables and nomograms in the handbook are now computer codes. The system is still used today to calculate the damage that would occur in a nuclear war.

Problems Solved and Not

Predicting Blast Damage

From the late 1940s to the early 1960s, knowledge about blast damage from nuclear weapons was encoded into governmental routines. Those in Air Force Intelligence responsible for predicting damage for use in nuclear war planning made it an early high priority to predict blast damage from nuclear weapons. This was a problem they chose to solve. In-house engineers in Air Force Intelligence turned to university-based researchers to develop the fundamental calculations that were then tested against data generated in the atmospheric nuclear weapons tests and simplified for routine use by government employees.

It was no coincidence that highly capable engineers were available to work on a challenging problem in the numerical calculation of structural response to dynamic forces. There was an obvious proximate cause: As part of the mobilization of science during World War II, these engineers had worked on targeting and blast damage and had met Grassy, the civilian who anchored PV after the war.

It was not inevitable that the engineers hired to solve this problem were so capable. Certainly the government could have hired less capable contractors who would have solved the problem of blast damage prediction poorly or not at all. However, the structure of civil engineering makes it unsurprising that leading academic engineers were interested in predicting blast damage from nuclear weapons. Understanding why buildings, along with bridges and other structures, stand up and fall down is at the historical core of civil engineering. (Think of the Roman aqueducts and Brunelleschi's Duomo in Florence.) By the mid-twentieth century, this old problem had become a newly interesting one that included the challenge of understanding and calculating the response of structures to *dynamic loads;* that is, forces on structures as a function of time. Dynamic loads are significant in such phenomena as earthquakes, high winds, and bomb damage. In modern civil engineering, the calculation of structural response to dynamic loads is basically the same whether the goal is to build structures to withstand forces or to predict the point at which those structures will sustain severe damage.

The basic problem of structural response to dynamic loads began to be understood by the early 1940s, and its application to blast damage was well developed by the end of World War II. However, there remained significant professional challenges and rewards in developing the numerical methods required to make the calculations, a challenge transformed by the advances in computing in the early postwar period. Air Force Intelligence and the academic engineers had a symbiotic relationship: For those in Air Force Intelligence, the engineers enabled the high-priority development of calculational routines to predict nuclear blast damage. For academic engineers, government-funded research on nuclear blast damage facilitated the solution of more fundamental calculational problems.

These professors of engineering were focused on the problem of developing methods for calculating how structures responded to abrupt forces (i.e., dynamic loads) applied to them—stated slightly more technically, on developing methods that would enable numerical calculation of structural response. This was a well-structured problem for Newmark and his colleagues. In their understanding, the calculation of structural response required a solution for a closely related *prior* problem: What were the dynamic forces on structures over time? In other words, they required a quantitative representation of the environment created by the blast wave. Newmark made a first, simple model of the blast wave and then turned to colleagues at RAND for more refined estimates and for "some assurance" that his initial model was adequate.[49]

One of these colleagues was physicist Harold Brode. Describing the blast wave was the first task Brode undertook when he started working at RAND in 1951. It was not an easy task. First, he needed computers that had the capacity to handle such calculations. He could not use the Los Alamos computers "because of the H-bomb design calculational needs," so he "waltzed around the country looking for machine time."[50] (He was able to borrow time on the IBM computer in New York, ENIAC in the Bureau of Standards, and ORDVAC at the Ballistic Research Labs.) Within two years, Brode wrote a code to calculate blast, though it took several years more to develop highly sophisticated algorithms.[51] Brode's formula, called a "forcing function," provided the basis for Newmark's calculations of structural response. In Brode's words, "The overpressure versus time from my calculations were used to define the blast load on structures being analyzed as potential targets."[52]

With Brode's description of the blast wave in hand, Newmark and his colleagues, working closely with Air Force Intelligence, developed the calculations underlying the VNTK system. Brode's results were not applied before late 1952 or early 1953.[53] By the mid-1950s, Newmark's problem was largely solved. (Brode continued to refine his predictive algorithms for the nuclear air blast environment. Within the nuclear weapons effects community, these algebraic approximations became an international standard known as "Brode-fits.")[54]

Failing to Predict Fire Damage

In the decade after World War II, organizational capability to predict mass fire damage from nuclear weapons followed a very different course. Predicting mass fire damage was not a priority for Air Force Intelligence, so no clear research agenda was set, no studies comparable to blast damage studies were conducted, and no outside experts were hired. The one effort Air Force Intelligence made to predict fire damage, a retrospective analysis of fire spread in World War II, stalled and then failed. This was not so much a personal failure on the part of the fire protection engineer hired to do the study, John Wolverton, as a reflection of the different professional structure and base of knowledge in the realm of fire damage.

As in the hiring of consultants to develop predictions of blast damage, the government had turned to an engineer who had had significant experience assessing fire damage in World War II. Although the methods used by fire protection engineers worked well to predict much incendiary bomb damage in World War II, they were not adequate to describe the course of wartime mass fires. (Nonetheless, fire protection engineers had been careful observers of these mass fires and understood their unprecedented magnitude.)

Fire protection engineering, unlike civil engineering, was not a well-established academic discipline; most fire protection engineers were trained as electrical, mechanical, or, especially, chemical engineers.[55] Wolverton was not based in a university and did not have a large ongoing research program that dovetailed with the concerns of Air Force Intelligence. Although neither Newmark nor Wolverton had the detailed disciplinary knowledge to describe the larger environment that acted on structures—in Wolverton's case, the physics that described the larger atmospheric fire environment—Newmark was able to draw on the intellectual resources available in the university and in the nuclear weapons effects community. Had Wolverton had the desire and contacts to draw on the resources of RAND, as had Newmark, the history might have been very different. In an apparent coincidence that would be too neat were this fiction, Brode, the physicist who modeled the blast environment for Newmark in the early 1950s, thirty years later led a team in modeling the fire environment. As it was, after Wolverton's attempt to predict fire damage, those in Air Force Intelligence made no further direct effort to predict damage from mass fire.

In sum, in the decade after World War II, the military had little interest in developing the capability to predict damage from mass fire in nuclear war planning. Why not? First, fire damage was not at the core of the doctrine of precision bombing. Were it to be considered at all, it would be as a "bonus" effect. Second, dating back to World War II and immediately after, government experts thought that mass fire, and damage from it, could not be predicted. Mass fire damage prediction was neither a problem the Air Force wanted to solve nor one it thought it could. Thus, it put almost no resources into trying to develop predictions of nuclear mass fire damage. In contrast, Air Force Intelligence was deeply interested in predicting nuclear blast damage and put considerable effort into developing the ability to do so. By the mid-1950s, blast damage could be predicted. Fire damage could not.

This early history could be a sufficient explanation for why U.S. nuclear war plans for the rest of the century did not incorporate predictions of damage from mass fire. We need only suppose that these early understandings about Air Force mission and the unpredictability of fire damage circulated as internal organizational accounts for decades, reinforcing and possibly embellishing earlier understandings of why it was sensible that the government did not make more effort to predict mass fire damage after the mid-1950s. Mass fire damage could not be predicted because it was seen as unpredictable; therefore it made sense not to try to predict it.

This explanation, a largely internal one in which earlier accounts informed later ones and later accounts reinforced earlier understandings, is consistent with the arguments made well into the 1990s by those concerned with predicting damage from nuclear weapons.

It is not, however, the whole explanation. At the same time that nuclear war planners wrote into their organizational routines predictions of blast damage but not fire damage, an expanded fire research community largely outside the military sphere reinforced the understanding of nuclear war planners that damage from mass fire was unpredictable. It is to this community that I now turn.

PREDICTING THE UNPREDICTABLE?
1955–2003

The Fire Research Community

Mass fires may occur in peacetime, too, started by such events as earthquakes or a rambunctious cow knocking over a lantern.

A. Broido, "Surviving Fire Effects of Nuclear Detonations,"
Bulletin of Atomic Scientists, March 1963

From the mid-1950s to the mid-1970s, government agencies far removed from Air Force Intelligence funded a small but far-flung net-
work of fire researchers to develop knowledge about the very large
fires that could occur in either peace or war. These fires included peacetime
forest and urban fires and wartime "firestorms" and "conflagrations." The
resulting knowledge was expected to be useful to help prevent or limit such
fires and to protect civilians from their effects.

The main government sponsor was the Federal Civil Defense Administration (FCDA; renamed the Office of Civil and Defense Mobilization in
1958 and the Office of Civil Defense in 1961). Other sponsors included the
Forest Service, the National Bureau of Standards (in the Department of
Commerce), and the military agency in charge of studying nuclear weapons
effects, the Armed Forces Special Weapons Project (AFSWP; renamed the
Defense Atomic Support Agency in 1959). They funded researchers at universities, applied research institutions, the Forest Service, and fire protection
laboratories. Some researchers held advanced degrees in chemical and mechanical engineering; others were trained as fire protection engineers or
foresters.

Through common sources of funding, overlapping concerns, and conferences, many of these researchers knew each other; they constituted the
"fire research community." Unlike the fire protection engineers in World War
II, whose main concern was predicting mass fire damage in war, this broader

community sought to understand the common dynamics of all very large fires—and to predict, among other things, fire damage from nuclear weapons. The community pursued many research topics, including fire chemistry, fire growth in houses, fire spread in forest fires, and the dynamics of nuclear mass fires. Fire researchers used many methods, including laboratory studies, outdoor experiments with forest fuels, analytically driven observation, and computer modeling. Because the military had little interest in mass fire damage, the fire research community did little research in the atmospheric nuclear weapons tests held after 1955. Such research was soon precluded by the U.S. moratorium on nuclear weapons testing from the fall of 1958 to the fall of 1961 and by the landmark Limited Test Ban Treaty in 1963, which banned nuclear weapons testing in the atmosphere (as well as in outer space and underwater—but not underground).

Unlike the physicists who drew a distinction between peacetime line fires subject to weather variables and wartime mass fires that created their own environments, fire researchers thought that the basic dynamics of all large fires were similar and that all were subject to unpredictable weather conditions. Fire researchers modeled what they could; for example, discrete mechanisms of fire spread within and between buildings. At the same time, they thought weather conditions such as ambient ground winds and humidity unpredictably influenced the course of all large fires. Fire researchers claimed progress in predicting fire damage, but they acknowledged their predictions were not yet reliable.

Given the military's inattention to fire damage from nuclear weapons, the fire research community gained an increasingly authoritative voice on the nature of nuclear mass fire and the feasibility of predicting mass fire damage. Its assumptions, methods, and findings played an important role in the military's own understanding of fire damage from nuclear weapons, both during this period and after.

Despite fire researchers' optimism about progress in understanding fire phenomena and predicting fire damage, their work reinforced the military's belief that fire damage was not predictable. First, fire research studies yielded neither a common definition of mass fire nor stable predictions about its occurrence. Second, fire researchers were forthright that they could not reliably predict fire damage. As a result, decades of fire research conducted largely in a civil defense context buttressed existing organizational understandings within the military and the broader nuclear weapons effects community that fire damage from nuclear weapons could not be predicted.

This raises several interesting questions. Why was the fire research community unable to develop predictions of fire damage from nuclear weapons? What shaped the course of their investigations and, in particular, their definition of the problem to include both wartime and peacetime large fires?

What effect did their inability to predict fire damage have on the later course of events?

The answers lie in the evolution of fire damage research from 1955 to the mid-1970s. Three main periods and research emphases can be discerned. From 1955 to 1961, the National Academy of Sciences' new Committee on Fire Research led a national effort to establish fire research as an academic field and to shape federally funded civilian research priorities. The research strategy favored by the academic engineers who set the committee's intellectual agenda was to probe the fundamental processes of fire ignition, growth, and spread, which they thought provided the basis for understanding very large fires in both war and peacetime.

In the early 1960s, the committee's activities were eclipsed by the Kennedy administration's boost in funding for civil defense and related fire research. These new funds revived and expanded the small community of contractors who, under the auspices of the FCDA and the Forest Service, had researched thermal radiation and ignition in the early to mid-1950s in the atmospheric nuclear weapons tests and in laboratory experiments.

By the late 1960s, fire researchers focused on a new question: How did the winds accompanying the nuclear blast wave affect fire ignition? These blast winds occur within tens of seconds of a nuclear detonation and are distinct from the inrushing fire-generated winds minutes later (see chapter 1). Throughout the 1970s the fire research community pursued the problem of the effect of blast winds on fire ignition largely through laboratory simulations. After a number of contradictory findings, a consensus emerged that the results were inconclusive. This reinforced the long-standing sense that mass fire and the resulting damage were not predictable.

Through the vagaries of funding from the mid-1950s through the 1970s, the fire research community managed to maintain a small core of researchers. They were to have a profound impact in subsequent decades when, for the first time, the military began to explore the feasibility of predicting fire damage from nuclear weapons.

National Academy Committee on Fire Research

In the early 1950s, representatives of the civilian Atomic Energy Commission and the military's AFSWP determined the experiments to be carried out in nuclear weapons tests. They also coordinated experiments with the FCDA and the U.S. Health Service. AFSWP, through its Panel on Thermal Radiation, sponsored experiments to increase understanding of and develop measures to defend against thermal radiation effects. These included ignition and other studies by the Forest Service on thermal attenuation, biomedical effects, and effects on military equipment. However, by 1956,

AFSWP had stopped sponsoring Forest Service projects in the atomic weapons tests, because "of the lack of military requirements for fire behavior data and fire growth studies."[1] FCDA activities in the nuclear weapons tests also declined. After its May 1955 experiments in TEAPOT APPLE-2 that simulated a "typical American community, complete with houses . . . automobiles . . . and mannequins dressed as family members," civil defense did not mount an equivalent operation.[2]

Shortly after the TEAPOT APPLE-2 shot, and probably anticipating that their participation in the nuclear weapons tests would decrease, the FCDA and the Forest Service began discussions with the National Academy of Sciences about increasing the Academy's involvement in the field of fire research. According to an Academy official, "The fire research that these Government agencies were talking about was not the research in the handling of the ordinary fires, but research looking towards better understanding and possible control of large spreading fires, such as forest fires and mass fires and fire storms that might result from atom bombs."[3] The imprecision in this quotation is significant, indicating the breadth of fire research that would fall under the Academy's purview. The fires caused by nuclear weapons would be neither clearly defined nor distinguished from other large fires. In particular, the simultaneous ignitions and fierce inrushing winds of mass fires would not be differentiated from more slowly developing fires that spread from a single fire source.

In December 1955, at the formal request of the FCDA, the National Academy of Sciences established a Committee on Fire Research with a broad mandate: "to stimulate and advise on research directed toward the development of new knowledge and new techniques that may aid in preventing or controlling wartime and peacetime fires."[4] Under the contract, the committee was to provide advice to the FCDA "in the field of planning and placing fire research," and to encourage cooperation among researchers in "both Government and private" research agencies. The Forest Service, the Department of Defense, and the National Bureau of Standards became early "supporting participants" of the committee.[5]

Hoyt Hottel was named chair of the new eight-member committee and also chair of its advisory group, the thirty-four-member Fire Research Conference. Hottel was a professor of fuel engineering at the Massachusetts Institute of Technology (MIT) who had headed the section of the National Defense Research Committee (NDRC) that had developed U.S. incendiary weapons in World War II. After the war, he headed AFSWP's Panel on Thermal Radiation from its origins in 1949 until 1956.[6] As the head of the Panel, Hottel had worked closely with fire researchers in the FCDA and the Forest Service in planning and coordinating experiments in the U.S. nuclear weapons tests.

Fire Research Committee members' professional activities reflected and reinforced the committee's concern with research on large peacetime fires. Besides Hottel, only one of the committee's eight members had been prominent in developing incendiary bombs or predicting damage from incendiaries in World War II: fire protection engineer Horatio Bond. During the war, Bond had recruited U.S. fire protection engineers to work in England on incendiary bomb damage assessment. He had then worked for the U.S. Strategic Bombing Survey (USSBS) as the head of fire damage assessment in Germany.[7] After the war, Bond had returned to his job as the chief engineer of the National Fire Protection Association, but he maintained a strong interest in the wartime experience of incendiary bombing. He felt he had a different perspective from others on the committee: "I didn't feel they were interested in the things that were necessary to come to grips with the problem. . . . They made some studies. But they were usually tied down to some little detail of fire prevention engineering. . . . Something like how combustible is a sheet of some quantity of paper? . . . They loved this kind of stuff."[8] Bond himself was more interested in understanding the conditions under which firestorms occurred and in predicting resulting damage and casualties.[9]

Bond was one of five committee members then professionally concerned with civilian fire prevention and control. The others were A. A. Brown, head of forest fire research at the U.S. Forest Service; Joseph Grumer, chief of flame research at the U.S. Bureau of Mines; J. B. Macauley, director of research and development at the Ethyl Corporation; and Walter T. Olson, head of fuels and combustion research at a laboratory of the National Advisory Committee for Aeronautics. The other three members were affiliated with major research universities: Hottel was professor of fuel engineering and director of the Fuel Research Laboratory at MIT; William H. Avery supervised research and development at the Applied Physics Laboratory affiliated with Johns Hopkins University; and Howard W. Emmons was professor of mechanical engineering at Harvard University.[10]

Hottel worked closely with Emmons, about ten years his junior. Emmons would succeed Hottel in 1956 as chair of the AFSWP Panel on Thermal Radiation and in 1967 as chair of the Committee on Fire Research. Emmons had begun as an assistant professor at Harvard in 1940, and by 1949 held a named professorship. He had first studied the chemistry and thermodynamics of fires; in the early years of the Committee on Fire Research, Emmons's research was on flame and combustion. He later turned his attention to fire protection and fire behavior, particularly in the home. According to the *Harvard University Gazette,* in the 1970s Emmons re-created "entire furnished rooms in a laboratory, setting them ablaze. . . . He documented how combustible materials systematically interact and how fires grow by stages until they rage out of control. . . . Emmons had individual rooms and even entire houses built to his specifications. These were then set afire to provide data for mathematical modeling."[11] In the mid-1970s, the modeling evolved into the well-known Harvard Computer Fire Code, also called the Harvard Fire Model.[12] By then, Emmons was known as "Mr. Fire Research."[13] His students liked him, and one, Jana Backovsky, remembered him as "wonderful . . . a classical American engineer. . . . He was absolutely fearless, sort of an optimistic guy who would just try things."[14] (Some in the fire research community felt less warmly toward him and called him "Mr. Know It All.")

According to Hottel, "There were almost no terms of reference for the new Committee; we were told to decide what the job was; and the crystallization of our reason for being was rather slow."[15] Hottel's chief interest was in developing a recognizable academic "field of fire research" that would stimulate "fundamental studies to understand fire growth and spread."[16] This represented a departure for the applied field of fire protection research, which focused on developing fire-fighting equipment and fire safety standards. But it meshed with a broader move in the early 1950s to make college and university engineering more scientific by placing greater emphasis on what were called the "engineering sciences," which included fluid mechanics, thermodynamics, and heat and mass transfer.[17] Hottel explained in diplomatic terms why the committee had decided to strengthen the research base rather than continue "the necessarily empirical approach to the solution of pressing fire problems[:] . . . There ultimately emerged a conviction that, although much vigorous and valuable effort went on in the fire [protection] field, that effort showed little influence of the Herculean strides that had been made in the fifteen-year period since the war in physical chemistry, in mathematics, in computational techniques, in fluid mechanics."[18]

Part of the committee's idea was "to attempt to persuade some of the 'purer' scientists that fire presents many challenging problems, and that involvement in fire research can be an honorable estate. . . . We believed, and still believe, that when enough able scientists and engineers start thinking hard about some of these interesting problems, they will not be stopped long by problems of funds."[19]

Hottel was interested in research on both wartime and peacetime fires; he did not focus the attention of the committee on the phenomenon of nuclear mass fire and resulting damage. Indeed, despite its primary support from the FCDA, the committee paid relatively little attention to developing knowledge about mass fire caused by nuclear weapons.

To shape the national agenda on fire research, the committee convened several large conferences attended by a broad range of fire researchers. The first, held in Washington, D.C., in November 1956, was primarily a show-and-tell about research in government agencies, including the U.S. Forest Service, the U.S. Weather Bureau, the National Bureau of Standards, and the military. The military research was on fire protection, not incendiary or nuclear weapons effects; the "Survey of Fundamental Knowledge of the Mechanics of Flame Extinguishment," presented at the conference, was typical.[20]

Hottel did not consider this initial attempt to develop a field of fundamental fire research to be successful. The first conference, he said, brought together "representatives of a wide range of disciplines, and includ[ed] pure scientists on the one extreme and practicing firemen on the other. It was found that although this mixing process had a few salutary effects, there was just too great a spread in background for much development of mutual interests."[21] Others were frustrated too. According to Wilbur Stump, a fire prevention engineer working for the Navy, "We can put out a fire in a house. We can put out a building fire. We can put out a block fire perhaps. But when we begin to get into these mass fires, we cannot do it. And we know doggone well we cannot. . . . If we ever have a mass attack upon any of the major cities of this country, we are lost. We have not a weapon or even a ghost of a show of controlling or suppressing such a fire."[22]

The committee's second conference, at the University of California, Los Angeles (UCLA), in May 1957, was on methods of studying mass fires. A half-dozen analysts sought information from "a group of individuals with fire-fighting and prevention experience as well as with knowledge of specific mass fires."[23] For this meeting, the committee did not distinguish between wartime and peacetime fires: "A mass fire is defined as a large area burning all at once and incapable of being extinguished by direct attack. A mass fire may be the result of many small fires ignited within a short period of time, or of a single fire whose growth or spread is uncontrolled."[24] The definition included that used by the USSBS: many simultaneous ignitions over a large area in war caused by incendiary or nuclear weapons. But it also included large forest fires, large peacetime urban fires, and large industrial fires, all of which could spread from a single source.

At the end of the meeting, Everett D. Howe, a professor of mechanical engineering at the University of California, Berkeley, concluded, "It seems that the most important first step is the clear definition of the term 'mass fire.'"[25]

Hottel was disappointed in this meeting, too, saying it "perhaps helped to paint a picture of the problems of forest fires, but it too apparently failed to cause new science-oriented individuals to enter the field of fire research."[26]

The committee's third large conference, in November 1959, was an international symposium on the use of models in fire research. By then, the committee had decided to concentrate on basic research, "quite specifically limiting the field to fire research of rather fundamental character and . . . not . . . concerned with ultimate applications to practice. We permit ourselves to wander as far afield as we wish—down various byways in our quest for the ultimate truth about fire."[27]

For this meeting, the committee assembled a group of more than 150 researchers involved in academic research, fire protection, civil defense, and nuclear weapons effects. Virtually everyone who was anyone in fire research was there. The roster included those who had participated in or analyzed incendiary warfare in World War II—Hottel, Bond, Orville J. Emory, Sr., Charles Walker, and John Wolverton—and a number who would become active members of the nuclear weapons fire research community in the 1960s and later. Among them were Perry Blackshear, professor of mechanical engineering at the University of Minnesota; Abraham Broido, from the U.S. Forest Service's Pacific Southwest Forest and Range Experiment Station in Berkeley; Robert M. Fristrom from the Applied Physics Laboratory affiliated with Johns Hopkins University; Stanley Martin from the U.S. Naval Radiological Defense Laboratory (later at United Research Services and the Stanford Research Institute); A. F. Robertson, chief of the fire protection section of the National Bureau of Standards; Arthur Takata and Frederick Salzberg from the Illinois Institute of Technology; and Fred M. Sauer from the Stanford Research Institute.[28]

Despite this impressive mobilization of research personnel, the Committee on Fire Research had sharply defined neither mass fire nor the scope of its interest, let alone developed solutions to controlling mass wartime fire. After its first five years, the committee did not try again to closely examine mass fire; no later meeting concentrated on the topic. In later references to mass fire, the committee reverted to the definition of the earlier USSBS, which emphasized "many simultaneous ignitions over a large area and the absence of strong [ambient] ground winds."[29] (The requirement for many simultaneous ignitions would be accepted by physicists working on the mass fire problem later, but the absence of strong ambient ground winds would not be considered a significant factor.)

By the early 1960s, the committee functioned mainly as a research clearinghouse, publishing abstracts on fire research and, from 1961 to 1978, eight editions of a *Directory of Fire Research*. The research projects in the latter had enormous breadth: the "listing of the projects alone yields a bewildering array of human curiosity."[30] The later editions grew to hundreds of entries, ranging from "alteration in physical properties of cottons caused by flame-retardant treatments" to "use of simplified sprinkler systems to provide selected fire protection."[31]

Increasingly, the committee turned its attention to fire protection, holding symposia on topics such as smoke generation and its medical effects, fire detectors, and arson.[32] According to Daniel Barbiero, an archivist at the National Academy of Sciences, the governing board of the National Research Council voted in 1977 to replace the Committee on Fire Research with a Committee on Fire Protection. However, "this latter body never actually came into being due to a failure to secure funding."[33]

Why had the Committee on Fire Research not focused more crisply on mass fire caused by nuclear weapons, a topic that clearly fell within its purview? Why had it not distinguished between large, spreading line fires, such as forest fires or peacetime urban conflagrations, and the mass fires of World War II, with their simultaneous ignitions and large-scale atmospheric perturbations?

First, there was no ongoing effort comparable to that undertaken to predict blast damage: no internal program to predict fire damage from nuclear weapons, no experiments on mass fire damage in nuclear weapons tests to provide a refined empirical base, no stream of funding to university-based academic researchers to develop knowledge-laden organizational routines. Instead, largely under the rubric of civil defense, government organizations interested in measures to predict, prevent, and fight many kinds of large fires funded the committee's work. The committee's incentive was not to distinguish large peacetime fires from wartime mass fires but to blur them together.

Further, most members of the committee were not interested in wartime mass fire per se but in an engineering agenda to "further the growth and development of fundamental research related to understanding fire [including] problems of ignition, fire growth, fire spread, convective movement of air into fire, radiation, and many other related phenomena" and in using "our growing knowledge of fluid mechanics, chemical kinetics, and transport phenomena."[34] The mass fire that would result from the use of nuclear weapons occurred at a much larger scale than the phenomena in which committee members were most interested. While wartime mass fire was related to their interests, it was not their primary concern.

Bond, who served on the committee from 1956 to 1965, recalled:

I had to fight with those guys. They all kept saying nobody knew anything about fire. I'd only been working on this for forty years. . . . The M.I.T. man [Hottel] didn't give me any trouble but the others all said . . . we're the first to do anything about this. . . . I knew better. I'd been through all the [National Fire Protection Association] publications on the subject back to the turn of the century. . . . They wanted an excuse to get appropriations for their schools so they could study about fires.[35]

Why had the committee not consulted outside its own engineering disciplines? Why, for example, had it not turned to physicists to model the large-scale dynamics of the nuclear fire environment, as Newmark had done earlier for the nuclear blast environment? Physicist Harold Brode answered:

> Why the fire researchers did not look beyond their comfortable patch is something of a mystery and, in my view, regrettable. It may be that fire research was a well established field. . . . They were mightily impressed (as was I) with how truly complex the whole subject of fire was, all the details of combustion dynamics, pyrolysis, the physical chemistry of ignition, propagation. . . . There was lots of room for research without entering the slightly distasteful subject of nuclear weapons effects. Especially when the popular notion was that fire was too unpredictable to be of use to the military.[36]

By convening meetings, influencing government funding, and publishing a widely available directory, the National Academy's Committee on Fire Research helped establish a broad field of fire research. But it did not distinguish between large peacetime fires and mass wartime fires: It characterized both in terms of chemistry and discrete mechanisms of ignition and spread. A similar approach would be used by fire researchers in the 1960s, when research on nuclear mass fire would, for the first time, be relatively well funded—not by the military out of concern for nuclear war planning but by the Office of Civil Defense.

"A *Big* Budget for Civil Defense"

In the early 1960s, President John F. Kennedy initiated dramatic changes in military spending, force posture, research priorities, and nuclear weapons testing.[37] In his first year in office, Kennedy increased Eisenhower's recommended military budget by more than 10 percent, from $45 to $51 billion for fiscal year 1962.[38] Kennedy also moved civil defense into the Department of Defense, renamed it the Office of Civil Defense (OCD), and increased its budget by $200 million. More than three-quarters of this increase was for a greatly expanded fallout shelter program that Kennedy requested during the Berlin Crisis in July 1961.[39]

Kennedy also requested significantly increased funding for civil defense research; at $13.5 million, it was more than triple the annual appropriations at the end of Eisenhower's term.[40] As part of this increase, OCD established a small but significant program of research into the fire effects of nuclear weapons. Throughout the 1960s, about $1 million a year was allocated for research on fire. This was peanuts compared to the total military budget, but it marked the beginning of "the major involvement of OCD in fire research."[41] Some additional funding on fire research was provided by the military's nuclear weapons effects agency, AFSWP's successor, the Defense Atomic Support Agency (DASA). Throughout the 1960s and most of the 1970s, however, the military services remained generally uninterested in pursuing research on the fire effects of nuclear weapons.

As with many large government programs, the funding pattern for civil defense research was not ideal. According to Brode,

> The Kennedy administration started off with a *big* budget for [the Office of] Civil Defense. They didn't know how to spend it, what kind of research to do. They didn't have the facilities developed and the contractors identified. And then each year, the amount was decreased. Well, the effective way to do it is to start with a little bit and build up as you gain confidence and build a staff. So they ran out of money on everything.[42]

In any case, the funding begun under Kennedy enabled the small number of contractors who had been involved in nuclear fire research in the 1950s, and many new contractors, to thrive for much of the 1960s. The increased civil defense funding, in the words of historian Stephen Pyne, "revitalized a moribund Forest Service fire research program."[43] Even more significant was the funding for numerous governmental and nongovernmental laboratories and research organizations, prominent among them the Naval Radiological Defense Laboratory, United Research Services, Illinois Institute of Technology Research Institute, and the Stanford Research Institute.[44] Ironically, this expanded community's initial research results reinforced earlier understandings that fire damage could not be predicted. The research would also have a considerable impact on the subsequent history of nuclear damage prediction.

"Nuclear Attack . . . Need Not Be Catastrophic"

The fire research of the 1960s should be understood in the context of the public rhetoric in which the importance and feasibility of civil defense was strongly affirmed. The 1961 congressional hearings on Kennedy's request to increase civil defense spending had the same "Leave It to Beaver" sensibility as the earlier civil defense experiments in the nuclear weapons tests Shot ANNIE and Shot APPLE-2.

At the hearings, an official from the government's leading fire research laboratory, the Naval Radiological Defense Laboratory, described a recent two-day test of habitability in a shelter to provide protection against nuclear weapons effects. The laboratory's previous experiments had involved only men, including inmates from a minimum security prison farm, but this test involved one hundred men, women, and children, including about a dozen preschoolers. Acknowledging that "we are not trying to maintain the present standard of living under thermonuclear attack," experimenters nonetheless tried to provide a strong semblance of normality.[45] Their report discussed the children, who "ate only jam, peanut butter, and candy" and showed photographs of family members in the shelter participating in "'Chow' Time," "Calisthenics," "Bedtime" and "Charades."[46] Guy Oakes recounts a similar episode of "nuclear housekeeping" broadcast in the late 1950s on *Retrospect,* a CBS television news series sponsored by U.S. civil defense, in which Mr. and Mrs. Brown from Topeka, Kansas, and their eight children spent a week in the CBS fallout shelter.[47] (To help children practice their survival skills, the FCDA had earlier provided schools with skits such as "Let's Plan What to Do Now," "Operation Family Car," and "Until the Doctor Comes.")[48] Historian Laura McEnaney explains that planners tried to "domesticate the bomb; FCDA planners made the bomb familiar by making it *familial*. . . . 'Domestication' as it was practiced by the FCDA was a rhetorical gambit to make the bomb and its attendant dangers more familiar, less threatening, thoroughly disassociated from war and militarism through an association with family."[49]

At the same 1961 hearings, Jerald E. Hill, a physicist at RAND, provided the clearest description to date of the state of knowledge regarding fire damage caused by nuclear weapons "in the unfortunate event of a nuclear attack on the United States." Although Hill had worked on nuclear weapons effects for the previous decade, he spoke on the basis of "a study which has been in progress for only a few weeks and is not yet complete."[50]

As with much work in civil defense, Hill tried to combat what he saw as undue pessimism about the effects of nuclear war. He opened by noting that as his study progressed, "I have become increasingly convinced that, while fire damage which might be caused by a nuclear attack on the United States could be very serious, it need not be catastrophic in the sense of preventing postwar recovery from rather heavy nuclear attacks." He concluded that the most pessimistic values were often used to estimate fire damage to urban and forested areas from a nuclear attack, and "this leads to gross overestimates of the damage likely to be experienced. By making the situation appear hopeless, such estimates do a great disservice by preventing actions which could do much to reduce the damage from a nuclear attack and help speed recovery during the postwar period."[51]

In the weeks in which he worked on his study, it is clear from his testimony that Hill had carefully studied the USSBS studies, Bond's *Fire and the Air War,* and reports from the civil defense experiments in the atmospheric nuclear weapons tests. Skipping over the muddled definitions of mass fire of the National Academy's Committee on Fire Research, Hill used the definitions developed in the USSBS. Like the Survey, he distinguished between firestorms that appeared to develop in conditions of "low natural wind velocity" and conflagrations in which fire "spread rapidly along a front driven by high natural winds."[52]

As did the USSBS and the Wolverton report, Hill emphasized the numerous variables and uncertainties involved in trying to predict damage from mass fire. Speaking in the context of civil defense planning, not war planning, he noted that, no matter which nuclear effects are being estimated, assumptions must be made regarding the enemy's choice of time and targets, and the number, yield, and burst altitude of weapons delivered in a nuclear attack. However,

> to estimate the fire damage, assumptions about a number of additional factors become important. Among these are: meteorological factors such as wind velocity, temperature, relative humidity, visibility, lapse of time since the last precipitation and presence or absence of inversion layers and cloud cover in the target area, fuel characteristics, . . . topography, . . . and finally numbers and distribution of sources of primary and secondary ignition. . . . The problem of estimating areas within which initial ignitions would occur for given weapon and target characteristics is relatively straight-forward, but estimating the spread of fire from these initial ignitions is much more difficult. . . . For example, the seasonal periods of worst fire danger are different in different areas of the country and the over-all conditions can vary markedly from year to year which means that careful study of the variations of these conditions for various climatological areas over long periods of time should be evaluated statistically.[53]

While prediction of fire spread and resulting damage was difficult, Hill testified at the hearings that he was relatively optimistic about the ability to ameliorate the effects of fire damage were the United States to be attacked. He acknowledged that in areas "severely damaged by blast, firefighting is virtually impossible." However, drawing on findings from the U.S. atmospheric nuclear weapons tests, he argued that

> A number of precautionary measures could greatly reduce the probability of primary ignitions in urban areas. Since combustible trash, such as scrap paper, excelsior and punky or rotten wood, are the fuels most easily ignited by thermal radiation, rigorously enforced regulations requiring that such trash be kept picked up and stored in tightly covered

metal containers would greatly reduce the chance of primary fires out-side the area of secondary ignitions resulting from blast damage. Also the proper care of exposed wood surfaces by painting is important.[54]

Hill added, "in very good residential areas with not a very large built-upness," ignition of a firestorm "would be less likely to happen." Hill con-cluded, "preliminary study indicates that fire damage to urban areas is likely to be confined largely to areas seriously damaged by blast. In relatively in-frequent weather situations fire may spread beyond the areas of blast dam-age."[55]

The large body of work conducted in the decades after Hill's testimony generally adopted the broad categorization of mass fires into firestorms and conflagrations. It also accepted that varying weather conditions could have a significant impact on mass fire ignition and spread. However, almost all of the work focused not on climatology and environmental variation, but on gaining a much more detailed understanding of the complex processes of fire ignition and fire spread.

Annual Meeting at Asilomar

With the funding of many new projects, in 1962 OCD began to convene an annual meeting of fire research contractors. The annual meeting provided an informal venue where fire researchers could schmooze and could stay abreast of current research efforts and the funding priorities of OCD. With some interruption in the mid-1970s and changes in research emphasis, these meetings continued through 1983. Almost all of the meetings were held at the Asilomar conference center in Pacific Grove, California.[56] Asilomar, originally a camp for the Young Women's Christian Association, was re-nowned for its white sand beach, pleasant accommodations, and bad food. Professional attendance generally averaged thirty to forty people, including researchers from the U.S. Forest Service, government laboratories, think tanks and contractors, and universities. Records of the meetings provide an invaluable resource for tracing the composition of the community and its re-search interests and results over a twenty-year period.[57]

Many of the fire research contractors who met at Asilomar were the same professionals who had been convened earlier by the National Acad-emy's Committee on Fire Research. There were proportionately fewer aca-demics and more contract researchers at the Asilomar meetings than at the earlier committee meetings, but both were dominated by the engineering community, with some foresters and a few physicists attending. Of the twenty-six organizations represented at the 1967 Asilomar meeting (the first meeting for which a written record exists), almost half (twelve), had been present at the Committee on Fire Research's 1959 meeting on the use of models. Six were governmental or government-chartered organizations: the Defense Atomic Support Agency; the Fire Research Section of the National Bureau of Standards; the Forest Service; the Office of Civil Defense; the U.S. Naval Radiological Defense Laboratory; and the National Academy of Sciences. Most of the remaining six specialized in contract research for industry or government. Several represented a relatively new kind of organization spawned by universities to capture income from contract research: the Illinois Institute of Technology Research Institute (IITRI), the Applied Physics Laboratory (APL) affiliated with Johns Hopkins University, the Stanford Research Institute (SRI), and the Southwest Research Institute, which had been spun off from IITRI. IITRI, founded in 1936 as the Research Foundation of the Armour Institute of Technology, was the oldest of these; APL was founded in 1942, SRI and the Southwest Research Institute after the war.[58]

Unlike the National Academy of Sciences' Committee on Fire Research, the community assembled at Asilomar did not wander "down various byways" in a "quest for the ultimate truth," but was engaged in the serious business of capturing and delivering on government contracts. Although the range of research undertaken by those attending Asilomar was broad, including "rapid extinguishment of mass fires," "fire department operations analysis," "critical fire weather patterns," and "simplified treatment of burns," it was much more focused on the thermal and incendiary effects of nuclear weapons than had been the Committee on Fire Research.[59] This was primarily because the fire research community convened at Asilomar had available to it the approximately $1 million dollars a year in OCD contracts for research on the fire effects of nuclear weapons.

To trace the fire research community's changing understanding of problems, research strategies, and state of knowledge, I turn to a few of their major projects of the early 1960s through the mid-1970s. Although the research did not result in consistent predictions of mass fire damage, the funding and research process did build a community of recognized experts on nuclear fire. These experts reinforced the military's understanding that nuclear fire damage could not be predicted.

Project Flambeau

No civil defense–funded program was more important to the revitalization of the "moribund Forest Service fire research program" than Project Flambeau, a series of experimental large fires set by the Forest Service under the initial sponsorship of OCD, with later additional support from the Defense Atomic Support Agency.[60] The project ran from 1962 through 1967.[61]

Clive Countryman, who had more than twenty years' experience in forest fire research with the U.S. Forest Service, was the first head of Project Flambeau.[62] Thomas Palmer, who succeeded Countryman as head of the project, noted that "the Project Flambeau experiments were the nearest approach to an instrumented experimental investigation of firestorms, mass fires and conflagrations that have [ever] been attempted."[63] However, Project Flambeau would fall short of its goal of creating, let alone measuring, mass fires.

Countryman and his colleagues in the Forest Service defined *mass fire* in terms similar to those of the USSBS: Mass fire included both inward spreading firestorms that occurred in the absence of strong ambient ground winds, and moving-front conflagrations that occurred in the presence of strong ambient winds.[64] However, unlike the USSBS authors who understood mass fire as a wartime phenomenon, these researchers thought mass fires could occur in war or peace. For these researchers, the relevant experiences for understanding mass fires caused by nuclear weapons were large forest fires, urban fires, and experiments like Flambeau that simulated nuclear weapons effects.

Shortly after Project Flambeau began, Countryman's colleagues in the Forest Service conducted a historical review for OCD. They examined records of almost two thousand wildland and urban conflagrations, from the Great Chicago Fire of 1871 to the Coal Pier Fire along a mile of New Jersey waterfront near Manhattan in 1961. The lead author, Craig Chandler, granted that "mass fires differ from the usual city or wildland fire in that large areas are actively burning *at the same time*." According to Chandler, "Admittedly mass fires following nuclear attack may be larger than any heretofore known. But there are several reasons for believing that the behavior and spread of such fires will be governed by the same factors, acting in the same way, as have affected large fires of the past." For example, even a very large firestorm "is exposed to the influence of all [atmospheric] factors that will affect fires, no matter how large."[65]

Flambeau's initial goals were to gain data—"to help alleviate the lack of quantitative information on the characteristics and behavior of mass fire"—and to develop a causal understanding—"to establish the relationship of fire spread, fire intensity, and other fire behavior characteristics of mass fire in relation to air mass, fuel, and topography and to determine the effect of the fire system itself on the environment surrounding it under various . . . conditions."[66]

The Forest Service first envisioned an ambitious "planned burn [of] one mile square, preceded by a number of exploratory smaller burns and well-designed laboratory tests."[67] Had the Forest Service carried out its plan, it would have burned an area approximately one-quarter the size of that destroyed by fire at Hiroshima. A simultaneously set fire this large would probably have created the characteristics of a mass fire: a large-scale rise in heated air and consequent inrushing air near ground level back into the fire zone. As it was, the largest fires set at Flambeau were 50 acres, less than a twelfth of the original plan of one square mile (640 acres). Still, 50 acres—roughly the area of forty-five football fields[68]—is equal in size to a subdivision of several hundred homes, and the fires of Flambeau were the largest experimental fires set up to that time by the U.S. government. Although the features of a mass fire might have been created fleetingly in the largest of the Flambeau fires, the scale, along with implementation and instrumentation problems, prevented examination of the environment characteristic of a mass fire.

In the initial phase, from April 1962 through June 1964, approximately fifteen test fires were "burned on isolated sites in California and Nevada" in the vicinity of the White Mountains northwest of Death Valley.[69] These experiments ranged from burning a single two-story wood-frame house to burning a plot of almost 4 acres covered in cut brush and felled trees.[70] According to Countryman, this first series of small-scale tests was "largely exploratory in nature. . . . A gradual stepping up of the size of test fires was decided on . . . because of the dearth of quantitative information about large fire behavior; even those factors to be measured, and the phenomena that might be significant were not known with any degree of certainty." Instrumentation was developed and tested concurrently: "No precedent existed for determining the kinds and amount of instrumentation needed and measuring systems that would succeed in large-scale tests."[71]

For the second phase, much larger plots were prepared, ranging from 5 to 50 acres, which were "designed to simulate urban conditions . . . rang[ing] in size from . . . 1 to 10 city blocks."[72] According to prominent fire researcher Stanley Martin, who participated in and observed some of the largest Flambeau fires, the Forest Service made piles, each containing "about 20 tons of combustible material . . . about the same amount of fuel as would be in wood frame structures." These were arranged in a very large "rectangular checkerboard pattern" separated by "streets." Martin said there were "a lot of variables. They had small fires, big fires, wide spacing, close spacing, heavy big piles."[73] The largest plots were composed of 250 to 420 fuel piles, representing tract homes in a subdivision.[74] Stephen Pyne notes that the fuel piles "resembled the suburban housing developments that were burning almost annually in . . . Southern California" and that the experiments "echoed their World War II antecedents, for which whole mock [Japanese and German] cities had been constructed and burned"[75] at Eglin Field and Dugway Proving Ground. The Flambeau test fires were lit by electrical starters in each pile, and some of the resulting fires were large. Martin recalled, "I actually flew through the convection column" of one of the Flambeau fires "shortly after they lit it off. . . . It was scary and it smelled like smoke. They were spectacular. . . . Those [winds] roared like a jet engine."[76]

Although considered costly, fire researchers thought the Flambeau fires "show[ed] a great deal of promise as a full-scale means of investigating mass fire characteristics."[77] Project Flambeau also generated related research by private fire research contractors funded by DASA, the Advanced Research Projects Agency (ARPA), and OCD. The Dikewood Corporation applied its "Firestorm Model" to findings of the Flambeau experiments to predict the consequences of fires resulting from a nuclear attack. IITRI studied the requirements for simulating urban area fires and analyzed data from Flambeau. Within the framework of Flambeau, Isotopes, Inc., studied biological hazards to occupants of shelters that would accompany mass fires.[78]

From these tests, the Forest Service learned a great deal about how to build and instrument large fires or, at least, how not to. Official reports do not make an overall judgment about the success or failure of Project Flambeau, but a subtle rewording of the goals in the final report indicates what was not achieved. In contrast to the earlier ambitions to "establish the relationship of . . . fire behavior characteristics of mass fire" to the environment and "to determine the effect of the fire system itself on the environment surrounding it," the final report stated less ambitious goals: "The study was not designed to develop cause-and-effect relationships, but rather to gain some insight into as many aspects as possible of mass fire."[79]

The final report recites a litany of instrument failures, only some of which were overcome. For example, measurements of air flow, thought to be a particularly important feature of the mass fires in World War II, were bedeviled by instrumentation problems. At first, commercially available anemometers and wind vanes were used, but they were "constructed of plastic or aluminum" and "failed to withstand the high temperatures encountered within a fire area." The Forest Service's Western Laboratory did develop an adequate anemometer for use in the Flambeau tests, but they could not develop a wind vane.[80] In another example, instruments to measure air pressure measurement failed, so "pressure data obtained in the fire tests were generally unsatisfactory." Although the first instrument used "worked well in the laboratory, its performance in the field was unsatisfactory. . . . The second sensor . . . gave a better signal . . . but did not respond well to very small pressure changes." A third type "performed well but had to be read manually so that continuous observations were not possible." Additionally, "under prolonged exposure to the elevated temperatures in the fire[,] the bare wires [of thermocouples to measure temperature] often burned badly and frequently parted under the vibration and strain of the turbulence within the fire." Thermocouples made of platinum gave rise to new problems that "were never entirely solved."[81] Other problems also developed. In the summary words of the final report, "The major problem in instrumenting a large experimental fire was the installation of a complete and work-able system. Each test plot presented new problems in terrain and soil con-ditions."[82]

Fire researcher Stanley Martin gave a mixed assessment of Project Flam-beau: "They were mighty good fires . . . They were very well done, but my criticism always was that the fuel load was too low. They weren't putting enough fuel in there to get a real firestorm." The fires did not have sufficient "power density . . . a measure of how much heat is being released by the fire per unit area of the fire. . . . They didn't have enough fuel to get that kind of a power density." As a result, the strong winds characteristic of a firestorm could not be simulated.[83] As Martin put it in an authoritative review shortly after Project Flambeau was completed, the "duration of very intense heat release was insufficient to duplicate the strong atmospheric perturbations that may have given those fires their alleged uniquely dramatic character. None of this detracts very much from the accomplishments of the Flambeau effort. It was, after all, an exploratory study."[84]

Many years later, Harold Brode, who was not part of the fire research contracting community that convened at Asilomar, referred to Project Flam-beau as "a disaster": "The Forest Service, at least the parts of the Forest Ser-vice that were involved in this, didn't know what research was. It was the most uncontrolled, cavalier experiment. It was a travesty." He recounted one of the experiments in which the Forest Service "simulated a city by stacking up wood products in piles. . . . But before they got around to the experiment, all of this was stacked and sat there through the winter. So these bricks of brush were full of snow that hadn't melted out when they got around to the experiment. . . . It didn't burn very well. And it was dismally instrumented. The records are very poor. Even the motion pictures taken weren't very good. So it was largely a wasted experiment. . . . So, I don't know that Flambeau taught us anything, really."[85]

Nevertheless, Project Flambeau bolstered the authority and prestige of the fire research community. More important than the results, or lack of re-sults, was that this well-funded large-scale undertaking put the Forest Ser-vice back into the fire research business and provided a focus of research for others. It was one of the few research projects from this period that is con-sistently mentioned in later fire research literature.[86]

Death by Hypothesis: The Five City Study

In the mid-1960s, OCD began what was formally, and at first secretly, called the "Five City Study." (Those within the fire research community also referred to it as the "Five Cities Study," or just the "Five Cities.") The Five City Study was not a single study, but an umbrella program for much of the research

funded by OCD between 1965 and 1969. Walmer (Jerry) Strope, head of research at OCD in the 1960s, led the program. He called the Five City Study "a
management tool" that allowed comparability among the numerous studies
contracted by OCD. Martin agreed: "Basically, it was a new requirement. . . .
If you do research, you'll have to do it in terms of the Five Cities."[87]

This research program had a considerable effect on the fire research community. It shifted the earlier research emphasis on ignition of materials in
experimental settings to the much more complicated processes of ignition
and fire spread in real cities. Martin characterized the Five City Study as a
"turning point" in his own work.[88] Before, "It was pretty much pure guess
and by gosh. . . . The Five City Study was the first time we really grappled
with a real-world problem."[89] As part of the Five City Study, OCD put
"quite a bit of funding" into developing the first computer models to predict fire damage from nuclear weapons.[90] Although these first computer
models were not entirely successful, the fire research community's involvement in computing added to its prestige. The Five City Study also gave rise
to a new line of inquiry on the possible effects of the nuclear blast wave on
fire starts—which sustained researchers' interest through the 1970s and had
a continuing impact on the discussion of nuclear fire effects.

OCD specified hypothetical nuclear attacks on five cities: Providence,
Detroit, New Orleans, Albuquerque, and San Jose. The specifications included yield, ground zero, height of burst, time of year and time of day, visibility, and cloud cover. They also included the distribution of air blast and
thermal radiation at given distances from the supposed detonation. These
specifications varied by city. For example, the San Jose attack was hypothesized to be a 5-megaton detonation at 14,500 feet above sea level occurring
in August just after sunset with visibility of 15 miles and scattered clouds.
The New Orleans attack was a 10-megaton surface burst occurring in August at night with visibility of 10 miles and no cloud cover.[91]

According to Martin, who did studies on San Jose and New Orleans, the
idea was to analyze what would happen to a city under nuclear attack, "brick
by brick, block by block" at a level of detail not attempted previously. The
studies brought together people "who didn't even know each other . . . people working on blast and working on fire and working on fallout and working on prompt radiation and this and that and the other thing and they
weren't talking to each other. They [had] hardly [been] aware that the other
people were doing this work."[92]

A variety of weapons effects were analyzed under the Five City Study,
but fire was the major concern. According to Strope, OCD "did do an awful lot of work on fire, more than on other areas."[93] The research related to
fire included detailed "fuel array" surveys of the combustibility and placement of buildings in sections of each city, careful calculation of the thermal

radiation to which structures and materials would have been exposed by the hypothetical detonation, estimates of initial fires that would occur and subsequent fire spread, and the first computer modeling of fire damage from nuclear weapons.[94]

Though seeking to predict urban damage from fire, Martin and other researchers presupposed that it was less predictable than blast damage: "Fire was way too sensitive to the environment. You could not be assured of destruction. The reason fire is of interest is because it's so complex and because you can do something about it, you can provide protection against it, reduce your vulnerability."[95] These understandings, deeply ingrained in the civil defense community, would not be changed by the Five City research program.

The initial scenarios focused empirical observation and data collection. According to a study that Martin led:

> In each sample area, selected buildings were surveyed on a room-by-room basis. The exposure of kindling fuels to thermal radiation was determined "on the spot" by observing and photographically recording the direction of the hypothetical fireball and the fraction of it that would be seen, and by estimating and recording the thermal exposure that would pass through windows and screens. This information, combined with the free-field thermal exposure at the given location and the best available information on ignition thresholds, indicated the number of initial ignitions in each room and each sample building.[96]

Physicist Harold Brode was then serving on the National Academy of Sciences' Committee on Civil Defense, which had endorsed the Five City Study. He said,

> The idea was to take the theorizing and hypothesizing by the presumed experts out of the realm of generalities and into real urban environments. . . . Instead of saying, "Well, fire can't be important, because some days it's raining, or it's cloudy," [the idea] was to pick specific weather conditions, specific burst points over specific cities and analyze in detail what the consequences would be. Well, if you know exactly where the burst was, you know which windows it shines through, you could go and look . . . through every window and see what it was that could ignite.[97]

Brode was disappointed in the results because "they ran out of money" before they could do all the detailed surveys that had been planned.[98] Only in a small number of sample areas were observations made of the actual fuels visible through windows in the line of the hypothetical fireball.[99] At least,

Brode said, researchers had begun to think "explicitly of what the consequences would be to five specific cities, which was a step in the right direction. . . . It was an opportunity to really get some good statistics. . . . It was
a useful exercise as far as it went. It just didn't go far enough."[100]

The First Computer Models

Perhaps most significant for the fire research community was that, as
part of the Five City Study, OCD sponsored the first "major development of
computerized . . . models" of fire damage from nuclear attacks on cities.[101]
The models drew on Forest Service studies of ignition threshold from the
mid-1950s nuclear weapons tests, U.S. Naval Radiological Defense Laboratory (NRDL) experiments on ignition of cellulose material, and IITRI experiments on fires in buildings and in scale models to study "the development
and spread of fire in . . . building types for any initial location of the fire."
(In buying interior furnishings for these experiments, IITRI became "the
biggest customer of Goodwill in Chicago.")[102] The models also drew on re-
analyses of World War II data on firestorms and on fire spread, and the survey work done in the Five Cities on the expected exposures of materials to
thermal radiation from a nuclear detonation.

Many of those who developed these early computer models to predict
nuclear fire damage were engineers who, like most of the engineers on the
National Academy's Committee on Fire Research, understood such fires in
terms of detailed processes of "diffusion of flames, combustion principles,"
and step-by-step spread from "inception through the various stages of
buildup."[103] While it was claimed that these models assessed the extent of
nuclear fire damage to urban areas and were complete, if preliminary, they
did not incorporate fire-generated winds. Thus, while they were models of
very large fires, they did not model wartime mass fires per se.

By 1968, fire researchers had developed three computer models that predicted fire spread from buildings ignited "by nuclear attack on urban areas"
and had applied their predictions to one or more of the five cities.[104] Crow-
ley and his associates at Systems Sciences, Inc. (SSI), based in Bethesda,
Maryland, developed "Firefly—A Computer Model to Assess the Extent of
Nuclear Fire Damage in Urbanized Areas." Martin, Ramstad, and Colvin at
United Research Service (URS) in San Mateo, California, developed an "Interim Fire Behavior Model," which incorporated "the URS Corporation
technique for calculating sustained fires and fire spread resulting from an attack on an urban area." They applied the predictions of their model to San
Jose and New Orleans. Takata and Salzberg at IITRI developed a "Complete Fire-Spread Model" and applied their calculations to the cities of Detroit, Albuquerque, and San Jose.[105]

These computer models predicted the initial ignitions of exposed materials from thermal radiation, the growth of fires in rooms and buildings, and the spread of fire between buildings through mechanisms such as radiation, firebrands, and convective heating. Fire spread was modeled step-by-step over time as the first buildings to burn spread fire to adjacent structures, which then spread to other structures, and so on. These calculations were extremely time-consuming to compute. When IITRI first began its modeling work in the early 1960s, the computing limitations were "such that the time required for one fire spread calculation in a tract of 100 buildings equaled or exceeded that which would occur in the real fire."[106] With improvements in computing capability, more fire-spread calculations could be done. By the late 1960s, URS was able to calculate short-range fire spread through four generations.[107]

However, the models developed in this period did not incorporate the hurricane-speed winds sucked into the fire zone by the mass of rising hot air caused by the many initial fires; these inrushing winds would fan, spread inward, and sustain a mass fire. Of course, researchers were aware of earlier descriptions of inrushing winds associated with firestorms, but they lacked a detailed understanding of the larger atmospheric involvement in nuclear fire and thus could not include such winds in their models. Fire-generated winds were not among the mechanisms of fire spread incorporated into the Takata and Salzberg model nor in the Martin, Ramstad, and Colvin model. Martin and his colleagues wrote at the time that among "the major limitations in the fire-behavior model" were "shortcomings in the state of the art of predicting . . . the coalescent effects of many structural fires burning simultaneously."[108] In a major review of the field of fire research written in the late 1960s, Martin said:

> Reliable descriptions of the behavior and characteristics of mass fires and the life hazards they produce are . . . lacking . . . as are their criteria of formation. . . . Strong fire induced wind velocities near ground level are frequently reported, although it is uncertain whether the high winds exist simultaneously over the whole fire-affected area or they are merely local manifestations of turbulence, of funneling by buildings or terrain irregularities, or of fire whirls.[109]

Without a way of modeling fierce fire-generated winds, researchers' models predicted gradual fire growth: "Fires initiated by the thermal radiation from the nuclear fireball will generally build up slowly, inasmuch as they typically evolve through a process of propagation of fire from a single kindling-weight fuel to heavier fuels."[110] In keeping with gradual fire growth and civil defense goals, IITRI developed a methodology "for predicting the number of [nuclear] fires which can be suppressed by self-help and brigades units" and included this "fire suppression methodology" in its fire damage model.[111] (In contrast, Bond, who had studied incendiary bomb damage to Germany in World War II, was skeptical about being able to fight such fires. He said later, "If you've got enough things burning, you wouldn't be able to do very much. . . . Nobody understands the limit of what a fire department can do." In a mass fire, "people there will be gone. No argument.")[112]

Those devising computer models in this period drew on the sometimes self-contradictory knowledge base to define firestorms. According to Martin's contemporary review: "Surprisingly little is known confidently about [firestorms]. Nothing illustrates the lack of understanding better than the fact that no clear and uniformly acceptable definition of the conditions for their formation and the unique characteristics they are said to exhibit exists after 25 years of study and debate. Some experts even deny that there is anything unique about them."[113]

In their study of hypothetical nuclear fire damage to San Jose, Martin and his colleagues weighed various criteria to determine whether fires initially ignited in downtown San Jose would result in a firestorm. According to the scenario with which they worked, downtown San Jose was 13 miles from a 5-megaton nuclear weapon detonation and would have been exposed to a thermal fluence of approximately 18 cal/cm², not quite twice the thermal fluence at the outer edge of mass fire at Hiroshima. Would these fires cause a mass fire that would burn down virtually all the structures in downtown San Jose? According to the authors, the conditions under which a mass fire would develop "unfortunately . . . is a very difficult question to answer with any reliability."[114] They wrote, "The present state of the art is not encouraging insofar as prediction of mass fires is concerned, and well-founded techniques are not likely to result from this study. A set of rules will be contrived, however, to give the best estimate possible concerning the existence of mass fires."[115] These rules would be derived from "available criteria for predicting fire storm development," which, however, "are empirical in nature and derived from a very limited sampling. The basic phenomena are not well understood and the criteria may be inappropriate."[116] The criteria specified some combination of fuel loading, area, heat released by initial ignitions, and ambient wind conditions.

Martin and his co-authors examined three studies providing such criteria. A 1955 civil defense technical manual concluded that a firestorm would generally require an area of 1 square mile or more in which 20 percent of the area was covered by buildings. A 1965 study done by Rodden, John, and Laurino at SRI specified conditions in which firestorms would develop that included: an area greater than 0.5 square miles, 8 pounds of combustibles per square foot, half of the structures initially on fire, surface winds of less than

8 miles per hour at the time of the attack, and an unstable atmosphere.[117]
A 1966 study by Lommasson and Keller at the Dikewood Corporation, another prominent fire research company in this period, analyzed the heat
release from large fires in World War II to develop a single quantitative criterion for firestorms.

Lommasson and Keller arrived at the remarkable conclusion that there
had not been a firestorm at Hiroshima. They used a concept of "power density," or heat release for a given area for a given period of time. This was
measured in British thermal units per square mile per second ($Btu/mi^2/sec$).
According to them, the fires that occurred in Germany, at Hamburg, Dresden, Heilbrun, and Darmstadt, had peak power densities of about 700 million $Btu/mi^2/sec$ and clearly qualified as firestorms. Lommasson and Keller
used a peak power density of approximately 500 million $Btu/mi^2/sec$ as the
criterion for a firestorm. In their analysis, thirteen other fires in Germany
and nine in Japan, plus the atomic bombings of Hiroshima and Nagasaki,
showed much lower peak power densities, ranging from 50 to 300 million
$Btu/mi^2/sec$, with Hiroshima and Nagasaki among the lowest, at less than
50 million $Btu/mi^2/sec$.[118]

Perhaps persuaded by their logic, Martin wrote that there is "some question as to whether or not a firestorm actually developed in Hiroshima.
Lommasson and Keller, on the basis of historical reports, estimates of fire
fatalities, and their own estimates of peak power density, conclude that a
firestorm did not occur in Hiroshima."[119] (Brode later dryly remarked, "Any
claim that it was not a 'firestorm' must rest on a very special definition of a
'firestorm.'")[120]

By the standards advanced in the first two studies, downtown San Jose
generally met the criteria for a firestorm. However, the power density calculation of the initial ignitions in downtown San Jose was approximately
250 million $Btu/mi^2/sec$; by the Dikewood criterion, "this value of power
density lies in the questionable region insofar as the development of a
firestorm is concerned."[121] On the basis of their analysis of initial fire
spread, Martin and his colleagues thought that the power density would
double to about 500 million $Btu/mi^2/sec$, meeting the Dikewood criterion.
Thus, Martin and his colleagues conservatively concluded that "the development of a fire storm appears to be a marginal possibility" in downtown
San Jose.[122]

Given an intellectual climate in which fire-generated winds were not incorporated into large-scale fire damage models, in which it was reasonable
for researchers to model the effects of fire brigades on suppressing fire damage caused by nuclear weapons, and in which Hiroshima, in which 4.4 square
miles burned to the ground, was not considered a firestorm (although it had
been defined as one by the fire analysts in the USSBS), it is not surprising that

the predictions of the three computer models by researchers at SSI, URS, and IITRI did not converge. "[The three] fire spread models prepared for OCD appear to give significantly different results in the number of ignitions, early fires, and rates of fire development."[123] OCD contracted with the Dikewood Corporation to analyze the conflicting results of the three models. According to the preliminary findings of the analysts at Dikewood,

> The results predicted by the models, under identical conditions, differ very markedly. This is true both for ignition and for fire spread. . . . It is suggested that progress in this area could be accelerated by the use of better reporting procedures. Obscure programming and fragmentary documentation do more than shorten final reports. They make evaluation, use and even understanding, of the models by other investigators very difficult, and thus lead to wasteful duplication of effort.[124]

There is no record that these inconsistencies were resolved at the time. Concerted work on computer models by this community would not begin again until a renewed interest by the government in fire effects in the late 1970s and early 1980s. At that point, the early models served as the point of departure, an indication that little work had been done after the late 1960s.

"Survival in a Brighter Light"

At the same time that the fire research community began to develop computer models of nuclear ignition and fire spread, they also asked how the nuclear blast wave would affect fire ignition and growth.[125] Fire researchers had long been aware that the blast wave could increase fire ignitions by exposing electrical equipment and by breaking open containers of volatiles such as gasoline; they called these "secondary" fire ignitions. (Brode and others would later call these "blast disruption" fires.) In the late 1960s, fire researchers began to examine two other phenomena that looked as though they might have the opposite effect, of decreasing fire ignitions. First, there was the possibility that the blast wave, arriving seconds to a minute after the thermal flash, could itself extinguish fires that had already been set by the flash. Second, there was the possibility that the blast wave would crush structures and create dense fields of debris; these debris fields could snuff out or retard the development and spread of incipient fires. These phenomena—secondary fire ignitions, extinction of fire by the blast wave, and collapsing structures—were studied under the rubric of "blast/fire interactions" and would figure in the fire community's research agenda into the 1970s and 1980s (see chapter 10).

Fire Extinction

In the late 1960s, researchers began to examine a question that had implications for their fire damage models: Could the blast wave extinguish
"young" fires just ignited by the thermal flash? Extinction of these fires was
thought possible because "ignition by thermal radiation occurs most readily in thin flammable material; and major fires develop only after some time
has passed." If fires could be suppressed by the blast wave, "the number of
persistent fires may be dramatically reduced. It could reduce the problem of
firefighting to manageable dimensions."[126]

Some research on blast extinction of fires had been done in the early
1950s when Forest Service researchers H. D. Bruce and Keith Arnold observed at the atomic weapons tests that fires initiated by the thermal pulse
were extinguished by the subsequent blast wave. In this same period, the Forest Service also sponsored laboratory simulations by Tramontini and others
at UCLA on airblast extinction of forest fuels, such as beds of pine needles
and some urban materials.[127] Both the atomic weapons studies and the simulations found that "fires in the open are blown out by modest levels of air-
blast overpressure" of 2 to 3 pounds per square inch (psi). A later assessment
of these studies said, "The ameliorative potential is profound, but the effect
has largely been discounted in fire damage assessments."[128]

The fire damage models of the Five City Study had not incorporated the
possibility that blast might extinguish incipient building fires; indeed, it was
not at all evident that fires in buildings, as opposed to those in the open,
could be extinguished as easily as the studies in the early 1950s had indicated. By the late 1960s, however, researchers considered the effects of air
blast on urban fire damage to be an important open question and began experiments to understand such effects. On the one hand, researchers noted
that "analyses of fire responses of urban targets in which blast interactions
have been neglected . . . predict a very high incidence of structurally damaging primary fires at modest overpressures—those which fall short of producing severe structural damage." In other words, if the blast wave did not
extinguish fire ignitions, the radius of thermally induced ignitions was predicted to extend significantly beyond the radius of severe blast damage. On
the other hand, "It is vitally important to know how much the initiation
process may be affected by blast and blast effects. If research reveals that
many of the predicted fire starts would not survive the blast environment,"
then damage would be considerably less. Researchers thought that recent experiments simulating the effects of nuclear air blast on fire ignition were "far
too preliminary in nature to permit drawing any firm conclusions. . . . No
substantial progress [has been] made toward understanding processes of
blast extinguishment or enhancement."[129]

In 1970, Thomas Goodale, a researcher at URS, produced what were considered to be the first decisive experimental results. The effort to replicate and interpret his results would occupy the fire research community over the next decade or more. Undertaking full-scale simulations with furnished rooms in the URS shock tunnel at Ft. Cronkite, in Marin County, California, Goodale found that "very moderate" airblast overpressures of 2.5 psi consistently extinguished the flames of incipient fires in rooms. At the same time, Goodale found that "kindlings that can support smoldering combustion will continue to smolder following extinction of the flame. Smoldering debris commonly resumed active flaming after delays ranging from minutes to hours."[130] Fire researchers argued that the smoldering material "can be very significant operationally because it allows more time for self-help fire fighting."[131]

The next year Goodale conducted more experiments in the same shock tunnel. One experiment examined the effects of blast overpressures of up to 9 psi on the smolder that remained after flames had been blown out. These findings, however, were not conclusive: "The higher overpressures did not produce a smolder-extinction counterpart to the blowout of flames. No trend was evident." Goodale also tested the likelihood of various materials smoldering. He found that "cotton batting may be especially susceptible to smolder" and concluded that eliminating such material could reduce a special nuclear fire hazard. Another experiment showed a very different outcome in which low blast pressure could increase fire spread. In this study, Goodale subjected burning curtains to blast overpressures of 1 psi "only to discover that transport of burning curtain fragments may become a considerable hazard under suitable conditions."[132]

Goodale's initial findings were considered important by fire researchers and stimulated much work. A report on the state of research on blast–fire interaction delivered at the 1973 meeting at Asilomar shows the impact:

> Thus, as we strive for a better comprehension of survival potential in a blast/fire environment, progress holds many surprises. Although some of these frustrate as we see old certainties disappear, each takes us a step closer to the truth. Fortunately, some put the whole picture of survival in a brighter light. Such was the discovery by Goodale that very moderate blast could extinguish ignitions. How many and under what conditions is not that clear.[133]

Many studies followed, but the results were inconclusive. One experiment undertaken in the spring of 1973, known as MIXED COMPANY, subjected twenty pans of burning fuel to blast overpressure of 5, 2, and 1 psi. The experimenters expected results consistent with Goodale's: At least some of the fires would be extinguished. Instead, "no fire at any of the three stations was extinguished by the shock wave." The authors noted that their result "seemingly contradicts the conclusion" of Goodale's experiment.[134] Later, it was reported that MIXED COMPANY "only added confusion to the questions of blast extinction."[135] Some experiments in the mid-1970s and early 1980s appeared to bear out Goodale's findings; others did not.[136]

"Buried in Debris"

In the late 1960s, fire researchers raised another concern about the "lack of information on the interaction of blast effects and fire behavior" in the models they had developed for the Five City Study: "For lack of a better approach, structures have been treated as though they were uncrushed." Researchers were aware that many buildings in which fires had started would collapse under the force of the blast wave. They reasoned that the "subsequent fire behavior in blast-damaged structures could be grossly different from that in undamaged buildings." Researchers noted that the "rearrangement of fuels" might cause fires to spread more readily as structures opened up and exposed more fuels; these were "secondary" ignitions.[137] However, in this period they became far more concerned that the blast could "squish everything."[138] "Clearly, incipient fires in kindling/tinder materials can be readily snuffed out when the fuel source is buried in debris."[139]

Because it was far more likely that structures would collapse at the higher overpressures near the detonation than farther away, researchers began to theorize a "hole in the doughnut" pattern: In the "doughnut hole," the area immediately surrounding the detonation, collapsed structures would prevent fires from burning or would extinguish incipient fires; farther away, fires would burn more vigorously. According to Martin, "Jim Kerr [director of research for the civil defense agency] would sometimes state: 'Let's separate the hole in the doughnut from the doughnut.'"[140] This was an understanding of fire dynamics based on researchers' laboratory findings and their theoretical extrapolation to nuclear weapons. Although at Hiroshima there was some evidence that the blast wave had extinguished a few fires, there was no "hole" near the detonation, nor was there evidence of such a hole at Nagasaki.[141]

The idea of the doughnut hole remained influential. In the late 1970s, as the civil defense agency rekindled its interest in fire damage, researchers envisioned "a 'hole-in-the-doughnut' model, applicable to areas of totally collapsed structures [and] continuous debris fields."[142] In the late 1980s and early 1990s, Pentagon planners concerned with the feasibility of predicting fire damage for use in nuclear targeting spoke of the "doughnut effect," in which mass fire would not rage in the area of severe blast damage because structures would collapse and smother ignitions; fires would, however, occur in a ring outside.[143]

In the 1970s, funding for civil defense and fire research declined and remained low until the end of the decade. James Kerr, the director of research at OCD, noted at Asilomar in 1971 that "budgetary fluctuations now appear to have damped out, but with the final reading unfortunately on the low side."[144] Matters were worse by 1973. Kerr noted "the steady decline in funding of research" for civil defense and a "tendency away from basic to applied studies. While [civil defense] has never gone in heavily for basic research, there has always been a respectable core program, but that is shrinking fast now." Kerr presented a bar graph showing the decline of spending for fire research from about $1.2 million annually in 1962 to just a third of that a decade later.[145] By 1974, the civil defense agency had moved even further away from fire research. Kerr noted that civil defense research now focused on "crisis relocation planning. . . . Work has slowed or stopped on room and full building fires."[146] Even more telling, no fire research meetings were held at Asilomar for the next three years. When the meetings resumed in 1978, they were no longer on fire research per se, but on blast–fire interactions. But by then, something new was afoot.

Chapter

The Physics and Politics of Mass Fire

It was kind of a lonely business actually, getting [the Defense Nuclear Agency] to pay serious attention to fire. . . . It's taken 10 years really to break through. It's kind of horrendous to think about changing the VN system. It's a big system, with a lot of people, money, capital assets. Now it's about to change. The trick we've used is to put fire damage in the same VN system so that they don't have to change the way they do business, they just have to change the numbers.

Harold Brode, August 11, 1989, and September 7, 1989

I n the late 1970s, physicist Harold Brode, then vice president of Pacific-Sierra Research (PSR), persuaded the government to support a substantial research program to predict fire damage from nuclear weapons. Brode first convinced the government's civil defense agency (called, since 1979, the Federal Emergency Management Agency, or FEMA) to fund development of a computer model of the physics of mass fire. Brode then persuaded a few key people at the Defense Nuclear Agency (DNA) to fund a national research program to predict nuclear fire damage. This program became the largest fire research program since the civil defense–funded research of the 1960s. The ultimate goal was to revise the knowledge-laden organizational routines used by nuclear war planners to predict blast damage—the VNTK system—to include predictions of fire damage.

By the late 1980s, Brode and his colleagues at PSR had developed a robust algorithm to predict both nuclear blast damage and nuclear fire damage. This was the first time since the invention of the atomic bomb that predictions of fire damage were developed that could be incorporated into nuclear war planning. In this same period, Brode and his colleagues persuaded a small number of key players involved in nuclear war planning at the Defense Intelligence Agency (DIA) and the Joint Strategic Target Planning Staff (JSTPS) that it was scientifically warranted and technically feasible to begin to incorporate fire damage into their war plans. By the early 1990s, the small group working on fire prediction in DNA, DIA, and JSTPS had come close to gaining government approval to incorporate a combined fire-blast vulnerability number (VN) into U.S. nuclear war planning. However, in early 1992, the program was halted and put on indefinite hold.

This chapter explains how the effort spearheaded by Brode almost succeeded. The next chapter explains why it did not. This is neither a story of inevitable success nor inevitable failure. Because it shows clearly what *almost* happened, we can learn a great deal about the requirements for organizational change. The change begun in this period was patterned differently from the other great period of organizational innovation after World War II.

Recall the origins of the VNTK system in the early 1950s, when civil servants in the Physical Vulnerability Branch in Air Force Intelligence, on their own initiative, sought the advice of experts outside the government to help them develop a knowledge-laden routine to predict nuclear blast damage. This time, Brode, a well-regarded member of the nuclear weapons effects community, tried to convince the government that they could and should incorporate predictions of fire damage into nuclear war planning routines. Brode was outside the government, which contributed to the independence of his perspective, but he had worked closely with government officials over many years, which contributed to his influence.

Why did Brode want to predict fire damage and why was he able to develop such predictions when others had not been able to? What explains the timing of his initiative? What was his strategy for changing how the government predicted damage from nuclear weapons? How did he almost succeed in marshaling support for this change? Why did he fail?

The answers to these questions will illuminate the fundamental question, How do knowledge-laden routines change? How do those in organizations change their approaches to problem solving—their understanding of what counts as a problem, their representation of problems, their strategies for solving problems, and their requirements for solutions? What are the sources of innovation in reconceptualizing problems and solutions? How are innovations developed and implemented? What are the requirements for such change?

Changing knowledge-laden routines is essential to larger-scale organizational change. The specifics of knowledge-laden routines can be changed without changing broadly articulated organizational goals,[1] but changes in organizational goals cannot be implemented without changing knowledge-laden routines. Stephen Rosen, for example, defines major innovation in military organizations as a change in mission, a "new way of war," *and* a change in operational procedures, "the tasks around which warplans revolve."[2] In my terms, these procedures and tasks are knowledge-laden routines. By examining how knowledge-laden routines change, we will gain insight into the requirements for far-reaching organizational change.

Organizational change is a hard problem. First, the usual explanation— an external shock that shakes up power in an organization or alters organizational understanding of the environment and the problems that must be solved—does not apply here. Of course, the environment surrounding key government agencies must be considered, including the continuing influence of the fire research establishment and the heightened Cold War under President Ronald Reagan in the 1980s. However, while both were important, neither provided an external shock that can explain why a new knowledge-laden organizational routine was developed. One might think that the *end* of the Cold War played an important role. However, Mikhail Gorbachev's global initiatives started *after* Brode had received substantial funding for research on nuclear mass fire and thus cannot explain the origins of the research program.

That is not to deny the possibility of world-scale influence on the internal organizational course of events: One of our tasks is to trace how interpretations and ramifications of such large-scale changes may have affected minute organizational routines. By the late 1980s, perceptions of a lessening Soviet threat led to anticipated decreases in U.S. nuclear weapons; this could have increased receptivity to Brode's arguments that, with fewer nuclear weapons in the U.S. arsenal, more accurate prediction of the damage they would cause was all the more important. But the dissolution of the Soviet Union and the Warsaw Pact caused significant decreases in the number of targets,[3] which, combined with decreases in U.S. military spending, could have lessened incentives for proceeding with Brode's methodology. In any case, external changes did not clearly determine a particular course of organizational action.

Another likely "external influence" explanation was publication of the landmark "nuclear winter" article in the December 1983 issue of the influential journal *Science*.[4] The article argued that smoke from nuclear weapons– ignited fires could cause catastrophic drops in temperatures and possibly extinguish life on earth. Public interest in nuclear winter did provide a rationale for government support for research on fire damage throughout the 1980s. However, nuclear winter became an issue several years after the government began funding research on nuclear fire damage and thus cannot explain the initial support.

Organizational change is a hard problem for a second reason: The definitions I have used and the historical argument I have developed imply the strong weight of the past. I have argued that *organizational frames* are approaches to problem solving that are largely shaped by understandings of mission, long-standing collective assumptions and knowledge about the world, and earlier patterns of attention to problem definitions and solutions. The very power of this approach in showing historical linkages between modes of problem solving before, during, and after World War II does not tell us how or why a major departure in problem definition occurred in the late 1970s, when government agencies began their first concerted research effort to predict fire damage from nuclear weapons. Analytically, I will need to unstick that which worked so well stuck together.

Can a conception of organizational frames embodying past understandings of problems help explain how this happened? In a sense, it cannot. The concept of organizational frames—problem representation and solution requirements within which are embedded organizational goals, assumptions and knowledge about the world, and traces of previous definitions of problems and solutions—simply does not explain *how* an organization changes its problem-solving focus. However, we can use our understanding of frames and the past embedded within to help us identify potential elements of organizational change.

We can begin by asking whether Brode or others tried to change organizational understandings of mission. Was there an effort to redefine the goal of destroying many *specific* installations, to one of destroying whole *areas*? It might seem that such a redefinition would be required to predict the vast damage that would result from mass fire. But there was no such redefinition. Brode and those he worked with in the government did not disturb the categories of what was to be damaged—these remained the same targeted structures as before. Unlike those who advocated fire bombing and area destruction in World War II, Brode worked within the assumptions of precision targeting. What changed was not an emphasis in targets or rationale, but the understanding and predictions of how those targets were to be destroyed. This continuity is important.

Did Brode's scheme for predicting fire damage challenge long-standing assumptions and knowledge about the world? Yes—Brode challenged understandings dating back to the end of World War II that fire damage from nuclear weapons was less predictable than blast damage. The problems he wanted to solve, and thought he could solve, were not dictated by past precedent. Why was Brode not bound by past understandings as others had been? And what would it mean for his strategy and chances of success that he challenged such long- and widely held understandings about the physical world?

Finally, was there continuity or discontinuity between earlier patterns of problem solving and Brode's later efforts to predict fire damage? His focus on predicting fire damage was by definition a departure from decades of focus on blast damage. However, Brode's approach also embraced continuities with past knowledge-laden routines. Just as he did not contest mission, he did not challenge the underlying accounting scheme and organizational routines developed in the VNTK system to predict blast damage. Instead, he modified the "blast VNTK" into a "fire-blast VNTK." The result was a radical change in how damage was predicted, but it did not challenge organizational mission or basic routine. We might think this was just good luck. In fact, the appearance of continuity was critical to Brode's strategy for organizational change.

In sum, the concept of organizational frame does not tell us how change occurs, but it sensitizes us to barriers to, and possibilities for, change. There is nothing inevitable about the pattern that occurred here. Sketching its broad outline indicates other possibilities in different historical contexts; for example, instead of incremental change, organizational goals can be changed and organizational routines radically reinvented.

A New Fire Research Program

The Changed Organizational Landscape

From the 1950s to the 1990s, key government agencies experienced change and continuity in three main areas: target intelligence for use in nuclear war planning, military research on nuclear weapons effects, and U.S. strategic nuclear war planning itself.

Throughout most of the 1950s, the Deputy Directorate for Targets (later the Directorate of Targets) in Air Force Intelligence was responsible for intelligence on structures to be targeted in U.S. nuclear war plans. Within the targeting directorate, the Physical Vulnerability Division maintained and updated the VNTK blast damage system. The Targets Analysis Division maintained the *Bombing Encyclopedia*, a compendium of information on potential targets worldwide. The military's Armed Forces Special Weapons Project (AFSWP), established in 1947, was responsible for research on nuclear weapons effects; among other things, it coordinated the military's experiments in the U.S. atmospheric nuclear weapons tests. The Air Force's Strategic Air Command (SAC) drew up the plans for action in the event of a nuclear war; they relied on Air Force Intelligence for information on target location and physical vulnerability. The invention of the Polaris nuclear submarine in the late 1950s and ongoing interservice disagreements about coordination of plans and target lists led in 1960 to new organizational arrangements for nuclear war planning.[5]

Many of the Air Force's target intelligence functions were transferred to a new Department of Defense agency, the Defense Intelligence Agency (DIA), established in the fall of 1961. DIA was to pull together the diverse and overlapping responsibilities of the separate service intelligence units. For those who had worked in target intelligence in the Air Force, there was more continuity than change: Many of the same people continued to do the same jobs they had done before, in DIA's Production Center, and later, in the Data Base Directorate (DB). Within DB, the Physical Vulnerability Branch in the Target Intelligence Division housed the analysts who maintained and updated the VNTK system. Another division of DB housed the large databases first developed by Air Force Intelligence for nuclear targeting, such as the *Bombing Encyclopedia,* and its successor, the Automated Installation File (AIF), as well as a more selective group of potential targets, the Target Data Inventory (TDI).[6]

There were fewer organizational changes for AFSWP. For more than fifty years it remained an independent agency of the Department of Defense, through several name changes: In 1959, it became the Defense Atomic Support Agency (DASA); in 1971, the Defense Nuclear Agency (DNA); and in 1997, the Defense Special Weapons Agency (DSWA). In 1998, it lost its autonomy and was absorbed into a new agency, the Defense Threat Reduction Agency (DTRA).

Like target intelligence, nuclear war planning was formally moved out of the Air Force. In 1960, all strategic nuclear targeting was brought under a single "joint" military organization called the Joint Strategic Target Planning Staff (JSTPS), which continued to work out of SAC Headquarters in Omaha, Nebraska. SAC had a large influence in JSTPS—the commander in chief of SAC was also the director of JSTPS—but all the services participated in JSTPS, and a Navy admiral ran the day-to-day operations. Although much of what JSTPS did was opaque to those it reported to, it was part of a broader planning process that included the President, the Secretary of Defense, and the Joint Chiefs of Staff.[7] In 1992, SAC was dissolved and replaced by the joint service organization called Strategic Command. At that point, the functions of JSTPS were absorbed into Strategic Command.

With these changes, action that had unfolded largely within the Air Force became located interorganizationally in DIA, DNA, and JSTPS. When Brode proposed new research to change the VNTK system, the process to change the system was different from earlier. In the early Cold War years, the VNTK system to predict blast damage had been developed and approved within the Air Force. In the early 1990s, approval had to come from those in charge of strategic nuclear war planning in the JSTPS and from high-level military officers reporting to the Joint Chiefs of Staff.

The Physics of Large Urban Fires

As a young physicist in his first job at RAND, Brode had modeled the nuclear blast environment, the "forcing function" used by Nathan Newmark as the basis of the VNTK system. Brode worked at RAND for twenty years, and left in 1971 to join the newly formed Los Angeles think tank R&D Associates (RDA), founded by two former RAND scientists, brothers Albert and Richard Latter. Brode headed the physics department at RDA. In 1979 he became vice president of another Southern California research firm, Pacific-Sierra Research. During his career, Brode served on more than twenty-five governmental advisory panels, groups, and committees; perhaps most important, he was a member of the Scientific Advisory Group (SAGE) to DASA/DNA, serving almost the entire period from 1961 to 1992, and chairing it from 1980 to 1992. As chair, Brode edited a major revision of DNA's *Effects Manual-1, Capabilities of Nuclear Weapons,* the authoritative multivolume source on nuclear weapons for those in the government, generally referred to as EM-1.[8] Not unlike many university-based scholars concerned with policy, Brode spent his career nurturing contacts, developing contracts, researching, writing, and briefing government officials. Much of his work has been classified, but some is publicly available in published articles or unclassified government reports.

Brode's research agenda was driven by the government's need for knowledge about a wide range of nuclear weapons phenomena and their effects on military systems. His methods for calculating blast pressure from nuclear explosions in the atmosphere, formulated in the early 1950s, became the standard description of blast used by the government. In the late 1950s, Brode participated in studies on how to maximize the survivability of U.S. missiles, whether through hardening of silos and equipment, increasing mobility, or dispersion. In 1961 he published with Robert Bjork the results of the first calculation of cratering action by a nuclear weapon burst on the surface of the earth.[9] In the 1960s, he became involved in studies on the "neutralization" of Soviet hardened missile sites, and in the 1970s to mid-1980s, he was also concerned with the targeting of "super-hard" command centers. Brode also used his calculational tools to study nuclear fireballs, high-altitude bursts, thermal radiation, nuclear cloud motions, explosions in cavities, shock propagation in tunnels, the design of hypervelocity launchers, and detonation and blast from chemical explosives.[10]

Brode's research agenda was also driven by his desire to understand and model the physics of a wide range of nuclear weapons effects:

For years, I was supported by DASA, DNA, DSWA contracts for work I proposed to do for them, usually to solve problems that they were aware of, or problems that they were *not* aware of, or had not considered important until I pointed out their significance to some military system or application. Fire damage was just one of these areas that for various reasons hadn't been vigorously pursued or not solved satisfactorily.[11]

It was DNA's policy to support high-caliber scientists and their organizations in order to keep them deeply involved in defense work. According to a high-level DNA official, "Brode was a first-class scientist. If Hal Brode wanted to work on fire, that was okay with us. . . . Brode was like Newmark and a few others. He was one of those talents it's important to keep [engaged]. . . . What Hal wanted to do was worth doing."[12] From Brode's perspective, it was not so rosy. "In truth, there was always high competition for DNA dollars, and budgets were always getting slashed."[13]

In the 1970s, Brode participated in "a study group of all sorts of notables" convened by DNA to review the radiation dose levels used by the Army in its plans to incapacitate enemy soldiers in tactical nuclear war. The committee was headed by Charles McDonald, a well-regarded scientist and colleague of Brode's at RDA. The question addressed by the McDonald committee was whether the Army's incapacitating dose criterion was too high. The human response to massive doses of nuclear radiation was not well understood, but Brode thought that the Army's criterion for an incapacitating dose was "totally cockeyed. . . . The Army, in wishing to instantly incapacitate the enemy tank crew before they could return fire, sought a guaranteed incapacitating dose. . . . In principle, as in so much planning for *assured* success, the multitude of conservative assumptions leading to a high probability of instant incapacitation required a very high dose."[14] This dose was 20,000 rads, which, according to Brode, was a dose at which "a soldier's blood is practically boiling."[15]

This study group renewed Brode's interest in the fire effects of nuclear weapons.[16] In the context of the McDonald committee, Brode briefed nuclear weapons scientists on "the so-called neglected effects" of nuclear weapons; that is, the consequences of nuclear bursts that had not been explicitly considered before. These included large-scale fires, along with smoke, ash, dust, fireball anomalies, dust-induced electromagnetic pulse (EMP) noise, intermediate radiation dose effects, crater ejecta, and blast-driven debris.[17] In the late 1970s, Brode gave the briefing under the auspices of DNA, "a briefing that made a kind of horror story."[18]

In the late 1970s and early 1980s, Brode won support from FEMA and DNA to do in-depth studies on the basic physics of mass fires caused by nuclear weapons and on methods for predicting fire damage that could be incorporated into nuclear war planning. His work proceeded in four phases over the 1980s and early 1990s: Brode and his colleagues (1) developed their basic model of the physics of mass fire, (2) began predicting fire damage to structures, (3) translated these predictions into the framework of the existing VNTK system, and (4) guided an interagency process aimed at radically revising the VNTK system to include both fire and blast damage.

Shortly after Brode left RDA for PSR in 1979, he began fundamental research to describe and model mass fire from nuclear weapons. Brode, along with his younger colleagues at PSR, Richard Small and Dale Larson, did most of this work under FEMA contract. Why FEMA? Because after leaving RDA, Brode "needed support right away," and FEMA was willing to fund him.[19]

It would be hard to overemphasize the break with past research inherent in Brode's approach, both in conception and in method. Decades of work by the fire research community had emphasized the similarity of mass fires to more common urban and forest fires, focused on detailed mechanisms of ignition and fire spread, and analyzed the plume rising above very large fires but not the inrushing hurricane-speed winds.

By contrast, in a study completed in March 1980, *Physics of Large Urban Fires,* Brode and Small emphasized "the unique properties of large area fires," focused on the macroscopic features, and made the inrushing winds a crucial part of their model. They approached mass fire as a large physical system dominated by the physics of heat release and fluid flow. They pointed to "the special significance of the scale of the event [in regard to] the physical dimensions and spatial heat release." These large area fires, or mass fires, "caused by multiple ignition points imply completely different physical phenomena than line fires."[20]

Instead of detailed descriptions of how conventional urban fires ignited and spread through rooms and buildings and across buildings, Brode and Small assumed that over a large area there would be a vast number of ignitions and concentrated instead on "those macroscopic features of urban type mass fires that set them apart from other fire experiences."[21] They strove for

> a general fire model which will predict the fire environment in a large section of an urban area, assuming that a given area is involved and a given fraction of the combustible structures are burning. The complexity involved in urban fire spread would thus be avoided. . . . Based on hydrodynamic and thermodynamic principles, a self-consistent physical model should be constructed which accounts for the unique properties of large-area fires.[22]

Brode and Small's fire model featured three components: (1) a large volume of heated air in the combustion zone; (2) "a violent, buoyant rise of air

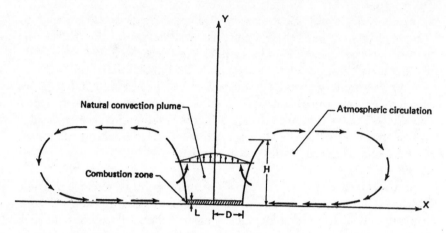

Figure 9.1. Harold Brode and Richard Small's schematic cross-section (slightly modified) of large area (mass) fire: combustion zone, convection plume, and atmospheric circulation causing inrushing winds. L = height of combustion zone; D = radius subject to fire; H = plume height. Source: R. D. Small and H. L. Brode, *Physics of Large Urban Fires*, PSR Report 1010, final report prepared for Federal Emergency Management Agency (Santa Monica, Calif.: Pacific-Sierra Research Corp., March 1980), p. 23, fig. 6.

and combustion products from the burning zone"; and (3) a large-scale re-circulation of the atmosphere outside the immediate area of the mass fire—a "recirculation flow field"—sucking hurricane-like winds back into the fire zone. Once in the fire zone, these winds would heat up, rise, and circulate back again (see Figure 9.1).[23]

Atmospheric circulation had not been seriously considered in earlier analyses by the fire research community, but, in Brode and Small's view, "its inclusion is essential in order to calculate the fire winds . . . and hence the rate of combustion." The recirculation flow field "accounts for the high velocity winds characteristic of firestorms observed in WW II fire bombings."[24] Brode explained the importance of these winds in a report later that year to DNA:

> Perhaps the most unusual and important consequence is the extremely high winds rushing into the burning region, further increasing burning rates. Such winds may exceed any experienced in natural meteorology. Indeed, the flames near the periphery may be laid nearly flat by the inrushing winds. Exceedingly fierce burning rates may result in the total combustion of all fuels within the fire area and the melting or destruction of many noncombustible structural materials.[25]

Brode and Small used a set of classical equations describing heat and fluid flow to predict the effects of the enormous amount of heat released into the atmosphere from a large burning area and the resulting upward flow of air. (Air, a gas, is considered to be a compressible fluid.) Gas, or fluid, dynamics describe a large number of phenomena, including the implosion within a nuclear weapon, traffic flows, heat rising in the atmosphere, and the propagation of nuclear blast waves. Generally, the equations that describe the physics for these phenomena cannot be solved exactly (i.e., they are not "closed-form" equations); instead, the solutions have to be approximated using iterative numerical methods, or "number crunching" on computers.

Using numerical methods, Brode and Small estimated the heat produced by the many ignitions in an urban mass fire, and then predicted what the temperature, air pressure, density, and air flow would be at various times and locations as the hot air rose. (At five minutes after ignition, one would estimate the temperature, air pressure, density, and air flow inside and outside the rising column of heated air at 50 feet above the ground, at 100, 200, 400 feet, and so on; at ten minutes after ignition, one would estimate the same variables at the same locations; etc.) To predict the values of these variables through time and space, each calculation depended on the one before—a "step-wise" or "time-marching" procedure "through a set of partial difference equations representing fluid or gas dynamics."[26] This involved many computations and cross-checks to ensure consistent results.

It was not until Brode went to PSR in early 1979 that he "[got] seriously into numerical calculations of large fires." Brode, Small, and a few others took a hydrodynamic code "generally available from Los Alamos [national laboratory]" and modified it specifically for the physics of mass fire: "All of the fire physics, equations of state for air and combustion products, and the balanced atmosphere had to be built in or added as subroutines."[27]

Could Brode have done this years before, or would it have been impossible given the lesser capacity of early computers? Brode said the basic computer programs he used were "the typical . . . hydrodynamics and radiation codes developed for bomb design work at the weapons labs and elsewhere to explore blast wave phenomena" decades earlier. Brode himself had pioneered such programs to model the blast environment in the 1950s. "By modern capabilities, my original programs (circa 1953–1968) were primitive," Brode said. "But both the blast calculation codes and the fire circulation calculations were basically numerical hydrodynamic (time-marching) programs."[28] In other words, although the programs he later used to model the fire physics environment were more sophisticated, the earlier programs could, at least in theory, have been used to develop a simple model.

Why did others not do similar modeling? According to Brode, the fire research community was "aware of the role of fire-induced winds—that's not anything new. Hamburg, Dresden, Hiroshima . . . dramatically illustrated that." But they had not had access to the early hydrodynamic codes developed in the weapons laboratories, nor to the later ones:

> The computer codes sufficiently sophisticated and powerful to accommodate the fire physics were not generally available. The weapons labs had enormous efforts going on code development, and it took me more than two years at RAND [1951–1953] to build mine. . . . By the time we got around to modeling the flow fields around mass fires, the codes had evolved into much more than my pioneering models. Still, some of the old fire researchers did not seem to have access to the modern computational tools, and their work seems to reflect that lack.[29]

Moreover, Brode said these computational tools were "not considered by the classical fire researchers as relevant or useful. . . . Actually, I think that most fire researchers were dependent on experiments—lab fires, room and house fires, and on the history of large fires."[30]

In mid-March 1980, Brode and Small asked DNA to fund a four-year program of fire research. The proposed program was substantial in terms of fire research, but from DNA's perspective, fire and other "neglected effects" were "not a major part of the budget. . . . Experiments were big money. Brode was not big money."[31] A DNA official explained that the underground testing program was "the crown jewel" of DNA's research program; also very important were studies on missile basing and silo hardness. "Those were important at DNA, big things. Fires weren't even cats and dogs—maybe just a cat."[32]

Brode and Small proposed four main research priorities: (1) model the large area fire environment, which PSR had already begun under FEMA sponsorship; (2) determine whether blast would extinguish a developing mass fire, as many in the fire research community thought; (3) develop models to predict fire spread from building to building; (4) develop procedures—algorithms—to predict damage from mass fires ignited by nuclear weapons.[33] The program reflected both Brode's own concerns with understanding the physics of fire and developing the ability to predict fire damage in U.S. nuclear war planning and the fire research community's concerns with blast–fire interaction, fire spread, weather, and so on. It was not a coincidence that Brode and Small proposed such an inclusive program. Given the fire research community's understanding that fire damage was not predictable, Brode thought a successful strategy would require

> an exhaustive modeling of every factor that was reputed to have an influence on fire damage: weather and climate effects (such as rain, snow,

heat, humidity, cloud cover above the burst or between the burst and the targets), fuel ignition variations, mitigation efforts (fire fighting and fire prevention), blast influences on fire such as blowing out ignitions or spreading ignited material, multiple window panes, influences of fire-generated winds on fire spread, etc.[34]

By March 1980 Brode and Small had a well-developed intuition of their later findings. First, they were impressed by the magnitude of fire damage. Even in the hedged, passive voice of scientific writing, their point was clear: "In many cases, damage from fire is anticipated to be greater and more encompassing than that from blast or nuclear radiation. It may also be that fires thus created can be far more devastating than any previous experience would lead us to believe." Second, contrary to common belief, they thought weather conditions would have little effect on the magnitude or predictability of mass fire. Finally, they were optimistic that a method for predicting damage from mass fire could be developed. "It is our conclusion that a well balanced careful research program can lead to a fire damage algorithm which could a priori predict potential target damage. . . . On the basis of our analysis, we anticipate that a predictive model that would enable calculation of thermal effects could be developed in five years."[35]

DNA accepted most of Brode's proposal and drew up a five-year plan of fire research to begin in the fall of 1981. DNA planned to fund research on the effects of weather, multiple bursts, and other variables on the development of mass fire and on initial conditions such as the distribution of "primary" and "secondary" fires, ignition thresholds, and blast–fire interaction. The greatest emphasis, however, was on the development of a fire damage model and the capability to predict fire damage to specific targets.[36] PSR received funding from DNA to study fire and other "neglected effects." At the same time, DNA's fire research program funded others and helped to revive the fire research community (see chapter 10).[37]

"A Simple Targeting Study"

At the same time that Brode, Small, and Larson began to model the physics of mass fire, Brode also began a pilot study funded by DNA to predict the damage that would result from nuclear use. This meant translating the results of their physical model—such as predictions of heat release rates and wind velocity—into the terms of nuclear targeting: Under given conditions, at what range would selected targets be damaged with a given probability? For example, if a 1-megaton bomb burst near the earth's surface on a clear day, at what range would typical urban industrial structures be severely damaged by fire with a 50 percent probability? How would the range of damage change if the bomb were detonated at various heights, under a variety of weather conditions, or if the probability of severe damage were set at 10 percent or 90 percent?[38]

From 1978 to 1983 Brode and his colleagues undertook "a simple targeting study" to examine "the possible consequences of including fire damage in [urban/industrial] targeting and damage assessments."[39] They tried to predict fire damage to structures from a 50-kiloton burst and a 1-megaton burst under various conditions. The study was briefed to DNA, reported to the JSTPS Scientific Advisory Group, and published as a DNA technical report, *Fire Damage and Strategic Targeting*, in June 1983.[40]

In this study, Brode and Small calculated the probability of fire damage on the basis of three sources of ignition: (1) direct exposure of materials to thermal radiation through uncovered windows, which would lead to rapid fire spread throughout an entire structure; (2) blast-induced disruptions such as ignitions resulting "from the spilling of volatile liquids located in industrial, commercial, and residential structures or vehicles, or from the disruption of hot or molten materials, sparks near volatile or explosive fuels, gas line ruptures, short circuits, reacting chemical mixtures, etc."; and (3) fire spread from one building to another, such as that caused by firebrands, or burning material, breaking off from one structure and carried by high winds to another.[41]

Brode and Small's nomenclature changed with this report. Earlier, they had used the term "primary ignitions" to mean thermal radiation–induced ignitions and "secondary ignitions" to mean blast-induced ignitions. Now they stopped using the terms "primary" and "secondary" ignitions in an effort to convey the holism of a mass fire: thermal ignition, blast disruption, and fire spread all inevitably occurred and all were important.

The focus on ignition sources may seem similar to the earlier calculations done by researchers at the Illinois Institute of Technology Research Institute (IITRI) on the probabilities of primary ignitions, secondary ignitions, and fire spread (discussed in chapter 8), but it was fundamentally different in that Brode and Small used a larger-scale, or regional, model that included the effects of fire-induced winds. This physical model then provided the framework into which they fit calculations of the probabilities of different types of ignitions.

Brode chose to present his findings in terms of ignitions from thermal radiation, blast disruption, and fire spread rather than at the aggregated regional level—a deliberate and effective rhetorical strategy. Casting PSR's results in terms familiar to those in the fire research community enabled Brode to address their concerns directly; it provided the framework within which he presented the results of his "exhaustive modeling."

Brode's rhetorical strategy did something else very important: Estimates of probabilities of specific damage mechanisms provided an apparent specificity similar to predictions of blast damage in the VNTK system, in which mechanisms of blast damage were differentiated into damage primarily from overpressure (P-type targets) or from dynamic pressure (Q-type targets). (By contrast, physicist Ted Postol, at Stanford University in the mid-1980s, working only with unclassified data and with fewer resources, focused on the physics of mass fire and the resulting total burnout within a large area. Postol cast his results in terms of the area within which mass fire would rage. To estimate the area, he used simple measures—the thermal fluence deposited at the outer edge of mass fire at Hiroshima, approximately 10 cal/cm^2, and, closer to the detonation, double the thermal energy, 20 cal/cm^2. Postol's rule-of-thumb measures had the virtue of encapsulating the physics of mass fire in a way that could be easily understood. His understanding of the physics of mass fire was the same as Brode's, and his aggregate results very similar. His approach, however, did not meet the requirements for specificity in the internal government debate.)

PSR's work on fire damage in the early 1980s was roughly analogous to the researchers' work of the early 1950s on blast damage. First, just as the physics of the blast environment had been translated into predictions of overpressure at various ranges ("effect to range"), so were the physics of mass fire translated by Brode and Small into predictions of thermal fluence at various ranges. Very rough estimates of thermal fluence had been done before, but the modeling of the physics of mass fire was new, as was Brode and Small's extensive sensitivity analysis to predict thermal fluence under varying conditions: different yields, burst heights, visibility conditions ranging from 1 to 50 miles, weather conditions such as snow or cloud cover above the burst or clouds below the burst, and possible civil defense measures.[42]

Second, just as Newmark had characterized the response of structures to overpressure and predicted the overpressures at which severe damage would occur, so too did Brode and Small characterize urban-industrial structures and the conditions under which thermal ignitions, blast-induced ignitions, and fire spread would cause severe fire damage. Just as Newmark's analysis of structural response was a prerequisite for the development of the VN system itself, so too did Brode and Small's early characterization of fire vulnerability precede the development of a system for predicting fire damage.

That is not to say that Brode and Small's work in the 1980s was as rudimentary as the work on blast damage in the 1950s. Nor is it to say that fire damage could not have been predicted long before. Reflecting on the earlier history, Brode thought predictions of fire damage comparable to blast damage could have been developed much earlier.

At the time Dick Grassy first made his "cookie cutter" calculations of blast damage in 1948?

"Yes, yes, of course."

At the time the first VN system was published in 1954?

"I cannot think of any reason why not."

At the time the first VNTK handbook was published in 1958?

"I think that all elements of fire damage VNs were known or could have been developed in the [late] 1950s . . . or early 1960s."[43]

But the standard was different two decades later: Fire prediction would require the sophistication not of the early VN system but of the far more refined VNTK system of the 1980s.

In this initial study, Brode and Small made simple but not unreasonable assumptions that conformed to historical data on Hiroshima and other mass fire attacks in World War II.[44] To estimate thermal ignitions, they assumed "a homogenous building type and uniform vulnerability . . . throughout the target area" and then designated thresholds for "sustained ignition" leading to full-scale fires.[45] For a 50-kiloton weapon, they assumed this ignition threshold to be 16 cal/cm^2, and for a 1-megaton bomb, they assumed it to be 22 cal/cm^2.[46] (The threshold was slightly higher for the 1-megaton bomb because higher-yield weapons deliver peak thermal energy more slowly than lower-yield weapons, causing slightly less damage for the same deposition of thermal energy.)[47] Given that the edge of mass fire of the approximately 20-kiloton bomb detonated at Hiroshima occurred at a threshold of about 10 cal/cm^2, these were conservative estimates.

For fires started by blast disruptions, Brode and Small made estimates based on recent work by fire researchers and used established indices of combustibility for typical urban building types and contents.[48] In an early briefing to DNA, Brode reported that in combining estimates of ignitions from thermal radiation and blast disruption for typical cases, he found that variation in weather, including "variations in cloud cover, snow cover and intervening clouds make relatively little difference since the secondary [blast disruption] fires act as a safety net below which the probability for fire damage will not fall."[49]

PSR's estimates for fire spread from building to building were even simpler; they assumed that "the probability of fire damage at any radius is doubled when spread is included. Thus, if 50 percent of the structures are burning, it is assumed that the fire will spread to all adjacent structures."[50] When added to the other two sources of ignition, this led to overall fire damage estimates that were broadly consistent with the historical data on damage from atomic bombing.

The combination of all three sources of ignition also meant that civil defense measures made relatively little difference in the range of fire. Even assuming that thermal ignitions could be "greatly reduced by some preparations [such as] removing flammable window coverings" and that blast-disruption fires could be halved "by turning off electricity and gas and removing cars, trucks and buses (because they have volatile fuels in them), putting out furnaces and all fires or pilot sources and shutting down industry and transportation," the overall probability of fires from thermal ignition, blast disruption, and fire spread meant that civil defense measures produced "only a rather modest reduction" in the range of fire.[51]

By 1983, Brode and Small could make simple predictions of the range of fire damage using the three major sources of ignition—thermal, blast disruption, and fire spread—and they had found that these predictions did not vary greatly when the many sources of variation, including yield, height of burst, snow, clouds, and civil defense measures, were taken into account. Uncertainties remained; there could be surprises when more variables were analyzed. Further, the characterization of targets was crude: they were all treated as "average" structures. Finally, Brode and Small had not yet developed a fire damage algorithm, let alone one that looked comparable to, or compatible with, the blast VNTK system. At this point, they did not know whether they would develop a separate designation for fire damage (fire vulnerability numbers) or a scheme that combined with the existing VNTK system and included both fire and blast damage (fire-blast vulnerability numbers). The choice would depend on whether they could translate PSR's results into the existing terms of the VNTK system. Still, Brode and Small thought the uncertainties were bounded, and they were optimistic that a procedure to predict fire damage could be developed.[52]

Brode and Small also emphasized that because fire damage had been left out of the VNTK system, the effects of nuclear weapons had been systematically underestimated: "In general, fire damage radii exceed those for moderate blast damage. . . . In addition . . . fire may cause more complete and permanent damage. A structure only moderately damaged by blast may be gutted and rendered useless by fire. Similarly, building contents may survive the blast but be destroyed by the fires." They concluded their study with an unusually frank and mordant critique of U.S. targeting procedures:

> The explicit exclusion of population, living space, and commercial and cultural edifices in targeting is at best confusing, since such nontargets are not avoided, and so are implicitly included, even though never counted in assessments of value destroyed. Both blast and fire will damage targets (industrial sites) and nontargets (apartments); but fire will generally go farther and cause more complete damage to both. . . . If "moderate damage" to "steel frame" buildings is the appropriate guide for destroying a city of a million or more inhabitants, then fire can only complete the job more effectively.[53]

We can cast this history in organizational terms. Unlike the research on blast damage, initiated by those in the government and understood to be a predictable phenomenon, the research on mass fire was initiated by a well-connected outside expert who had to convince those in the government that fire damage could be predicted at all. At first, Brode did not seek to alter the blast damage frame and organizational routines of DIA and JSTPS, but to change the knowledge base that underlay their approach to problem solving. Brode and his colleagues Small and Larson modeled the physics of the larger fire environment in a way broadly parallel to Brode's description of the blast environment in the 1950s. Their results, however, ran contrary to decades of accumulated understanding within the fire research and nuclear weapons effects communities that mass fire was not predictable. By establishing a robust model of the physics of mass fire, Brode began to make a case that the organizations concerned with nuclear war planning should broaden their approach to problem solving to include predictions of fire damage. Fire damage could not count as a problem unless and until it could be represented as a problem that could be solved.

Once he had modeled mass fire, Brode's strategy was to translate the physics into terms relevant to nuclear war planning. He modeled damage mechanisms and estimated their effects on specific targets. Brode and Small's *Fire Damage and Strategic Targeting* claimed that the mechanisms of damage—ignitions caused by thermal radiation, blast disruption, and fire spread, especially in the aggregate—were relatively insensitive to variations in weather and other conditions. This provided one requirement for solution: that the range of uncertainty be bounded and the predictions stable. The study did not, however, meet other requirements for a solution: It did not describe the structures themselves in detail or by type, nor did it provide an algorithm to predict fire damage.

Where There's Smoke There's Fire

Nuclear Winter

Shortly after Brode and Small completed their targeting study on nuclear fire damage for DNA, public controversy erupted over the potentially catastrophic consequences of nuclear war on the global climate. The catalyst was the article "Nuclear Winter: Global Consequences of Multiple Nuclear Explosions," published in *Science* in late December 1983. Its five authors were Richard Turco, Owen Toon, Thomas Ackerman, Jonathan Pollack, and Carl Sagan—often collectively referred to as TTAPS.

Nuclear winter was predicated on fire caused by nuclear detonations. The central claim was that in a number of possible scenarios of nuclear war, the large fires set in cities and in nonurban areas could loft vast clouds of black smoke and dust that would absorb or scatter so much sunlight that the surface of the earth would be darkened and chilled to catastrophically cold temperatures: "even in summer, subfreezing land temperatures" could persist "for months." These and other drastic climatic effects could severely disrupt agriculture, affect animal life, "place severe stresses on the global ecosystem," and "pose a serious threat to human survivors and to other species."[54]

Despite the public brouhaha over nuclear winter—one of the most publicized science policy controversies of the decade—and that few people knew of Hal Brode's work to predict fire damage from nuclear weapons, the two were connected. The authors drew to some extent on Brode's work. There were also strong professional connections between some of the authors and Brode and others at PSR. Finally, the public controversy over nuclear winter would lead to greater government funding of research on nuclear fire damage.

The climate modeling study that formed the core of the nuclear winter study was influenced by the scientific backgrounds of the co-authors: (Sagan and Pollack) in planetary science, (Toon) in physics, (Turco) in physics and electrical engineering, and (Ackerman) in climate.[55] Both Pollack and Toon had been graduate students of Sagan; Pollack had become a distinguished senior scientist at NASA's Ames Research Center. At the time of the study, Turco was at RDA in Southern California; Toon and Ackerman worked in Pollack's group at the Ames Research Center in Northern California; and Sagan was at Cornell University. The nuclear winter study was informed by Sagan and Pollack's earlier study of a large global dust storm on Mars and by the Alvarez hypothesis that dust raised by a meteor impact had cooled the earth's climate and caused the extinction of dinosaurs. By the spring of 1982, the authors had begun to estimate the properties and effects of the dust that could be raised into the atmosphere in a nuclear war. Their attention expanded beyond dust as they learned of a forthcoming study to be published in mid-1982 in a special issue of *Ambio*, an environmental science and policy journal, on the effects of global nuclear war. The article, by the atmospheric chemists Paul Crutzen and John Birks, was subtitled "Twilight at Noon" and described the smoke that would result from a nuclear war, particularly from forest fires and oil and gas well fires. The article did not receive wide public attention at the time, but later was considered to be the first of the nuclear winter studies.[56]

The nuclear winter debate of the early 1980s coincided with the Reagan administration's suggestion that nuclear war was winnable—with "enough shovels" and a "Star Wars" defense against incoming missiles.[57] Critics sought to show the American public that nuclear war would have dire effects. Jonathan Schell published his eloquent *The Fate of the Earth* in 1982, and the organizations Ground Zero and Physicians for Social Responsibility launched public mobilization campaigns. Policy prescriptions included the U.S. Catholic Bishops' 1983 pastoral letter on war and peace, the nuclear freeze campaign, and, inside the beltway, campaigns for no-first-use, deep cuts, and build-down.[58]

Nuclear winter was very much part of this political stew, providing perhaps the single most vivid image of the dire consequences of nuclear war. Turco, Toon, and Ackerman began the study, but it was their famous co-author, Carl Sagan, who effectively crafted a strategy to gain maximum political impact. That strategy was to publish serious science, aim for wide scientific interest and endorsement, make policy recommendations that went beyond the science, and energetically publicize both the science and policy implications.[59]

Shortly after the article in *Science* was published, Sagan spelled out policy implications in *Foreign Affairs*.[60] While the *Science* article clearly acknowledged the uncertainties of the authors' climate change model, and couched its findings in the "coulds," "mays," and "can alsos" of scientific writing, Sagan's article in *Foreign Affairs*, "Nuclear War and Climatic Catastrophe," sounded far more certain: "The study . . . for the first time demonstrates that severe and prolonged low temperatures would follow a nuclear war. . . . The new results have been subjected to detailed scrutiny, and half a dozen confirmatory calculations have now been made. A special panel appointed by the National Academy of Sciences to examine this problem has come to similar conclusions."[61] While the *Science* article said there may be a low "threshold for major optical and climatic consequences" that could cause massive smoke emissions and subfreezing land temperatures, Sagan said "A threshold exists at which the climatic catastrophe could be triggered." This, he wrote, leads to "one apparently inescapable conclusion: the necessity of moving as rapidly as possible . . . to a small percentage of the present global strategic arsenals."[62]

Although Sagan's strong statements incurred the wrath of some fellow scientists, the carefully couched climate modeling effort and the boldly stated policy recommendations worked as a piece. Without the science, the policy positions would have had far less force; without the public relations effort orchestrated by Sagan, the science would likely have remained obscure.

There are striking differences and some similarities between the public nuclear winter campaign and Brode's partly classified research program to predict nuclear fire damage.

Sagan was playing an "outside game," aiming at large audiences: the public, the scientific community, and government staffers and officials who read, or read about, articles in *Science*.[63] The purpose of the nuclear winter campaign was to make vivid the possible effects of fighting a nuclear war. The ultimate goal was not to provide a basis for war planning or war policy, but to build public and political support for deep cuts in the U.S. nuclear weapons arsenal and to turn opinion against programs such as the Star Wars "shield" first advocated by President Reagan in March 1983. Nuclear winter modeled global effects that were necessarily speculative.

By contrast, Brode was engaged in an "inside game." His audience was the nuclear weapons effects community: several government agencies such as DNA, DIA, JSTPS; a small number of government-funded researchers; and a few university-based researchers attentive to such issues. In contrast to the mighty news coverage of nuclear winter, a computer search of newspapers in the 1980s produced not a single contemporary news story on Brode's work on the physics of mass fire or on the prediction of fire damage. Brode aimed to help the government better understand nuclear weapons effects to provide a sounder basis for policy and war planning.[64] Brode's scope was not global but regional, which could be modeled with more confidence.

Yet these efforts did not exist in different worlds. The nuclear winter study published in *Science* aimed to model nuclear weapons effects and to influence government policy. The study calculated that nuclear weapons would cause widespread fires in forests and, especially, in cities (the most important source of black sooty smoke); TTAPS cited, among others, the work of Brode and his colleagues. However, TTAPS did not draw in depth on Brode's studies, positing conservatively that there would be "fire storms" in only 5 percent of urban fires, whereas Brode predicted "mass fire" in "almost any nuclear attack on a city (as . . . in Hiroshima and Nagasaki)."[65]

There were personal connections as well. Turco worked in the physics department at RDA that Brode headed from 1971 to 1979. Indeed, Turco and Sagan asked Brode if he wanted to participate in the original nuclear winter study, but Brode was skeptical about what he later termed "the nuclear winter doomsday hooha."[66]

Brode, however, was not uninterested in issues of dust and smoke effects from nuclear weapons. In the mid-1970s, he and a colleague at RDA had tried to estimate how much dust and smoke would be lofted into the atmosphere and whether it would be enough to affect the sunlight reaching the earth. "Even with the vast uncertainties involving lofting, particle sizes, dwell time, distribution, [and] optical properties" significantly diminished sunlight "did not look to us as sufficiently probable to merit . . . immediate attention. . . . Rather than play Chicken Little, we opted to wait for better data."[67]

Brode lacked confidence in the calculations that provided the basis for

nuclear winter, but he was concerned about public understanding of the devastation to urban areas that nuclear weapons could wreak. Indeed, he had
been an advisor for the November 1983 ABC television movie, *The Day After*, about the effects of a nuclear attack on Lawrence, Kansas. Brode, however, had been an "unsuccessful advisor"; he had "tried to get them to
represent some of the effects more realistically," but the makers understated
them and he withdrew his name as a consultant.[68]

The public and congressional interest in nuclear winter had consequences for government funding of fire research. By mid-1984 DNA had established a Global Effects Program to fund research on nuclear winter and
related effects, including fire. Total annual funding for the program went as
high as $5 million.[69]

The First Fire VN

DNA's research agenda had been influenced by a briefing Brode gave in
January 1984, just a few weeks after the nuclear winter article in *Science*.
Brode provided a detailed overview of the fire research that had been funded
by DNA so far, and he proposed a multiyear, multimillion dollar program
for fire research. Though still concerned with modeling the physics of mass
fire—including, not coincidentally, predicting smoke generation from nuclear fires—Brode was now far more focused on a program to develop "fire
damage algorithms" and then a "fire VN system" comparable to the blast
VN (i.e., VNTK) system.[70] For Brode and his team, the increased funding
by DNA "opened up a few million dollars of research . . . into the global effects . . . oriented toward fires to some extent. And we profited from that a
little."[71] Some of the funds supported work by Brode's team at PSR on nuclear winter; joining the scholarly debate in *Science*, *Ambio*, and other publications, the team arrived at estimates of smoke emission that were not
nearly as great as those in the TTAPS study.[72] These same funds also supported Brode's research to develop a method to predict fire damage from nuclear weapons.[73]

In October 1985 Brode developed the first fire VN for commercial and
residential structures. In an exploratory study, Brode reanalyzed the atomic
fire damage to four typical types of residential and commercial structures at
Hiroshima and Nagasaki and compared that damage to predicted blast
damage to similar structures. These structures ranged from vulnerable single-story wood-frame buildings to strong multistory reinforced-concrete
structures. Brode concluded that all of the structures were as vulnerable to
severe fire damage as the most vulnerable single-story wood-frame building
was to severe blast damage alone.[74] For a 200-kiloton nuclear weapon,
strong multistory residential complexes that were predicted to sustain severe

blast damage at a range of 0.9 miles from the detonation would be vulnerable to severe fire damage at a range of 2.2 miles from the detonation.[75] On this basis, Brode assigned all structures the same VN as the most vulnerable structure to blast damage, 6Po.[76]

This was not, strictly speaking, a fire VN, or, more accurately, a fire-blast VN, but a translation of predictions of fire damage into the terms of the blast VN system. For the first time, however, Brode realized that he could modify the VNTK system into one that would include predictions of both blast damage and fire damage.

> I just put it together in pieces . . . by just empirically taking a bunch of yields and seeing what each one gave and then finding if they were averageable . . . to give an adjusted [fire] VN. . . . And I was really gratified. . . . The nicest part about the invention is that I was able to couch it in precisely the same terms they currently used for the blast VNs by simply changing the VNs to accommodate fire damage, which made it more understandable and more acceptable, both at DIA and JSTPS. . . . So, if there's any ingenuity to it, it's just that we have refused to change the system.[77]

Real Targets and High-Level Briefings

The Fifty-Target Study

An important new phase of work began in 1988. Under contract to DNA, and in close cooperation with two other government agencies, Brode and others at PSR began to develop VNs that would, for the first time, account for both blast and fire damage to a set of almost fifty "example installations"; that is, actual structures targeted in U.S. nuclear war plans that were typical of many similar structures.[78] (These VNs always included both fire damage and blast damage. They were sometimes called "fire VNs," or, more accurately, "fire-blast VNs" or "FBVNs.") According to Brode, the new phase of work "aimed at the targeting issue: how to include fire damage in assessing nuclear damage to particular targets. The trick was to look at particular installations rather than at a city or area."[79]

DIA and JSTPS joined DNA in the fire targeting research. An earlier ad hoc working group from the three agencies had agreed that for future work incorporating fire damage into nuclear war planning, JSTPS would nominate a set of targets, DIA would concur, and DNA would "develop a vulnerability characterization" of those targets.[80] The arrangement made organizational and political sense: Predicting fire damage from nuclear weapons would not be meaningful in an organizational context unless it solved a problem that those responsible thought should be solved. DNA supported research on nuclear weapons effects, and this included any research that would be required to revise the VNTK system. Part of the job of DNA officials was to see that the research they supported "met perceived needs" at government agencies concerned with nuclear weapons issues.[81] The agency was "always . . . on the lookout" for "customers" to justify the investment by DNA.[82]

The "customers" for fire research were JSTPS and DIA. JSTPS drew up the actual plans for waging nuclear war: the Single Integrated Operational Plan (SIOP). Officers at JSTPS decided which weapons went where and when, and they relied on DIA's characterizations of target vulnerability to do so. DIA maintained and updated target databases, including the VNTK designations of target vulnerability.

Both DIA and JSTPS would have to be convinced that predicting fire damage was a good idea: a problem they wanted to solve and could solve. They would have to be convinced that predictions would be valid and could be integrated into their organizational routines. (Cost considerations would come later: If an algorithm to predict fire damage could be developed for organizational use, would the benefits of more accurate prediction outweigh the costs in terms of time and budget?)

Of course, the cooperation did not happen by itself. According to Brode, Eugene Sevin, an assistant deputy director at DNA, "made it happen"; he "brought it all together at the working group level" and then saw it through at higher levels. This, said Brode, "required considerable tact. . . . Gene was outstanding."[83]

By early 1988, JSTPS and DIA had agreed on the set of example targets, and in February 1988, Brode and his colleagues at PSR—George Fisher, Peter Konopka, Armas Laupa, and Gene McClellan—began their analysis under contract to DNA. This was the real thing: If it proved feasible to develop "fire-blast" VNs for this many targets, it could be the beginning of the inclusion of fire damage in the routines used in nuclear targeting. Fire-blast VNs could affect how targeteers went about planning nuclear war, including both "the designation of ground zeros and burst heights for weapon laydowns" and "damage assessment" (i.e., how the expected damage from those plans would be evaluated in the absence of actual use).[84]

The study marked an important step in the implementation of a new organizational approach to damage prediction. It demonstrated for the first time that fire damage could be predicted for a small number of "real" targets and that the prediction could be grafted onto the VNTK system using the "same numerology and terminology."[85]

The two-volume analysis, *Fire Damage to Urban/Industrial Targets*, was published in July 1989. The unclassified version of this remarkable document provides the fullest available description of government-sponsored research showing the much greater magnitude of damage from combined fire and blast effects than from blast effects alone. Analysts at PSR examined the fire vulnerability of open fields and forested areas and forty-one of the original forty-eight targets designated for study. The targets included oil storage and distribution facilities; nuclear weapons storage sites; manufacturing facilities; energy production and transmission facilities; heavy industrial facilities; leadership, training, and control facilities; residential complexes; ammunition depots and military repair installations; and railroad yards.[86]

Brode and researchers at PSR analyzed each installation individually and exhaustively. DIA supplied the required information on each installation: for example, "What's the floor space? How many floors is it? Can we determine how much window fraction is on the outside?"[87] Based on their earlier work modeling the physics of mass fire and their simple targeting study of the early 1980s, Brode and his colleagues developed computer programs to calculate for each target the probability that the structure would be severely damaged by fire. As Brode and Small had done five years earlier, the PSR team calculated the probability of fire on the basis of three ignition sources— direct exposure to thermal radiation, blast disruption, and fire spread from one building to another—and then combined these into an overall probability of fire damage. They then combined the probability of fire damage with the probability of severe damage from blast, already encoded in the blast VNTK system, and came up with a combined fire-blast vulnerability number (FBVNTK).

Variations in many conditions would affect the probability of fire damage. For this study, Brode and his colleagues expanded their examination from the nine variables in the 1983 targeting study, which had included visibility, snow or cloud cover, and possible civil defense measures, to more than fifty. These variables included some easily determined, such as the type of installation, building height, distance to neighboring structures, and VN for severe blast damage, as well as some more difficult to estimate, such as the percentage of windows in external walls and internal ignitables and atmospheric conditions.[88]

To average out the variations in the conditions that could affect the probability of fire, for each target the computer program calculated the probability of fire damage "at each of a series of ground ranges (every tenth of a nautical mile), for five burst heights (from 1 to 700 feet scaled height of burst [SHOB]), . . . for eight yields (from 20 KT [kilotons] to 5 MT [megatons])" and for "three protective activity levels potentially able to mitigate fire damage (none, some, and heroic)."[89]

Brode defined "no mitigation" as no measures taken to make structures or cities less flammable. He defined "some, or moderate, mitigation" as "when you do the best you can but still keep things operating. The lights are on and the fires are lit and so forth," but window shades would be down and "you've cleaned up as best you can." Heroic mitigation was when "you . . . really shut things down and cover things up": Almost all structures would be emptied of fuel, and cars and trucks would be moved away "so you wouldn't have vehicle fires being spread to the structure."[90]

Heroic mitigation might not quite replicate the efforts made in the atmospheric nuclear weapons tests at shots ANNIE and APPLE-2 in the 1950s, when structures not only had been stripped of appliances and emptied of fuel but painted white and built of fire-resistant materials, but it was the same general idea. The ostensibly technical term, "heroic mitigation," slyly indicated Brode's skepticism about achieving such a level of protective activity. Brode thought even a "moderate" level of mitigation would understate fire damage and that "no mitigation" was the most realistic of the scenarios. He reported results for each level of mitigation and for the average of all three.[91]

Calculating the effects of relevant parameters on each target at varying ground range, height of burst, yield, and mitigation level "amount[ed] to 5,000 to 20,000 separate calculations of the fire probabilities for each target." In addition, like the K factor indicating how blast damage varied with yield, developed in the 1950s, Brode determined a K factor for the fire-blast VN that indicated how fire and blast damage varied with yield.[92]

Based on the thousands of calculations and the new K factor, Brode derived an average fire-blast VN over all burst heights and levels of mitigation for each target.[93] The detailed executive summary was presented in the unclassified but coded terms of blast VNs and fire-blast VNs. The lower the VN, the more vulnerable the target and the greater the range of damage. The authors found that, overall, the combined fire-blast VN was less than half of the blast VN. In the understated language of the unclassified report, the comparison "leads to the observation that inclusion of fire damage can make a significant increase in the vulnerability of many urban targets."[94]

These were dramatic results. As summarized the next year in an authoritative independent study for DNA: "Current DNA sponsored research indicates fire damage may be no more uncertain than is airblast for selected types of targets. . . . The evolving fire damage methodology is exhibiting damage radii which are 2 to 5 times larger than determined for airblast effects"[95]—that is, areas damaged by fire are 4 to 25 times larger than by blast alone.

We can understand the results more vividly by examining the damage to groups of specific targets. One group consisted of nine typical manufacturing facilities. These facilities included plants making power equipment, ball bearings, "miscellaneous" research and development equipment, electronic components, tractors, radios, and computers.[96] Brode's analysis showed that, for a 300-kiloton bomb burst near the surface, if only blast damage were taken into account, on average these facilities would be severely damaged when subjected to 19.2 psi, which would occur a mile from the detonation. However, when damage from fire was also included (assuming average mitigation), these same installations were far more vulnerable: They would be severely damaged by fire and blast at a fraction of the overpressure, just 2.8 psi, and at distances more than three times as far from the detonation, 3.1 miles.[97] In other words, Brode's fire-blast VN predicted severe damage to manufacturing structures within an area almost ten times greater than when damage from blast alone was considered. (The area increases by the square of the radius.)

The difference, of course, resulted from the physics of mass fire—the bomb's vast output of heat that would cause a multitude of ignitions, rising air, atmospheric recirculation, and winds rushing back into the fire area. At 1.0 mile from ground zero, the distance at which the government's VNTK methodology predicted severe damage by blast, the deposition of thermal fluence on structures and surroundings would be 280 cal/cm^2, about twenty-eight times the thermal fluence at the outer edge of mass fire at Hiroshima (10 cal/cm^2). At 3.1 miles from ground zero, where Brode's team predicted severe damage from blast and fire, the thermal fluence would be 26 cal/cm^2, a conservative estimate that was well over twice the thermal fluence deposited at the edge of mass fire at Hiroshima.

Similar results obtained for five leadership, training, and control facilities (largely multistory office buildings) and for five heavy industrial installations, which included two coke oven batteries and plants producing iron and steel, sulfuric acid, and nitrogen fertilizer. Indeed, for all but one category—underground nuclear weapons storage facilities impervious to fire effects—significantly greater damage was predicted when fire effects were included.[98]

PSR's analysis was published in the summer of 1989, but it had been largely completed and briefed earlier in the year. Indeed, in early 1989, key government support mounted for the study. In January 1989, PSR's technical monitor at DNA, Paul Rohr, briefed members of a working group within the JSTPS Scientific Advisory Group (SAG) on the thirty-nine targets analyzed to that point.[99] (The JSTPS's scientific advisory group, SAG, should not be confused with DNA's scientific advisory group, SAGE.) SAG included government officials and nongovernment experts. One government official who attended the briefing recalled that SAG members "liked it a lot. It was sort of the rage."[100] It seems likely that the deputy director of DIA, Gordon Nigas, and the deputy director of DNA, Marv Atkins, both members of SAG, were among those briefed. According to an analyst close to the study, "Both deputy directors supported the fire effort."[101]

That spring, Atkins himself briefed the full SAG. The SAG members "were encouraged by the initial results and wanted to press forward and see if they could bring this thing towards implementation if it was feasible."[102] Atkins sent a summary of PSR's fire targeting results to the vice director of JSTPS, Rear Admiral R. M. Eytchison, with a strong endorsement. He claimed that "the methodology represents a major breakthrough. . . . It accounts for fire damage . . . in terms of a modified vulnerability number (VN). Hence, it can be readily incorporated within the mathematical framework of the current strategic targeting procedures."[103]

Hundreds of Targets

In the spring of 1989, SAG and the three agencies involved in the fifty-target study decided to proceed with a much larger study in which DNA, DIA, and JSTPS would evaluate "nearly 300 sample targets."[104] The goal was to determine the feasibility of scaling up the fire-blast VN methodology for use in nuclear war planning. Could DIA assign fire-blast VNs to so many targets? Did it have the data on the approximately fifty variables required for each target? Was the method sufficiently straightforward that DIA analysts could work with it reliably? And, even if the method could be applied on a large scale, were the differences in resulting damage sufficient to warrant the time and cost? If, for example, most of the targets were isolated underground missile silos, fire damage would probably not be important. If, however, many targets in a representative target set were command and control facilities located in and near urban areas, fire damage could be very important.

Brode and his colleagues at PSR were involved in this study, but less directly than in the earlier fifty-target study. The earlier study had been undertaken to demonstrate that PSR's fire-blast VN methodology could be applied to actual targets. This study was intended to demonstrate that DIA could apply PSR's methodology to a much larger number of targets; as before, each fire-blast VN was tailored to a specific target.

For this study, JSTPS would pick "the targets considered appropriate and representative [as] an honest target set."[105] DIA would assign fire-blast VNs to the chosen targets. JSTPS would do a sample war plan—a "weapon laydown"—in which it planned the delivery of nuclear weapons to detonate near the designated targets and assess "the impact such VN changes might have on the allocation of weapons."[106] In other words, could fewer weapons be used to achieve the same levels of damage? Such a study was also relevant to answer a different question: Should some weapons or designated ground zeros be changed so that "undesired collateral damage" (i.e., destruction by fire of the surroundings of a targeted facility) would not occur?[107] DNA funded the project and was kept informed, but it was not as actively involved as in the prior study.[108]

By the summer of 1989, JSTPS had chosen the target set, and in one small "shop" in DIA, Army Lieutenant Colonel Bob Ryan began to direct the construction of the hundreds of fire-blast VNs. Ryan led the Nuclear Weapons Effects Section in the Physical Vulnerability Branch. The branch, headed by Richard "Red" Seaward, was one of several in the Target Intelligence Division, which was in DB, the largest directorate within DIA. The Physical Vulnerability Branch was the direct descendant of the Physical Vulnerability Division in Air Force Intelligence (see figure 4.1), which had been transferred to DIA in the early 1960s. Over the next year, Ryan and a member of his section, Air Force Captain Ed O'Connell, trained military intelligence reserve officers on active duty to collect the data necessary to construct the fire-blast VNs. The officers "jerked the target folders"—the information collected on each target over many years, much of it not stored on computer and some of it "incredibly classified"—and scoured them for the information required. They would then enter the information into a database that Ryan had constructed to accommodate PSR's methods for calculating the fire-blast VNs. According to one analyst, "this methodology asks for the world" and required detailed information that "there was no requirement to collect in the past." Collecting the data represented "several man years" of work.[109]

By early 1990, support had built for the fire-blast VN methodology and some were optimistic about its chances of being adopted. One DNA official explained that some at DIA were "reluctant at first. They didn't want to change horses in midstream after riding the same one for 30 or 40 years. . . . The senior civilian level said to go ahead."[110] In addition to important high-level support, those working directly on the project were also won over. According to one analyst:

> When you would brief people as to what all was involved and the type data that you needed and the assumptions that needed to be made if you didn't know for sure what the data was, people at first blush would kind of roll their eyeballs: "Sounds uncertain to me." And I think the people that worked with it longer and were more involved with it thought that uncertainties could be overcome.[111]

Brode recalled that by the spring of 1990, he and his colleagues at PSR had convinced DIA that the methodology was viable. By then, "the small group at DIA involved were comfortable with the procedure, and were successful at turning out VNs with fire damage included according to our methodology."[112]

An authoritative technical guide on nuclear targeting, dated January 1990, was optimistic about adoption:

> There are very few cases where "neglected" effects could prove to offer a major advantage over airblast for objective targets [targets designated for destruction]. The most noteworthy exception to this rule has been the explicit omission of fire damage as an offensive target damage mechanism. This is likely to change within the next few years, however, as DNA-sponsored research moves toward completion of a fire damage methodology.[113]

A colleague of Brode's at PSR, George Fisher, wrote the computer program that analyzed material from DIA's database and maintained the "day to day" contact with DIA to ensure everything was running smoothly. Once all the data was entered for any target, a DIA analyst could compute the fire-blast VNTK by "push[ing] the button . . . and this program would go in on that target . . . , pull out all of the data, run it though the models, and it would start spitting out computer printouts, a couple pages per target. Then the bottom line was: here's . . . your [fire-blast] VTNK."[114]

By July 1990, DIA had determined the fire-blast VNTK values for several hundred targets. JSTPS then planned a hypothetical attack on these targets to see if the previously achieved level of damage could now be achieved with fewer weapons.[115] According to a government official who had been at DNA in this period, the effect of fire "was rather profound. For certain targets it was incredibly effective. For some, not. . . . The question was: how will we know what's really true?" There were disagreements about the level of mitigation that would occur. Some claimed that "depending on . . . warning, [the enemy] might take heroic steps." Ultimately, DNA and JSTPS agreed to analyze fire-blast VNs at the "moderate" level of mitigation. According to the DNA official, in this "more conservative approach . . . certain target classes were still vulnerable to fire and you could take credit for it. In my opinion, it vindicated the methodology."[116]

Seeking Military Approval

It was one thing for some in DNA and DIA to have confidence in the fire-blast VN method. It was another thing to gain military approval. The question was: Would the Joint Chiefs of Staff think the fire-blast VN methodology feasible to use in nuclear war planning? As part of a formal review requested by the Joint Chiefs of Staff, in early December 1990, DIA and JSTPS briefed officers on the Joint Staff directly responsible for nuclear war planning. (These officers were lieutenant colonels and colonels and naval

commanders and captains—the O-5 and O-6 level—in the Chemical Nuclear Division ["Chem Nuc"], in J-5, Strategic Plans and Policy, of the Joint
Staff.) DNA analysts also attended. Briefing at this level is considered a "dry
run." The officers being briefed would decide "was this thing good enough,
had it progressed enough" to be briefed at higher levels. They decided that
it was and scheduled a briefing "fairly high up in the chain" for early January 1991.[117]

Many consequential military decisions are made not by the Joint Chiefs
of Staff—all four-star generals and admirals—but by two- and three-star
generals and admirals working under their authority within the Joint Staff
structure. One very important group consists of the three-star officers appointed by each service chief as his operations deputy. These officers, along
with the director of the Joint Staff, form the body known as the Operations
Deputies or "Ops Deps." The Ops Deps make final decisions or review very
important decisions before they reach the Joint Chiefs level. Just below the
Ops Deps is a group called the Deputy Operations Deputies ("Dep Ops
Deps"), composed of two-star officers and the vice director of the Joint
Staff. The Dep Ops Deps may make final decisions or forward issues to the
Operations Deputies.[118]

The early January 1991 briefing was to the Deputy Operations Deputies,
the two-star deputies of the three-star deputies of the four-star Joint Chiefs
of Staff. As in December, DIA and JSTPS did the briefing, with DNA "sit-
ting in." The Dep Ops Deps then scheduled a briefing at the three-star Op
Deps level. This last briefing occurred just before Operation Desert Storm
began on January 16. Brode's impression of the January briefings was that
the military had decided to go ahead with the methodology and that this decision had been confirmed at higher levels.[119] However, according to one
participant, the Operations Deputies were not so definite. They did agree to
continue the project, but "they were putting off a decision on it for probably about another year. They wanted some additional work done. . . . They
didn't make a decision as to whether to implement it. Questions were raised
that they wanted answered on uncertainties." One of the issues had to do
with the definitions of levels of damage, that is, damage criteria. The damage criteria then being used were "blast-oriented. They incorporated damage from blast, ground shock, and cratering effects. Well, if you were going
to implement fire effects, you would need to redo your damage definitions
to account for what constituted severe or moderate damage, based on a combined suite." One might think this would be fairly simple to change, but revising definitions of damage for all the target types was, at least from a DIA
perspective, "a significant task." Shortly after the briefing, Desert Storm
began. This "wiped out" work on the fire-blast methodology for several
months.[120]

For over a decade, Brode's strategy of research and persuasion was shaped by his own goals and by the concerns of established fire research contractors and nuclear war planners. Through the beginning of 1991, the strategy was largely successful. At the same time, the established fire research community was revitalized by the increased funding of the era, and they questioned and challenged Brode's methods and findings. They were not as well connected to defense officials, at least not to those at DNA, but the arguments of the fire research community impressed others in the government and—as we will see in chapter 10—affected the final decision on whether to incorporate predictions of fire damage into nuclear war planning.

Chapter

10

ENCORE and After

It's now almost forty years since nuclear weapons were first used in warfare, and still we know very little about the fire effects.

Stanley Martin, "Fire in an Air Blast Environment," 1982

t the same time the government was funding Harold Brode's extensive nuclear fire research from the late 1970s to the early 1990s, it also
provided a new infusion of funds to the fire research community. Fire
researchers at organizations such as Science Applications International Corporation (SAIC), Stanford Research Institute (SRI), and Stan Martin & Associates began new analyses of and experiments on blast–fire interaction.[1]
They began to revise their computer models of fire damage to incorporate
new digital databases, to build on recent findings about blast–fire interaction, and to update predictions of fire damage from nuclear weapons. As a
result of new funding and research, the fire research community enjoyed a
renewed authority and influence.

Fire researchers embraced Brode's broad definition of the problem to be
solved—the incorporation of fire effects into the damage predictions used
in nuclear war planning—but they drew on different physical understandings than the ones used by Brode and his colleagues, and they arrived at different results. Building on a long research tradition of laboratory and
small-scale experiments and close empirical observation of large fires, fire
researchers conceptualized nuclear mass fire as similar to other very large
fires, which are strongly affected by environmental influences. Because of the
many variables that affected other large fires, they were skeptical that the
probability and range of mass fire could be reliably predicted, and at various times they directly challenged Brode's methods and conclusions. Indeed,

they viewed Brode's models as "computer fantasies to a large extent. . . . There's very little foundation for them experimentally. . . . We [in the fire research community] didn't hold much high regard for that kind of stuff."[2]

Although Brode appeared to have the inside track in the government, several people in the fire research community were also highly regarded by government officials concerned with nuclear weapons effects. These fire researchers had the advantage that their ideas about the unpredictability of mass fire were consistent with widely accepted and long-held understandings dating back to World War II. Brode's work was very nearly adopted, but, as we will see in this chapter, in 1992 the fire research community's doubts about the predictability of fire damage would prevail.

The "ENCORE Effect"

Asilomar Reconvened

After a hiatus of several years, the fire research community reconvened at Asilomar in the spring of 1978. As before, they met under the auspices of civil defense—the Defense Civil Protection Agency (DCPA) in 1978 and 1979 and, after that, the new agency into which DCPA functions had been folded, the Federal Emergency Management Agency (FEMA). During the 1980s, fire researchers also received funding from the Defense Nuclear Agency (DNA) and other government agencies, including the office in the Pentagon responsible for civilian oversight of strategic nuclear war planning by the military, then called the Strategic Forces Policy Office.

DCPA asked the 1978 Asilomar participants to formulate a "feasible" program of research into the fire effects of a nuclear war; DCPA wanted to begin funding this program immediately. Of the twenty-two participants, seven were from government agencies including DCPA, DNA, the Defense Intelligence Agency (DIA), and Lawrence Livermore national laboratory; most of the others were research contractors from SRI, Illinois Institute of Technology Research Institute (IITRI), TRW, and Scientific Services, Inc. The usual suspects included Ray Alger, Tom Goodale, Stan Martin, and John Rempel from SRI and Andy Longinow and Tom Waterman from IITRI. Perhaps most prominent among them was Martin, who, since 1969, had managed fire research at SRI, only a small part of which was concerned with nuclear weapons.[3] Years later, one contractor at another firm referred to Martin as "very respected." A Defense Department official said that "Stan Martin and Hal Brode are probably the two names that stand out in my mind of, say, the old pioneers. . . . I believe that there are two camps. There is a significant camp that says the fire VN is not possible. And there's Hal Brode [who] believes that a fire VN is possible. . . . I'd say Stan Martin probably is in the other camp [from Brode]. . . . Have you talked to Stan?"[4]

Brode, who did not share the same orientation as most in the fire research community and who was described by one fire researcher as "sort of on the fringes," also attended the 1978 meeting; he was then at R&D Associates (RDA).[5] At this first meeting, the conferees laid out a broad research agenda. The overall goal was to develop "reliable estimates of the incendiary out-come of a nuclear attack on the United States" to aid the DCPA in planning for relocation of population and "countermeasures such as firefighting" in the event of nuclear war. As explained in the conference report, developing better predictions of fire damage from nuclear attack entailed two things: a better understanding of certain phenomena, particularly the impact of the blast wave on incipient and developing fires, and the development of more sophisticated computer models to predict fire damage.[6]

This agenda was not inconsistent with Brode's push to understand mass fire phenomena and develop computer algorithms to predict fire damage. Brode was not uninterested in blast–fire interaction, but he was far more in-terested in phenomena of atmospheric perturbation and resulting fire-in-duced winds.

The fire research community took a sharply different approach to dam-age prediction from Brode's. For example, instead of a single regional model of the physics of mass fire, the fire research community developed two sep-arate models: a "general urban fire-distribution/spread model for areas of light-to-moderate building damage" and a "hole in the doughnut" model (discussed in chapter 8), applicable to areas of heavy damage in which the very high blast overpressures near the detonation and resulting debris from collapsed buildings were expected to snuff out incipient fires.[7] (Brode did not expect a "hole in the doughnut" close to the detonation but rather an in-tense fire there.) Until about the mid-1980s, the fire research community fo-cused more on understanding blast–fire interaction than on developing extensive computer models of damage because "unfortunately, little progress can be made [on predictive models of damage] until the basic blast/fire interactions are understood."[8]

"Flames Gushed Out"

Based on a number of experiments simulating nuclear blast and fire ef-fects, the general understanding in the fire research community in the mid-1970s was that blast waves could blow out incipient fires in structures at overpressures as low as 2 psi.

These findings were thrown into serious question at the 1981 Asilomar conference. Martin and some of his colleagues at SRI had begun to reexamine results of the atomic weapons test Operation UPSHOT–KNOTHOLE, Shot ENCORE, on May 8, 1953.[9] At ENCORE, the Forest Service had set up two block houses, each with a picture window (see chapter 6). According to Martin, "It was a full-scale living room . . . a little bit small, but full scale . . . and they had couches and chairs and lampshades and various things."[10] The items in one of the living rooms included "venetian blind, wood slats, and cotton tape," "wood chair, padded with cotton, chintz cover," and "low table with newspapers." The other living room contained more fire-resistant materials of vinyl and wool.[11] The block houses were located at a distance from the detonation where they would be subjected to thermal fluence of 17 cal/cm² and overpressure of 5 psi; the blast wave would arrive 4 seconds after the detonation. Martin said that the Forest Service expected "that they would get a little fire in a few of the items in there and it would eventually develop into a flashover [a fire engulfing the whole room] in 5 to 20 minutes. . . . Well, they got a surprise."[12]

Instead of a slow buildup of fire that could be blown out by the blast wave, one of the structures instantaneously flashed over and immediately burned down. Further, the "flames gushed out all the way to the camera and blinded" it. The camera was 18 feet away and recorded only a very bright flash. An hour after the detonation, the other structure, containing more fire-resistant materials, was "scorched and charred"; the plastics in the drapery, chair seat, and lamp shade were melted, and fire burned in a wall. The immediate flashover was significant because it indicated, in Martin's words, "a fairly high certainty that the building was going to be destroyed by fire." If a large percentage of structures flashed over at about 20 cal/cm², the probability of destruction by fire in a nuclear attack was much higher than researchers had expected, both because such fires were extremely unlikely to be blown out by the blast wave and because there would not be time for fire fighters to arrive and quell the fire. However, at the time of Shot ENCORE, "it was described in the [test] report as an anomalous response. This won't happen again. It just happened. We don't know why." It was completely ignored, Martin said, virtually forgotten, until Tom Waterman of IITRI asked at the 1980 Asilomar conference, "What happened at ENCORE?" Martin and others began to think about it.[13]

By the 1981 Asilomar conference, Martin referred to the immediate flashing over of the block house as the "ENCORE effect": "This remarkable event received little subsequent attention; in retrospect, from a vantage point that now includes observations of how easily the flames of a single, incipiently burning fuel item can be blown out, the question of whether this room response was an anomaly or not has far-reaching significance. Nearly 30 years later, we still cannot say."[14]

Although it may seem surprising that fire researchers would consider it anomalous that a structure burned down quickly when exposed to thermal fluence of 17 cal/cm^2, approximately twice the exposure at the limit of mass fire at Hiroshima, experimental data had indicated that flames could be easily blown out, and that fire growth in structures was a gradual process. In the words of Martin and his colleague Robert McKee: "Nuclear-effects predictive models customarily treat the incipient fire, prior to flashover, as a relatively feeble (indeed, blast extinguishable) stage in the growth process. . . . Only much later, following a growth process that may take from many minutes to an appreciable fraction of an hour, does the enclosure's heat-conserving character manifest itself in a flashover response."[15]

The renewed interest in the ENCORE effect led to a 1-kiloton high-explosive simulation called DIRECT COURSE, at White Sands, New Mexico, in October 1983. It was designed specifically to investigate whether the short flashover times at ENCORE could be replicated. Four structures, similar to those at Shot ENCORE, were built and exposed to similar blast pressure and heat. As at ENCORE, half of the structures exhibited "dramatic flashover behavior," in which flames shot explosively out of the windows, and the structures immediately burned up. According to Martin, the flames "came out and blinded the camera. . . . It was . . . spooky, it was so much like the original situation." In the other two structures, flashover occurred after a period of gradual burning. In one, the result was the complete consumption of the combustibles. In the other, smoldering and dense smoke changed after a half hour to flaming and "developed rapidly to a classical flashover . . . consum[ing] all the combustibles in the room."[16]

The authoritative analysis on ENCORE was written by a young Harvard Ph.D. in engineering, Jana Backovsky. Backovsky had been a student of "Mr. Fire Research," Harvard professor Howard Emmons. After completing her dissertation, a mathematical model of how flame enhances fire spread, she had gone to work for Martin at SRI in late 1979.[17] (Martin left SRI in 1982 to form Stan Martin & Associates; he consulted with Backovsky at SRI on the DIRECT COURSE simulation.) According to Backovsky's report, "With the DIRECT COURSE flashover behavior, the ENCORE phenomenon can no longer be considered an anomaly but a phenomenon that can be produced readily in a real or simulated nuclear scenario."[18]

Backovsky attempted to simulate on a computer the rapid onset of flashover observed at ENCORE and DIRECT COURSE, using "the most sophisticated mathematical model" available for fire growth in structures, the Harvard Fire Model.[19] (Backovsky was familiar with the code, having worked on an early version of it for Emmons in the summer of 1975.)[20] However, she was not able to simulate the flashover with the Harvard Fire Model. She observed that the code's predictive power failed, at least in part, because of the "rapid changes of conditions during some phase of the fire."[21] She noted that the kind of rapid fire growth observed at ENCORE and DIRECT COURSE had not been previously recognized as a problem in fire modeling:

> Initial ignition by a large amount of intense radiant energy is not a common fire experience in peace time and hence has not been studied, theoretically or experimentally. The very high rates of energy deposition (the initial irradiation) and ventilation (shock wave penetration) results in fire growth that is untypical and cannot be accurately predicted at present. In fact, in the past, this problem has not even been recognized as an important part of nuclear fire modeling.[22]

For Martin, the whole thing was getting curiouser and curiouser. After EN-CORE was determined not to be an experimental anomaly, Martin noted: "We have evidence that fires are easily blown out, on the one hand, and are virtually immune to blowout, on the other. It is far from clear at this time how this gross uncertainty is to be resolved."[23] He also pointed out the incongruity between the atomic attacks on Japan and current fire models: "Hiroshima was totally burned out to about 6000 feet from ground zero, and despite collapse of the majority of structures in that same area, a mass fire developed within 20 minutes of the explosion. . . . It is extremely hard to reconcile the high incidence of fires in the Japanese cities with the implied ease of extinguishment by blast. . . . This suggests serious inadequacies of the models."[24]

State-of-the-Art Modeling

An Attack on Washington

Beginning in 1985, mainly under contract to DNA, but also to the Pentagon's Strategic Forces Policy Office, fire researchers began to revise their models to predict nuclear fire in urban areas. The models from which they worked dated from the late 1960s and had been developed under civil defense's Five City Study (discussed in chapter 8); with very little funding available to develop them further, the models had not changed much since. Fire researchers were acutely aware of the shortcomings of these models, developed at a time when computers had much less capacity and before much attention had been paid to the complexities of blast–fire interaction. They noted that among the phenomena not modeled were the extinguishing effects of air blast on incipient fires; the instantaneous flashover that would prevent fires from being extinguished; the fire behavior in areas of collapsed buildings and debris (the "doughnut effect"); and the "effects of wind, either ambient or fire-induced."[25]

Now funding resumed to enable fire researchers to update the older models into "state-of-the-art" fire models. The first major study, *Nuclear Weapon Induced Urban Fires and Smoke Injection,* published in 1987, hypothesized a nuclear attack on Washington, D.C., similar to the attack discussed in chapter 1 of this book. The differences in predicted damage, however, are striking. Instead of a very large area engulfed in mass fire, the study predicted only small areas of firestorm.

The study was done jointly by Roger Craver at SAIC, a major military research contractor, and Stan Martin & Associates. At a time when government funding was available for research on nuclear winter, *Nuclear Weapon Induced Urban Fires and Smoke Injection* modeled smoke output from large urban fires.[26] To model smoke injection into the atmosphere, the authors first predicted fire starts and fire spread in urban structures and then modeled smoke injection. However, they concentrated far more on predicting fire damage to structures in large urban fires than on modeling smoke release in the atmosphere. This was not a coincidence. One of the study's sponsors, the Pentagon's Strategic Forces Policy Office, provided oversight of nuclear war planning.[27] The authors were tasked to make the structural types "parallel to the descriptions of the *Physical Vulnerability Handbook—Nuclear Weapons* printed by the Defense Intelligence Agency . . . the basic reference document for damage analysis within the Department of Defense."[28]

The authors hypothesized an attack on Washington using up to three 500-kiloton nuclear weapons: one surface burst on the Pentagon and the others air bursts about a half-mile above the White House and above Andrews Air Force Base. Visibility was 6 miles.[29] The authors used computer-generated data from the Defense Mapping Agency, which enabled them to map "structure and occupancy types in considerable detail . . . along with the associated fuel loading factors . . . and heat release values" of those structures.[30] The digital mapping of structures had been used in programming cruise missiles to avoid man-made objects on their way to their targets ("clobber analysis"). The Strategic Forces Policy Office was interested in knowing if these same databases could be used to help model fire damage in strategic nuclear war planning.[31]

The database was quite new, but the authors noted that "the fire model used is not state-of-the-art."[32] Instead, the authors used a modified version of a thermal ignition fire-start model developed in the mid-1960s in the civil defense–funded Five City Study, and added to it algorithms to estimate blast-disruption fire starts (the authors called them "secondary" fire starts) and fire spread to neighboring structures. The authors wrote "The insights of those 20-year-old studies still serve us well,"[33] though they acknowledged that their report dealt "in an ad hoc way" with the ENCORE effect and other potentially important issues such as thermal radiation shielding by neighboring buildings and multiburst interactions. However, the authors thought that "some of the omitted . . . factors may counterbalance one another." For example, they thought that their neglect of air-blast blowout and the thermal screening of window shades and draperies might to some degree offset "the unaccounted impact of the ENCORE effect. But until the sensitivity of incendiary outcome to these factors is much better known that it is now, we can only speculate on how successfully we have balanced the model's shortcomings, one against another."[34]

For a surface burst of a 500-kiloton bomb on the Pentagon, the authors found that a firestorm would be set in only a very small area in downtown Washington and downtown Rosslyn, Virginia. (See Figure 10.1.)[35]

For a combined attack of two 500-kiloton bombs on the Pentagon and the White House, the authors found somewhat greater areas of firestorm. (Farther away, Andrews Air Force Base had only a negligible effect on Washington.) The detailed six-color maps, included in the study, showed not vast areas but relatively small pockets of mass fire.[36] (See Figure 10.2.) According to the authors, "The period of high rates of heat release [associated with firestorms] appears to last only an hour or so. Areas supporting fires of such intensity are: downtown D.C.; Rosslyn; Crystal City [Virginia]; and a few small areas of commercial warehousing."[37]

The authors based their firestorm predictions on an exceptionally conservative measure of heat-release rates, with a power density of 250 kilowatts per square meter (kW/m^2). This was even higher than the 1966 Lommasson and Keller study (discussed in chapter 8), long relied on by the fire research community, that set a power density criterion of approximately 200 kW/m^2 for a firestorm; they calculated that the fires that had raged at Hiroshima and Nagasaki had power densities of approximately 20 kW/m^2 and that therefore (as reported by Martin) "a firestorm did not occur in Hiroshima."[38] The criterion of 250 kW/m^2 was two and a half times Brode's criterion of 100 kW/m^2 for mass fire, published in an article at about the same time as *Nuclear Weapon Induced Urban Fires*.[39] According to the authors of the latter, "These high heat-release rates [250 kW/m^2] coincide with densely built-up areas of commercial land use inside the 4-psi peak overpressure contours, and there only. . . . In any case, the period of high rates of heat release appear to last only an hour or so."[40] Had the authors used Brode's criterion, they would have predicted a far greater incidence of mass fire. (Figure 10.3, using Theodore Postol's conservative criterion for mass fire of thermal fluence of 20 cal/cm^2, is much closer to Brode's predictions of mass fire.)

Indeed, another measure used by the authors to predict fire damage— percentage of buildings burned out—yielded very different results.[41] In the same combined attack on the Pentagon and the White House, which showed only small areas of firestorm, the authors found and noted without comment that 76 to 100 percent of the buildings in a large area—almost all of the structures within 3 miles of the White House, including all structures between the Pentagon and the White House—were burned out.[42] (See Figure 10.4.)

How did the authors of *Nuclear Weapon Induced Urban Fires* judge that almost all the buildings in a very large area would be burned out but at the same time predict that only small pockets of buildings would be consumed in a firestorm? In addition to its very conservative criterion for a firestorm, the study did "not attempt to account for effects of wind, either ambient or fire-induced."[43] Without the hurricane-force winds at the core of their fire model, the authors predicted a very large number of structures burning down without causing a mass fire.

Lieutenant Colonel Gary Betourne, of the Pentagon office that commissioned the study, wrote to the authors that "your study . . . has convinced us that we may have the ability (someday) to approximate the damage caused by such fire."[44] This was a decidedly longer-range notion of when fire damage could be predicted than envisaged by Brode and his colleagues. It was, however, consistent with the authors' own understanding. In one briefing slide, the authors said: "No need to trivialize fire phenomena by force-fitting fire VNTKs," a critical reference to Brode's "fitting" of fire damage predictions to the VNTK system. It also said, "Leaves only the weather problem."[45] While upbeat, this indicated that "the weather problem" could not yet be solved, thus disputing Brode's claims that weather parameters were bounded and could be incorporated into fire damage predictions.

A Fire-Start Model

Around the same time, Martin developed a new fire-start computer code for DNA: the Nuclear Weapon Fire Start (NWFS) model. Martin used a thermal ignition model similar to the one used in the recently completed study of the attack on Washington; his innovation was to combine that model with "a secondary [blast disruption] fire start model of recent development."[46] Characteristic of the fire research community's style of work, Martin was attentive to the tremendous variation in the causes of blast-disruption fires. Shortly after, he wrote about the difficulty of modeling such fires: "The causes of fire in structurally damaged industrial operations are . . . varied . . . ranging from the rupture of hot furnaces to the release of reactive chemicals. . . . Earthquake experience shows, in general, that much of the associated fire incidence and its causes, even in residences, might be categorized as freak accidents. Though different from earthquake-caused fires, secondary fires of nuclear explosions would seem to have much the same chance-event character."[47]

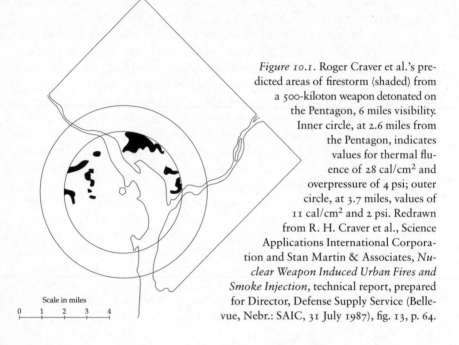

Figure 10.1. Roger Craver et al.'s predicted areas of firestorm (shaded) from a 500-kiloton weapon detonated on the Pentagon, 6 miles visibility. Inner circle, at 2.6 miles from the Pentagon, indicates values for thermal fluence of 28 cal/cm^2 and overpressure of 4 psi; outer circle, at 3.7 miles, values of 11 cal/cm^2 and 2 psi. Redrawn from R. H. Craver et al., Science Applications International Corporation and Stan Martin & Associates, *Nuclear Weapon Induced Urban Fires and Smoke Injection,* technical report, prepared for Director, Defense Supply Service (Bellevue, Nebr.: SAIC, 31 July 1987), fig. 13, p. 64.

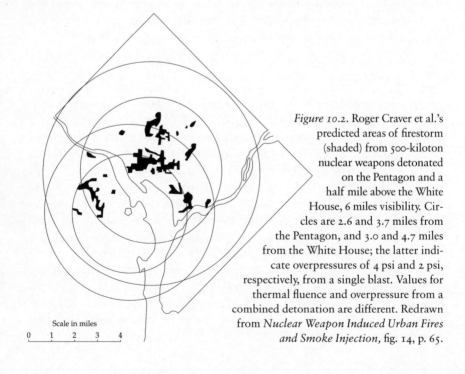

Figure 10.2. Roger Craver et al.'s predicted areas of firestorm (shaded) from 500-kiloton nuclear weapons detonated on the Pentagon and a half mile above the White House, 6 miles visibility. Circles are 2.6 and 3.7 miles from the Pentagon, and 3.0 and 4.7 miles from the White House; the latter indicate overpressures of 4 psi and 2 psi, respectively, from a single blast. Values for thermal fluence and overpressure from a combined detonation are different. Redrawn from *Nuclear Weapon Induced Urban Fires and Smoke Injection,* fig. 14, p. 65.

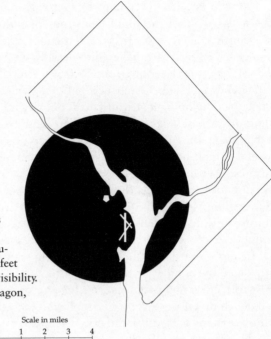

Figure 10.3. Theodore Postol's predicted area of mass fire (shaded) from a 300-kiloton nuclear weapon detonated 1,500 feet above the Pentagon, 10 miles visibility. Circle, 3.5 miles from the Pentagon, indicates value for thermal fluence of 20 cal/cm² and overpressure of 2.2 psi.

Scale in miles
0 1 2 3 4

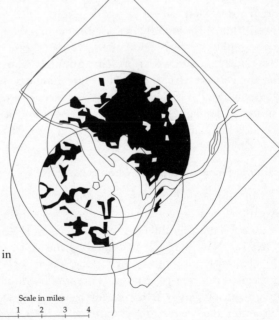

Figure 10.4. Roger Craver et al.'s predicted area of 76-percent to 100-percent of structures burned out (shaded) from 500-kiloton nuclear weapons detonated on the Pentagon and a half mile above the White House, 6 miles visibility. Circles around the Pentagon and the White House are the same as in Figure 10.2. Redrawn from *Nuclear Weapon Induced Urban Fires and Smoke Injection*, fig. 11, p. 62.

Scale in miles
0 1 2 3 4

Martin finished his "completely restructured" fire-start code in August 1987, shortly after the simulation study of nuclear attack on Washington was finished.[48] He wrote that the new code "reflects recent experimental insights and is, therefore, believed to be fully state of the art."[49]

Martin was referring to the ENCORE effect, the probability that room contents would immediately be consumed by fire. He modeled the ENCORE effect by developing a measure that compared the rapidity and intensity of ignition of materials to the speed of air-blast arrival. If fire were already established by the time the blast wave arrived, the ENCORE "flashover" effect would hold. If not, Martin had further procedures to "calculate the number of fires surviving after the passage of the blast wave."[50] It appears that Martin did not have sufficiently detailed data to provide an empirical basis for determining whether the ENCORE effect would occur. Instead, he posited scenarios in which immediate flashover either occurred or did not; the user would decide which scenario to use. The example Martin provided, fire starts for a 1-megaton nuclear bomb airburst 5,000 feet over the Kremlin, predicted the number of thermal ignitions that would occur both with the ENCORE effect and without. Over the area encompassing Moscow, Martin predicted that if the ENCORE effect held there would be over one and a half times as many fires as if it did not.[51]

NWFS did not model mass fires (in Martin's terms, conflagrations and firestorms) or the effects of such fires (in Martin's terms, long-range fire spread). Commenting later on the capabilities of NWFS, Martin wrote: "The threats left out—those of long-range fire spread, conflagrations, and firestorms—can greatly increase fire damage, but they are weather dependent, highly stochastic outcomes, whose criteria of onset of quantification are poorly established at present. Any user whose application requires offensive conservatism [i.e., nuclear war planners at the Joint Strategic Target Planning Staff (JSTPS)] would be expected to reject such uncertain measures of damage."[52] This was again an implicit but direct criticism of Brode's fire damage estimates.

Adding Fire Spread to the Model: NWFIRES

In August 1987, shortly after completing a draft of the revised Nuclear Weapon Fire Start code, Martin assembled a team of consultants to develop a comprehensive, state-of-the-art code for DNA called Nuclear Weapon Fires, or NWFIRES. This combined the just-completed fire-start model, NWFS, with an improved fire-spread model called FISAT. NWFIRES was presented in a 174-page technical report in March 1990 and published virtually unchanged by DNA in May 1991.[53] Like the study that hypothesized an attack on Washington completed in 1987, this study also used the Defense Mapping Agency's unclassified digital databases.[54] The goal was to develop a "computer program that will forecast, at city-block resolution, both blast and fire damage . . . as functions of weapon, urban-makeup, and weather variables."[55] NWFIRES was by far the most ambitious fire model ever undertaken by the fire research community; it drew on the combined expertise of a dozen experts, many of whom had been active in fire and blast effects research since the early 1950s.[56]

The task was similar to Brode's concurrent efforts: to develop a comprehensive computer algorithm to predict fire and blast damage caused by nuclear weapons. Indeed, Brode's work shaped the context for NWFIRES. The authors of NWFIRES generally followed Brode's lead in form, if not in content. For example, in a departure for the fire research community, NWFIRES was designed to "parallel the mathematics of the current DIA vulnerability number (VNTK) system."[57] And, like Brode, the authors derived fire VNs from their modeling work and performed sensitivity analyses to test for consistency in their results. Further, some of the data for the fire VNs in NWFIRES were based on Brode's fifty-target study (see chapter 9).[58]

At the same time, the authors criticized Brode's methods. In an appendix, Clive Countryman, who had headed Project Flambeau in the 1950s (see chapter 8), and Tom Goodale, whose experiments in the early 1970s had demonstrated that blast waves could extinguish incipient fires more easily than previously thought, agreed "that it is unrealistic to model the burning of an urban area as an extensive flat, uniformly hot surface, with flow from the perimeter as the sole source of air supporting the fire. To anyone that has observed even a relatively small area fire it is obvious that rate of heat production and fire characteristics vary greatly over the fire area."[59]

The main innovation in NWFIRES was its "major upgrade" in fire-spread modeling,[60] most notably its treatment of fire-induced winds as a factor in fire spread. The author of the fire-spread subprogram of the overall model was Arthur Takata, now one of Martin's associates. For many years, Takata had worked at IITRI and was the author of three earlier models for IITRI undertaken as part of the Five City Study. Martin referred to Takata's fire-spread models at IITRI as "perhaps [the] most ambitious and computationally sophisticated" at the time.[61]

Martin and his co-authors made a variety of claims about the fire-spread modeling in NWFIRES, from the very ambitious to the extremely modest:

- The treatment of the "effects of fire-induced winds on fire spread is a singular unprecedented contribution to the advance of large-scale urban fire technology."[62]
- NWFIRES "makes a genuine attempt to represent fire-induced winds and effects on fire spread."[63]

- "The principal difficulty to be addressed is the still unsettled question of fire-induced winds, and how these winds can affect fire behavior and ultimate fire damage."[64]
- "Fire-induced winds are a vital part of fire modeling, but understanding of the phenomena is still in its formative stage."
- "Fire spread models still have major uncertainties—in part due to a strong coupling with weather variables."[65]
- "In the case of mass fires and wind related fire spread . . . at the present time, despite significant improvement of our understanding of these phenomena, it is virtually impossible to estimate the contribution of these fire spread mechanisms in a reliable quantitative way."[66]

How could the authors claim their fire-spread model was a "singular unprecedented contribution" but that reliable prediction of fire spread was "virtually impossible"? A close look at Takata's separate report on how he modeled fire spread for NWFIRES shows that these claims were not necessarily inconsistent: The predictability of fire-induced winds was indeed poor, but the developers considered the model itself to be a significant advance over past models done by the fire research community.

In Takata words, "In areas of intense highly-concentrated fire, fire-induced winds will enhance fire spread within and between buildings. Unfortunately, such winds are much too unpredictable to afford fire spread predictions. As a result, two arrays . . . were introduced into the code to provide the user with means for altering the calculated rates of fire spread." The calculated rates will depend on the user's input as to "whether a tract's buildings burn independently . . . or are exposed, respectively, to downdrafts . . . or [to] updrafts . . . generated by very intense fires."[67]

In other words, in the absence of the ability to predict the fire-induced winds characteristic of mass fire, the user could choose to vary the rates of fire spread on the basis of some preference or knowledge not embedded in the code. Thus, while the authors did not have a physical basis for predicting fire spread, their model did incorporate the effects of fire-induced winds on fire spread on the basis of user input.

The authors argued that "the analysis of primary fire starts is considered to be at least as sound as that for blast, so offers a good level of confidence in a lower-bound estimate of fire damage. . . . Secondary fires and fire spread by mass fires, fire-induced winds, firebrands, and the mechanism of spotting, cannot be treated with the same level of confidence."[68]

Unlike Brode and his colleagues at Pacific-Sierra Research (PSR), the authors of NWFIRES did not develop a combined fire-blast vulnerability number, but instead used their model to devise separate fire vulnerability numbers (FVNs). In their view, "the introduction of these FVNs would mean that each installation would require at least two VN descriptions in the target data base: one for blast and one for fire." Further, if more detail were wanted, three VNs might be required: one blast VN and a choice of two fire VNs, depending on whether the user thought the dominant fire damage was from thermal ignition or fire spread.[69]

The authors did not do the thousands of calculations that PSR's researchers did for each target to test the sensitivity to variation. In any case, their results were not as stable as Brode's. Unlike Brode, Martin and his colleagues found "significant swings" that varied with assumptions regarding the conditions of targets, including "efforts at mitigation (such as 'hard' window coverings), daytime versus nighttime . . . , meteorological conditions, snow and cloud cover." They concluded that "the magnitudes [of the variation in results] seem to be sufficiently large to be of concern to those who develop and assess major operational nuclear attack plans in which the conditions of the particular day (and time) of attack cannot be foreseen in advance."[70] In other words, the most advanced model developed by the fire research community could not reliably predict fire damage under a wide variety of conditions.

NWFIRES was the last comprehensive nuclear weapons fire damage model developed by the fire research community. It did not appear to be anywhere near as powerful a predictor of mass fire damage as Brode's model, but its insistence that the uncertainties of weather and other local conditions made the prediction of mass fire and resulting fire damage infeasible was to prove influential in the government's consideration of fire damage over the next year.

"The Trouble with Fire"

From the mid-1980s to the early 1990s, DNA and other government agencies were funding two distinct streams of research on fire damage. Brode and his PSR colleagues had developed a methodology they claimed would enable nuclear war planners to predict both fire and blast damage. At the same time, Stan Martin & Associates had developed a "state of the art" model that incorporated mechanisms of fire start and fire spread, but did not include wind-related fire spread "in a reliable quantitative way."

By the beginning of 1991, Brode saw good prospects for incorporating fire damage into the algorithm used to predict damage in nuclear war planning. He was confident of his model and thought that knowledgeable advocates in the government could persuade the military to adopt it.

In the fall of 1991, even skeptics in the government thought Brode's methodology well on its way to being adopted. One government defense intelligence analyst said "the effort really is to get comfortable" with including fire in damage assessment. "People are comfortable with the way we target with blast, particularly because we've done testing. . . . Well, somehow we have to get comfortable with fire effects."[71]

Still, the idea that fire damage was not predictable was widespread in the government, and as it turned out, shaped the decision not to introduce fire damage into nuclear weapons damage predictions. The work of the fire research community had become the stuff of common sense; government officials drew on this common sense as they evaluated Brode's ambitious claims.

In the fall of 1990, one Pentagon official, who was familiar with and informed by the work of those in the fire research community and involved in the civilian oversight of nuclear war planning, explained why he believed fire damage was unpredictable:

> The trouble with fire . . . is that it's not quantifiable, the amount of fire that's produced depends very much on the weather at the time and the cloud cover. . . . You can't count on it. . . . At the end of the day . . . although we tried manfully to try to get our arms around this, [the problem] was not one that we were able to really solve to our satisfaction. . . . For other than population targets, which we don't attack, fire is really almost a minor player. . . . Unfortunately, blast is very simple. I say unfortunately because then blast effects tend to dominate because you can calculate them.[72]

In the summer of 1991, another Pentagon official familiar with recent fire research explained that he too wanted to get his "arms around being able to calculate something if it can be calculated." However, he was concerned about uncertainties due to local weather conditions, exposed fuels, and "the impacts of the blast itself. . . . Would it blow out something that just ignited? Would the blast blow it down and cover the fuel?"

> At least from my perspective, there isn't a decision to be made out there. I don't see the fire VNs as being mature enough to be useful, because of all the variables involved. And it's just a tough problem, really tough. . . . Some in the scientific community have bet their scientific reputations on this. I'm not convinced. . . . Nobody can convince me that fire VNs are the way to go and they provide anything that's useful. I know that things will catch on fire. . . . But will ignition sustain? I haven't a clue. . . . What exactly is the material that's hanging over the window? How much moisture does it have in it? What's the humidity for the day?. . . . You start building yourself a long litany of assumptions. And pretty soon . . . well, we could have a fire and we could not have a fire. So you say, how can I use that?[73]

By the fall of 1991, the same government intelligence analyst who said officials were trying to "get comfortable" with including fire in damage prediction, explained why he was still not convinced. "We can't really test it. We can only test little pieces of it. . . . The example I . . . use as a counterexample is [the large fire at] Yellowstone. They couldn't put it out, but when the first snows came, it all went out. So, to a novice like me, a practical applicator, it's clear that the weather and environment have a major impact." He also questioned whether blast-disruption fires would occur, referring to them as the "shake, rattle, and roll aspect" of building fires. "Can you set fires in a building as a result of things breaking? There was widespread devastation in Armenia with the [recent] earthquake, but there were no fires." The breakup of buildings in Armenia did not occur in the midst of a nuclear attack, and I did not respond. The analyst said that at meetings when he gives such examples, "This results in what just happened: silence."[74]

End Game

"Terminated"

In mid- to late 1991, a number of people close to the DNA-DIA-JSTPS study of target vulnerability using the fire-blast VN method did not know how the decision would be made on whether to incorporate fire damage into U.S. nuclear war plans. They knew there would be more high-level briefings to the military. Several thought that General Lee Butler, the head of SAC and also the director of JSTPS, the organization in charge of nuclear targeting, would then make the key recommendation to the Joint Chiefs of Staff as to whether or not to proceed.[75] As it turned out, the vice director of JSTPS, Vice Admiral Michael Colley, made the decision to halt the work on fire damage, with the concurrence of General Butler. According to Colley, "I told him about it. He said, 'You're right, let's spend the money elsewhere.'"[76]

Toward the end of 1991 there was another round of briefings to the military on the current state of the fire damage methodology. This time, DIA and DNA did the briefings, and JSTPS attended. (JSTPS had continued to study the methodology, but they were not taking the lead; at this point, they were "trying to stay smart.")[77] Again, the briefings began with the "underlings"—the lieutenant colonels and colonels who worked on nuclear war planning for the Joint Staff—and worked up to the very high-level briefing for the three-star Operations Deputies (Ops Deps), on December 18, 1991. The briefings focused less on the differences in predicted damage when fire was included than on the kinds of data required and the demands on intelligence. At the briefing, the Ops Deps did not make a decision on whether to proceed with the study, but, according to a colonel close to the study, they "just weren't interested. It just didn't excite them."[78]

What followed is clear in the paper trail, although this is only part of the decision-making process. As Colley said, "Of course, I had had telephone and face-to-face conversations with all of the principals . . . in advance of the various memos, letters, etc."[79]

On December 30, the director of the Joint Staff and chair of the Operations Deputies, Lt. General Henry ("Butch") Viccellio, Jr., wrote an unclassified memo on revalidating the fire-blast VN method to assess target vulnerability—now termed the Fire Vulnerability Study—to the vice director of JSTPS, Vice Admiral Michael Colley. (Copies were sent to the directors of DIA and DNA.)[80]

As vice director, Colley was formally responsible for implementing the director's policies and running the day-to-day operation of JSTPS. General Butler, however, did not micromanage Admiral Colley. In Colley's words, Butler "really gave me the opportunity to do whatever was needed down there, as long as I made sure he knew what I was doing."[81]

In his memo to Colley, Viccellio wrote that despite the excellent briefing to the Ops Deps on December 18, "the competition for shrinking resources requires us to focus our efforts on measures that offer the greatest potential return. That competition, as well as ongoing changes in the international environment and our consequent changing priorities, suggests now is an appropriate time to reassess the Fire Vulnerability Study time line." Viccellio requested that JSTPS take the lead in reviewing the schedule for the study "in the light of competing demands on JSTPS, DIA, and DNA resources" and recommend a revised schedule if necessary.[82] In other words, without denigrating the quality of the work on fire vulnerability, the memo suggested that continuing the study on the present schedule might not be worth the investment. The vice director of JSTPS was ostensibly being asked to review the schedule, not the program itself.

On January 10, 1992, Colley wrote to the directors of DNA and DIA and asked for their inputs. On January 31, Colley pulled the plug. In a memo to the Director of the Joint Staff, along with similar letters to the directors of DIA and DNA, Admiral Colley wrote: "I recommend the Fire Vulnerability Study be terminated and request that the requirements set in current milestones be removed."[83] On February 11, a memo by the vice director of the Joint Staff, Major General Rudolph "Mike" Ostovich III, concurred with Colley's assessment "that the cost of proceeding with the Fire Vulnerability Study currently outweighed any foreseeable benefit." Thus, the Joint Staff "terminated" the Fire Vulnerability Study but recommended the study record be "retained as a point of departure in the event that future circumstances dictated a renewal of the analysis."[84] In theory, then, the study could be revived at some later date.

Why had Admiral Colley written the letter, not General Butler? How had the decision really been made? What was the admiral's thinking? Colley explained: "I don't know how familiar you are with the military way of doing these things, but see, if I write the letter to the director and then somebody gets upset, in this building [the Pentagon] let's say, 'Now, wait a minute, fire is important, what are those idiots out in Omaha thinking of?' then we can always say that it was me and Viccellio. And Butler can square it with [Chairman of the Joint Chiefs of Staff] Colin Powell."[85]

(In 1998, General Butler told me that he could not remember a fire vulnerability study. He said Colley may have brought it to his attention, but, if so, he could not remember it, and in any case, it would have been one of many studies to which he could not have paid close attention. Butler referred to the vice director of JSTPS as "the God of targeting"; he himself simply did not spend his time at this level of detail.)[86]

"Fire Is Gravy"

Why had Colley decided to terminate Brode's fire research program— which had been funded for years, gained considerable support, increased the power of its predictions, and looked feasible to the multiagency team involved? In a very cordial, three-hour interview in late 1993 in a small office in the Pentagon, Admiral Colley explained his thinking to me.

First, like many in the government, Colley had not been persuaded that fire could be predicted. He acknowledged the considerable fire damage at Hiroshima and Nagasaki.

> But you know in Russia, or other countries over that region, the time of the year, the vegetation, the petroleum distribution system, the natural gas distribution system, all of those things have to be in a fire algorithm somehow, and there's no way to do it, in all honesty . . . to come up with some kind of an algorithm that [makes] sense. . . . Time of year, day of the week, whether it rained yesterday or not, I mean it just [is] too cumbersome. . . . There are too many variables.[87]

Had Admiral Colley not found the materials from the December 18 briefing persuasive?

> The briefing, in all honesty, Lynn, was not important to me. . . . It was my evaluation that we could spend our money better elsewhere. . . . To me, it was just one more of this continuing pileup of things that we

ought not to be spending money on, because we didn't need to. It didn't
add anything to our effectiveness. The attack was *devastating* and complete as it was.

I understood Colley's argument that the nuclear attack being planned by
the U.S. government was devastating and complete. But I was puzzled that
he did not think predicting additional damage from fire would add to the
understood effectiveness of the attack.

In part, the answer lay in the broader context of the decision. Vice Ad-
miral Colley, a submariner, had come out to Omaha as the vice director of
JSTPS in August 1991. As the "new kid" in targeting, Colley began to review
JSTPS research priorities. Of course, JSTPS was not a research organization. Important research was done for JSTPS by other agencies, particularly
DNA. Colley examined the annual tasking letter by JSTPS to DNA in which
the targeting organization listed its research priorities "to make sure that
DNA's efforts were focused on what we really needed." He said, "It was a
great relationship. It was their [DNA's] money . . . but you needed to do an
annual update of this priority list."

Colley asked his staff why each of about a dozen projects on the list was
being funded. He then visited with the newly appointed director for operations at DNA, Air Force Major General Kenneth Hagemann, in Washington
that fall and discussed priorities. Then as "the new guy stirring the pot . . .
I threw some things off the list entirely, because I thought they were just not
productive and not necessary. I added some things that I thought would help
us." From Colley's perspective, "We [didn't] need the fire thing to help us,
because it's already a very, very devastating attack. I believe, as a public ser-
vant, that stewardship of the taxpayer dollar is important. Further expenditure along this very difficult path [was] just not wise."

Colley's reexamination of research priorities occurred at a time of significant changes in war planning and organizational upheaval at SAC. These
changes were not imposed from the outside but initiated by the SAC commander, General Butler. From the beginning of his tenure as SAC commander in January 1991, Butler thought that the changing international
environment and the inevitable cutback in funding for U.S. strategic nuclear
forces—what he termed the "kinder and gentler strategic modernization
program"—called for a change in U.S. nuclear war plans and a refocusing
of SAC's mission. Butler had been director of plans and policy for the Joint
Chiefs of Staff when the Berlin Wall fell, and had become highly knowledgeable about U.S. nuclear war planning. He was not happy with what he
saw. At the time he became head of SAC, he said, those involved in devising
the Cold War Single Integrated Operational Plan (SIOP; the nuclear war
plan) "with tens of thousands of weapons going down" had "lost track of

the large picture." He later said that as the head of SAC, he had been "responsible for war plans with over 12,000 targets, many struck with repeated nuclear blows, some to the point of complete absurdity."[88]

Butler began a serious revision of the war plan. In the spring and summer of 1991—in the aftermath of the fall of the Berlin Wall and the reunification of Germany, and as the Warsaw Pact dissolved and the Baltic states declared their independence—nuclear war planners at JSTPS pulled approximately three thousand targets out of the war plan so that eastern and central Europe would not automatically be attacked in a war with the Soviet Union. Although this was a large cut, roughly seven thousand Soviet targets still remained in the attack plans.[89] After the formal dissolution of the Soviet Union at the end of the year, JSTPS further revised options so that former Soviet republics would not automatically be targeted in an attack on Russia. They could, however, be targeted separately; this was called "republic purity."[90]

By the time Colley arrived as vice director of JSTPS in August 1991, Butler had decided to make great organizational changes at SAC. Undoubtedly on the basis of Butler's planning and recommendations, President George H. W. Bush announced on September 27, 1991, that the Strategic Air Command—an icon of the Cold War—would be dissolved and replaced on June 1, 1992, by Strategic Command, a drastically reconfigured joint command in charge of nuclear war planning and all strategic nuclear weapons.[91] (When Butler became the head of SAC, he had intended a far-reaching restructuring of nuclear war planning, but he did not begin with the idea of ending SAC as a separate entity. A joke circulating at SAC about this time was "Who killed SAC?" The answer was: "The Butler did it.")[92]

Recall that the organization that planned nuclear war, JSTPS, was a separate multiservice organization, a "free-standing organization with an Air Force Command wrapped around it." The targeting staff reported to the vice director of JSTSP, a three-star admiral, who formally reported to the director, the commander in chief of SAC (CINCSAC). But in "reality . . . CINCSAC was so busy on other things" that it was "the three-star admiral who interfaced with Washington."[93] In the reorganization, JSTPS would lose its name and autonomy; its functions would be folded into the planning directorate (J-5) of Strategic Command. But Strategic Command would be much smaller than SAC. It would no longer command the bomber force—or, indeed, any forces, in peacetime. It would, however, gain command of all strategic nuclear forces, including submarine forces, in war.

Colley understood his job as not only overseeing large changes in target selection but also changing the entire operation of war planning.

[The war plan had become] a lot more complicated, [and] it had to be much more responsive to handle these changes that seemed to be happening all the time. . . . We needed to get away from this very cumbersome monolithic attack plan. It really did take too long to produce and it was difficult to change in a timely manner. Militarily this was not good, but also the huge mainframe computer operation was very expensive [in terms of] people and hardware. We needed to go to a "workstation" computing system and a living attack plan which was amenable to continuous change. . . . We call it now the living SIOP.[94]

(This ghoulish oxymoron—no deadlier plan has ever been devised in the history of humanity—came not out of the black humor of war planners but the language of computing, in which programs that can be very quickly changed are called adaptive, dynamic, or living.)

To move toward computing workstations required shifting money away from the large companies that had made "huge investments" in developing and managing the proprietary and highly classified software that ran on the mainframes. These companies had offices near Offutt Air Force Base. Colley recounted that "one day, I was talking to General Butler, and I said, 'Good gravy, they're living off us here. They've even got their own buildings right outside the gate.' So I looked into it. I don't remember what the number was. . . . Ridiculous, *ridiculous*. So we chopped them off. I went up to Butler with a shopping list. I said, 'I don't need this anymore. I don't need this.' Boy, were they irritated." (According to the respected defense reporter R. Jeffrey Smith, Butler "supported canceling the development of new nuclear weapons systems worth $40 billion, and told an astonished group of senior defense industrialists that the command would no longer need their products.")[95]

As part of this shift in priorities, "getting rid of these software leeches outside Offutt, getting off the mainframe computer," Colley "look[ed] hard at the money we were spending for DNA studies. All of that was on my shopping list to make this place more efficient, more cost effective and drive down the resources that we needed."[96]

Even though budget cutting seemed not unreasonable and suggested that Colley was more concerned with reallocating and managing resources than with developing more accurate predictions of damage caused by nuclear weapons, this did not fully explain why, as targets decreased and the U.S. attack got smaller, funding of a research program to ensure that U.S. forces would be used most effectively was not continued. And given that U.S. targeteers planned "withholds" (i.e., options not to attack) from urban population centers, was it not important to try to predict the full extent of damage so that millions of civilians would not inadvertently be killed?

To both questions, Colley's response was informed by his military experience in nuclear war planning and nuclear operations. Although in theory "it would seem obvious that as the attack gets smaller, it would be interesting to think that we were using the best measures of effectiveness available," he said, in practice, the attack being planned was still very large. "We are talking literally about weapons of mass destruction. They are designed to destroy targets with brute force." Colley did not think that "nuances such as small errors in accuracy, height of burst, time of day [and] year" would make much difference in the damage that would result.[97] "In the general scheme, you're using thousands of weapons anyway."[98]

But the deeper point was that although in theory efficiency may be desirable, in this case it was beside the point. JSTPS could achieve its damage goals without fire. For Colley and others involved in nuclear war planning, issues of organizational success are played out in an annual highly classified reporting process within the Department of Defense. Before the revised SIOP goes into effect, usually on October 1, the predicted results of executing the war plan—computer simulations known as the "consequences of execution"—are briefed in what is known as the revision or "rev" report. In this process, the question was not, Have you been as efficient as humanly possible? Rather, the question was, Do your computer simulations show that you have met the very high thresholds of damage expected against enemy targets?[99] Although Colley explained there had been "a couple of wobbles" in the predicted damage in the U.S. nuclear war plan completed on October 1, 1991, as both targets and forces decreased, he did not think he needed *more* damage. From his perspective, what mattered was whether there was enough destruction in the war plan without fire, and in his opinion, there was. That is what he meant when he said,

> The attack is very very conservative already. . . . We don't need the fire thing to help us, because it's already a very, very devastating attack. . . . It didn't *add* anything to our effectiveness. . . . And while Sierra-Pacific [did] lots of good analysis and all that, we didn't need it. . . . Again, the attack is *so* conservative, that, to my mind, fire is gravy. Whatever you can get from fire just makes everything worse. And you don't need to particularly measure it. It's just there.[100]

Still, what about inflicting too much damage? If Colley didn't "need" fire damage, did he not need to know about it so that he could avoid the many targets in or near cities for which fire damage could extend much farther than blast damage? Colley began to answer this question with stated government policy and then explained the pragmatic considerations that effectively negated that policy:

> To the best of my knowledge, our country has never had a stated policy of attacking cities or people. Unfortunately, the Russians build highly

valuable, hard, legitimate targets in cities. And so it's been, I think, a tough job for our policy people and our guidance people and our targeteers to weigh that in their minds. So that [sometimes] you have to go after this one site, even though it's in an area where you would normally practice urban restraint.[101]

Still, would it not be important to understand the degree of damage one might inadvertently inflict? Colley responded: "I consider the whole issue of urban polygons and withholds to be in the realm of political policy, not nuclear effects."[102] This statement puzzled me, but Colley explained what he meant. He said "as a junior officer I was at sea and knew where these 'packages' were going." (He had earlier spoken of the "Moscow package.") Being involved in nuclear operations in a submarine "is not just doing research at Stanford on a . . . dry subject. . . . When you're out there in the lonely ocean," he paused, "you think about it." But at high policy levels, he said, they don't like to think about this.

We don't like hitting cities, we don't like killing people. So we have a philosophy of mass destruction, yes, but aimed at military targets. So it's politically comfortable and morally comforting for political leaders of our country to espouse "urban polygons" or "city withholds," so we can tell the world, hey, we don't hit cities. So I put this in the realm of political policy, not military effects. Because there are military targets all over the world that are in or near cities. . . . The emotion, the politics, is very, very important.

"Emotion?" I asked.
Colley replied, "We're not targeting cities and that makes us feel better. I call that emotion."[103]
Admiral Colley had just taken me through the self-contradictory world of nuclear strategy and operations, a world in which potential horror, political nostrums, and mundane organizational problem solving are all mixed together. In Colley's words, "Nuclear war is irrational and unthinkable. *But,* if you're going to believe in deterrence, you have to have a war plan which makes sense, is executable—and devastating."[104] The logic of nuclear strategy requires a fully executable and devastating plan, but politicians generally do not like to acknowledge the extent of devastation. Thus, they espouse "limited" mass destruction in executable plans that would be irrational and unthinkable to carry out. What many comfortingly call the "paradox" of nuclear strategy is perhaps better understood as the "nonsense" of nuclear strategy—literally, that which does not make sense.

"Deck Chairs on the Titanic*"*

Early 1992 marked the end of Harold Brode's fifteen-year campaign to include fire damage in U.S. nuclear war planning. For those closely involved in the process, the prediction of nuclear fire damage appeared to be feasible. Some who were more skeptical acknowledged that previous objections had been satisfied.[105] One DNA official noted that there were "so many things [to take into account]: are shutters open or not, is it raining or sunny or cloudy. . . . But we found we *could* calculate fire." By then, however, "it wasn't worth the expense." Echoing Colley's logic, though not his tone, he said, "If we meet our damage goals, moderate or severe—and it's generally severe—then we don't give a hoot if we incinerate everything in the area."[106]

In many ways, Brode and his colleagues had gone quite far in turning a potential organizational frame into a knowledge-laden organizational routine. They had won government resources to predict fire damage. They had built considerable organizational expertise. They had developed a solution that, while challenging long-held assumptions that fire could not be predicted, was consistent with previous procedures for evaluating damage to individual structures. The solution built on and extended the existing blast VNTK system, which made it seem familiar and possible to implement. Finally, they had provided strong evidence of the feasibility of their solution. Nevertheless, the problem of predicting fire damage was overwhelmed by the collapse of the Soviet Union, changes in the SIOP's target base, and SAC's scramble to reinvent itself as budgets and weapons decreased.

Still, the outcome is filled with contingency: *if* the Soviet Union had not dissolved at the same time that the fire damage study was being revalidated; *if* General Butler had taken a personal interest in the issue; *if* Admiral Colley had not had other more pressing concerns regarding war planning; and, perhaps most likely, *if* Admiral Colley had been personally convinced that it was feasible to predict fire damage, then the Fire Vulnerability Study might have survived. Instead, the problem of predicting nuclear fire damage by this time was like "moving deck chairs on the *Titanic*."[107]

It Ain't Over Till It's Over

The multiagency effort spearheaded by Brode had failed. After the Fire Vulnerability Study was put on hold by the Joint Chiefs of Staff in early 1992, Brode did little further work on fire damage. His formal contract with DNA ran until the end of September 1994.[108] As part of his contractual obligations, Brode wrote a long final report, enclosed a computer program on a floppy disk "dressed up" with Windows 3.1 pull-down menus, and submitted six copies to DNA in May 1995. DNA then "lost" it "for a year or more."[109]

Yet, largely out of Brode's view, analysts at what was now Strategic Command were interested in fire and other kinds of damage that they might be able to "take credit for" as they set about to "remanufacture" the U.S. nuclear war plan.[110] The impetus seems to have come from Theodore Hardebeck, a mathematician and high-level analyst who had been at SAC since 1981. After Strategic Command was established, Hardebeck became the associate director for strategic planning in J-5, Plans and Policy, where war planning was now located; in this capacity, he headed the "re-engineering" of the SIOP.[111] Precisely when Hardebeck became interested in fire and other forms of damage is not clear, though it seems likely to have dated from the late 1980s.

In any case, if Hardebeck's interest was necessary, it was not sufficient. Only with high-level "ownership," could the issue regain prominence. General Butler's successor as commander in chief of Strategic Command, Admiral Henry Chiles, was not interested in exploring such issues, but Chiles's successor, Air Force General Eugene Habiger, and his successor, Admiral Richard Mies, were interested.[112] Habiger headed Strategic Command from February 1996 to the end of June 1998; Mies from June 1998 to November 2001.

Like Colley, Habiger's understanding of the issue was shaped by his experience. As a young officer, Habiger had been stationed at Fairchild Air Force Base near Spokane, Washington, when Mount Saint Helens erupted in 1980 on the other side of the state. The volcano had spewed a half inch of dust over the base, causing people to get sick and damaging the radar so that it had to be shut down. Reportedly, Habiger was aware that similar damage could occur in a nuclear war, but that the United States did not "take credit" for such damage.[113] It seems likely that the experience made him more receptive to later arguments about examining unaccounted-for damage.

The British Cultivate a Field

By late 1996, about six months into his term as the head of Strategic Command, Habiger learned in some detail that the British had done exceptionally good modeling of fire damage and that they included it in their nuclear war plans.[114] Indeed, it appears that the British took into account several nuclear weapons effects that the United States did not: fire effects; "non-ideal surface blast effects," that is, the shadow effects of hills and the effects of structures on blast propagation; and possibly electromagnetic pulse (EMP). This led Strategic Command to be all the more interested in modeling such effects. This was a powerful demonstration of feasibility: not only could it be done, it had been done. Strategic Command's analytical effort continued under Admiral Mies.[115]

How long had the British predicted fire damage in their nuclear war planning? Given their commitment to incendiary bombing in World War II, it seems possible that, while the United States developed the ability to predict nuclear blast damage shortly after World War II, the British had developed nuclear fire damage predictions. If that were the case, however, why would no other commander in chief of SAC or Strategic Command before Habiger have been impressed by British predictions?

The waxing and waning of Anglo-American cooperation on nuclear weapons during World War II and after is the subject of careful historical scholarship.[116] Close wartime cooperation was followed by a significant chill when the United States passed the McMahon Act of 1946, which prohibited the country from sharing nuclear weapons information. Cooperation increased in the 1950s, most importantly in a far-reaching 1958 agreement to share information. In April 1959, the United States and Britain further agreed to exchange information on twenty specific subjects related to nuclear weapons, from health physics to the metallurgy of plutonium, and to set up fifteen joint working groups (JOWOGs) in areas of common interest, such as antiballistic missile defense, warhead design, and underground and outerspace testing. This system provided the basis for a "quiet, highly complex, flexible, and largely secret nuclear relationship that has remained in place for the past forty years."[117]

Lorna Arnold, the author of an authoritative history of the British hydrogen bomb, writes that the British strategy was to "identify a particular field in which the Americans had done little work, so that the British scientists could cultivate it to good effect themselves."[118] The assessment of fire damage from nuclear weapons was such a field. Precisely when the joint working group on fire damage, JOWOG 43, was formed is not clear. (Indeed, I have found no written reference to it.) However, over the decades, as many of the JOWOGs have become inactive, JOWOG 43 has remained vital.[119]

In the 1980s, whether through JOWOG 43 or some other venue, U.S. defense officials "talked with colleagues in the UK about . . . mutual areas of research" regarding fire. For example, would the signals that the United States meant to convey with "limited options" or "withholds" be "obscured" by mass fire damage? In 1987, according to one official, although the British "had done an awful good look at some of these questions . . . at the end of the day, everybody sort of has this feeling [that] fire's going to play some role—but you can't tell what it is."[120]

There were other contacts. A delegation from England visited Brode in Southern California in the early 1990s, before the U.S. Fire Vulnerability

Study had been terminated. At that point, the British had done extensive research, "they were underway, but they didn't have a going system" to predict
fire damage. The British "did not use the VN system; they had different
weapons and different target objectives." The British delegation and Brode
had some disagreements about blast-disruption fires and fire spread. The
British "weren't comfortable" with how Brode modeled fire spread. However, despite different methodologies, they agreed on many things.[121]

At the same time that the U.S. Fire Vulnerability Study was shelved and
Brode's final report to DNA misplaced, the British greatly improved their capability to predict fire damage and other effects. According to one observer,
it was in this period that the British ability to predict fire damage "put the
shame to Strat Com [Strategic Command]" and spurred their interest.[122]

Is Fire Damage in the U.S. Nuclear War Plan?

Coinciding with the renewed interest in fire damage prediction at Strategic Command, Brode's report was "found" at DNA in 1996. By now, however, there was a problem: Brode's program, written for Windows 3.1, would
not run on Windows 95. In 1997 DNA's successor, the Defense Special
Weapons Agency (DSWA), "put the cattle prod" to Brode to update the
computer program and submit the accompanying final report. In late 1997,
at the urging of Strategic Command, DSWA turned to Gilbert Binninger and
his colleagues Joseph McGahan and Suzanne Wright at SAIC to translate
the earlier program to Windows 95.[123] According to Binninger, the program
"wasn't converting to Windows 95. The problem was not in Hal's work, but
in some Microsoft proprietary material so Windows 95 wouldn't translate
it. It had to be fixed and corrected." It took three or four weeks to rewrite
the program. It was completed in late 1997 or early 1998.[124] Brode's final report, *Fire Targeting Methodology, Improvements and Automation,* was
published in April 1998. It was a synthesis of the years of work on the fire-
blast VNTK system; the floppy disk for Windows 95 was tucked in the
back.[125]

Before Habiger retired as the head of Strategic Command, he was reported to have ordered that both fire effects and EMP be included in the
SIOP to take effect on October 1, 1998.[126] But was fire damage included? I
have been told contradictory things. In any case, the effort to incorporate
fire damage continued under Admiral Mies.[127]

On July 9, 1998, just after Mies became the head of Strategic Command,
three analysts from Strategic Command flew to Southern California and met
with Brode for a full day. At the meeting, they discussed aspects of Brode's
model, including how fire-spread and blast-disruption fires were calculated.
On fire spread, the analysts were particularly concerned with whether Brode

and his colleagues included shadows, wind, and firebrands.[128] Earlier, the military's interest in fire damage had been driven by a concern for greater effectiveness: covering targets by including more effects. "Then the targets disappeared." By this meeting, the military's interest was primarily about "collateral," or undesired effects. The primary concern was no longer with targets such as power plants in urban conglomerations but with single targets, such as buried bunkers for chemical or biological or nuclear weapons. But even if single targets were destroyed, fire could still spread; the military wanted to "find out about it" so they could minimize it.[129]

But has fire damage been incorporated into the war plan? In late October 2000, Strategic Command ran an unclassified ad for a lieutenant or captain (an O2 or O3) to "assist in development of the fireblast effects assessment model," "advise the fire program manager of potential model shortfalls and gaps, and recommend fixes to improve usability and fidelity," "assist in developing [concepts related to] the 'firespread' phenomenon," and "integrate the fireblast model with an alternative model to more accurately predict firespread and collateral damage due to initial and secondary fires."[130]

The ad reveals several things. First, it indicates that, more than half a century after Hiroshima and Nagasaki were burned to the ground, prediction of fire damage had not been incorporated into the U.S. strategic nuclear war plan. A decade after an algorithm to predict both fire and blast damage had been developed and applied to hundreds of targets, a "fireblast effects assessment model" was still "in development." How serious the model's "shortfalls and gaps" were thought to be we cannot tell, but perhaps not too serious since part of the advertised job was to recommend "fixes" to improve the model's "usability and fidelity."

Second, the ad suggests that the analysts at Strategic Command were working with both Brode's and British methods. The "fireblast model" surely refers to Brode's work on the fire-blast VNTK. "An alternative model to more accurately predict firespread" almost certainly refers to British methods. Apparently part of Brode's method had been accepted, but not his methods for predicting fire spread. At this point, the goal was to integrate the two methods.

Finally, the term "fireblast effects assessment model" may indicate that the goal was not to incorporate fire damage prediction into the war plan itself to help determine where weapons would detonate—as blast damage prediction is used—but to assess in an auxiliary way what further damage might occur. The main concern was most likely the calculation of fire damage to reduce collateral damage. Of course, it is all to the good to try to "minimize" fire damage, but if fire damage prediction is not built into the sinews of the war plan and given the same status as blast damage, more weapons than otherwise may be allocated to destroy targets. And, if history is a guide, it will always be possible to set the predicted "collateral" damage aside as unfortunately unavoidable. In any case, the ad indicates both that the issue of fire damage prediction was being studied yet again and that it was not considered to be developed enough to be used as a standard measure comparable to the blast VNTK.

At the end of November 2001, Admiral James O. Ellis, Jr., succeeded Admiral Mies as the commander in chief of Strategic Command. It seems likely that the analysts at Strategic Command will continue to pursue the issue of fire damage prediction. As of spring 2003, it appears that fire damage has not been incorporated into the U.S. strategic nuclear war plan. According to one well-informed person, every year analysts draw up lists of what they would like to be able to include, but nothing has come of fire damage. "It's not in. . . . There seems to be a warming trend, but it will be years away. . . . It's like the cherry blossoms around here [Washington, D.C.]. They come out every spring and they go away."[131]

Conclusion: Routine Surprises

hole World on Fire is a history of the knowledge and knowledge-laden organizational routines made—and not made—about nuclear weapons damage. Four interwoven processes compose this history. First, military organizations concerned with nuclear war planning and target intelligence focused on increasing knowledge about nuclear blast damage. Second, these same organizations paid little attention to predicting nuclear fire damage. Third, this disparity in knowledge was self-reinforcing: The contrast between the military's ability to predict blast damage and its inability to predict fire damage confirmed for many the inherent unpredictability of fire damage. The failure by U.S. civil defense–funded researchers to predict fire damage further confirmed its unpredictability. Finally, despite this disparity in attention and knowledge, the seeds of organizational innovation lay within, and a significant capacity to predict fire damage was developed, although not adopted at the time it was proposed.

Organizational attention to blast damage predated by decades the invention of nuclear weapons. The U.S. air force (then the Army Air Corps) developed doctrine in the 1920s and '30s that emphasized the destruction of an enemy's ability and will to fight by the precision bombing of specified targets. Such operations would be conducted with high-explosive, not incendiary, bombs. This initial setting of ends and means—which entailed the building of an arsenal of high-explosive bombs, planes configured to carry such bombs, and training centered on handling such bombs—structured for many years to come the problems that airmen and others would work to solve. In other words, they worked within an organizational "blast damage frame" that shaped how problems were represented and the constraints and requirements placed on possible solutions. During World War II, mathematicians, structural engineers, and operations analysts working within the blast damage frame greatly increased organizational capabilities to predict such damage. This new knowledge drew on the existing knowledge base of professionals and researchers and also significantly added to their expertise.

The invention of the atomic bomb and the extraordinary blast and fire damage wreaked on Hiroshima and Nagasaki in 1945 did not disrupt the pre-atomic dynamics. After the bomb, organizational goals remained concentrated on the destruction of specific targets, and government analysts, many of whom had served in the war, continued to understand blast damage as more certain, hence more predictable, than fire damage. In short, analysts "saw" atomic weapons as "blast weapons."[1] In the early post-war period, analysts in air target intelligence worked with university-based research engineers and others to develop systematic predictions of atomic blast damage. By 1954, the government had codified damage prediction in the knowledge-laden organizational routine known as the VN system. By the late 1950s, analysts were able to take into account the much higher yields of the hydrogen bomb in the VNTK system.

The continuities in goals, personnel, and problem focus did not preclude significant innovation. If the broad problem of predicting blast damage carried over from the war, the specifics did not. The new scale of war planning and the new physics of atomic and hydrogen bombs presented great challenges: making a compendium of targets, carrying out experiments in nuclear weapons tests, devising new routines to predict nuclear blast damage. Meeting these challenges required bureaucratic creativity, a significant mustering of resources, large-scale coordination, and the creativity and hard work of individuals. Some of the people involved were little known, some famous. This is, however, not an actor-centered story; always these individuals worked within organizations that provided the context for their activities.

In the same period, a second, inverse, historical process unfolded. Within the military, incendiary bomb damage prediction received no attention before World War II, relatively little during the war, and virtually none after. U.S. air doctrine before the war had led to an arsenal with almost no incendiaries, but as World War II proceeded, some incendiary bombs were developed and incorporated into selected operations. A "fire damage frame" developed alongside the blast damage frame, but it involved many fewer resources and people. Fire protection engineers, a different professional group from those who predicted blast damage, were mobilized to predict fire damage. Working mainly with the British and drawing on knowledge based in fire insurance and fire fighting, they were able to develop effective practical predictions of incendiary bomb damage. However, this knowledge was not as important to the U.S. war effort, nor was it codified.

After the war, the disparity became even greater. The same government organization, Physical Vulnerability in Air Force Intelligence, that developed predictions of atomic blast damage funded only a single study to predict fire damage. Despite the practical predictions made during the war, the study, by fire protection engineer John Wolverton, failed to generalize wartime findings. Fire protection engineers were not university-based; they were not well connected to physicists deeply knowledgeable about nuclear weapons effects; they did not have access to computers; and they did not use numerical computational techniques to model the fire environment.

Thus, organizational determination to predict blast damage during World War II led to the organizational capacity to do so, which provided the basis for building more capacity after the war. In contrast, lack of attention to the prediction of fire damage led to the allocation of fewer resources. Even less attention after the war resulted in a total incapacity to predict nuclear fire damage: no recognized experts, no manuals, no knowledge-laden organizational routines.

Third, the disparity in knowledge about blast damage and fire damage was self-reinforcing. The increasing contrast between the ability to predict nuclear blast damage and the inability to predict nuclear fire damage contributed to the sense that fire damage was inherently unpredictable. Analysts read the past and present state of knowledge as a confirmation of the state of nature.

In addition, the disparity in attention and resources that led to the understanding that blast damage could be predicted and that fire damage could not was further reinforced by the very resources that *were* devoted to fire damage. This seeming contradiction is explicable. With a few exceptions, fire studies were funded primarily by U.S. civil defense. Unlike nuclear war planning, civil defense planning was not an operational undertaking. If nuclear war could not be won, it could be "fought": Forces could be launched with devastating consequences. However, civil defense—evacuation, protection, and recovery from nuclear war with the Soviet Union—simply could not be done. Instead, the purpose of research was to provide the *appearance* of research; in sociologist Lee Clarke's terms, to provide the appearance of "solving problems for which there are no solutions."[2]

Because civil defense research on fire was not part of a highly focused operational effort, the research was diffuse. Civil defense funded many projects on many topics by many contractors; there was no penalty when methods and findings were inconsistent. Further, fire researchers—generally trained as chemical engineers, fire protection engineers, or foresters—developed their ideas primarily from their knowledge of urban building fires and forest fires. As a result, they had neither the intuition nor the disciplinary tools to model the large regional atmospheric flows that drive nuclear mass fires. Although the fire research community was distant from the war planning process, the inconclusive results of their research reinforced war planners' sense that fire damage could not be predicted.

All three historical processes together exhibit what social scientists call "path dependence," in which the effects of learning, high research costs, interdependence, and self-reinforcing expectations reinforce choices already made. For blast damage, expert knowledge was encoded into routines that continually built more organizational capacity to predict blast damage. For fire damage, expert knowledge was not translated into organizational routines, and predictive capacity was not built. Blast damage prediction, once woven into the routines used in nuclear war planning, did not prevent change, but it meant that the initial investment would sharply constrain any future change. Perhaps most significant, participants made sense of the increasing divergence of organizational capability to predict blast damage and incapability to predict fire damage by understanding it to demonstrate that fire damage could not, in fact, be predicted. Thus, the choice made to solve problems of blast damage prediction but not fire damage prediction seemed to be based not on prior choices but grounded in nature itself. This became, in turn, a self-fulfilling prophecy.[3]

These three interrelated historical processes could, in theory, provide a full account of why predictions of nuclear blast damage were developed, why predictions of nuclear fire damage were not, and why the disparity has persisted for over a half century. Indeed, had this account been written at any time from the mid-1950s to the early 1980s, this would look like a classic story of organizational inertia, or "lock-in," in which choices once made are inflexible and cannot be reversed. Frequently cited examples are the lock-in of inferior choices: the adoption of the QWERTY keyboard (named after the top left row of letters) over the apparently more efficient Dvorak keyboard (named after its inventor) and of the VHS videotape standard over the reputedly better Betamax standard. A different kind of lock-in example is the decision to launch the *Challenger* space shuttle. In sociologist Diane Vaughan's words, "Socially organized and history-dependent, it is unlikely that the decision they reached could have been otherwise."[4]

Yet, as we saw—and this is the fourth historical strand—by the early 1980s, physicist Harold Brode and several collaborators had begun research to predict fire damage for use in nuclear war planning. Long before, Brode had modeled the nuclear blast environment and contributed to the understanding of a variety of nuclear weapons effects. He had an entirely different perspective from the fire research community. Brode did not extrapolate from large conventional urban or forest fires but developed a regional model of the nuclear fire environment created by the heat rising from many simultaneous ignitions. Consistent with the physics of the fire environment, he then developed algorithms to predict fire damage that incorporated both the form and content of existing blast damage algorithms. In short, Brode worked within a "fire-blast damage frame," and enlarged the blast VNTK system to the fire-blast VNTK system.[5] This was a significant innovation that in many cases predicted far greater damage: On average, damage from fire reached two to five times farther than damage from blast alone. At the same time, the procedure was made palatable and "useable" by preserving the VNTK system and by conforming to expectations that predictions took the form of damage to specific structures. The effort was well-funded by the

Defense Nuclear Agency, the government organization then responsible for research on nuclear weapons effects. Over about a dozen years, the research yielded increasingly powerful predictions and looked likely to become incorporated into war planning. However, the effort was halted in 1992, though evidently revived in different form later.

Clearly, the organizations involved in nuclear war planning had the potential for generating significant innovation. Given the deep entrenchment of routines to predict blast damage, the development of a method to predict fire damage was certainly not inevitable; indeed, it seems unlikely. Without the determination of a single researcher who was well connected and bureaucratically savvy, nuclear fire damage would have continued to look utterly unpredictable.

How does this innovation square with the institutional persistence expected in path-dependent processes? Although much of the history above is self-reinforcing, in two respects it does not conform to important scholarly understandings about path dependence. Perhaps not coincidentally, these are the earliest and most recent aspects of the history, where issues of change are particularly salient.

Scholars have argued that the origins of path-dependent processes lie in random events. For economist Brian Arthur, history itself is equated with "random historical sequence," "historical chance," and "the small elements outside our economic model that we must treat as random."[6] For sociologist Jack Goldstone, historical "outcomes are related stochastically to initial conditions.'"[7]

History as "random"—this is a remarkably ahistorical approach to history. As we saw, the origins of U.S. precision bombing doctrine and its emphasis on blast weapons were structured by the past; for example, a long-standing political aversion to "promiscuous bombing" and a service tradition of precision marksmanship. If the development of U.S. precision bombing doctrine does not seem inevitable—as what history does?—neither does it seem random. No wonder that historians have opted for weaker notions of path dependence, claiming only that "what has happened at an earlier point in time will affect the possible outcomes of a sequence of events occurring at a later point in time," an idea that denies stochastic origins.[8]

Regarding change, scholars are divided on how "locked-in" are path-dependent processes. In the strong version, path-dependent processes "set into motion institutional patterns or event chains that have deterministic properties." Like inertia, "once processes are set into motion . . . [they] tend to stay in motion" and to "reproduce a particular institutional pattern over time."[9]

Political scientist Kathleen Thelen critiques this strong version of path dependence as "both too contingent and too deterministic . . . too contingent in . . . the initial choice" in not emphasizing, among other things, antecedent conditions and "too deterministic in that once the initial choice is made . . . the argument becomes mechanical."[10]

Political scientist Paul Pierson argues for a less deterministic version: "Path dependent analyses need not imply that a particular alternative is permanently locked in following the move onto a self-reinforcing path. . . . Asserting that the social landscape can be permanently frozen hardly is credible, and that is not the claim. Change continues, but it is bounded change—until something erodes or swamps the mechanisms of reproduction that generate continuity."[11]

Self-reinforcing processes and bounded change characterize the innovations made over decades in the VNTK system to predict blast damage. However, erosion or swamping—presumably some form of external pressure or shock—is not the mechanism at work in the recent past. The external environment mattered—whether in political mobilization around nuclear winter issues or the end of the Cold War. Those involved in predicting nuclear weapons damage used these events as political resources to bolster their own claims. But the key to potential change was not the external environment but an internal incubator of innovation: the government agency responsible for research on nuclear weapons effects, the Defense Nuclear Agency. At the same time, far-reaching innovation was anything but guaranteed.

In sum, path dependence powerfully describes much of the self-reinforcing history of nuclear weapons damage prediction. But it does less well as a description of origins or of more recent innovation. Wherever one cuts into the history, whether the earliest origins of bomb damage prediction before and during World War II or the post–World War II development of nuclear damage prediction, random processes are not a good characterization. And, more recently, the history looks neither locked-in along a predetermined path nor jolted off that path by external change.

The Science of Destruction Is Social

I want to return to a theme that has run throughout the book: how deeply social is the enterprise to understand nuclear weapons effects and predict weapons damage. Of course, nothing could be more powerful in its facticity than the effects of nuclear weapons. Yet understanding such effects is a social enterprise in at least four respects.

First, as we have seen, nature is read from inside institutions. These include institutions of science and engineering, which bring to bear distinctive intellectual orientations and tools, and organizations with goals and frames that shape how problems are represented and solutions conceived.

Two examples from the text suffice to show how organizations embed the social in the understanding of nuclear weapons effects. "Target hardness" is not simply a characterization of the strength of structures. The phrase is meaningless without a specification of social purpose, which is indicated by the type and degree of damage sought. Take an example of a heavy industrial structure containing steel or chemical production. If the goal is to collapse some supporting walls to preclude use of the building until major repairs are made ("moderate" blast damage), then the structure is rated as less hard, or more vulnerable, than if the goal is to turn the structure into matchsticks ("severe" blast damage). Many structures and installations have two such ratings (or more if "light" damage is also included). If fire damage is considered, the structure will be rated as more vulnerable than if fire is ignored. Thus, how hard a target is considered to be depends not only on its physical construction but on the level of damage sought and the kind of damage that "counts."

Similarly, the predictability of mass fire and resulting fire damage depends not only on whether variation in weather conditions significantly affects the probability and range of mass fire, but on the criteria, or social requirements, for prediction. Weather itself illustrates the social aspects of prediction. For purposes of packing my suitcase, I know that in the summer, I should pack for much warmer weather in Washington, D.C., than in San Francisco, and I know that it is extremely unlikely that I will need an umbrella in Los Angeles. For these purposes, the weather can be predicted with high probability. On the other hand, if I want to know if I can wear suede shoes in January in San Francisco, I probably will think that the weather cannot be predicted very well. Thus, it is only meaningful to say that something can or cannot be predicted against some understanding of purpose. Regarding the predictability of fire damage, the requirements for solution were critical. If nuclear war planners had accepted a solution in which area damage was predicted (e.g., the area corresponding to the perimeter of mass fire at Hiroshima), a robust prediction of mass fire, and resulting damage, could have been developed in the first decades after World War II. But because war planners thought it necessary to characterize the vulnerability of specific structures to fire damage, in a way consistent with how blast damage was predicted, a method to do so was not developed until the 1980s.

Second, the institutions dedicated to planning and predicting nuclear destruction are sites of great sociability. We have seen the rivalry and exasperation of wartime service; the camaraderie of office life; the hard work and sly strategies involved in mobilizing bureaucratic support; and the drama of high-level briefings in the protected room in the Pentagon known as the "tank." This sociability is seen in the jokes and slang used at the time (e.g., "If we meet our damage goals . . . then we don't give a hoot if we incinerate everything in the area");[12] in unpublished manuscripts and private publications such as Jerry Strope's "Autobiography of a Nerd" and Frank Shelton's *Reflections of a Nuclear Weaponeer;* and in published articles and books. (We should not forget that this social world was a highly compartmentalized and secret one—but secrecy involves its own social interactions. Henry Nash, for example, who worked in target intelligence in the early 1950s to identify government control targets, did not speak to the analysts who identified atomic power targets. Richard Grassy, for many years the head civilian in the group that analyzed the physical vulnerability of structures, did not discuss his work with his family.)[13]

Third, through omission, abstraction, classification, disembodiment, a focus on physical forces, specialized vocabularies, and whole systems of knowledge, nuclear war planners engage in a social construction of the asocial.[14] The very social world in which nuclear war planners live, both at work and outside, is entirely omitted from the environment they make plans to destroy. As if to anticipate the effect for which they plan—the utter effacement of human society—the environment they consider is abstracted from and devoid of the buzz and hum of human activity. The world of nuclear weapons damage is generally an unpeopled one of physical objects—structures, installations, and equipment.

In this world, buildings are structures that house war-making activities, not people per se; structures are targets; targets are categorized in census-like classifications, identified by numerical designators, located by latitude and longitude, and keyed to specially constructed maps. Specific buildings, installations, and equipment are classified as structural types; structural types are rated by how they respond to the physical forces, such as duration and drag, that act on them; physical forces are studied and described, as are the very large physical environments created by the blast, fire, and other effects of nuclear weapons. The effects of nuclear weapons on plants, animals, and people are studied in terms of material and physiological response. Nuclear weapons are allocated for maximum efficiency in a language of cost, requirements, and transportation logistics (weapons, for example, are "deconflicted" so that a warhead detonating does not destroy another aimed at the same or a nearby location). Each aspect is part of an edifice of disciplinary understanding, empirical study, and particular bodies of knowledge created to solve specialized problems. Much of this knowledge has been put in the form of computer codes and embedded in organizational routines. Such abstraction is inevitable in war planning and, indeed, in any planning, but it is not the less striking for it.

When the social is brought into nuclear war planning via considerations of civil defense, the effect is comic, an unintentional parody of the planning process that emphasizes the inability of planners to incorporate the social aspects of destruction. In civil defense planning, human society is neither omitted nor obliterated. Rather, it endures in a fantasyland of normalcy where a few buildings and mannequins represent a "typical American community"; the family car provides some protection "against the radiation, heat, and blast of a nuclear bomb"; "fireproof housekeeping" is efficacious; prompt rescue and recovery operations are possible; and families in protective shelters consume peanut butter and play charades. Even acknowledgment of the limits of civil defense planning parody it, as in the statements made in congressional testimony in the early 1960s that "we are not trying to maintain the present standard of living under thermonuclear attack," or that while "nuclear attack on the United States could be very serious, it need not be catastrophic."

Fourth, the meaning of "conventionalization," a term coined by Hans Morgenthau to characterize thinking about nuclear weapons as though they were conventional weapons, should be rethought. Robert Jervis argues that conventionalization is psychologically attractive because it denies what is disturbing about nuclear weapons and intellectually attractive because it allows analysts to use familiar strategic concepts.[15] The concept is lodged in the individual psyche. However, conventionalization should not be understood primarily as a fallacy of thought. It is much more powerfully understood as a social phenomenon residing in organizational capabilities and knowledge-laden routines in which nuclear weapons are treated as though they were conventional weapons—as though they cause damage to specific structures and do not lay waste to vast areas, as though they cause damage by blast and not by mass fire or other less "conventional" means, as though their destructive power should be measured as so many tons of dynamite, and so on. Conventionalization lies in the problems organizations seek to solve and in their routines, not in individuals' minds. The implications for change are significant. The point is not to change thinking or attitudes or psychological acuity but to change the problem-focus of organizations in building knowledge and routines.

Organization-Made Disasters

These ideas—organizational frames, path dependence, the deep embeddedness of the social in our readings of nature, and the social construction of the asocial—illuminate the particularities of the history represented in *Whole World on Fire*. I want now to step outside this history to explore briefly some broader implications.

In the introduction I said that the partial prediction of nuclear weapons damage is a case of poorly understood or unanticipated physical processes whose resulting representation of the physical world in documents, technologies, and routines is inaccurate or incomplete. I mentioned some other examples: the shipbuilder's lack of understanding of how brittle the steel was in the *Titanic;* Grumman's lack of understanding of the severity of potholes on New York City streets and their effect on newly designed buses; and the engineers' and architects' lack of anticipation and understanding of the effects of burning jet fuel inside the towers of the World Trade Center.

These are also examples of problem solving consistent with the best contemporary standards of professional practice: There was no suppression of evidence or disregard of a well-understood body of knowledge. (Grumman may not have been engaged in best practice, but the company did not suppress evidence or lie, and it quickly took responsibility for its design errors.)[16] To say this is to adumbrate four categories of organizational approaches to problem solving (see Table C.1).

In the first category, physical processes are well understood by organizational problem solvers, and organizational actions are consistent with best practice. Consequently, resulting technologies and knowledge-laden routines are reliable and safe. This is the world each of us hopes to live in all the time, a world in which ships float, buildings are structurally sound, elevators are safe, airplanes fly as expected, and mushrooms and meat in the supermarket are untainted.

Second, there is the "dark" side of organizations, the world of corporate wrongdoing and crime, in which physical processes are well understood, but organizational approaches to problem solving fly in the face of contemporary best practice: Organizational actors neglect, suppress, or lie about evidence and the state of knowledge. In these cases, the pursuit of craven organizational interests in profit or, rarely, organizational or national pride, cause people in positions of responsibility to ignore physical processes that they could, and should, understand. Examples include the cigarette industry after about 1960, when the connection between lung cancer and cigarette smoking had been clearly established and the industry both denied the state of knowledge and suppressed and twisted evidence; the suppression of evidence of danger in the Corvair automobile that rolled over; the decision not to change the design of the Ford Pinto gas tank that exploded; and the continued manufacture and sale of Firestone tires that shredded. Other examples include French officials who did not prevent contamination of their national blood supply by the HIV virus; builders in India who did not construct buildings to code, which led to disastrous collapses in a large earthquake in early 2001; and British manufacturers dumping in Europe thousands of tons of feed suspected of causing mad cow disease after the feed had been banned in the United Kingdom. According to one editorial, the dumping was "morally unforgivable even if legal."[17]

Third is the "dumb and dark" side of organizations in which problem solvers poorly understand relevant physical processes, and their approaches

TABLE C.1.
ORGANIZATIONAL APPROACHES TO PROBLEM SOLVING

Category	Physical processes well understood?	Organizational actions consistent with best practice?	Potential results	Examples
1. Ideal	Yes	Yes	Technologies and knowledge-laden routines are reliable and safe	Ships float; buildings stand up; food is safe
2. "Dark" side	Yes	No	Dire consequences as organizational actors neglect, suppress, or lie about the state of knowledge, usually for profit	Cigarette industry after 1960; Ford Pinto gas tanks; Firestone tires
3. "Dumb and dark" side	No	No	Dire consequences, but was there negligence in organizational actors' interpretation of evidence?	Mad cow disease; Cerro Grande fire; *Challenger* explosion
4. "Ignorant but upright"	No	Yes	Dire or potentially dire consequences due to poorly understood physical processes reflected in knowledge-laden routines	*Titanic*; effects of burning jet fuel in World Trade Center; partial prediction of nuclear weapons damage; but disaster averted at Citicorp Center

to problem solving are apparently inconsistent with contemporary best practice. These cases often raise difficult questions about what could and should have been known, whether evidence was interpreted poorly, and if action was taken without proper precaution. Was there negligence, in other words, and if so, to what degree, and why? Examples include the very profitable use of sheep remains in cattle feed in Britain in the 1970s in the face of some early warnings of risk, which resulted in what we now know as mad cow disease; and the conduct of clinical trials for an asthma study at Johns Hopkins medical school that resulted in the death of a participant. The study "failed to obtain published literature about the known association between hexamethonium [the drug used in the study] and lung toxicity," which was "readily available," and violated federal regulations that required, among other things, the convening of face-to-face meetings of medical review boards overseeing such studies.[18]

Another example is the accidental burning by the U.S. Park Service of 48,000 acres (75 square miles) in the Cerro Grande fire near Los Alamos National Laboratory in May 2000. Eighteen thousand residents were evacuated, hundreds of homes were destroyed or damaged, and total damage was estimated at about $1 billion. In a contingency never planned for, the nuclear weapons laboratory itself was threatened, and forty laboratory structures were destroyed.[19] This gigantic wildland fire resulted from a deliberately set, or prescribed, fire going out of control. First, the prescribed fire burned beyond its boundaries and then, to contain it, a backfire was introduced that, in conjunction with the wind and seasonal conditions, was disastrous.[20] A National Park Service board of inquiry found that "questionable judgment was exercised" but that there were "no violations of policy."[21] It is clear that Park Service fire managers did not understand the risks, and this was due partly to procedural problems in risk assessment. The National Weather Service did not predict winds in their three- to five-day forecast due to constantly changing conditions, and Park Service personnel evidently took that to mean high winds were not expected. Indeed, the Park Service official in charge "said that if he had better information on the wind . . . he would not have introduced fire . . . into the burn area."[22] Yet, a General Accounting Office (GAO) study said, "This time of year typically brings high winds, [further,] the area was in the midst of a 3-year drought. . . . Also, during the 2-week period before the fire was started . . . four prescribed fires got out of control in that region.[23] Another procedural problem was that the fire complexity ratings for prescribed fires had been mistranscribed on the web site used by National Park Service fire managers, resulting in a significant underestimate of the difficulties that could be encountered. Given evident incompetence and inadequate procedures, the GAO recommended that prescribed burn plans "need to be 'peer-reviewed' by independent, knowledgeable individuals."[24]

Another example is the U.S. space shuttle program's understanding of the behavior of the O-rings that sealed in the hot propellant gases in the shuttle's booster rockets—the failure of which resulted in the explosion of the *Challenger* on January 28, 1986. The engineers did not understand the mechanisms of sealing in cold weather (although they thought they did), nor did they clearly see the correlation of cold temperature and erosion of the O-rings by hot gases. But were they negligent in not understanding these complicated processes? On the one hand, they believed they were following best practice, and in many respects they were. On the other hand, in part due to design compromises (and all projects have design compromises), the difficulty of understanding the sealing mechanisms, and the scale and complexity of the whole enterprise that caused them not to know what they did not know, they unwittingly departed from best practice in a process Diane Vaughan terms the "normalization of deviance." It appears that the catastrophic failure of the *Columbia* space shuttle on February 1, 2003, reflects a similar "incremental descent into poor judgment."[25]

In these examples, organizational history and goals contributed to incompetent problem solving for physical processes that were not well understood. Explicit or implicit pressure from the top to proceed seems likely. In addition, in the short term, precaution can be mind-bogglingly expensive (though not as costly as the failure that may result).[26]

Best Practice, Mostly Bad Outcomes

Finally, let us turn to the fourth category in which poorly understood physical processes, embodied in knowledge-laden technologies and routines, combine with best contemporary practice to produce dire or potentially dire consequences. In addition to the partial prediction of nuclear weapons damage and cases mentioned above—the *Titanic*'s steel, the potholes on New York City streets, and the effects of burning jet fuel in the World Trade Center—there are other striking examples. These include ignorance about the spread of childbed, or puerperal, fever in the eighteenth and nineteenth centuries—"the most serious, deadly, and terrifying of all the complications of childbirth and the most common cause of maternal deaths" in this period;[27] not understood dynamic loads on suspension bridges in the early twentieth century that resulted in the sudden collapse of the Tacoma Narrows Bridge on November 7, 1940; and the failure to calculate certain forces on New York's Citicorp Center and Boston's John Hancock Tower in the 1970s, which could have resulted in catastrophic collapses.

These examples—and there are many others—are especially troubling because they involve no willful misinterpretation of evidence or obvious deviation from best practice. This suggests that incentives to engage in best practice or punitive measures to inhibit such actions will not be effective since competent, even preeminent, practitioners are already doing the best they can and acting with integrity.

This does not mean that nothing can be done. These examples represent a wide range of outcomes. In these cases, the understanding that paves the way to solution can occur after persistent failure (childbed fever) or a single failure (*Titanic,* Tacoma Narrows Bridge, World Trade Center). Dire consequences can also be averted (Citicorp Center, John Hancock Tower) or may remain unrecognized (underestimates of nuclear weapons damage). Thus, these cases have implications both for understanding dire consequences and for preventing disaster.

Let us begin with childbed fever. In the eighteenth and nineteenth centuries, lying-in hospitals for women in childbirth became widespread in Europe. These hospitals provided rest and nutrition for women, professional delivery by midwives and doctors, and training facilities for midwives and medical students. One problem associated with these hospitals was the very high rate of childbed fever. Within a few days after delivery, affected mothers began to suffer from terrible shivers and fevers, excruciating abdominal pain, and, often, death. Sometimes entire maternity wards would suffer epidemics in which "nearly every patient died."[28]

Drawing on current medical knowledge, doctors tried to understand the problem. French doctors who did postmortems on the affected women observed a milky white substance covering the intestines and omentum and theorized that breast milk had metastasized to the abdominal cavity. An English doctor thought it was due to the "putridity" of the indoor atmosphere in which, deprived of an essential ingredient, the air became "vitiated." Others thought childbed fever was due to miasmas—odorless materials in the air emanating from vegetable decomposition—or to "mental depression, malnutrition, or its opposite," gluttony.[29]

Outbreaks of childbed fever were sometimes associated with particular midwives and doctors, but until the early 1850s, no one thought that midwives and doctors themselves might play a role. However, as part of their training, medical students performed postmortem examinations and then routinely went from examining cadavers to delivering women—without washing their hands. And they went from mother to mother delivering babies—again without washing their hands.[30] Their knowledge-laden childbirth routines did not include hand washing for the same reason that we do not routinely stand on our heads before taking tests: They could see no causal connection. It was not until the last quarter of the nineteenth century, after the development of the germ theory and its incorporation into hospital practices of antisepsis and sterilization—thanks largely to the physician Joseph Lister—that incidents of childbed fever, caused primarily by streptococcal bacteria, declined dramatically.[31] Until the germ theory was developed, the theoretical knowledge base from which to derive a solution was beyond not only practitioners in hospitals but all contemporaries.

The ship *Titanic*, which sank in 1912 when it hit an iceberg in the North Atlantic, is similar in one regard: Knowledge of the time was inadequate to prevent catastrophe or to directly address it after. The proximate cause of disaster was the flooding of the forward five compartments in the ship, which as every moviegoer now knows, had been designed to withstand flooding in the first four. The design itself, which set new marks for safety, cannot be faulted by contemporary standards. For many years the prevailing theory held that the iceberg had torn a large continuous gash in the side of the ship. But when the ship was found at the bottom of the ocean many years later, it turned out that the iceberg had not forcefully punctured the side; rather, the pressure of the iceberg had caused the ship's inch-thick steel plates to buckle and to open in several thin discontinuous slits. The plates had buckled because they were brittle in cold water.[32]

Contemporaries understood that brittle metal was a problem in shipbuilding. For that reason, the *Titanic*'s steel plates were not made by the Bessemer process, which produced brittle steel, particularly at low temperatures (due to its high nitrogen content). Indeed, according to an authoritative study, the steel used in the *Titanic* was "probably the best . . . ship plate available in the period of 1909 to 1911." The only other manufacturing method available was the open-hearth process, which was most commonly done in acid-lined tubs. The acid-lined tubs produced steel with a high sulfur content and other chemicals that, as it turned out, also embrittled steel and produced a hull "not suited for service at low temperatures."[33]

Given the lengths to which the *Titanic*'s builders went to design and build a safe ship, it seems highly unlikely that they were aware of the effects of their manufacturing methods. Whether steel makers and metallurgists did not understand how the acid-lined tubs interacted with the steel being produced, or could not analyze the steel content and/or the embrittling effects of certain chemicals, it seems likely that no one understood the vulnerability of the steel produced for the *Titanic*. If the required knowledge regarding content or effects of steel content was not beyond the theoretical knowledge base of the time (and I do not know whether it was or was not), in all likelihood it was beyond the knowledge base available to the organizations and practitioners involved in steel production.

Three other cases illustrate failure to understand physical processes within a context of high professional standards. In the Tacoma Narrows Bridge collapse in 1940 and in the serious design errors in the Citicorp Center and the John Hancock Tower in the 1970s, the required understandings of physical processes were well within the knowledge base of contemporaries and, hence, were much more amenable to solution. In these cases, the failures lay in the problems engineers sought to solve, and the problems they did not.

At the time it was built, the Tacoma Narrows Bridge near Seattle was the third longest suspension bridge in the world (after the Golden Gate Bridge in San Francisco and the George Washington Bridge in New York). From the time it opened in 1940, the bridge, known as "Galloping Gertie," undulated in the wind. Flexible suspension bridges were not unusual in this period and were frequently stiffened after construction. Engineers observed the bridge and began to take steps to reduce the sway, but no one expected a catastrophic failure. A few months after it opened, in a light wind in early November, the bridge not only swayed but began to twist, the sides of the roadway seesawing. Within a short time, the bridge tore itself apart and collapsed.[34] Fortunately, the bridge was closed to traffic that day, and no one was killed.

The bridge had been designed by an eminent engineer, Leon Moisseiff, who worked within well-established suspension bridge design principles of the period. Modern engineers had developed what appeared to be robust design algorithms that calculated wind forces on bridges as static, or steady, forces rather than as dynamic forces. Using this method, they worked within a "design climate" in which they focused on principles of structural simplicity and aesthetics to produce "ever longer, slenderer, and lighter suspension bridges."[35] The methods they used had been successful in the George Washington Bridge, built in the 1920s, and in later suspension bridges. However, the algorithms poorly represented the forces on the bridges, although bridge engineers were unaware of it at the time. Engineers modeled the wind forces pushing sideways on the roadway, but they did not take into account the forces that could lift the road and drag it down, much like an airplane wing. It was these forces that would cause the Tacoma Narrows Bridge to twist and collapse.[36]

Clearly, the effects of dynamic forces on bridges were beyond bridge designers' understanding at the time. But the new field of aerodynamics, used in the design of airplanes in the 1930s, provided precisely the dynamic analysis that was needed for suspension bridge building. Indeed, engineer W. Watters Pagon published a series of eight articles on aerodynamics in the 1930s—the first titled "What Aerodynamics Can Teach the Civil Engineer." However, according to author-engineer Henry Petroski, "the whole series seems largely to have been ignored by the bridge builders," in large part because "bridge building was becoming so highly specialized that there was the 'danger of losing contact with the other branches of engineering and with allied sciences.'"[37] In this case, a fully developed knowledge base was available, but bridge builders did not make use of it.

Two recent cases illustrate other oversights. To accommodate a church on a corner of the building site of the fifty-nine-story Citicorp Center in New York, the structural engineer William J. LeMessurier decided to support the building's steel skeleton on four massive columns placed at the center of each side rather than at the corners as was usually done; he also used an innovative system of steel braces to provide strength against the wind. But when an engineering student challenged the strength of the completed structure, LeMessurier found, to his great surprise, that the steel braces were not as strong as he had expected against winds hitting the building from the corners, called quartering winds. The New York City building code required only that the perpendicular winds pushing face-on to the structure be calculated, but LeMessurier had also calculated quartering winds in the design; in particular, the massive columns placed in the center of each side were unusually strong against them. Although the engineer's recalculations showed that the strain on the braces was greater than anticipated, it was well within the margin of safety, all other things being equal.[38]

But all other things were not equal. In his reexamination, LeMessurier also discovered that the joints that held together the building's steel girders had not been built to his original specifications. Instead, his office had approved a change recommended by the construction company that the joints be bolted instead of welded, on the grounds that welds were stronger than necessary. This was not a question of improper procedure or shoddy construction. The problem was that in designing the bolts, LeMessurier's office had not considered the sensitivity to quartering winds. This, plus another "subtle conceptual error," meant that the Citicorp building could fail catastrophically in a "sixteen-year storm"—a storm with a probability of occurring once every sixteen years.

After contemplating silence or suicide, LeMessurier explained the problem to the building's lawyers, architects, insurers, and owners. Emergency repairs were made, and disaster averted.

Somewhat similarly, in 1975 a renowned structural engineer, Bruno Thurlimann, determined that under certain wind conditions the new John Hancock Tower in Boston could fall over, not on its face but on its "narrow edge . . . as if a book standing upright on a table were to fall on its spine."[39] (This is the same building notorious for window panes falling out.) Like the Citicorp Center, the John Hancock Tower was an innovative design that met all building codes. And like the Citicorp building, the structure was scrutinized by fellow engineers. As with Citicorp, analysis revealed the problem, and it was corrected immediately.

We might be tempted to say that the structural engineers in these two cases were not adhering to best practice, since best practice would dictate that buildings be not so vulnerable to wind forces. Yet, as with the Tacoma Narrows Bridge, the engineers involved were at the top of their profession, they *defined* best practice, and their oversights were not obvious at the time. However, the understanding of the physical processes involved was well within the knowledge base of civil engineering. In both buildings, when the errors were pointed out by other engineers, those responsible immediately understood the problem. The framing of problems is clearly what caused a lack of attention to particular wind loads on these structures.

Finally, the effects of burning jet fuel inside the towers of the World Trade Center may seem like a failure to anticipate the social environment rather than the physical one. It is hard not to agree with National Security Advisor Condoleezza Rice's statement that "I don't think anybody could have predicted that these people would take an airplane and slam it into the World Trade Center."[40] Yet, Leslie Robertson, the engineer in charge of the structural design of the towers, did consider the contingency of the largest jet aircraft of the time, a Boeing 707, hitting the building, and he designed the building to withstand its impact.[41] He did not, however, design for "thousands of gallons of fuel being put inside the building," according to a prominent structural engineer, Abolhassan Astaneh-Asl.[42] Why not? According to Robertson himself, after designing for the impact of an aircraft,

> The next step would have been to think about the fuel load, and I've been searching my brain, but I don't know what happened there, whether in all our testing we thought about it. Now we know what happens—it explodes. I don't know if we considered the fire damage that would cause. Anyway, the architect, not the engineer, is the one who specifies the fire system.[43]

Aircraft impact, force, and structural response were anticipated, but potential fire damage was overlooked.

State of Knowledge, Problem Recognition, Secrecy

We see in these examples a range of determinants of understanding of physical processes. At one extreme are the spread of childbed fever and the brittleness of the *Titanic*'s steel plates, which were beyond the ability of every contemporary to understand. In such cases, the background state of knowledge about the physical world defines and delimits how problems are cast.

In the other examples, the requisite knowledge base about the physical world was, at least in theory, available to contemporaries. In these cases, the key lay in how problems were represented and solutions were defined—organizational frames. For example, had the designers of suspension bridges been familiar with aerodynamics, they could have much more quickly understood the forces on the Tacoma Narrows Bridge and would have solved structural design problems differently. Had the *Challenger*'s engineers been deeply grounded in statistical analysis or graphical analysis, they would have seen the danger of launching the *Challenger* shuttle in record-cold weather.[44] It is not my goal to explain how these particular organizational frames developed. Indeed, satisfying explanations have already been written. I simply want to say that these are the questions to be asked and answered.

We have seen that feedback from the environment can indicate that a severe problem exists, but contemporaries may be unable to diagnosis the problem or solve it (childbed fever). On the other hand, contemporaries may have the ability to recognize a problem before there is any direct indication that a problem exists (Citicorp).[45]

We can see that environmental feedback is *always* mediated through social expectations, whether at the organizational or societal level. For example, at the organizational and professional level, the flexibility of suspension bridges, even the galloping of Gertie, did not lead bridge designers to think there was a serious problem in their calculations of forces. They expected the swaying and thought they understood its causes. Similarly, the *Challenger* space shuttle's engineers reinterpreted the increasing erosion of the O-rings as normal and not dangerous.[46] We might think that mobilization for safety occurs when the threat to life is obvious. But even potential or actual deaths are not good predictors of the social expectations of the acceptability of failures. Why do important problems in airline safety not get addressed until after crashes bring them to public attention? Why have large numbers of deaths from routine medical mistakes persisted for so long?[47]

Understanding that physical signs must always be socially interpreted also allows us not to make the mistake of using later understandings to read back into earlier situations our own superiority and participants' apparent stupidity. As a member of the commission investigating the *Challenger* disaster, physicist Richard Feynman's famous and rhetorically effective demonstration that O-rings stiffen in ice water was, in terms of our understanding of what space shuttle engineers understood, beside the point. The *Challenger*'s engineers knew that O-rings stiffen in cold temperature.[48] They had *not* understood, among other things, that the backup that they had thought would compensate for O-ring behavior in cold temperature was inadequate. Feynman and the rest of the commission did not understand the complicated organizational context that had led to these interpretations of O-ring behavior. No one did until the painstaking research and original interpretation by Diane Vaughan.

Finally, to what extent were people other than organizational problem solvers aware of a problem and empowered to address it? As we have seen, transparency of technology and design to a wide professional community can raise awareness of problems and prevent disaster. Catastrophic failure can also make widely known what was not and can bring others into the process. This is not automatic. Under conditions of extreme secrecy and lack of democratic accountability, even disaster can be made invisible. For example, in 1979 a military biological weapons laboratory in Sverdlovsk in the Soviet Union accidentally released airborne anthrax spores that killed sixty-six people. Soviet officials lied and claimed that people had died of gastrointestinal and cutaneous anthrax due to consumption of contaminated meat and contact with diseased animals. Questions were raised over many years, but it was not until a decade and a half later that the matter was fully resolved as to the kind of anthrax and the source of the release.[49]

Nuclear Weapons Damage

These cases give us a comparative context in which to understand the half century in which the U.S. government did not predict nuclear fire damage for decades and then chose not to incorporate such predictions into knowledge-laden organizational routines. Clearly, the failure to predict fire damage lies at an extreme of persistence (not to say potential consequence), at least among known contemporary examples.

One possible explanation does not hold here: The contemporary knowledge base did not foreclose the possibility of prediction. Although most considered nuclear mass fire and resulting damage so complex as to defy prediction, an understanding of the basic physical processes involved was well within the knowledge base of physicists, and had been for many years. The applied knowledge required for damage prediction was not so ready-made as in the case of Citicorp or the John Hancock building or even the Tacoma Narrows Bridge: It was not circulating among practicing professionals. Instead, it had to be made, just as all knowledge about nuclear weapons effects had to be made. The physics of the fire environment had to be modeled. The potential variables contributing to fire damage had to be analyzed. The results had to be translated into organizational routines that were consistent with and built on past damage-predicting routines. As this book has demonstrated, the key lay in organizational frames, the approaches to problems by those in organizations, which influenced the mobilization of expertise, resources, and resulting knowledge-laden routines.

One might think that the mass fires at Hiroshima and Nagasaki would have been sufficient indication that fire damage mattered. However, the issue was not understood to be whether nuclear fire damage would sometimes occur, but whether it would occur with enough regularity that it could be robustly predicted. The answer was thought to be no. Nothing occurred after the war to shake confidence in the adequacy of this answer. But a counterfactual or two demonstrates the role that environmental feedback could have played. Had one of the atomic bombs dropped over the Nevada Test Site gone astray and accidentally burned down Las Vegas—approximately 65 miles away—or had the United States inadvertently burned down Moscow in a "limited" nuclear exchange, it seems likely that war planners would have reevaluated the necessity and feasibility of predicting nuclear fire damage. Fortunately for the world, these scenarios never occurred.

Unfortunately, as we have seen, it is often catastrophes that make known what was not known, or widely known, and that put the pressure of public accountability on internal organizational processes. Although professional standards within the nuclear weapons effects community have been high, the issue of nuclear fire damage has been nearly invisible to the public. There has been very little mention in the press or discussion by scholars of its importance or omission in war planning, and no discussion until now of how this has come about.[50] The lack of visibility resulted from both formal secrecy and opacity. The world of nuclear war planning is a secret one separated from practicing professionals and ordinary citizens.[51] To a large extent, this is a self-policing system in which those with classified knowledge pledge not to divulge it.

Still, it may not be the formal secrecy that has kept the issue from public awareness so much as opacity: Even unclassified information is not widely understood. Unlike building design, the technical issues are not familiar to a broad community of practicing professionals. With the notable exception of MIT physicist Theodore Postol, few outside the government-sponsored nuclear weapons effects community have paid attention to these issues or been available to explain them to journalists, scholars, and the wider public. The organizational processes that have determined which problems are solved and which are not are no less important, and these too have been hidden from the public.

No wonder, then, that the lack of prediction of nuclear fire damage has been so persistent. These are largely self-reinforcing organizational processes, sealed off from the public through secrecy and opacity. And since World War II, the consequences of these weapons have been in the realm of the hypothetical.

What we have seen is paradoxical: Organizations should think about what they are not thinking about—a kind of organizational walking and chewing gum at the same time. It is not that organizations should simply do worst-case analysis well. They should figure out what problems they are not trying to solve and examine how those could lead to consequences worse than the worst case being considered. The engineer LeMessurier's advice is instructive: "Any time you depart from established practice, make ten times the effort, ten times the investigations. Especially on a very large-scale project."[52] Of course, organizations do not think; people think and approach problems in ways that are structured by organizational history, capacity, and routines. As we have seen, it can be extremely difficult to change organizational approaches to problem solving. Dominant understandings, not surprisingly, dominate. Organizations that do not encourage alternatives to, or questioning of, dominant approaches to problem solving may overlook important problems. (In FBI agent Coleen Rowley's words after the September 11 attacks, this is the "don't rock the boat, don't ask a question" problem.)[53] Queries from the top of an organization, or from outside, regarding technology and the physical world may be answered in ways that simply reflect ongoing approaches to problem solving. Further, change cannot simply be mandated from the top or from outside. To be fully effective, change must be implemented at the level of knowledge-laden routines, algorithms that both represent problems and embody solutions.

The only alternative to learning from catastrophe is learning from smaller failures, near failures, and scenarios of possible failure and unforeseen consequences. Precaution regarding the unforeseen is particularly important in a world in which the full consequences of our actions will not be fully known until much later. We have experienced many unforeseen consequences of twentieth-century innovation, from the miracle mineral asbestos that has proved dangerous to human health to the miracle drugs that are steadily losing their effectiveness in promoting human health. What will the twenty-first century hold? The consequences will be great indeed if, among other things, we do not anticipate the social and ecological consequences of huge construction projects (like the Three Gorges and Narmada dams), if we do not exercise precaution in proceeding with genetically engineered organisms, and if we do not understand the effects of our actions on global warming.

In all of our interactions with the physical world, organizational integrity and intelligence is critical. Visibility of organizational actions to independent professionals and scholars is necessary. Comprehensibility of organizational processes to a wider public is essential. Democratic accountability is indispensable.

Notes

INTRODUCTION

1. Kistiakowsky quote from memorandum for the president from the special assistant to the president for science and technology, 25 November 1960, annex to note by the Secretaries to the Joint Chiefs of Staff on Strategic Target Planning, JCS 2056/208, 27 January 1961, 3205 Target Systems (17 Aug 59) Sec. 9, Record Group 218, Records of the Joint Chiefs of Staff, Modern Military Records, National Archives at College Park, Md. (NACP); document declassified through Freedom of Information Act request by National Security Archive, George Washington University. Bethe quoted in Mary Palevsky, *Atomic Fragments: A Daughter's Questions* (Berkeley: University of California Press, 2000), p. 33.

2. Thom Shanker, "12 Million Could Die at Once in an India-Pakistan Nuclear War," *New York Times,* May 27, 2002; according to the article, the "deaths caused by urban firestorms" were "subsequent deaths," like "deaths from long-term radiation, or the disease and starvation expected to spread"—in other words, not very predictable. See also Elisabeth Bumiller and Thom Shanker, "Bush Presses Pakistan on Kashmir and Orders Rumsfeld to Region," *New York Times,* May 31, 2002; Todd S. Purdum with Seth Mydans, "U.S. Envoys Ready to Press Two Foes in Kashmir Crisis," *New York Times,* June 3, 2002. The estimate was prepared by the Defense Intelligence Agency, an organization that figures heavily in the history that follows.

3. Some important targets in nuclear war plans are not located in suburban or urban areas, but a large number of military, command, industrial, and political targets are co-located there. See, e.g., Ashton B. Carter, "Assessing Command System Vulnerability," in Carter, John D. Steinbruner, and Charles A. Zraket, eds., *Managing Nuclear Operations* (Washington, D.C.: Brookings Institution, 1987), pp. 561–563, 571–572.

4. Gilbert Binninger, Roger Craver, and Suzanne Wright, *Staff Officers' Guide for Targeting Uncertainties,* DNA-TR-89-115, prepared for Director, Defense Nuclear Agency, Washington, D.C. (n.p., January 1990), p. ix; discussed in chapter 9.

5. I draw heavily on Wiebe E. Bijker's definition of "technological frame" in Bijker, *Of Bicycles, Bakelites, and Bulbs: Toward a Theory of Sociotechnical Change* (Cambridge: MIT Press, 1995). See chapter 2.

6. See, e.g., Edwin Hutchins's study of ship navigation, *Cognition in the Wild* (Cambridge: MIT Press, 1995), esp. pp. 317–351, and Diane Vaughan, *The Challenger Launch Decision: Risky Technology, Culture, and Deviance at NASA* (Chicago: University of Chicago Press, 1996).

7. *James Cameron's Titanic Explorer* (Fox Interactive CD-ROM, 1997); Katherine Felkins, H. P. Leighly, Jr., and A. Jankovic, "The Royal Mail Ship *Titanic:* Did a Metallurgical Failure Cause a Night to Remember?" *JOM* [formerly *Journal of Metals*] 50, no. 1 (1998): 12–18, available at www.tms.org/pubs/journals/JOM.

8. James Barron, "Builder of Buses Says City Roads Cracked Frames," *New York Times,* December 16, 1980; Judith Cummings, "Questions and Answers about the Grumman Buses,"

New York Times, December 17, 1980; "Testing of City Buses Faulted in U.S. Study," *New York Times,* June 22, 1981; David W. Dunlap, "Grumman Finds Perfectly Aged Potholes for Testing Buses," *New York Times,* October 10, 1981; Suzanne Daley, "All Grumman Buses to Be Put Off Streets in City Permanently," *New York Times,* February 8, 1984.

9. Abolhassan Astaneh-Asl, interviewed by Terry Gross, *Fresh Air,* National Public Radio, October 16, 2001; John Seabrook, "The Tower Builder," *New Yorker,* November 19, 2001, 64–73.

10. On the concept of closure, see Trevor J. Pinch and Wiebe E. Bijker, "The Social Construction of Facts and Artifacts: Or How the Sociology of Science and the Sociology of Technology Might Benefit Each Other," in Bijker, Thomas P. Hughes, and Pinch, eds., *The Social Construction of Technological Systems: New Directions in the Sociology and History of Technology* (Cambridge: MIT Press, 1987); H. Tristram Engelhardt, Jr., and Arthur L. Caplan, *Scientific Controversies: Case Studies in the Resolution and Closure of Disputes in Science and Technology* (Cambridge: Cambridge University Press, 1987).

11. See Donald MacKenzie, *Inventing Accuracy: A Historical Sociology of Nuclear Missile Guidance* (Cambridge: MIT Press, 1990); and Vaughan, *Challenger Launch Decision.*

12. R. W. Apple, Jr., "A Lesson from Shultz," *New York Times,* December 9, 1986.

CHAPTER 1. COMPLETE RUIN

1. I have written this chapter in close consultation with Theodore A. Postol. Sources include: Samuel Glasstone and Philip J. Dolan, eds., *The Effects of Nuclear Weapons,* 3d ed. (Washington, D.C.: U.S. Government Printing Office [GPO], 1977); Theodore A. Postol, "Possible Fatalities from Superfires following Nuclear Attacks in or near Urban Areas," in Fredric Solomon and Robert Q. Marston, eds., *The Medical Implications of Nuclear War* (Washington, D.C.: National Academy Press, 1986), pp. 15–72; Theodore A. Postol, "Targeting," in Ashton B. Carter, John D. Steinbruner, and Charles A. Zraket, eds., *Managing Nuclear Operations* (Washington, D.C.: Brookings Institution, 1987), pp. 373–406; Lachlan Forrow et al., "Accidental Nuclear War—A Post–Cold War Assessment," *New England Journal of Medicine* 338, no. 18 (1998): 1326–1331; R. D. Small and H. L. Brode, *Physics of Large Urban Fires,* PSR Report 1010, final report for Federal Emergency Management Agency, Washington, D.C. (Santa Monica, Calif.: Pacific-Sierra Research Corp., March 1980); Harold L. Brode and Richard D. Small, *Fire Damage and Strategic Targeting,* PSR Note 567, sponsored by Defense Nuclear Agency, Washington, D.C. (Los Angeles: Pacific-Sierra Research Corp., June 1983); H. L. Brode, G. P. Fisher, P. F. X. Konokpa, A. Laupa, and G. E. McClellan, *Fire Damage to Urban/Industrial Targets,* vol. 1, *Executive Summary,* and voluminous unclassified material from vol. 2, *Technical Report,* PSR Report 1936, prepared for Headquarters Defense Nuclear Agency, Washington, D.C. (Los Angeles: Pacific-Sierra Research Corp., 25 July 1989).

2. Glasstone and Dolan, *Effects of Nuclear Weapons,* lists the yield of the bomb at Hiroshima as 12.5 kilotons; U.S. Department of Energy, *United States Nuclear Tests, July 1945 through September 1992,* DOE/NV—209-Rev. 15 (Las Vegas, Nev.: U.S. Department of Energy, Nevada Operations Office, December 2000), p. xi, lists the yield at Hiroshima as 15 kilotons; available at www.nv.doe.gov/news&pubs/publications/historyreports/pdfs/DOENV 209_REV15.pdf. Both publications list the yield of the Nagasaki bomb as 21 kilotons.

3. Many weapons in modern arsenals have yields of 300 kilotons or more. In the United States, the Minuteman IIIa, MX/Peacekeeper, and Trident II systems are estimated to have warhead yields of 335, 300, and 475 kilotons respectively. Robert S. Norris et al., "NRDC Nuclear Notebook: U.S. Nuclear Forces," *Bulletin of the Atomic Scientists* 59, no. 3 (2003): 76.

Russian ICBM warheads range from 550 to 750 kilotons; Russian submarine warheads, from 100 to 200 kilotons. Robert S. Norris et al., "NRDC Nuclear Notebook: Russian Nuclear Forces, 2003," *Bulletin of the Atomic Scientists* 59, no. 4 (2003): 72, both available at www .thebulletin.org. From the mid-1950s to the early 1960s, the United States introduced into its arsenal thousands of very high-yield nuclear weapons, ranging from 1 megaton (1,000 kilotons) to 10–15 megatons. Thomas B. Cochran et al., *Nuclear Weapons Databook,* vol. 2, *U.S. Nuclear Warhead Production* (Cambridge, Mass.: Ballinger, 1987), pp. 10–11; Thomas B. Cochran, William M. Arkin, and Milton M. Hoenig, *Nuclear Weapons Databook,* vol. 1, *U.S. Nuclear Forces and Capabilities* (Cambridge, Mass.: Ballinger, 1984), pp. 10–11, 39; Robert Berman and Bill Gunston, *Rockets and Missiles of World War III* (New York: Exeter Books, 1983), p. 31. In the same period, the Soviet Union introduced into its arsenal thousands of warheads with yields from 1 to 20 megatons. Thomas B. Cochran et al., *Nuclear Weapons Databook,* vol. 4, *Soviet Nuclear Weapons* (New York: Harper and Row, 1989), pp. 3–4, 99; Neta Crawford, *Soviet Military Aircraft,* vol. 2 of *World Weapon Database,* ed. by Randall Forsberg (Lexington, Mass.: Lexington Books, 1987); Berman and Gunston, *Rockets and Missiles.* See also the fine compendium by Robert S. Norris and Thomas B. Cochran, *US-USSR/Russian Strategic Offensive Forces, 1945–1996,* Nuclear Weapons Databook (Washington, D.C.: Natural Resources Defense Council, January 1997).

4. Washington has long been a favorite hypothetical target. See Vance O. Mitchell, "The Formative Years of Air Force Intelligence, 1945–1950," in *Society for History in the Federal Government, Occasional Papers,* vol. 1 (Washington, D.C., 1997), p. 43; "Preview of the War We Do Not Want," special issue of *Collier's* (October 27, 1951); and chapter 10.

5. Unattributed, phone conversation with author, February 23, 1999.

6. Postol, "Possible Fatalities from Superfires," pp. 59–66.

7. Brode and Small, *Fire Damage and Strategic Targeting,* pp. 10–21; Brode et al., *Fire Damage to Urban/Industrial Targets,* vol. 1.

8. See Seymour Hersh, "Missile Wars," *New Yorker,* September 26, 1994, 86ff.; William J. Broad, "Antimissile Testing Is Rigged to Hide a Flaw, Critics Say," *New York Times,* June 9, 2000, p. 1; Gary Taubes, "Postol vs. the Pentagon," *Technology Review* 105, no. 3 (2002): 52–61.

9. The award cited Brode's "pioneer[ing] research on nuclear effects in the atmosphere through computer simulations of the phenomena," his "seminal computations," his "landmark nuclear blast wave solution," and his "methodology for assessing damage from fire started by nuclear fireballs and blast waves." Defense Special Weapons Agency Lifetime Achievement Award to Dr. Harold L. Brode, 7 February 1997, signed by Gary L. Curtin, Maj. Gen., USAF, Director.

10. On Tokyo, see U.S. Strategic Bombing Survey [USSBS], Physical Damage Division [PDD], *Effects of Incendiary Bomb Attacks on Japan, a Report on Eight Cities* (n.p., April 1947), pp. 65–117. On Hamburg, see Postol, "Possible Fatalities from Superfires," pp. 52–53; and the broader treatment by Horatio Bond, "The Fire Attacks on German Cities," in Bond, ed., *Fire and the Air War* (Boston: National Fire Protection Association, 1946), pp. 76–97. Bond headed the analysis of fire damage in Europe for the Physical Damage Division of the USSBS.

11. On the power of a single forest fire, see the American classic by Norman Maclean, *Young Men and Fire* (Chicago: University of Chicago Press, 1992). On the Great Lakes fires, see Stephen J. Pyne, *Fire in America: A Cultural History of Wildland and Rural Fire* (Princeton: Princeton University Press, 1992), pp. 199–218; Barry T. Hill, General Accounting Office,

"Fire Management: Lessons Learned from the Cerro Grande (Los Alamos) Fire and Actions Needed to Reduce Fire Risks," testimony before the House Subcommittee on Forest and Forest Health, Committee on Resources, 106th Cong., 2d sess., August 14, 2000, available at www .fire.nps.gov/fireinfo/cerrogrande/reports.htm.

12. U.S. Geological Survey, Department of the Interior, *The San Francisco Earthquake and Fire of April 18, 1906 and Their Effects on Structures and Structural Materials,* U.S. House, 60th Cong., 1st sess., Document No. 719 (Washington, D.C.: GPO, 1907), p. 138.

13. Postol, "Possible Fatalities from Superfires," p. 53.

14. Pyne, *Fire in America,* p. 206.

15. Later editions of the book from 1895 to 1932 were titled *Hydrodynamics.* See the entry on Horace Lamb by K. E. Bullen, in Charles Coulston Gillispie, ed., *Dictionary of Scientific Biography,* vol. 7 (New York: Charles Scribner's Sons, 1973), pp. 594–595. T. E. Faber, *Fluid Dynamics for Physicists* (Cambridge: Cambridge University Press, 1995), provides a clear verbal explanation for lay readers.

16. Richard Rhodes, *The Making of the Atomic Bomb* (New York: Simon and Schuster, 1988), p. 544. See also William Aspray, *John von Neumann and the Origins of Modern Computers* (Cambridge: MIT Press, 1990), pp. 27–34; N. Metropolis and E. C. Nelson, "Early Computing at Los Alamos," *Annals of the History of Computing* 4, no. 4 (1982): 348–357. Von Neumann was a crucial figure in early computing; he was also interested during and after World War II in numerical computation of hydrodynamic weather processes. See Aspray, *John von Neumann,* pp. 121–154; Paul N. Edwards, "The World in a Machine: Origins and Impacts of Early Computerized Global Systems Models," in Agatha C. Hughes and Thomas P. Hughes, eds., *Systems, Experts, and Computing: The Systems Approach in Management and Engineering, World War II and After* (Cambridge: MIT Press, 2000), pp. 221–254.

17. H. L. Brode, *Review of Nuclear Test Peak-Overpressure Height-of-Burst Data,* PSR Note 353 (Los Angeles: Pacific-Sierra Research Corp., November 1981), pp. 13, 52–54.

18. Brode and Small, *Fire Damage and Strategic Targeting,* pp. 32, 22.

19. These calculations assume reduced visibility for the entire distance from the rising fireball to the target area and result in conservative estimates of thermal fluence delivered.

20. These figures are based on a decade of hourly weather observations at Reagan National Airport. See Federal Climate Complex, Asheville, N.C., U.S. Navy-U.S. Air Force, Department of Commerce, *International Station Meteorological Climate Survey,* prepared under authority of Commander, Naval Oceanography Command, Version 1.0, October 1990. I thank Benjamin Olding for finding these data and putting them in an easily comprehensible form.

21. Harold Brode, phone conversation with author, August 11, 1989; see also Small and Brode, *Physics of Large Urban Fires,* p. 18; and H. L. Brode and R. D. Small, "A Review of the Physics of Large Urban Fires," in Solomon and Marston, *The Medical Implications of Nuclear War,* p. 83. Robert Nathans, "Making the Fires That Beat Japan," in Bond, *Fire and the Air War,* p. 141.

22. Bruce G. Blair, John E. Pike, and Stephen I. Schwartz, "Targeting and Controlling the Bomb," in Stephen I. Schwartz, ed., *Atomic Audit: The Costs and Consequences of U.S. Nuclear Weapons since 1940* (Washington, D.C.: Brookings Institution, 1998), p. 242.

23. I draw on a copy of the handbook marked "unclassified" (originally classified as Confidential) from the late 1960s and early 1970s. The handbooks, in order of publication, are Physical Vulnerability Division, Directorate for Intelligence, Headquarters United States Air Force, *Target Analysis for Atomic Weapons,* AF-628202, PV TM-14, 30 June 1954; Physical Vulnera-

bility Division, Director for Targets, Assistant Chief of Staff, Intelligence, Headquarters United States Air Force, *Nuclear Weapons Employment Handbook (U)*, AFM 200-8, 1 May 1958 (both cited in Gilbert C. Binninger, Paul J. Castleberry, Jr., and Patsy M. McGrady, *Mathematical Background and Programming Aids for the Physical Vulnerability System for Nuclear Weapons,* DI-550-27-74 [Washington, D.C.: Defense Intelligence Agency, 1 November 1974], p. 1); *Nuclear Weapons Employment Handbook,* AFM 200-8 (Washington, D.C.: Physical Vulnerability Branch, Targets Division, Air Force Intelligence Center, Assistant Chief of Staff, Intelligence, Headquarters United States Air Force, 1 September 1961); *(U) Physical Vulnerability Handbook—Nuclear Weapons,* PC 550/1-2-63 (Washington, D.C.: Defense Intelligence Agency [DIA] Production Center, 1 September 1963); DIA, *Physical Vulnerability Handbook—Nuclear Weapons* AP-550-1-2-69-INT (Washington, D.C.: Defense Intelligence Agency, 1 June 1969, with change 1 [1 September 1972] and change 2 [28 January 1974]); hereafter, DIA, *Physical Vulnerability Handbook* (1969–1974); and DIA, *Physical Vulnerability Handbook for Nuclear Weapons (U),* Defense Intelligence Reference Series, prepared by the Target Intelligence Division, Directorate for Research, Defense Intelligence Agency, OGA-2800-23-92, January 1992.

24. See chapter 7 for discussion of how VNs were used to produce the VNTK system, which has been used in all the physical vulnerability handbooks after 1954. See also the explanation of the VN system in the detailed study of U.S. nuclear war planning by Matthew G. McKinzie, Thomas B. Cochran, Robert S. Norris, and William M. Arkin, *The U.S. Nuclear War Plan: A Time for Change* (New York: Natural Resources Defense Council, June 2001); also available at www.nrdc.org.

25. DIA, *Physical Vulnerability Handbook* (1969–1974), p. I-3.

26. Ibid., p. I-20.

27. Ibid., p. I-17. I am using the *Physical Vulnerability Handbook*'s assignment of a vulnerability number of 10P0 for "light damage" to nose-on oriented light fighters and bombers. The *Handbook*'s examples are Soviet MIG-21, MIG-15, MIG-17, and YAK-25, but we would not expect them to be parked at Reagan National Airport!

28. At 1 mile from the detonation, the blast wave would be accompanied by 500-mph winds, which would generate wind forces on the buildings almost 100 times those of hurricane-force winds. At 1.2 miles, the accompanying winds would be 400 mph, and they would create forces 50 times that of hurricane force.

CHAPTER 2. ORGANIZATIONAL FRAMES

1. Jerald E. Hill, "Problems of Fire in Nuclear Warfare," statement before the Military Operations Subcommittee of the House Committee on Government Operations, *Civil Defense—1961, Hearings,* 87th Cong., 1st sess. (Washington, D.C.: GPO, 1961), August 9, 1961, pp. 345–346.

2. Not for attribution, interview with author, Washington, D.C., July 19, 1989.

3. Vice Admiral Michael C. Colley (USN, ret.), interview with author, Washington, D.C., November 8, 1993.

4. An incisive discussion of classical theories of choice that assume "decisions will be uniquely determined by environmental constraints" is James G. March, "Decisions in Organizations and Theories of Choice," in Andrew H. Van de Ven and William F. Joyce, eds., *Perspectives on Organizational Design and Behavior* (New York: Wiley, 1981), pp. 207–210.

5. Arguing that we must not confuse the physical world independent of human beings ("brute facts") with human agreement about those facts is John Searle, *The Construction of Social Reality* (New York: Basic Books, 1995).

6. Not for attribution, interview, July 19, 1989.

7. U.S. Strategic Bombing Survey [USSBS], Physical Damage Division [PDD], *A Report on Physical Damage in Japan* (n.p., June 1947), p. 175.

8. USSBS, PDD, *The Effects of the Atomic Bomb on Hiroshima, Japan,* vol. 1 (n.p., May 1947), p. 16.

9. Ibid., p. 17; see also USSBS, Chairman's Office, *The Effects of Atomic Bombs on Hiroshima and Nagasaki* (Washington, D.C.: GPO, 30 June 1946), pp. 8–9. The exact blast damage radii are listed in chapter 4.

10. Ted Postol, conversation with author, San Francisco, Calif., January 23, 1993.

11. Samuel Glasstone, ed., *The Effects of Atomic Weapons* (Washington, D.C.: GPO, June 1950), p. 45. Glasstone noted social ramifications: "Because of its primary importance in atomic warfare, the subject of air blast has received more intensive investigation and, in consequence, is better understood than the other characteristics of a nuclear explosion" (p. 45).

12. For data on fire-damaged buildings, see USSBS, PDD, *The Effects of the Atomic Bomb on Hiroshima, Japan,* vol. 2 (n.p., May 1947), p. 5. In a ghoulish piece of bureaucratic understatement, the same volume offered a more social reason why the cause of atomic fire was so difficult to assess: for one-third of combustible buildings studied, "The probable cause of initial ignition . . . was not determined inasmuch as few people, present at the time of detonation of the atomic bomb, were available for interrogation" (p. 74).

13. Brode's reanalysis of the Hiroshima and Nagasaki data is in Brode et al., *Fire Damage to Urban/Industrial Targets,* vol. 2, *Technical Report,* PSR Report 1936, prepared for Headquarters Defense Nuclear Agency, Washington D.C. (Los Angeles: Pacific-Sierra Research Corp., 25 July 1989), pp. 28–35, 189–196; Harold Brode, phone conversation with author, April 13, 1990.

14. Harold Brode, interview with author, Los Angeles, September 7, 1989; Brode, phone conversation, April 13, 1990.

15. Michael May, discussion with author, Stanford University, May 15, 1996.

16. This argument has been made to me persuasively by George Bunn, former dean of the University of Wisconsin Law School, now consulting professor at the Institute for International Studies at Stanford University.

17. Michael S. Sherry, *The Rise of American Air Power: The Creation of Armageddon* (New Haven: Yale University Press, 1987), p. 287. On moral issues, see also Ronald Schaffer, *Wings of Judgment: American Bombing in World War II* (New York: Oxford University Press, 1985).

18. General Curtis E. LeMay with MacKinlay Kantor, *Mission with LeMay: My Story* (Garden City, N.Y.: Doubleday, 1965), p. 384.

19. Fred Reed, "Hypocrisy and the Smithsonian," *Air Force Times,* November 7, 1994, p. 78.

20. This is broadly parallel to the argument that chemical weapons were banned because of a long-standing revulsion against the use of poison. For a refutation of the poison argument, see Richard M. Price, *The Chemical Weapons Taboo* (Ithaca: Cornell University Press, 1997).

21. LeMay, *Mission with LeMay,* p. 384. Similarly, Commanding General of the Army Air Forces in World War II "Hap" Arnold commented shortly after the bombing of Dresden, "We must not get soft—war must be destructive and to a certain extent inhuman and ruthless" (quoted in Sherry, *Rise of American Air Power,* p. 262).

22. Morton H. Halperin, with the assistance of Priscilla Clapp and Arnold Kanter, *Bureaucratic Politics and Foreign Policy* (Washington, D.C.: Brookings Institution, 1974).

23. On interests, see Brian Barry, *Political Argument: A Reissue with a New Introduction* (Berkeley: University of California Press, 1990 [first pub. 1965]), pp. 173–186; Hanna Fenichel Pitkin, *The Concept of Representation* (Berkeley: University of California Press, 1967), pp. 155–167; Clifford Geertz, *The Interpretation of Cultures* (New York: Basic Books, 1973), pp. 201–203.

24. For the sake of brevity, I have not distinguished between two types of interest-based approaches. Each provides different answers to the questions, How do actors know what their interests are? and How do they know how to achieve them? One approach is structural: Given the structure of a situation, whether it be competitive markets, political rules of the game, or the imperatives of international competition, actors generally "read" their situations correctly and have little choice but to act as they do in advancing organizational interests. Such arguments generalize about the situations confronting types of organizations. Broad classes of expected behavior can then be deduced from the type of situation and used to predict or explain the actions of a particular organization. The power of such an approach is that with minimal assumptions about human rationality—in particular, that actors seek to achieve advantage in the future—it holds across many situations. Mediating ideas and practices are deeply subordinated to the constraints and incentives derived from the environment. Variations in ideas and practices may explain odd outcomes, but are not essential in explaining most situations. In security studies, interest-based explanations are often structural. Scholars have culled these ideas from the organizational literature and have used them deductively to explain military doctrine, procurement, and organizational bias. See Barry R. Posen, *The Sources of Military Doctrine: France, Britain, and Germany between the World Wars* (Ithaca: Cornell University Press, 1984); Jack Snyder, *The Ideology of the Offensive: Military Decision Making and the Disasters of 1914* (Ithaca: Cornell University Press, 1984). A vigorous challenge to this approach is Elizabeth Kier, *Imagining War: French and British Military Doctrine between the Wars* (Princeton: Princeton University Press, 1997). This approach is more context-specific and actor-oriented, focusing on how particular actors understand future advantage and how best to achieve it; historical contingency, not generalization, is emphasized. In such an approach, statements of interest adhere closely to the historical context, explaining in specific terms how members of organizations think they can achieve their ends and what ends they want to achieve. Either approach can explain actors' behavior on the basis of cold calculation of the consequences of carrying out certain kinds of actions or on the basis of predispositions and deeply held assumptions that may not be articulated at the time.

25. Halperin, *Bureaucratic Politics and Foreign Policy*, pp. 26–28. Halperin and others deploy "essence" in a minimalist way, only slightly increasing the assumptions or information required to make broad deductions about expected behavior.

26. This argument is less deductive than it may appear. An identical conception of interests in which the Air Force wanted more nuclear weapons to secure organizational advantage in the future could lead to the prediction of opposite behavior: The Air Force would *seek* evidence of damage from fire in order to demonstrate the effectiveness of nuclear weapons. The greater the effectiveness of nuclear weapons, the more sensible an investment in them could appear to be to those in the Executive Branch and Congress—leading to greater procurement of those weapons. Political scientist Jack Snyder made this prediction to me in conversation (Washington, D.C., June 9, 1992). This is an example of how general statements of interest, dominant in security studies over the past decade and a half, do not serve as guides to under-

standing action "in the absence of specific understandings as to how [interests or objectives] are to be achieved" (Richard R. Nelson and Sidney G. Winter, *An Evolutionary Theory of Economic Change* [Cambridge: Harvard University Press, Belknap Press, 1982], p. 56).

27. On founding processes and the origins of organizational goals, see Herbert A. Simon, *Administrative Behavior: A Study of Decision-Making Processes in Administrative Organization,* 3d ed. (New York: Free Press, 1976 [first pub. 1945]), pp. 315–334; Arthur L. Stinchcombe, "Social Structure and Organizations," in James March, ed., *Handbook of Organizations* (Chicago: Rand McNally, 1965), pp. 142–193; John F. Padgett, "Organizational Genesis, Identity, and Control: The Transformation of Banking in Renaissance Florence," in James E. Rauch and Alessandra Casella, eds., *Networks and Markets* (New York: Russell Sage Foundation, 2001), pp. 211–257.

28. I draw on Wiebe Bijker's definition of a "technological frame." I use a somewhat broader notion, explicitly place it in organizational context, and emphasize the organizational determinants of what problems are to be solved. See Wiebe E. Bijker, "The Social Construction of Bakelite: Toward a Theory of Invention," in Bijker, Thomas P. Hughes, and Trevor J. Pinch, eds., *The Social Construction of Technological Systems* (Cambridge: MIT Press, 1987), pp. 159–187; and Wiebe E. Bijker, *Of Bicycles, Bakelites, and Bulbs* (Cambridge: MIT Press, 1995), esp. pp. 122–127.

29. See Karl E. Weick, *Sensemaking in Organizations* (Thousand Oaks, Calif.: Sage, 1995); Karl E. Weick, *The Social Psychology of Organizing,* 2d ed. (New York: Random House, 1979).

30. Pinch and Bijker, "The Social Construction of Facts and Artifacts," in Bijker, Hughes, and Pinch, *The Social Construction of Technological Systems,* p. 18. A fine overview of constructive arguments is Jan Golinski, *Making Natural Knowledge: Constructivism and the History of Science* (Cambridge: Cambridge University Press, 1998).

31. Walter W. Powell, "Expanding the Scope of Institutional Analysis," in Walter W. Powell and Paul J. DiMaggio, eds., *The New Institutionalism in Organizational Analysis* (Chicago: University of Chicago Press, 1991), pp. 188–189. In sociology, see also W. Richard Scott, *Institutions and Organizations* (Thousand Oaks, Calif.: Sage, 1995). In political science, see James G. March and Johan P. Olsen, *Rediscovering Institutions: The Organizational Basis of Politics* (New York: Free Press, 1989); Kathleen Thelen, "Historical Institutionalism in Comparative Politics," *Annual Review of Political Science* 2 (1999): 369–404.

32. Ludwik Fleck, *Genesis and Development of a Scientific Fact* (Chicago: University of Chicago Press, 1979 [first pub. 1935]), p. 20.

33. On path dependence, see esp. Paul A. David, "Clio and the Economics of QWERTY," *American Economic Review* 75, no. 2 (1985): 332–337; W. Brian Arthur, *Increasing Returns and Path Dependence in the Economy* (Ann Arbor: University of Michigan Press, 1994); Paul Pierson, "Increasing Returns, Path Dependence, and the Study of Politics," *American Political Science Review* 94, no. 2 (2000): 251–267.

34. Levi quoted in Pierson, "Increasing Returns," p. 252.

35. Pierson, "Increasing Returns," p. 252. Emphasis in original.

36. This broadly follows Brian Arthur's arguments regarding large set-up costs, coordination effects, learning effects, and self-reinforcing or self-fulfilling expectations. I have taken liberty with the last category, in which Arthur and Pierson stress expectations of future use. I stress self-fulfilling rationales that lead to future use. See Arthur, *Increasing Returns and Path Dependence,* p. 112, and Pierson, "Increasing Returns," p. 254.

37. James Mahoney, "Path Dependence in Historical Sociology," *Theory and Society* 29, no. 4 (2000), pp. 507–515. Arguing similarly about initial conditions is Jack A. Goldstone,

"Initial Conditions, General Laws, Path Dependence, and Explanation in Historical Sociology," *American Journal of Sociology* 104, no. 3 (1998): pp. 829–845.

38. Thomas H. Greer, *The Development of Air Doctrine in the Army Air Arm, 1917–1941* (1955; reprint, Washington, D.C.: Office of Air Force History, 1985), p. 57.

39. Posen, *Sources of Military Doctrine*, pp. 13, 14. Emphasis in original.

40. I draw on broadly similar arguments in the organizational literature. See Simon, *Administrative Behavior;* Richard M. Cyert and James G. March, *A Behavioral Theory of the Firm* (Englewood Cliffs, N.J.: Prentice-Hall, 1963); Neil Fligstein, *The Transformation of Corporate Control* (Cambridge: Harvard University Press, 1990).

41. James G. March and Herbert A. Simon, *Organizations* (New York: Wiley, 1958), p. 165.

42. Stephen Peter Rosen, "New Ways of War: Understanding Military Innovation," *International Security* 13, no. 1 (1988): 134–168; Stephen Peter Rosen, *Winning the Next War: Innovation and the Modern Military* (Ithaca: Cornell University Press, 1991).

43. See Stephen Skowronek, *Building a New American State: The Expansion of National Administrative Capacities, 1877–1920* (Cambridge: Cambridge University Press, 1982); Fligstein, *Transformation of Corporate Control;* William H. Sewell, Jr., "A Theory of Structure: Duality, Agency, and Transformation," *American Journal of Sociology* 98, no. 1 (1992): 1–29.

44. This is a form of "coercive isomorphism" discussed by Paul J. DiMaggio and Walter W. Powell, "The Iron Cage Revisited: Institutional Isomorphism and Collective Rationality in Organizational Fields," *American Sociological Review* 48, no. 2 (1983): 147–160; reprinted and slightly revised in Powell and DiMaggio, *The New Institutionalism in Organizational Analysis*, pp. 63–82.

45. Martin J. S. Rudwick, *The Great Devonian Controversy: The Shaping of Scientific Knowledge among Gentlemanly Specialists* (Chicago: University of Chicago Press, 1985); Matthew H. Edney, *Mapping an Empire: The Geographical Construction of British India, 1765–1843* (Chicago: University of Chicago Press, 1997); Thomas P. Hughes, *Networks of Power: Electrification in Western Society, 1880–1930* (Baltimore: Johns Hopkins University Press, 1983); Bruno Latour and Steve Woolgar, *Laboratory Life: The Construction of Scientific Facts* (Princeton: Princeton University Press, 1979); Donna Haraway, *Primate Visions: Gender, Race, and Nature in the World of Modern Science* (New York: Routledge, 1989); Karin Knorr Cetina, *Epistemic Cultures: How the Sciences Make Knowledge* (Cambridge: Harvard University Press, 1999); Peter Galison, *Image and Logic: A Material Culture of Microphysics* (Chicago: University of Chicago Press, 1997); Paul N. Edwards, *The Closed World: Computers and the Politics of Discourse in Cold War America* (Cambridge: MIT Press, 1996); Hugh Gusterson, *Nuclear Rites: A Weapons Laboratory at the End of the Cold War* (Berkeley: University of California Press, 1996); Donald MacKenzie, *Inventing Accuracy* (Cambridge: MIT Press, 1990); Stefan Helmreich, *Silicon Second Nature: Culturing Artificial Life in a Digital World* (Berkeley: University of California Press, 1998).

46. Simon, *Administrative Behavior*, pp. xxxvii, xxxix; March and Simon, *Organizations*, p. 165. Recent work has reformulated earlier insights to connote a fuller, more interconnected symbolic world than do the analytical images of "premises" and "filters"; e.g., Mary Douglas's social cognition approach to classification in Douglas, *How Institutions Think* (Syracuse, N.Y.: Syracuse University Press, 1986); and Fligstein, *Transformation of Corporate Control.* On routines as carriers of knowledge, as opposed to the basically dumb standard operating procedures portrayed in Graham T. Allison's *Essence of Decision: Explaining the Cuban Missile Crisis* (Boston: Little, Brown, 1971), see Nelson and Winter, *Evolutionary Theory of Economic Change*, pp. 96–136; Edwin Hutchins, *Cognition in the Wild* (Cambridge: MIT Press,

1995), esp. pp. 317–351; Diane Vaughan, *The Challenger Launch Decision* (Chicago: University of Chicago Press, 1996); Martha S. Feldman, "Organizational Routines as a Source of Continuous Change," *Organization Science* 11, no. 6 (2000): 611–629; Martha S. Feldman and Anat Rafaeli, "Organizational Routines as Sources of Connections and Understandings," *Journal of Management Studies* 39, no. 3 (2002): 309–331. See also the related discussion on rules as carriers of knowledge: James G. March, Martin Schulz, and Xueguang Zhou, *The Dynamics of Rules: Change in Written Organizational Codes* (Stanford, Calif.: Stanford University Press, 2000). On organizational learning and knowledge, see Barbara Levitt and James G. March, "Organizational Learning," *Annual Review of Sociology* 14 (1988): 319–340; the articles from *Organization Science* collected in Michael D. Cohen and Lee. S. Sproull, eds., *Organizational Learning* (Thousand Oaks, Calif.: Sage, 1996); and Ikujiro Nonaka and Toshihiro Nishiguchi, eds., *Knowledge Emergence: Social, Technical, and Evolutionary Dimensions of Knowledge Creation* (Oxford: Oxford University Press, 2001).

47. E.g., Stinchcombe, "Social Structure and Organizations"; Powell, "Expanding the Scope of Institutional Analysis"; MacKenzie, *Inventing Accuracy*.

48. Bijker, "The Social Construction of Bakelite," and Bijker, *Of Bicycles, Bakelites, and Bulbs*. In organization theory the discussion has been more implicit, but see Wanda J. Orlikowski and Debra C. Gash, "Technological Frames: Making Sense of Information Technology in Organizations," *ACM Transactions on Information Systems* 12, no. 2 (1994): 174–207.

49. The exemplary work drawing on both literatures is Vaughan, *The Challenger Launch Decision;* and Diane Vaughan, "The Role of the Organization in the Production of Techno-Scientific Knowledge," *Social Studies of Science* 29, no. 6 (1999): 913–943; see also Wanda J. Orlikowski, "The Duality of Technology: Rethinking the Concept of Technology in Organizations," *Organization Science* 3, no. 3 (1992): 398–427; and Orlikowski, "Using Technology and Constituting Structures: A Practice Lens for Studying Technology in Organizations, *Organization Science* 11, no. 4 (2000): 404–428.

50. See, e.g., the rewarding article by James G. March, Lee S. Sproull, and Michal Tamuz, "Learning from Samples of One or Fewer," *Organization Science* 2, no. 1 (1991): 1–13, reprinted in James G. March, *The Pursuit of Organizational Intelligence* (Oxford: Blackwell, 1999), pp. 137–155.

51. But see Feldman, "Organizational Routines."

52. Important exceptions include Douglas, *How Institutions Think;* Fligstein, *Transformation of Corporate Control;* Vaughan, *The Challenger Launch Decision.*

53. Exceptions include MacKenzie, *Inventing Accuracy;* Graham Spinardi, *Polaris to Trident: The Development of U.S. Fleet Ballistic Missile Technology* (Cambridge: Cambridge University Press, 1994); Thomas P. Hughes, *Rescuing Prometheus: Four Monumental Projects That Changed the Modern World* (New York: Pantheon Books, 1998).

54. In work on later inventions, large-scale organizations are more prominent. E.g., Edward W. Constant II, in *The Origins of the Turbojet Revolution* (Baltimore: Johns Hopkins University Press, 1980), uses as his main unit of analysis communities of technological practitioners, which may be in, or span, organizations. Constant, however, does not explore in detail the impact of organizational assumptions or routines on invention, or the impact of invention on organizational routines.

CHAPTER 3. DOCTRINE AND DAMAGE THROUGH WORLD WAR II

1. John E. Burchard, "Knowledge Is a Weapon, Too!" in Burchard, ed., *Rockets, Guns and Targets: Rockets, Target Information, Erosion Information, and Hypervelocity Guns Devel-*

oped during World War II by the Office of Scientific Research and Development, *Science in World War II*, [the official history of the] *Office of Scientific Research and Development* (Boston: Little, Brown, Atlantic Monthly Press, 1948), p. 239.

2. Burchard, *Rockets, Guns and Targets*, p. 241.

3. James K. McElroy, "The Work of the Fire Protection Engineers in Planning Fire Attacks," in Horatio Bond, ed., *Fire and the Air War* (Boston: National Fire Protection Association, 1946), p. 131.

4. Curtis E. LeMay with MacKinlay Kantor, *Mission with LeMay* (Garden City, N.Y.: Doubleday, 1965), p. 384.

5. Pascal Vennesson, "Institution and Airpower: The Making of the French Air Force," *Journal of Strategic Studies* 18, no. 1 (1995): 36; see also Pascal Vennesson, *Les chevaliers de l'air: aviation et conflits au XXe siècle* (Paris: Presses de la Fondation nationale des sciences politiques, 1997), esp. pp. 183–203.

6. On the cult of the offensive, see Jack Snyder, "Civil–Military Relations and the Cult of the Offensive, 1914 and 1984," *International Security* 9, no. 1 (1984): 108–146; Tim Travers, *The Killing Ground: The British Army, the Western Front and the Emergence of Modern Warfare, 1900–1918* (London: Unwin Hyman, 1989), pp. 37–61; Stephen Van Evera, *Causes of War: Power and the Roots of Conflict* (Ithaca: Cornell University Press, 1999), pp. 193–239.

7. Trenchard quoted in Sir Charles Webster and Noble Frankland, *The Strategic Air Offensive against Germany, 1939–1945*, vol. 1, *Preparation* (London: Her Majesty's Stationery Office, 1961), p. 46; Lord Weir's letter, written in September 1918, quoted in Andrew Boyle, *Trenchard* (London: Collins, 1962), p. 312.

8. Malcolm Smith, *British Air Strategy between the Wars* (Oxford: Clarendon Press, Oxford University Press, 1984), p. 63.

9. Portal quoted in Denis Richards, *Portal of Hungerford* (London: Heinemann, 1977), p. 165. On the shift in British strategy from May 1940 through November 1941, see Webster and Frankland, *Strategic Air Offensive*, vol. 1, pp. 144–187; Tami Davis Biddle, *Rhetoric and Reality in Air Warfare: The Evolution of British and American Ideas about Strategic Bombing, 1914–1945* (Princeton: Princeton University Press, 2002), pp. 176–203.

10. Webster and Frankland, *Strategic Air Offensive*, vol. 1, pp. 181–182, 252, 267.

11. Ibid., pp. 252–253.

12. Report of British Bombing Survey Unit, *The Strategic Air War against Germany, 1939–1945*, p. 48. Copy courtesy of Tami Davis Biddle.

13. Webster and Frankland, *Strategic Air Offensive*, vol. 1, p. 253.

14. Robert C. Ehrhart, Thomas A. Fabyanic, and Robert F. Futrell, "Building an Air Intelligence Organization and the European Theater," in John F. Kreis, ed., *Piercing the Fog: Intelligence and Army Air Forces Operations in World War II* (Bolling Air Force Base, Washington, D.C.: Air Force History and Museums Program, 1996), p. 135.

15. U.S. Strategic Bombing Survey [USSBS], Area Studies Division Report No. 31 (n.p., 1945), p. 4, quoted in Stephen A. Garrett, *Ethics and Airpower in World War II: The British Bombing of German Cities* (New York: St. Martin's Press, 1993), p. 16.

16. USSBS, Physical Damage Division [PDD], *Physical Damage Division Report (ETO)* (n.p.,. April 1947), p. 100.

17. Ehrhart, Fabyanic, and Futrell, "Building an Air Intelligence Organization," p. 138.

18. McElroy, "Work of the Fire Protection Engineers," p. 123.

19. Webster and Frankland, *Strategic Air Offensive*, vol. 1, pp. 267–268, 473–474, 486–

488; Sir Charles Webster and Noble Frankland, *The Strategic Air Offensive against Germany, 1939–1945*, vol. 2, *Endeavour* (London: Her Majesty's Stationery Office, 1961), pp. 245–247; Ehrhart, Fabyanic, and Futrell, "Building an Air Intelligence Organization," pp. 138–139; John Wyndham Mountcastle, "Trial by Fire: U.S. Incendiary Weapons, 1918–1945" (Ph.D. diss., Duke University, 1979), p. 139.

20. The Gorrell plan quoted in Mark Clodfelter, "Pinpointing Devastation: American Air Campaign Planning before Pearl Harbor," *Journal of Military History* 58, no. 1 (1994): 80.

21. Kenneth P. Werrell, *Blankets of Fire: U.S. Bombers over Japan during World War II* (Washington, D.C.: Smithsonian Institution Press, 1996), p. 8.

22. Stephen L. McFarland, *America's Pursuit of Precision Bombing, 1910–1945* (Washington, D.C.: Smithsonian Institution Press, 1995), p. 83.

23. Thomas H. Greer, *The Development of Air Doctrine in the Army Air Arm, 1917–1941* (1955; reprint, Washington, D.C.: Office of Air Force History, 1985), p. 57.

24. On the development of U.S. strategic air doctrine, see also Biddle's outstanding *Rhetoric and Reality in Air Warfare*; Robert A. Pape, *Bombing to Win: Air Power and Coercion in War* (Ithaca: Cornell University Press, 1996); Conrad C. Crane, *Bombs, Cities, and Civilians: American Airpower Strategy in World War II* (Lawrence: University of Kansas Press, 1993); and the older very good accounts in Michael S. Sherry, *The Rise of American Air Power, The Creation of Armageddon* (New Haven: Yale University Press, 1987); Ronald Schaffer, *Wings of Judgment: American Bombing in World War II* (New York: Oxford University Press, 1985); Gary Joseph Shandroff, "The Evolution of Area Bombing in American Doctrine and Practice" (Ph.D. diss., New York University, 1972); and Wesley Frank Craven and James Lea Cate, eds., *The Army Air Forces in World War II*, vol. 1, *Plans and Early Operations, January 1939 to August 1942* (Chicago: University. of Chicago Press, 1948).

25. Hansell, "The Development of the U.S. Concept of Bombardment Operations," lecture at Air War College, Air University, 19 September 1951, quoted in Greer, *Development of Air Doctrine*, p. 80.

26. Greer, *Development of Air Doctrine*, p. 80.

27. Baker quoted in McFarland, *America's Pursuit of Precision Bombing*, p. 81.

28. Biddle, *Rhetoric and Reality in Air Warfare*, pp. 163–164.

29. McFarland, *America's Pursuit of Precision Bombing*, p. 82.

30. Tami Davis Biddle, "British and American Approaches to Strategic Bombing: Their Origins and Implementation in the World War II Combined Bomber Offensive," *Journal of Strategic Studies* 18, no. 1 (1995): 111; Werrell, *Blankets of Fire*, p. 12.

31. Greer, *Development of Air Doctrine*, p. 57. On the Army's tradition of marksmanship, see Thomas L. McNaugher, *The M16 Controversies, Military Organizations and Weapons Acquisition* (New York: Praeger, 1984).

32. This paragraph is drawn from Clodfelter, "Pinpointing Devastation," pp. 88–91.

33. Constance McLaughlin Green, Harry C. Thomson, and Peter C. Roots, *The Ordnance Department: Planning Munitions for War, The United States Army in World War II* (Washington, D.C.: Office of the Chief of Military History, Department of the Army, 1955), pp. 454–455.

34. Mountcastle, "Trial by Fire," p. 151; Horatio Bond, "Applying Fire Experience to the Air War," in Bond, *Fire and the Air War*, p. 192.

35. McFarland, *America's Pursuit of Precision Bombing*, p. 76; see also p. 83.

36. Ibid., p. 242, n. 11; H. H. Arnold, *Global Mission* (New York: Harper, 1949), p. 150.

37. Charles W. McArthur, *History of Mathematics*, vol. 4, *Operations Analysis in the U.S.*

Army Eighth Air Force in World War II (Providence, R.I.: American Mathematical Society, 1990), p. 294.

38. J. E. Zanetti, "Strategy of Incendiaries," *Chemical Warfare Bulletin* 27 (April 1941): 41–44, quoted in Mountcastle, "Trial by Fire," p. 136.

39. Mountcastle, "Trial by Fire," pp. 67–70, 100–102; Leo P. Brophy and George J. B. Fisher, *The Chemical Warfare Service: Organizing for War, The U.S. Army in World War II* (Washington, D.C.: Office of the Chief Historian, Department of the Army, 1959), pp. 1–17, 22–23, 45.

40. Bond, "Applying Fire Experience," p. 192.

41. Mountcastle, "Trial by Fire," pp. 99, 141, 146.

42. Leo P. Brophy, Wyndham D. Miles, and Rexmond C. Cochrane, *The Chemical Warfare Service: From Laboratory to Field, The U.S. Army in World War II* (Washington, D.C.: Office of the Chief Historian, Department of the Army, 1959), pp. 168–170; on wartime production and production problems, pp. 167–190, 342–352.

43. Mountcastle, "Trial by Fire," p. 101.

44. Bond, "Applying Fire Experience," p. 192 (emphasis added).

45. Brophy and Fisher, *Organizing for War,* p. 46; Brophy, Miles, and Cochrane, *From Laboratory to Field,* p. 49; Mountcastle, "Trial by Fire," pp. 100, 146–147; Schaffer, *Wings of Judgment,* p.108; Sherry, *Rise of American Air Power,* p. 226.

46. The best accounts of how problems were solved regarding incendiaries are in Mountcastle, "Trial by Fire," pp. 146–156; Brophy, Miles, and Cochrane, *From Laboratory to Field,* pp. 167–190, 342–352; E. P. Stevenson, "Incendiary Bombs" and "Incendiary Fuels," both in W. A. Noyes, Jr., ed., *Chemistry: A History of the Chemistry Components of the National Defense Research Committee, 1940–1946, Science in World War II,* [the official history of the] *Office of Scientific Research and Development* (Boston: Little, Brown, Atlantic Monthly Press, 1948), pp. 388–409, 410–419.

47. Ehrhart, Fabyanic, and Futrell, "Building an Air Intelligence Organization," p. 136.

48. Ibid., p. 138.

49. Schaffer, *Wings of Judgment,* pp. 74–75.

50. Ehrhart, Fabyanic, and Futrell, "Building an Air Intelligence Organization," pp. 136–137.

51. See Barry M. Katz, *Foreign Intelligence: Research and Analysis in the Office of Strategic Services, 1942–1945* (Cambridge: Harvard University Press, 1989), pp. 97–136.

52. Ehrhart, Fabyanic, and Futrell, "Building an Air Intelligence Organization," p. 137.

53. Ibid., p. 138.

54. Carl Kaysen, interview with author, Cambridge, Mass., October 18, 1989. On the Committee of Operations Analysts, see ibid., pp. 152–53; Schaffer, *Wings of Judgment,* pp. 110–112.

55. Ehrhart, Fabyanic, and Futrell, "Building an Air Intelligence Organization," p. 136.

56. Katz, *Foreign Intelligence,* p. 115.

57. Ehrhart, Fabyanic, and Futrell, "Building an Air Intelligence Organization," pp. 138–139.

58. Mountcastle, "Trial by Fire," p. 137; McArthur, *Operations Analysis,* p. 65.

59. Sara E. Wermiel, *The Fireproof Building: Technology and Public Safety in the Nineteenth-Century American City* (Baltimore: Johns Hopkins University Press, 2000), pp. 81–82.

60. Ibid., pp. 210–211.

61. Horatio Bond, interview with author and Ted Postol, Hyannisport, Mass., October 21, 1989.

62. McElroy, "Work of the Fire Protection Engineers," p. 122.

63. Bond, interview, October 21, 1989.

64. McElroy, "Work of the Fire Protection Engineers," p. 122.

65. Ibid., pp. 122–135.

66. Horatio Bond, "The Fire Attacks on German Cities," in Bond, *Fire and the Air War*, pp. 95–96.

67. McElroy, "Work of the Fire Protection Engineers," pp. 129–130; see also Bond, "Applying Fire Experience," p. 191.

68. Bond, interview, October 21, 1989.

69. Bond, "The Fire Damage Caused by Air Attacks," in Bond, *Fire and the Air War*, p. 9; Horatio Bond, phone conversation with author, April 2, 1990; Bond, "Applying Fire Experience," p. 189.

70. Horatio Bond to Col. R. D. Hughes, quoted in Mountcastle, "Trial by Fire," p. 140; Arnold quoted in Mountcastle, "Trial by Fire," p. 141.

71. Horatio Bond and James K. McElroy, "Some Observations and Conclusions," in Bond, *Fire and the Air War*, p. 245, citing *Incendiary Attack on Industrial Targets*, by Horatio Bond and Norman J. Thompson, Division 11, National Defense Research Committee (July 1943). According to their account, Bond prepared these notes in February and March 1943.

72. Theodore A. Postol, "Possible Fatalities from Superfires following Nuclear Attacks in or near Urban Areas," in Fredric Solomon and Robert Q. Marston, eds., *The Medical Implications of Nuclear War* (Washington, D.C.: National Academy Press, 1986), p. 52.

73. On the Hamburg firestorm, see Horatio Bond, "Fire Casualties of the German Attacks," in Bond, *Fire and the Air War*, pp. 112–121. See also Hans Brunswig, *Feuersturm über Hamburg* (Stuttgart: Motorbuch Verlag, 1978); Sherry, *Rise of American Air Power*, pp. 153–155; Richard Rhodes, *The Making of the Atomic Bomb* (New York: Simon and Schuster, 1988), pp. 472–474; W. G. Sebald, *On the Natural History of Destruction*, trans. Anthea Bell (New York: Random House, 2003).

74. Postol, "Possible Fatalities from Superfires," p. 51.

75. Mountcastle, "Trial by Fire," pp. 142, 145–146.

76. Schaffer, *Wings of Judgment*, pp. 64–73.

77. On Hamburg, Kassel, and Darmstadt, see Bond, "Fire Attacks on German Cities," pp. 82, 85; on Cologne, see Webster and Frankland, *Strategic Air Offensive*, vol. 1, p. 407.

78. Werrell, *Blankets of Fire*, pp. 38–39.

79. Mitchell quoted in Sherry, *Rise of American Air Power*, p. 58. Mitchell had been a U.S. Army General. He was court-martialed in 1925 for insubordination in his advocacy of air power.

80. Chennault quoted in Werrell, *Blankets of Fire*, p. 41, and in Sherry, *Rise of American Air Power*, p. 102; Arnold quoted in Werrell, *Blankets of Fire*, p. 41.

81. I draw heavily on John F. Kreis, "Planning the Defeat of Japan: The A-2 in Washington, 1943–1945," in Kreis, *Piercing the Fog*, pp. 349–392.

82. Kreis, "Planning the Defeat of Japan," pp. 364–365; Schaffer, *Wings of Judgment*, pp. 109–110.

83. Schaffer, *Wings of Judgment*, pp. 110–111; see also Kreis, "Planning the Defeat of Japan," pp. 365–366.

84. Werrell, *Blankets of Fire*, pp. 52–53.

85. Schaffer, *Wings of Judgment,* pp. 113–116.

86. Kreis, "Planning the Defeat of Japan," pp. 357, 367–368; Lincoln R. Thiesmeyer, "Analysts of Air Attack—Selecting Bombs and Fuzes," in Lincoln R. Thiesmeyer and John E. Burchard, *Combat Scientists, Science in World War II,* [the official history of the] *Office of Scientific Research and Development* (Boston: Little, Brown, Atlantic Monthly Press, 1947), p. 191.

87. Thiesmeyer, "Analysts of Air Attack," p. 191. See also the report by J. Bronowski, RE 8, "The Work of the Joint Target Group," June–July 1945, decimal file no. 142.6601-5, U.S. Air Force Historical Research Agency (AFHRA), Maxwell Air Force Base, Alabama.

88. Bronowski, "Work of the Joint Target Group," pp. 1–2.

89. Schaffer, *Wings of Judgment,* pp. 60–62, 80–106; Sherry, *Rise of American Air Power,* pp. 229, 266.

90. Hansell quoted in Sherry, *Rise of American Air Power,* p. 258.

91. Ibid., pp. 256–258, 266–267, 273–284; see also Schaffer, *Wings of Judgment,* pp. 124–148; Werrell, *Blankets of Fire,* pp. 159–163; USSBS, PDD, "Effects of Incendiary Bomb Attacks on Japan, a Report on Eight Cities" (n.p., April 1947), pp. 65–117.

92. See the official history of the Office of Scientific Research and Development by James Phinney Baxter III, *Scientists against Time* (Boston: Little, Brown, Atlantic Monthly Press, 1948); and the concise overview by W. A. Noyes, Jr., "The Organization of the National Defense Research Committee: General Plan," in Noyes, *Chemistry,* pp. 3–14.

93. G. B. Kistiakowsky and Ralph Conner, "Introduction to the History of Division 8," in Noyes, *Chemistry,* p. 24.

94. G. B. Kistiakowsky and Ralph Conner, "Research on Detonation and Shock Waves," in Noyes, *Chemistry,* p. 60.

95. Burchard, *Rockets, Guns and Targets,* pp. 260–262.

96. My account draws heavily from Burchard, *Rockets, Guns and Targets,* pp. 239–302, quotation of Burchard at p. 241; see also John Burchard, *Q.E.D.: M.I.T. in World War II* (New York: John Wiley), pp. 51–52.

97. Burchard, *Rockets, Guns and Targets,* p. 247.

98. Ibid., pp. 244–246, 302.

99. William J. Hall, Professor Emeritus of Civil Engineering, University of Illinois, letter to author, October 8, 1996.

100. Burchard, *Q.E.D.,* p. 52.

101. Burchard, *Rockets, Guns and Targets,* pp. 292–295.

102. Richard Grassy, interview with author, Lac du Flambeau, Wisc., May 21, 1995.

103. Burchard, *Rockets, Guns and Targets,* p. 287–291.

104. Mountcastle, "Trial by Fire," pp. 146–149; Stevenson, "Incendiary Bombs," p. 392.

105. Schaffer, *Wings of Judgment,* p. 115; see also Crane, *Bombs, Cities, and Civilians,* pp. 91–92, 127.

106. A report prepared by Capt. William H. Baldwin, "Development of Incendiary Bombs," quoted in Mountcastle, "Trial by Fire," p. 148.

107. Stevenson, "Incendiary Bombs," p. 393.

108. Ibid., p. 393.

109. Jack Couffer, *Bat Bomb: World War II's Other Secret Weapon* (Austin: University of Texas Press, 1992), pp. 208–209. Couffer participated in a remarkable project to release large numbers of live bats carrying tiny incendiary bombs. His memoir is a gem, a real-life *Catch-22.*

110. Stevenson, "Incendiary Bombs," pp. 393–394.

111. The best overview of the Survey is Biddle, *Rhetoric and Reality in Air Warfare,* pp. 271–280; see also the detailed discussion in David MacIsaac, *Strategic Bombing in World War II* (New York: Garland, 1976). On staffing the fire damage studies, see Bond, "Fire Attacks on German Cities," p. 78, and Bond and McElroy, "Some Observations and Conclusions," p. 242.

112. USSBS, PDD, *Fire Raids on German Cities,* 2d ed. (n.p., January 1947), pp. 35–36.

113. Forrest J. Sanborn, "Fire Protection Lessons of the Japanese Attacks," in Bond, *Fire and the Air War,* pp. 177–178.

114. A 1965 study by Rodden, John, and Laurino, discussed in chapter 8, specified a relatively low fuel loading of 8 pounds of combustible per square foot; Harold Brode, phone conversation with author, August 11, 1989.

115. Bond, "Fire Attacks on German Cities," pp. 94–96.

116. Robert Nathans, "Making the Fires that Beat Japan," in Bond, *Fire and the Air War,* pp. 141, 143–144; Sanborn, "Fire Protection Lessons," p. 178.

117. USSBS, PDD, *A Report on Physical Damage in Japan* (n.p., June 1947), p. 96.

118. Samuel Glasstone, ed., *The Effects of Atomic Weapons* (Washington, D.C.: GPO, June 1950), p. 217.

119. USSBS, PDD, *Report on Physical Damage in Japan,* p. 96.

120. Glasstone, *Effects of Atomic Weapons* (June 1950), p. 218 (emphasis added).

121. Sanborn, "Fire Protection Lessons," p. 181.

122. USSBS, PDD, *Report on Physical Damage in Japan,* p. 96 (emphasis added). This functional understanding has been reflected in subsequent historical accounts. Sherry, for example, writes that as the fires "merged and intensified, their greed for oxygen sucked in the fresher air from the fringes of the cauldron" (*Rise of American Air Power,* p. 153). Rhodes writes, "Small fires had coalesced into larger fires and, greedy for oxygen, had sucked air from around the coalescing inferno" (*Making of the Atomic Bomb,* p. 473).

CHAPTER 4. EARLY POSTWAR ATOMIC PLANNING

1. On expanded U.S. interests, see Melvyn Leffler, *A Preponderance of Power: National Security, the Truman Administration, and the Cold War* (Stanford: Stanford University Press, 1992). There was not unanimity on those interests. The major competing visions were a European-oriented internationalism and a more Asian-oriented isolationism grounded in U.S. regional domestic political economy; see Bruce Cumings, *The Origins of the Korean War,* vol. 2, *The Roaring of the Cataract, 1947–1950* (Princeton: Princeton University Press, 1990). Air Force interests were aligned with Republican isolationism; see Lynn Eden, "Capitalist Conflict and the State: The Making of United States Military Policy in 1948," in Charles Bright and Susan Harding, eds., *Statemaking and Social Movements: Essays in History and Theory* (Ann Arbor: University of Michigan Press, 1984).

2. A small secondary literature has transformed the understanding of U.S. nuclear war planning; it emphasizes the operational realm and shows that deterrence theory has been less influential than previously thought. The two foundational works are David Alan Rosenberg, "The Origins of Overkill: Nuclear Weapons and American Strategy, 1945–1960," *International Security* 7, no. 4 (1983): 3–71; and Rosenberg, "Toward Armageddon: The Foundations of United States Nuclear Strategy, 1945–1961" (Ph.D. diss., University of Chicago, 1983). On the early period, see also Fred Kaplan, *The Wizards of Armageddon* (New York: Simon and Schuster, 1983); Steven T. Ross, *American War Plans 1945–1950* (New York: Garland, 1988);

Marc Trachtenberg, "A 'Wasting Asset': American Strategy and the Shifting Nuclear Balance, 1949–1954," *International Security* 13, no. 3 (1988/89): 5–49; and the fifteen-volume set of facsimile atomic war planning documents in Steven T. Ross and David Alan Rosenberg, eds., *America's Plans for War against the Soviet Union, 1945–1950* (New York: Garland, 1989–1990). The best concise synthesis on nuclear war planning from the late 1940s through the 1980s is Scott D. Sagan, *Moving Targets: Nuclear Strategy and National Security* (Princeton: Princeton University Press, 1989), pp. 10–57.

3. Rosenberg, "Origins of Overkill," pp. 9–10; David Alan Rosenberg, "Reality and Responsibility: Power and Process in the Making of United States Nuclear Strategy, 1945–68," *Journal of Strategic Studies* 9, no. 1 (1986): 36–37.

4. Rosenberg, "Origins of Overkill," p. 11.

5. David Alan Rosenberg, "American Atomic Strategy and the Hydrogen Bomb Decision," *Journal of American History* 66, no. 1 (1979): 64–66; Rosenberg, "Origins of Overkill," p. 12.

6. Col. Dale O. Smith, "Operational Concepts for Modern War," *Air University Quarterly Review* 2, no. 2 (1948): 6, 14. On "killing a nation," see esp. Robert Frank Futrell, *Ideas, Concepts, Doctrine: A History of Basic Thinking in the United States Air Force 1907–1964*, 2d ed. (Maxwell Air Force Base, Ala.: Air University, 1974), p. 122; see also Rosenberg, "American Atomic Strategy," p. 67.

7. Rosenberg, "Origins of Overkill," p. 15.

8. Ibid., p. 9; see also Rosenberg, "Toward Armageddon," pp. 162–166.

9. Stanley Lawwill, letter to author, November 21, 1991.

10. Stanley Lawwill, phone conversation with author, September 26, 1991; Lawwill, phone conversation with author, November 6, 1991; Lawwill, letter, November 21, 1991.

11. Lawwill, letter, November 21, 1991.

12. Stanley Lawwill, letter to author, October 15, 1991.

13. Lawwill, letter, October 15, 1991. Lawwill was Zimmerman's deputy.

14. Stanley Lawwill, letter to author, September 9, 1991; Carroll L. Zimmerman, *Insider at SAC, Operations Analysis under General LeMay* (Manhattan, Kans.: Sunflower University Press, 1988), p. 55.

15. Lawwill, phone conversation, November 6, 1991.

16. Except for port facilities, this list is from war plan TROJAN, approved for planning purposes by the Joint Chiefs of Staff in December 1948, as described in Rosenberg, "Toward Armageddon," p. 117.

17. Lawwill, phone conversation, November 6, 1991.

18. Rosenberg, "Origins of Overkill," p. 17.

19. Rosenberg, "Toward Armageddon," pp. 116–117, quoting SAC's Emergency War Plan 1–49 (SAC's air war plan in support of TROJAN) in early 1949.

20. David Alan Rosenberg, "'A Smoking Radiating Ruin at the End of Two Hours': Documents on American Plans for Nuclear War with the Soviet Union, 1954–1955," *International Security* 6, no. 3 (1981/82): 11; Navy captain quoted on p. 25.

21. Rosenberg, "Origins of Overkill," p. 9, and Rosenberg, "Toward Armageddon," pp. 162–166. When available, the fullest treatment of target intelligence will undoubtedly be Vance O. Mitchell, *The History of Air Force Intelligence, 1946–1963* (unpublished book manuscript for U.S. Air Force History Support Office currently undergoing declassification review). For now, see Vance O. Mitchell, "The Formative Years of Air Force Intelligence, 1945–1950," in *Society for History in the Federal Government, Occasional Papers*, vol. 1 (Washington, D.C., 1997), pp. 29–52.

22. The phrase is from James Lowe, "The Intelligence Basis of Selection of Strategic Target Systems," lecture presented to the students of the Air War College, Maxwell Air Force Base, Montgomery, Ala., on 13 November 1947, p. 1, in file no. K 239.716247–50, Air Force Historical Research Agency (AFHRA), Maxwell Air Force Base, Montgomery, Ala. I am grateful to Tami Davis Biddle for providing me with a copy.

23. Richard Grassy, phone conversation with author, February 1, 1996.

24. Lawwill, phone conversation, September 26, 1991; Lawwill, letter, September 9, 1991.

25. A good discussion is Herman S. Wolk, *Planning and Organizing the Post-war Air Force, 1943–1947* (Washington, D.C.: Office of Air Force History, United States Air Force, 1984).

26. Vance O. Mitchell, phone conversation with author, April 8, 1996. I am indebted to Vance Mitchell for clarifying for me the organization of Air Force Intelligence in this period.

27. Richard Grassy, interview with author, Lac du Flambeau, Wisc., May 21, 1995.

28. Lincoln R. Thiesmeyer, "Analysts of Air Attack—Selecting Bombs and Fuzes," in Lincoln R. Thiesmeyer and John E. Burchard, *Combat Scientists* (Boston: Little, Brown, 1947), p. 182.

29. Lowe quoted in Richard G. Grassy, "History of the Physical Vulnerability Division" (n.p., n.d. [spring 1995]), p. 1. This is a thirteen-page single-spaced typescript. I am grateful to Edgar (Bud) Parsons for providing me with a copy and to Dick Grassy for permission to cite and quote.

30. Grassy, interview, May 21, 1995.

31. Ibid.

32. Henry Nash, interview with author and Barry O'Neill, Pigeon Cove, Mass., May 6, 1988.

33. Grassy, "History," p. 1; Grassy, interview, May 21, 1995.

34. Grassy, phone conversation, February 1, 1996; Grassy, "History," pp. 7, 2.

35. Grassy, interview, May 21, 1995.

36. Ibid.

37. "Fifth Meeting of the Air Board," 5–6 June 1947, p. 93, available in the Air Force History Support Office, Bolling Air Force Base, D.C. Document courtesy of Vance Mitchell.

38. Grassy, interview, May 21, 1995.

39. Ibid.

40. Henry T. Nash, "The Bureaucratization of Homicide," in E. P. Thompson and Dan Smith, eds., *Protest and Survive* (New York: Monthly Review Press, 1981), p. 150. I am grateful to Carol Cohn for drawing the essay, and Mr. Nash himself, to my attention.

41. Grassy, interview, May 21, 1995.

42. Nash, interview, May 6, 1988.

43. Air Targets Division, Directorate of Intelligence, [U.S. Air Force], "History of the Air Targets Division, January 1950 thru 30 June 1950," p. 1, obtained under Freedom of Information Act request.

44. Grassy, interview, May 21, 1995.

45. Director of Intelligence [U.S. Air Force], organization chart for January 1955, in "United States Department of the Air Force Organization and Functions, January 1955," on file in Air Force History Support Office. These three functional areas were delineated much earlier; see, e.g., the minutes of the "Fifth Meeting of the Air Board," 5–6 June 1947, p. 93.

46. Hugh Lehman, phone conversation with author, October 19, 1991; Grassy, interview, May 21, 1995. On code breaking, see Robert Louis Benson and Michael Warner, eds., *Venona:*

Soviet Espionage and the American Response, 1939–1957 (Washington, D.C.: National Security Agency/Central Intelligence Agency, 1996), p. xiii.

47. Administrative Services Office, Air Force Intelligence Center, "Semiannual History, Air Force Intelligence Center (AFCIN-3), Assistant Chief of Staff, Intelligence, 1 July 1959 thru 31 December 1959," pp. 5, 10, obtained under Freedom of Information Act request; Grassy, interview, May 21, 1995.

48. Grassy, interview, May 21, 1995; [Deane J. Allen], *Defense Intelligence Agency, 35 Years: A Brief History* (Washington, D.C.: DIA History Office, 1996), pp. 6, 16.

49. The "Fifth Meeting of the Air Board," 5–6 June 1947, p. 93, refers to the project as "A Bombing Encyclopedia of the World"; see also Lowe, "Intelligence Basis," p. 5. The title *Bombing Encyclopedia* was changed in the late 1960s or early 1970s to *Basic Encyclopedia*. In 1973 publication was discontinued and the *B.E.* was converted to a computerized database used to compile the Automated Installation File (AIF), the DIA master target list used for nuclear targeting (Raymund E. O'Mara, Br. Gen., USAF, DCS, Strategic Planning and Analysis, letter to author, 13 December 1989).

50. "Fifth Meeting of the Air Board," 5–6 June 1947, p. 93.

51. Vance Mitchell, phone conversation with author, June 4, 1990.

52. Memoranda for Chief, Air Intelligence Division, From William H. Mee, Captain, Air Corps, Executive, Strategic Vulnerability Branch, Air Intelligence Division, Subject: Daily Activity Report, 16 January 1946 and 12 July 1946, both under Daily Activity Reports, Air Intelligence Division, 1945–47, microfilm roll 1036, AFHRA.

53. "Fifth Meeting of the Air Board," 5–6 June 1947, pp. 94–95.

54. Nash, interview, May 6, 1988. Nash worked in target intelligence from 1950 to 1956, but the description also applies to the earlier period.

55. *Bombing Encyclopedia,* Alphabetical Listing, 6th ed., vol. 1 (Washington, D.C.: Directorate of Intelligence, Headquarters, U.S. Air Force, and Office of Naval Intelligence, Navy Department, April, 1952), p. v, in file no. K 142.6-1, vol. 1, April 1952, AFHRA. The unclassified sections of it are the front and inside front cover through p. viii.

56. Not included in this edition were all countries in the Western Hemisphere, the British Isles, Iceland, Greenland, Japan, Australia, and New Zealand (*Bombing Encyclopedia*, vol. 1, April 1952, inside cover, and pp. ii–iii, vii).

57. Given the large number of targets in the *B.E.* and the very small number of nuclear weapons available, one must surmise that the *B.E.* was a master list for both conventional and nuclear weapons. On the nuclear stockpile, see David Alan Rosenberg, "U.S. Nuclear Stockpile, 1945 to 1950," *Bulletin of Atomic Scientists* 38, no. 5 (1982): 25–30.

58. "SIOP-62 Briefing, JCS 2056/281 Enclosure, 13 September 1961," in Scott D. Sagan, "SIOP-62: The Nuclear War Plan Briefing to President Kennedy," *International Security* 12, no. 1 (1987): 44. Before 1960, each service developed its own plan to use nuclear weapons. Unwieldy military conferences were then held to "coordinate" these separate plans. In 1960 President Eisenhower ordered the development of a single plan (Rosenberg, "Origins of Overkill," pp. 14–15, 64–65).

59. *Bombing Encyclopedia,* vol. 1 (April 1952), pp. vii–viii.

60. Ibid., p. v.

61. *The Bomber's Baedeker: Guide to the Economic Importance of German Towns, Cities, and Industries* (Ministry of Economic Warfare, Enemy Branch, January 1943), decimal file no. 512.611-39, AFHRA, p. 1.

62. *Bomber's Baedeker,* pp. 3ff. The *Baedeker* provided the analytical underpinnings to

the more diagrammatically arranged "Blue Books" kept by Sir Arthur Harris, the head of the British Bomber Command. The "Blue Books" were "evidence of Harris's commitment to city bombing" (Biddle, *Rhetoric and Reality in Air Warfare*, p. 217).

63. Richard Grassy, phone conversation with author, September 4, 1997.

64. Grassy, "History," p. 3; Grassy, phone conversation, February 1, 1996.

65. "Planning Factors for Atomic Bomb Requirements," n.d. [1947], DCS/Ops, Asst for Atomic Energy 1947 TS, 471.6 Outline of Planning Factors for Atomic Bomb, RG 341, Records of the Headquarters, U.S. Air Force, Modern Military Records, National Archives at College Park, Md. (NACP), declassified August 24, 1998, and released on August 6, 1999, six and a half years after I requested declassification under the Freedom of Information Act. Another targeting study, a mobilization plan prepared by the war planners on the staff of the Joint Chiefs of Staff, was also under way in the summer of 1947. I am grateful to David A. Rosenberg for clarifying the concurrent war plans in the summer of 1947 and helping me figure out that PV's study was for the Air Staff. On the Air Staff study, see also L. Wainstein et al., *The Evolution of U.S. Strategic Command and Control and Warning, 1945–1972 (U)* (Arlington, Va.: Institute for Defense Analyses, June 1975, declassified 15 September 1992), p. 14.

66. Steven T. Ross, *American War Plans, 1945–1950*, p. 56. The plan was JWPC 486/7, 29 July 1947.

67. Grassy, phone conversation, February 1, 1996.

68. Richard Grassy, letter to author, n.d., received February 8, 1996.

69. Grassy, phone conversation, February 1, 1996.

70. Grassy, interview, May 21, 1995.

71. Ibid.

72. Grassy, "History," p. 3.

73. Grassy, interview, May 21, 1995.

74. U.S. Strategic Bombing Survey [USSBS], Chairman's Office, *The Effects of Atomic Bombs on Hiroshima and Nagasaki* (Washington, D.C.: GPO, 30 June 1946). Later reports provided figures consistent with those in the 1946 summary report: USSBS, Physical Damage Division [PDD], *The Effects of the Atomic Bomb on Hiroshima, Japan*, vols. 1–3 (n.p., May 1947), originally classified Secret; USSBS, PDD, *Effects of the Atomic Bomb on Nagasaki, Japan*, vols. 1–3 (n.p., June 1947), originally classified Secret; and the systematic overview, USSBS, PDD, *A Report on Physical Damage in Japan* (n.p., June 1947), originally classified Restricted (a lower classification than Confidential, and not to be confused with Restricted Data). The reports added extensive information on the damage at Hiroshima and Nagasaki, including some information on fire. The PV analysts did not use these reports, almost certainly because they became available too late for them to incorporate into their analysis.

75. The USSBS building types were broadly based on Joint Target Group categories used in World War II (see USSBS, PDD, *Report on Physical Damage in Japan*, p. 4).

76. Grassy, interview, May 21, 1995.

77. Grassy, phone conversation, February 1, 1996.

78. USSBS, PDD, *Report on Physical Damage in Japan*, p. 8.

79. Grassy, interview, May 21, 1995 (emphasis added).

80. Grassy, "History," p. 4.

81. Rosenberg, "Toward Armageddon," pp. 95–98, 107; Ross, *American War Plans*, pp. 61, 71, 86–90.

82. Richard Grassy, phone conversation with author, April 28, 1995.

83. Grassy, "History," pp. 3–4.

84. On Penney, see Lorna Arnold with Katherine Pyne, *Britain and the H-Bomb* (Basingstoke: Palgrave, 2001).

85. USSBS, PDD, *Report on Physical Damage in Japan,* p. 202; Frank H. Shelton, *Reflections of a Nuclear Weaponeer* (Colorado Springs, Colo.: Shelton Enterprise, 1988), pp. 2-23–2-32.

86. Grassy, interview, May 21, 1995; see also Grassy, "History," p. 4.

87. USSBS, PDD, *Effects of the Atomic Bomb on Hiroshima, Japan,* vol. 1, p. 16.

88. Grassy, interview, May 21, 1995.

89. Ibid.

90. Ibid.

91. Lawwill, letter, October 15, 1991.

92. PV tackled other important problems in this period that required substantial mathematical sophistication, but they are beyond the scope of our concern here (Grassy, interview, May 21, 1995).

93. Samuel Glasstone, ed., *The Effects of Atomic Weapons* (Washington, D.C.: GPO, June 1950).

94. Grassy, interview, May 21, 1995.

95. Ibid.

96. Grassy, phone conversation, September 4, 1997.

97. Horatio Bond, interview with author and Ted Postol, Hyannisport, Mass., October 21, 1989.

CHAPTER 5. NEW INQUIRY ABOUT BLAST

1. James G. March and Herbert A. Simon, *Organizations* (New York: Wiley, 1958), p. 165.

2. Barton C. Hacker, *The Dragon's Tail: Radiation Safety in the Manhattan Project, 1942–1946* (Berkeley: University of California Press, 1987), p. 137; Frank H. Shelton, *Reflections of a Nuclear Weaponeer* (Colorado Springs, Colo.: Shelton Enterprise, 1988), p. 2-46.

3. Hacker, *Dragon's Tail,* pp. 138–147; Jonathan M. Weisgall, *Operation CROSSROADS: The Atomic Tests at Bikini Atoll* (Annapolis, Md.: Naval Institute Press, 1994), pp. 240–243, 259–261.

4. These are standard definitions drawn from civil engineering and physics. I have drawn my discussion from Samuel Glasstone and Philip J. Dolan, eds., *The Effects of Nuclear Weapons,* 3d ed. (Washington, D.C.: GPO, 1977), pp. 127–136, 154–157. By definition, pressure = force/area (e.g., 5 pounds per square inch, or 5 psi); and force = pressure × area. An overpressure of 5 psi exerts a force in excess of air pressure at sea level of 720 pounds per square foot (5 pounds × 12 inches × 12 inches) and 72,000 pounds of force on a wall measuring 10 feet by 10 feet, or 100 square feet.

5. Samuel Glasstone, ed., *The Effects of Atomic Weapons* (Washington, D.C.: GPO, June 1950), p. 114.

6. Ibid., pp. 114–116. The terminology may be confusing: Because both overpressure and drag pressure have duration, the "dynamic analysis" of forces, as discussed in chapter 3 (done by civil engineers Hansen, Newmark, and White during and after World War II), refers to both overpressure and drag pressure. Here, "dynamic pressure" refers only to drag pressure.

7. Shelton, *Reflections of a Nuclear Weaponeer,* pp. 2-27, 2-38.

8. Glasstone, *Effects of Atomic Weapons* (June 1950), pp. 129, 133, 139, 147.

9. Shelton, *Reflections of a Nuclear Weaponeer,* pp. 2-31–2-32; Wolfgang Panofsky, conversation with author, Stanford, Calif., July 2, 1996.

10. Shelton, *Reflections of a Nuclear Weaponeer,* pp. 2-38–2-39; Defense Nuclear Agency [DNA], *Operation CROSSROADS 1946,* U.S. Atmospheric Nuclear Weapons Tests, Nuclear Test Personnel Review [NTPR], DNA 6032F (Washington, D.C.: DNA, 1984), pp. 27, 1.

11. DNA, *Operation SANDSTONE 1948,* U.S. Atmospheric Nuclear Weapons Tests, NTPR, DNA 6033F (Washington, D.C.: DNA, 1982), p. 97.

12. Glasstone, *Effects of Atomic Weapons* (June 1950), p. 130.

13. Ibid., p. 45.

14. Richard G. Grassy, "History of the Physical Vulnerability Division" (n.p., n.d. [spring 1995]), pp. 3–4.

15. Ibid., p. 3.

16. DNA, *Operation CROSSROADS,* p. 1.

17. Grassy, "History," pp. 4–5.

18. See Stephen L. Rearden, *History of the Office of the Secretary of Defense,* vol. 1, *The Formative Years* (Washington, D.C.: Historical Office, Office of the Secretary of Defense, 1984), pp. 96–103; on the Research and Development Board, see Herbert F. York and G. Allen Greb, "Military Research and Development: A Postwar History," *Bulletin of Atomic Scientists* 33, no. 1 (1977): 13–26.

19. Grassy, "History," p. 5; Richard Grassy, interview with author, Lac du Flambeau, Wisc., May 21, 1995.

20. Grassy, "History," p. 5.

21. Ibid.; Grassy, interview, May 21, 1995; Shelton, *Reflections of a Nuclear Weaponeer,* pp. 4-7–4-8, 5-18.

22. Grassy, "History," p. 6; Grassy, interview, May 21, 1995.

23. Grassy, interview, May 21, 1995.

24. Grassy, "History," p. 6; Grassy, interview, May 21, 1995.

25. Grassy, interview, May 21, 1995.

26. Shelton, *Reflections of a Nuclear Weaponeer,* p. 4-7.

27. Ibid., p. 4-1.

28. Barton C. Hacker, *Elements of Controversy: The Atomic Energy Commission and Radiation Safety in Nuclear Weapons Testing, 1947–1974* (Berkeley: University of California Press, 1994), p. 37.

29. Shelton, *Reflections of a Nuclear Weaponeer,* p. 4-8.

30. "Historical Summary, Physical Vulnerability Branch, 1 July–31 December 1950," app. C to Air Targets Division (DI/USAF-ONI), "Historical Summary for period 1 July 1950–31 Dec. 1950," pt. I, p. 5, obtained under Freedom of Information Act request.

31. Curtis Lampson chaired the structures panel; members included H. L. Bowman, Roy W. Carlson, a professor at the University of California, and Nathan M. Newmark. Lampson and Bowman were also on the ad hoc panel on the optimum height of burst. Shelton, *Reflections of a Nuclear Weaponeer,* pp. 4-7–4-8.

32. Ibid., p. 4-8.

33. Grassy, "History," p. 6; Richard Grassy, phone conversation with author, November 4, 1996.

34. Grassy, "History," pp. 5–6; Grassy, phone conversation, November 4, 1996; Richard Grassy, phone conversation with author, September 4, 1997.

35. Grassy, "History," pp. 3, 7, 9; Grassy, phone conversation, November 4, 1996.

36. "Historical Summary, Physical Vulnerability Branch, 1 July–31 December 1950," p. 2.

37. Merit P. White, phone conversation with author, August 22, 1991.

38. See Matthys Levy and Mario Salvadori, *Why Buildings Fall Down: How Structures Fail* (New York: Norton, 1992), app. A, "Loads."

39. N. M. Newmark, "Analysis and Design of Structures Subjected to Dynamic Loading," *Proceedings, Conference on Building in the Atomic Age* (Cambridge: MIT Press, 1952), pp. 34–47, at p. 34. My emphasis.

40. Grassy, phone conversation, November 4, 1996.

41. William J. Hall, letter to author, October 8, 1996.

42. White, phone conversation, August 22, 1991.

43. Grassy, interview, May 21, 1995.

44. White, phone conversation, August 22, 1991; not for attribution, phone conversation with author, August 27, 1991. See also W. J. Hall, "Nathan M. Newmark: Biography [and Bibliography]," in Hall, ed., *Structural and Geotechnical Mechanics: A Volume Honoring Nathan M. Newmark* (Englewood Cliffs, N.J.: Prentice-Hall, 1977), pp. 1–2; R. A. Kingery, R. D. Berg, and E. H. Schillinger, *Men and Ideas in Engineering: Twelve Histories from Illinois* (Urbana: University of Illinois Press, 1967), pp. 14–16.

45. Gilbert Binninger, interview with author, Alexandria, Va., July 19, 1991.

46. N. M. Newmark, "Methods of Analysis for Structures Subjected to Dynamic Loading," report to Physical Vulnerability Branch, Air Targets Division, Directorate of Intelligence, U.S. Air Force, Washington, D.C., 17 November 1949, revised 18 December 1950 [95 pp.], p. 1. I am grateful to William J. Hall for providing me with a copy of this unpublished document and several articles.

47. N. M. Newmark, "Methods of Analysis for Structures Subjected to Dynamic Loading," p. 67.

48. Grassy, phone conversation, November 4, 1996.

49. White, phone conversation, August 22, 1991.

50. Ibid.

51. Ibid.

52. Ibid.; not for attribution, phone conversation, August 27, 1991.

53. White, phone conversation, August 22, 1991.

54. Grassy, interview, May 21, 1995.

55. Grassy, "History," p. 9; also Grassy, interview, May 21, 1995.

56. "A Classification of Structures Based on Vulnerability to Blast from Atomic Bombs (U)," PVTM-4, Physical Vulnerability Branch, Air Targets Division, Directorate of Intelligence, Headquarters United States Air Force (HQUSAF), 2 March 1951. I was not able to get this document declassified (the "U" in the title indicates that the title itself is not classified), but the document is well described in Marc Peter, Jr., and Andrew Marshall, *A Re-examination of Hiroshima-Nagasaki Damage Data*, RM-820 (Santa Monica, Calif.: RAND, 1 May 1952), p. 8; Gilbert C. Binninger, Paul J. Castleberry, Jr., and Patsy M. McGrady, *Mathematical Background and Programming Aids for the Physical Vulnerability System for Nuclear Weapons*, DI-550-27-74 (Washington, D.C.: Defense Intelligence Agency, 1 November 1974), p. 3; Grassy, "History," p. 9; and Grassy, interview, May 21, 1995.

57. *Target Analysis for Atomic Weapons*, AF-628202, Physical Vulnerability Division, Directorate for Intelligence, HQUSAF, PVTM-14, 30 June 1954. See Binninger, Castleberry, and McGrady, *Mathematical Background and Programming Aids*, p. 1.

58. The account that follows is based on the only detailed written account: Grassy, "History," p. 9; also Grassy, interview, May 21, 1995.

59. Grassy, "History," p. 9. The report was Los Alamos Report No. LA-743R. According

to Frank Shelton, this report was by F. B. Porzel, F. Reines et al., "Height of Burst for Atomic Bombs," Los Alamos, Report No. LA-743R, 3 August 1949 (Shelton, *Reflections of a Nuclear Weaponeer*, p. 5-23).

60. Grassy, "History," p. 9; Peter and Marshall, *Re-examination of Hiroshima-Nagasaki Damage Data*, p. 8.

61. Grassy, "History," p. 9; Grassy, phone conversation, November 4, 1996.

62. Peter and Marshall, *Re-examination of Hiroshima-Nagasaki Damage Data*, p. 8; Grassy, interview, May 21, 1995.

63. Grassy, "History," p. 9.

64. Grassy, interview, May 21, 1995; see also Grassy, "History," p. 9.

65. Grassy, interview, May 21, 1995.

66. Richard Grassy, letter to author, n.d., received February 8, 1996. The basic VN was referenced to a weapon yield of 20 kilotons. VNs for other yields were calculated by an "adjusted VN"; see Hugh R. Lehman, Lt. Col., USAF, and John J. Plunkett, Capt., USA, Physical Vulnerability Branch, Targets Division, AFCIN-3K, *(U) Development of the K Factor in the VN System*, PV 105-61, 25 January 1961 (prepared by Air Force Intelligence Center for the Assistant Chief of Staff, Intelligence, HQUSAF), originally classified as Confidential, p. 22. I am grateful to Bill Burr, National Security Archive, George Washington University, for finding this document.

67. Binninger, Castleberry, and McGrady, *Mathematical Background and Programming Aids*, pp. 3–8.

68. Richard Grassy, phone conversation with author, February 1, 1996.

69. Drawn from Defense Intelligence Agency [DIA], *Physical Vulnerability Handbook— Nuclear Weapons* (Washington, D.C.: Defense Intelligence Agency, 1 June 1969, with change 1 [1 September 1972] and change 2 [28 January 1974]).

70. Harold Brode, phone conversation with author, August 11, 1989; Gilbert Binninger, interview with author, Alexandria, Va., May 13, 1994.

71. Brode, phone conversation, August 11, 1989.

72. Grassy, interview, May 21, 1995.

CHAPTER 6. NUCLEAR WEAPONS TESTS

1. See the excellent discussion in Chuck Hansen, *U.S. Nuclear Weapons: The Secret History* (Arlington, Tex.: Aerofax, 1988), pp. 50–89.

2. U.S. Department of Energy [DOE], *United States Nuclear Tests, July 1945 through September 1992*, DOE/NV—209-REV 15 (U.S. Department of Energy: December 2000), pp. 2–9.

3. Harold Brode, phone conversation with author, August 11, 1989.

4. Calculated from DOE, *United States Nuclear Tests*, REV 15, pp. 2–3.

5. Barton C. Hacker, *Elements of Controversy: The Atomic Energy Commission and Radiation Safety in Nuclear Weapons Testing, 1947–1974* (Berkeley: University of California Press, 1994), p. 56.

6. Frank H. Shelton, *Reflections of a Nuclear Weaponeer* (Colorado Springs, Colo.: Shelton Enterprise, 1988), p. 4-32.

7. Hacker, *Elements of Controversy*, p. 56.

8. Richard Rhodes, *Dark Sun: The Making of the Hydrogen Bomb* (New York: Simon and Schuster, 1995), p. 508.

9. Hacker, *Elements of Controversy*, pp. 86–87.

10. Rhodes, *Dark Sun,* pp. 509–510.

11. Federal Civil Defense Administration [FCDA], *Operation CUE, the Atomic Test Program of the Federal Civil Defense Administration in cooperation with the Atomic Energy Commission, Nevada Test Site, Spring 1955* (Washington, D.C.: GPO, 1955), p. 74.

12. Theodore A. Postol, "Possible Fatalities from Superfires following Nuclear Attacks in or near Urban Areas," in Fredric Solomon and Robert Q. Marston, eds., *The Medical Implications of Nuclear War* (Washington, D.C.: National Academy Press, 1986), pp. 27–28.

13. Ted Postol, conversation with author, Cambridge, Mass., October 23, 1996.

14. Defense Nuclear Agency [DNA], *Operation GREENHOUSE 1951,* U.S. Atmospheric Nuclear Weapons Tests, Nuclear Test Personnel Review [NTPR], DNA 6034F (Washington, D.C.: DNA, 1983), pp. 98, 157, 111.

15. Richard Grassy, phone conversation with author, November 4, 1996.

16. Richard G. Grassy, "Semi-Annual Historical Summary, Physical Vulnerability Branch, Air Targets Division, DI-USAF/ONI, 1 January thru 30 June 1951," app. C to "Air Targets Division (D/I, USAF-ONI), Historical Summary for period 1 Jan. 1951–30 June 1951," p. 7, obtained under Freedom of Information Act request.

17. N. M. Newmark, "Methods of Analysis for Structures Subjected to Dynamic Loading," report to Physical Vulnerability Branch, Air Targets Division, Directorate of Intelligence, U.S. Air Force, Washington, D.C., 17 November 1949, revised 18 December 1950, p. 67.

18. Grassy, phone conversation, November 4, 1996.

19. Richard G. Grassy, "History of the Physical Vulnerability Division" (n.p., n.d. [spring 1995]), p. 6; Grassy, "Semi-Annual Historical Summary, Physical Vulnerability Branch, 1 January thru 30 June 1951," p. 7; Merit White, phone conversation with author, August 22, 1991.

20. Richard Grassy, phone conversation with author, April 25, 1997.

21. Grassy, "History," p. 7.

22. DNA, *Operation BUSTER–JANGLE 1951,* U.S. Atmospheric Nuclear Weapons Tests, NTPR, DNA 6023F (Washington, D.C.: DNA, 1982), pp. 93–94; Grassy, "History," p. 7.

23. DNA, *Operation TUMBLER–SNAPPER 1952,* U.S. Atmospheric Nuclear Weapons Tests, NTPR, DNA 6019F (Washington, D.C.: DNA, 1982), p. 86.

24. DNA, *Operation UPSHOT–KNOTHOLE 1953,* U.S. Atmospheric Nuclear Weapons Tests, NTPR, DNA 6014F (Washington, D.C.: DNA, 1982), pp. 31–32.

25. Development Office, Policy and Management Group, "Semi-Annual History, Deputy Director for Targets, Directorate of Intelligence, 1 Jan–30 Jun 1953," chap. 3, "Physical Vulnerability Division," p. 44, obtained under Freedom of Information Act request.

26. Grassy, "History," p. 7.

27. DNA, *Operation UPSHOT–KNOTHOLE 1953,* p. 92.

28. Shelton, *Reflections of a Nuclear Weaponeer,* pp. 6-15, 6-18.

29. Grassy, phone conversation, November 4, 1996; Richard G. Grassy, ed., "Semi-Annual Historical Summary, Physical Vulnerability Branch, Air Targets Division, DI-USAF/ONI, 1 January thru 30 June 1952," Tab to "Air Targets Division (DI USAF-ONI), Historical Summary for period 1 January 1952–30 June 1952," p. 217, obtained under Freedom of Information Act request.

30. Grassy, "Semi-Annual Historical Summary, Physical Vulnerability Branch, 1 January thru 30 June 1952," p. 224.

31. Development Office, Policy and Management Group, "Semi-Annual History, Deputy Director for Targets, Directorate of Intelligence, 1 July 1953 thru 31 December 1953," chap.

3, "Physical Vulnerability Division," p. 55, obtained under Freedom of Information Act request.

32. *Index of Selected Publications of RAND, 1946–1962,* vol. 1 (Santa Monica, Calif.: RAND, 1962).

33. Physical Vulnerability Division, Directorate for Intelligence, Headquarters United States Air Force, *Target Analysis for Atomic Weapons,* AF-628202, PVTM-14, 30 June 1954.

34. Shelton, *Reflections of a Nuclear Weaponeer,* p. 5-23.

35. Ibid., p. 4-20.

36. Grassy, phone conversation, November 4, 1996.

37. Shelton, *Reflections of a Nuclear Weaponeer,* pp. 4-19–4-20, 4-22.

38. Ibid., p. 5-23; DNA, *Operation BUSTER–JANGLE 1951,* p. 26.

39. Shelton, *Reflections of a Nuclear Weaponeer,* pp. 5-23–5-24; see also DNA, *Operation TUMBLER–SNAPPER 1952,* p. 27.

40. Shelton, *Reflections of a Nuclear Weaponeer,* p. 5-25.

41. The quotation is David Rosenberg's paraphrase of the memorandum. David Alan Rosenberg, "The Origins of Overkill: Nuclear Weapons and American Strategy, 1945–1960," *International Security* 7, no. 4 (1983): 24–25.

42. Grassy, "Semi-Annual Historical Summary, Physical Vulnerability Branch, 1 January thru 30 June 1952," pp. 192, 195.

43. Memorandum for: N. E. Bradbury, From: F. Reines (LASL [Los Alamos Scientific Laboratory]) and E. Cox (Sandia Corp.), Subject: The Implication of the BUSTER–JANGLE Blast Measurements, 29 January 1952 [formerly Restricted Data], pp. 2, 3 in [Box 63] 2-22500 to 2-22599, entry 214, Deputy Chief of Staff, Operations, Director of Intelligence, Top Secret Control and Cables (TSC&C), RG 341, Records of the Headquarters U.S. Air Force, Modern Military Records, National Archives at College Park, Md. (NACP). I thank Vance O. Mitchell for guiding me into this record group and for drawing my attention to this document.

44. Memo: Reines and Cox to Bradbury, pp. 3, 4, 5.

45. DNA, *Operation TUMBLER–SNAPPER 1952,* pp. 27–28.

46. Shelton, *Reflections of a Nuclear Weaponeer,* p. 5-25.

47. Ibid.

48. Samuel Glasstone and Philip J. Dolan, eds., *The Effects of Nuclear Weapons,* 3d ed. (Washington, D.C.: GPO, 1977), p. 95; Shelton, *Reflections of a Nuclear Weaponeer,* p. 5-26.

49. Shelton, *Reflections of a Nuclear Weaponeer,* p. 5-26.

50. Glasstone and Dolan, *Effects of Nuclear Weapons* (1977), p. 125.

51. Plans and Program Office, Policy and Management Group, "Semi-Annual History, Deputy Director for Targets, Directorate for Intelligence, 1 July thru 31 December 1952," chap. 3, "Physical Vulnerability Division," p. 21, document no. 3-389, entry 214, RG 341, NACP.

52. [John M. Wolverton], Physical Vulnerability Division, Deputy Director for Targets, Technical Memorandum No. 16, *Fire Spread in Urban Areas,* PVTM-16, AF-688816 (Washington, D.C.: Directorate of Intelligence, Headquarters United States Air Force, 30 September 1955), ca. 100 pp. I am grateful to Hal Brode for providing me with a copy of this document. The project can be traced in the official histories, cited below. Richard Grassy did not remember the study.

53. Grassy, "Semi-Annual Historical Summary, Physical Vulnerability Branch, 1 January thru 30 June 1951," p. 8.

54. Horatio Bond and James K. McElroy, "Some Observations and Conclusions," in Ho-

ratio Bond, ed., *Fire and the Air War* (Boston: National Fire Protection Association, 1946), p. 242.

55. W. G. Berl, ed., *International Symposium on the Use of Models in Fire Research,* sponsored by the Committee on Fire Research and the Fire Research Conference, National Academy of Sciences, November 9–10, 1959 (Washington, D.C.: National Academy of Sciences–National Research Council, 1961), "Participants," p. 317.

56. Richard G. Grassy, "Semi-Annual Historical Summary, Physical Vulnerability Branch, Air Targets Division, DI-USAF/ONI, 1 July thru 31 December 1951," app. C to "Air Targets Division (DI/USAF-ONI), Historical Summary for period 1 July 1951–31 Dec. 1951," p. 8, document no. 2-22556, entry 214, RG 341, NACP; Grassy, "Semi-Annual Historical Summary, Physical Vulnerability Branch, 1 January thru 30 June 1952," p. 227; Plans and Program Office, "Semi-Annual History, Deputy Director for Targets, 1 July thru 31 December 1952," chap. 3, "Physical Vulnerability Division," p. 59; Management Office, Policy and Management Group, "Semi-Annual History, Deputy Director for Targets, Directorate of Intelligence, 1 July 1955 thru 31 December 1955," chap. 3, "Physical Vulnerability Division," p. 71, obtained under Freedom of Information Act request.

57. Wolverton, *Fire Spread in Urban Areas,* pp. 1, 2.

58. On Berlin and "fire division mapping," see James K. McElroy, "The Work of the Fire Protection Engineers in Planning Fire Attacks," in Bond, ed., *Fire and the Air War,* pp. 125–129.

59. Wolverton, *Fire Spread in Urban Areas,* pp. 7–8.

60. Ibid., p. 2.

61. Ibid., p. 70.

62. Ibid., p. 2.

63. Ibid.

64. Ibid., p. 70.

65. Ibid., p. 19.

66. Ibid., p. 71.

67. Ibid., p. 6.

68. "Semi-Annual History, Deputy Director for Targets, 1 July 1955 thru 31 December 1955," p. 66.

69. Wolverton, *Fire Spread in Urban Areas,* p. 70.

70. Ted Postol, conversation with author, San Francisco, Calif., January 23, 1993.

71. This arrangement went into effect after Operation CROSSROADS. See DNA, *Operation SANDSTONE 1948,* U.S. Atmospheric Nuclear Weapons Tests, NTPR, DNA 6033F (Washington, D.C.: DNA, 1982), p. 89.

72. *First History of AFSWP [Armed Forces Special Weapons Project], 1947–1954,* vol. 3, *1950,* chap. 3, "Headquarters" (AFSWP, n.d.), p. almost illegible but probably 3.2.75. I am grateful to Bill Burr for providing me with declassified portions of AFSWP histories from the National Security Archive.

73. Maj. Gen. Edward B. Giller (USAF, ret.), phone conversation with author, September 29, 1991.

74. On the earliest Desert Rock exercises, see DNA, *Operation BUSTER–JANGLE 1951,* pp. 1-5, 46-57; Hacker, *Elements of Controversy,* pp. 67-81.

75. Samuel Glasstone, ed., *The Effects of Atomic Weapons,* rev. ed. (Washington, D.C.: GPO, September 1950), p. 199.

76. Giller, phone conversation, September 29, 1991.

77. Ibid.

78. Ibid.

79. On aircraft, e.g., see DNA, *Operation CROSSROADS 1946*, U.S. Atmospheric Nuclear Weapons Tests, NTPR, DNA 6032F (Washington, D.C.: DNA, 1984), pp. 27, 63; see also DNA, *Operation GREENHOUSE 1951*, pp. 178–179; DNA, *Operation BUSTER–JANGLE 1951*, p. 66; DNA, *Operation TUMBLER–SNAPPER 1952*, pp. 86–87; DNA, *Operation UPSHOT–KNOTHOLE 1953*, pp. 108–111, 119–120; DNA, *Operation TEAPOT 1955*, U.S. Atmospheric Nuclear Weapons Tests, NTPR, DNA 6009F (Washington, D.C.: DNA, 1981), pp. 103–106.

80. DNA, *Operation BUSTER–JANGLE 1951*, p. 60.

81. Ibid., p. 68.

82. Ibid., pp. 68–69. At the same shots, the Naval Radiological Defense Laboratory investigated burn damage to rats from thermal radiation (pp. 68–69). Further experiments included studying "the production of skin burns in pigs." DNA, *Operation TUMBLER–SNAPPER 1952*, pp. 90–92.

83. DNA, *Shots ENCORE to CLIMAX: The Final Four Tests of the UPSHOT–KNOTHOLE Series, 8 May–4 June 1953*, U.S. Atmospheric Nuclear Weapons Tests, NTPR, DNA 6018F (Washington, D.C.: DNA, 1982), p. 155.

84. Stephen J. Pyne, *Fire in America: A Cultural History of Wildland and Rural Fire* (Princeton: Princeton University Press, 1982), pp. 287–288, 395–396, 175–177, 477–480.

85. DNA, *Operation BUSTER–JANGLE 1951*, p. 61.

86. Pyne, *Fire in America*, pp. 480–481, 609 n. 44.

87. DNA, *Operation TUMBLER–SNAPPER 1952*, p. 100.

88. Ibid., p. 103.

89. Ibid., pp. 87–88.

90. Ibid., p. 101.

91. DNA, *Operation UPSHOT–KNOTHOLE 1953*, pp. 120, 124.

92. Ibid., p. 124.

93. Stanley Martin, interview with author, Redwood City, Calif., June 29, 1998; DNA, *Operation UPSHOT–KNOTHOLE 1953*, p. 124.

94. Giller, phone conversation, September 29, 1991.

95. Samuel Glasstone, ed., *The Effects of Nuclear Weapons* (Washington, D.C.: U.S. Atomic Energy Commission, 1957), pp. 318–319.

96. The dimensions of the miniature houses and block houses are in H. D. Bruce, U.S. Dept. of Agriculture, Forest Service, Forest Products Laboratory (Madison, Wisc.), *Operation UPSHOT–KNOTHOLE, March–June 1953, Project 8.11a, Incendiary Effects on Building and Interior Kindling Fuels,* report to the test director, WT-774 (Sandia Base, Albuquerque, N.Mex.: Headquarters Field Command, AFSWP, December 1953), p. 17; Glasstone, *Effects of Nuclear Weapons* (1957), p. 319.

97. Stanley Martin, interview, June 29, 1998.

98. Glasstone, *Effects of Nuclear Weapons* (1957), pp. 316–317.

99. *History of the Armed Forces Special Weapons Project (Latter Period, 1955–1958)*, pt. II, *Headquarters*, chap. 7, "Divisions and Offices," section 7-4: "Weapons Effects Division (through 1957)" (AFSWP, n.d.), p. 49.

100. A very good discussion of civil defense and the American state is Andrew D. Grossman, *Neither Red nor Dead: Civilian Defense and American Political Development during the Early Cold War* (New York: Routledge, 2001), chap. 2.

101. Lee Clarke, *Mission Improbable: Using Fantasy Documents to Tame Disaster* (Chi-

cago: University of Chicago Press, 1999), pp. 12–14. The single best book on U.S. civil defense is Laura McEnaney, *Civil Defense Begins at Home: Militarization Meets Everday Life in the Fifties* (Princeton: Princeton University Press, 2000). See also the interesting discussion of "emotion management" in Guy Oakes, *The Imaginary War: Civil Defense and American Cold War Culture* (New York: Oxford University Press 1994), and the superb documentary film *The Atomic Cafe* (1982). Older useful work is James J. Kerr, *Civil Defense in the U.S.: Bandaid for a Holocaust?* (Boulder, Colo.: Westview Press, 1983); Paul Boyer, *By the Bomb's Early Light: American Thought and Culture at the Dawn of the Atomic Age* (New York: Pantheon Books, 1985), chap. 26; Allan M. Winkler, *Life under a Cloud: American Anxiety about the Atom* (New York: Oxford University Press, 1993), chap. 5.

102. DNA, *Operation BUSTER–JANGLE 1951*, p. 74.

103. FCDA, *Operation DOORSTEP, AEC Atomic Proving Ground Yucca Flat, Nevada March 17, 1953* (Washington, D.C.: GPO, 1953), p. 2; see esp. McEnaney, *Civil Defense Begins at Home*, pp. 54–55.

104. Richard G. Hewlett and Jack M. Holl, *Atoms for Peace and War, 1953–1961: Eisenhower and the Atomic Energy Commission* (Berkeley: University of California Press, 1989), pp. 147–148.

105. Hewlett and Holl, *Atoms for Peace and War*, pp. 147–148; Glasstone, *Effects of Nuclear Weapons* (1957), p. 126 and p. 319, referring to pp. 125–128, 293–295.

106. FCDA, *Operation CUE* (1955).

107. DNA, *Shot APPLE-2, TEAPOT Series, 5 May 1955*, U.S. Atmospheric Nuclear Weapons Tests, NTPR, DNA 6012F (Washington, D.C.: DNA, 1981), p. 52.

108. DNA, *Shot APPLE-2, TEAPOT Series*, p. 52.

109. Philip A. Randall, *Operation TEAPOT, Nevada Test Site, February–May 1955, Project 31.1, Damage to Conventional and Special Types of Residences Exposed to Nuclear Effects* (Washington, D.C.: [Office of Technical Services, Department of Commerce], April 12, 1961), p. 17.

110. Glasstone, *Effects of Nuclear Weapons* (1957), pp. 129–140. DNA, *Shot APPLE-2, TEAPOT Series*, p. 52.

111. Glasstone, *Effects of Nuclear Weapons* (1957), p. 125.

112. Oakes, *Imaginary War*, pp. 109–110.

113. Compare the summary in Glasstone, *Effects of Atomic Weapons*, rev. ed. (September 1950), p. 199, and Glasstone, *Effects of Nuclear Weapons* (1957), pp. 293, 294.

114. Harold Brode, e-mail to author, August 8, 2001.

115. Hacker, *Elements of Controversy*, p. 96, quoting a joint AEC-DOD press release, 18 April 1953.

CHAPTER 7. THE HYDROGEN BOMB AND DAMAGE CODES

1. Marc Peter, Jr., and Andrew Marshall, *A Re-examination of Hiroshima-Nagasaki Damage Data*, RM-820 (Santa Monica, Calif.: RAND, 1 May 1952), p. 55.

2. Physical Vulnerability Division, Director for Targets, Assistant Chief of Staff, Intelligence, Headquarters United States Air Force, *Nuclear Weapons Employment Handbook (U)*, AFM 200-8, 1 May 1958. See chapter 1, note 23 for fuller discussion.

3. Curtis E. LeMay with MacKinlay Kantor, *Mission with LeMay* (Garden City, N.Y.: Doubleday, 1965), p. 384; William A. Adams, Col., USAF, Director of Intelligence, Strategic Air Command Headquarters, to Director of Intelligence, Headquarters USAF, Washington, D.C., Subject: Plan for Strategic Vulnerability Branch Detachment Detailed to Strategic Air

Command on M-Day, 13 Mar 50, Tab D to Col. H. E. Watson, Chief, Strategic Vulnerability Branch, Air Intelligence Division, Memorandum for Record, 17 November 1948 [formerly Top Secret], document no. 2-14777, entry 214, Top Secret Control and Cables (TSC&C), RG 341, National Archives at College Park, Md. (NACP).

4. *Public Papers of the Presidents of the United States: Harry S. Truman, 1950* (Washington, D.C.: GPO), January 31, 1950, p. 138.

5. Merit P. White, phone conversation with author, August 22, 1991.

6. William Hall, phone conversation with author, May 11, 1997.

7. White, phone conversation, August 22, 1991.

8. Nathan M. Newmark, "An Engineering Approach to Blast Resistant Design," *Proceedings, Separate No. 306, American Society of Civil Engineers* [ASCE] 79 (October 1953): 1–15; more formally published as Nathan M. Newmark, "An Engineering Approach to Blast-Resistant Design," *Transactions of the American Society of Civil Engineers* 121 (1956): 45–64.

9. Hugh R. Lehman, Lt. Col. USAF, and John J. Plunkett, Capt. USA, Physical Vulnerability Branch, Targets Division, AFCIN-3K, *(U) Development of the K Factor in the VN System*, PV-105-61, 25 January 1961 (prepared by Air Force Intelligence Center for the Assistant Chief of Staff, Intelligence, HQUSAF), originally classified as Confidential, pp. 14, 18. The study drew directly on Newmark's work.

10. Newmark, "Engineering Approach to Blast Resistant Design," *Transactions ASCE*, pp. 46–48.

11. William Hall, letter to author, October 8, 1996.

12. Hall, phone conversation, May 11, 1997. An early statement of the Beta method is N. M. Newmark, "Computation of Dynamic Structural Response in the Range Approaching Failure," in C. Martin Duke and Morris Feigen, eds., *Earthquake and Blast Effects on Structures, Proceedings of the Symposium* ([Los Angeles]: [UCLA], 1952), pp. 114–129; the definitive statement is Nathan M. Newmark, "A Method of Computation for Structural Dynamics," *Transactions of the American Society of Civil Engineers* 127 (1962, pt. I), pp. 1406–1435 (copy to author courtesy of William Hall).

13. Samuel Glasstone, ed., *The Effects of Atomic Weapons* (Washington, D.C.: GPO, June 1950), p. 116.

14. Newmark, "Engineering Approach to Blast Resistant Design," *Transactions ASCE*, pp. 48–52.

15. Hall, phone conversation, May 11, 1997.

16. Lehman and Plunkett, *Development of the K Factor*, p. 22.

17. Newmark "Engineering Approach to Blast Resistant Design," *Transactions ASCE*, p. 57; Lehman and Plunkett, *Development of the K Factor*, pp. 71–72. The equation formally became known as the Damage Pressure Level Equation (William J. Hall and John D. Haltiwanger, fax to author, August 20, 2002).

18. Quotation: Management Office, Policy and Management Group, "Semi-Annual History, Deputy Director for Targets, Directorate of Intelligence [U.S. Air Force], 1 July 1955 thru 31 December 1955," chap. 3, "Physical Vulnerability Division," p. 61, obtained under Freedom of Information Act request; J. W. Melin and S. Sutcliffe, approved by J. D. Haltiwanger and N. M. Newmark, *Development of Procedures for Rapid Computation of Dynamic Structural Response*, final report on Contract AF 33 (600)-24994 for Physical Vulnerability Division, Deputy Director of Targets, Directorate of Intelligence, Headquarters, USAF, Washington, D.C. (Urbana, Ill.: Civil Engineering Studies, University of Illinois, Structural Research Series

No. 171, n.d. [January 1959 according to Lehman and Plunkett, *Development of the K Factor,* p. 66]), copy to author courtesy of William Hall.

19. Richard Grassy, phone conversation with author, November 4, 1996.

20. Richard G. Grassy, "History of the Physical Vulnerability Division" (n.p., n.d. [spring 1995]), p. 9; Grassy, phone conversation, November 4, 1996.

21. Richard Grassy, interview with author, Lac du Flambeau, Wisc., May 21, 1995; Grassy, phone conversation, November 4, 1996.

22. Grassy, "History," p. 9; Grassy, phone conversation, November 4, 1996.

23. Hugh Lehman, phone conversation with author, October 29, 1991.

24. Peter and Marshall, *Re-examination of Hiroshima-Nagasaki Damage Data,* pp. 55–56.

25. Development Office, Policy and Management Group, "Semi-Annual History, Deputy Director for Targets, Directorate of Intelligence, 1 July 1954 thru 31 December 1954," chap. 3, "Physical Vulnerability Division," pp. 51–54, obtained under Freedom of Information Act request.

26. Physical Vulnerability Division, *Target Analysis for Atomic Weapons,* 30 June 1954.

27. Development Office, "Semi-Annual History, Deputy Director for Targets, 1 July 1954 thru 31 December 1954," chap. 3, "Physical Vulnerability Division," pp. 53–54. Emphasis added.

28. Caroll L. Zimmerman, *Insider at SAC, Operations Analysis under General LeMay* (Manhattan, Kans.: Sunflower University Press, 1988), p. 55.

29. Grassy, interview, May 21, 1995.

30. Development Office, "Semi-Annual History, Deputy Director for Targets, 1 July 1954 thru 31 December 1954," chap. 3, "Physical Vulnerability Division," pp. 52, 54.

31. Ibid., p. 51.

32. Ibid., p. 54.

33. Grassy, interview, May 21, 1995.

34. Fred Gross, phone conversation with author, November 6, 1991.

35. Development Office, "Semi-Annual History, Deputy Director for Targets, 1 July 1954 thru 31 December 1954," chap. 3, "Physical Vulnerability Division," pp. 55–56; Samuel Glasstone and Philip J. Dolan, eds., *The Effects of Nuclear Weapons,* 3d ed. (Washington, D.C.: GPO, 1977), pp. 172–174.

36. I am grateful to Gil Binninger for first drawing these tests to my attention and explaining their significance (Gilbert Binninger, interview with author, Alexandria, Va., July 19, 1991).

37. U.S. Department of Energy, *United States Nuclear Tests, July 1945 through September 1992,* DOE/NV—209-REV 15 (U.S. Department of Energy, December 2000), p. 7.

38. Glasstone and Dolan, *Effects of Nuclear Weapons* (1977), p. 174.

39. DOE, *United States Nuclear Tests,* REV 15, p. 7.

40. Glasstone and Dolan, *Effects of Nuclear Weapons* (1977), p. 175.

41. Gross, phone conversation, November 6, 1991.

42. Management Office, Policy and Management Group, "Semi-Annual History, Deputy Director for Targets, Directorate of Intelligence, 1 July 1955 thru 31 December 1955," chap. 3, "Physical Vulnerability Division," p. 60, obtained under Freedom of Information Act request.

43. Management Office, Policy and Management Group, "Semi-Annual History, Deputy Director for Targets, Directorate of Intelligence, 1 January 1956 thru 30 June 1956," chap. 3,

"Physical Vulnerability Division," pp. 69–70, 81, obtained under Freedom of Information Act request.

44. Management Office, Directorate of Targets, "Semi-Annual History, Directorate of Targets, Assistant Chief of Staff, Intelligence [U.S. Air Force], 1 July 1957 thru 31 December 1957," chap. 3, "Physical Vulnerability Division," p. 100, obtained under Freedom of Information Act request; Management Office, Directorate of Targets, "Semi-Annual History, Directorate of Targets, Assistant Chief of Staff, Intelligence [U.S. Air Force], 1 July 1958 thru 31 December 1958," chap. 3, "Physical Vulnerability Division," p. 118, obtained under Freedom of Information Act request.

45. Gross, phone conversation, November 6, 1991.

46. Lehman and Plunkett, *Development of the K Factor,* pp. 1, 31–65.

47. Clear expositions are in Gilbert Binninger, Roger Craver, and Suzanne Wright, *Staff Officers' Guide for Targeting Uncertainties,* DNA-TR-89-115, prepared for Director, Defense Nuclear Agency, Washington, D.C. (n.p., January 1990), p. 8; H. L. Brode et al., *Fire Damage to Urban/Industrial Targets,* vol. 2, *Technical Report,* PSR Report 1936, prepared for Headquarters Defense Nuclear Agency, Washington D.C. (Los Angeles: Pacific-Sierra Research Corp., 25 July 1989), pp. 121–123.

48. See chapter 1, note 23.

49. Harold Brode, e-mail to author, February 25, 1999.

50. Harold Brode, e-mail to author, April 19, 2001.

51. Harold Brode, e-mail to author, February 27, 2001; Harold Brode, letter to author, June 10, 1999.

52. Harold Brode, letter to author, September 22, 1998.

53. Brode, e-mail, February 25, 1999. The first publication on Brode's resume is *A Method of Predicting the Blast from an Air-Burst Atomic Bomb with Corrections for Nonuniform Atmosphere Effects and Reflections,* RM-1074 (Santa Monica, Calif.: RAND, April 20, 1953).

54. Citation accompanying Defense Special Weapons Agency Lifetime Achievement Award to Dr. Harold L. Brode, 7 February 1997, signed by Gary L. Curtin, Maj. Gen., USAF, Director.

55. Horatio Bond, phone conversation with author, April 2, 1990.

CHAPTER 8. THE FIRE RESEARCH COMMUNITY

1. *History of the Armed Forces Special Weapons Project [AFSWP] (Latter Period, 1955–1958),* pt. II, *Headquarters,* chap. 7, "Divisions and Offices," section 7-4: "Weapons Effects Division (through 1957)" (AFSWP, n.d.), p. 49.

2. Defense Nuclear Agency [DNA], *Shot APPLE-2, A Test of the TEAPOT Series* (Washington, D.C.: DNA, 1981), p. 52.

3. Louis Jordan, National Academy of Sciences–National Research Council, "Introduction and Background," in *First Fire Research Correlation Conference,* sponsored by the Committee on Fire Research and Fire Research Conference, Washington, D.C., November 8 and 9, 1956 (Washington, D.C.: Division of Engineering and Industrial Research, National Academy of Sciences–National Research Council, 1957), pp. 4–5. See also Stephen J. Pyne, *Fire in America* (Princeton: Princeton University Press, 1982), p. 482.

4. Committee on Fire Research of the National Academy of Sciences–National Research Council, Division of Engineering and Industrial Research, *A Study of Fire Problems,* a study held at Woods Hole, Massachusetts, July 17 to August 11, 1961 (Washington, D.C.: National Academy of Sciences–National Research Council, 1961), back cover.

5. Jordan, *First Fire Research Correlation Conference,* p. 5.

6. *First History of AFSWP, 1947–1954,* vol. 2, *1949,* chap. 3, "Headquarters" (AFSWP, n.d.), p. 3.2.6.

7. Horatio Bond, interview by author and Ted Postol, Hyannisport, Mass., October 21, 1989.

8. Bond, interview, October 21, 1989.

9. Horatio Bond, "The Fire Damage Caused by Air Attacks," in Bond, ed., *Fire and the Air War* (Boston: National Fire Protection Association, 1946).

10. *First Fire Research Correlation Conference,* p. ix.

11. "Howard W. Emmons, Authority on Fire Safety, Dies at 86," *Harvard University Gazette,* December 3, 1998, www.news.harvard.edu/gazette/1998/12.03/emmons.html.

12. "Howard W. Emmons," *Harvard University Gazette.*

13. Jana Backovsky, telephone conversation with author, August 3, 2000.

14. Ibid.

15. H. C. Hottel, "Introduction and Background," in W. G. Berl, ed., *International Symposium on the Use of Models in Fire Research,* sponsored by the Committee on Fire Research and the Fire Research Conference, National Academy of Sciences, November 9–10, 1959 (Washington, D.C.: National Academy of Sciences–National Research Council, 1961), p. 3.

16. Hottel, in Berl, *International Symposium on the Use of Models,* pp. 4, 3.

17. Eugene S. Ferguson, *Engineering and the Mind's Eye* (Cambridge: MIT Press, 1992), pp. 159–161. An insightful discussion comparing knowledge in engineering science and in science is Walter G. Vicenti, *What Engineers Know and How They Know It: Analytical Studies from Aeronautical History* (Baltimore: Johns Hopkins University Press, 1990), pp. 134–135.

18. Hottel, in Berl, *International Symposium on the Use of Models,* p. 3.

19. Ibid., p. 4.

20. *First Fire Research Correlation Conference,* p. vi.

21. Hottel, in Berl, *International Symposium on the Use of Models,* p. 4.

22. Wilbur Stump, "Discussion," *First Fire Research Correlation Conference,* p. 261.

23. *Methods of Studying Mass Fires,* Second Fire Research Correlation Conference, sponsored by Committee on Fire Research and Fire Research Conference in cooperation with Department of Engineering, UCLA, May 26, 27, 28, 1957 (Washington, D.C.: Division of Engineering and Industrial Research, National Academy of Sciences–National Research Council, 1958), p. vii.

24. Alexander W. Boldyreff, Chairman, Second Fire Research Correlation Conference, foreword to *Methods of Studying Mass Fires,* p. vi.

25. Everett D. Howe, "My Reactions to the Conference," *Methods of Studying Mass Fires,* pp. 17–18.

26. Hottel, in Berl, *International Symposium on the Use of Models,* p. 4.

27. Ibid.

28. Berl, *International Symposium on the Use of Models,* "Participants," pp. 306–317.

29. Committee on Fire Research, *A Study of Fire Problems,* p. 24.

30. Carl W. Walter, Chairman, foreword to Committee on Fire Research, Division of Engineering, National Research Council, *Directory of Fire Research in the United States, 1971–1973,* 7th ed. (Washington, D.C.: National Academy of Sciences, 1975), p. v.

31. Committee on Fire Research, *Directory of Fire Research in the United States, 1971–1973,* index of subjects, pp. 321, 344.

32. National Academy of Sciences, National Academy of Engineering, IM, and National

Research Council, *Annual Report FY 1974–75* (Washington, D.C.: GPO, referred to the Committee on Labor and Public Welfare, 94th Cong., 2d sess., Senate Document No. 94–155, February 6, 1976), p. 144.

33. Daniel Barbiero, associate archivist, NAS-NRC Archives, e-mail to author, December 28, 1998.

34. Committee on Fire Research, *A Study of Fire Problems,* p. 9; see also Howard W. Emmons, "The Phenomenological Aspects of Fires and Fire Fighting," *Methods of Studying Mass Fires,* pp. 5–9.

35. Bond, interview, October 21, 1989.

36. Harold Brode, e-mail to author, February 25, 1999.

37. Robert Frank Futurell, *Ideas, Concepts, Doctrine: A History of Basic Thinking in the United States Air Force, 1907–1964* (Maxwell Air Force Base, Ala.: Air University, 1971), pp. 329–335.

38. Futurell, *Ideas, Concepts, Doctrine,* p. 338.

39. *Public Papers of the Presidents of the United States: John F. Kennedy, 1961* (Washington, D.C.: GPO, 1962), July 25, 1961, pp. 536–537; House of Representatives, Subcommittee on Military Operations of the Committee on Government Operations, *Civil Defense—1961, Hearings,* 87th Cong., 1st sess. (Washington, D.C.: GPO, 1961), p. 131 [hereafter, *Civil Defense—1961, Hearings*]; Allan M. Winkler, *Life under a Cloud* (New York: Oxford University Press, 1993), pp. 125–127.

40. *Civil Defense—1961, Hearings,* pp. 9, 131, 398.

41. James W. Kerr, OCD, and Mathew G. Gibbons, USNRDL, eds., *OCD Research Report No. 12, Technical Summary, 5th Annual OCD Fire Research Contractors Meeting, Asilomar, California,* April 2–6, 1967 (Office of Civil Defense [OCD], Office of the Secretary of the Army, Department of Defense: October 15, 1967), p. 1.

42. Harold Brode, interview with author, Los Angeles, September 7, 1989.

43. Pyne, *Fire in America,* p. 489.

44. See, e.g., Committee on Fire Research, Division of Engineering, National Academy of Sciences National Research Council, *Directory of Fire Research in the United States,* 3d rev. ed., 1965 (Washington, D.C.: National Academy of Sciences National Research Council, 1966), pp. 292–293.

45. Statement of Walmer E. Strope, associate scientific director, U.S. Naval Radiological Defense Laboratory, San Francisco, in *Civil Defense—1961, Hearings,* August 8, 1961, pp. 248–249, 237.

46. Robert L. Olson et al., "Food Supply for Fallout Shelters," in *Civil Defense—1961, Hearings,* app. 10, p. 492, discussing the same habitability test; Strope, in *Civil Defense—1961, Hearings,* pp. 250–253.

47. Guy Oakes, *The Imaginary War* (New York: Oxford University Press, 1994), pp. 123–127.

48. Andrew D. Grossman, *Neither Dead nor Red* (New York: Routledge, 2001), p. 84.

49. Laura McEnaney, *Civil Defense Begins at Home* (Princeton: Princeton University Press, 2000), pp. 69, 73.

50. Jerald E. Hill, "Problems of Fire in Nuclear Warfare," statement before the House of Representatives, in *Civil Defense—1961, Hearings,* August 9, 1961, p. 345. I thank Ted Postol for drawing this testimony to my attention.

51. Hill, "Problems of Fire," pp. 345, 358.

52. Ibid., pp. 349, 350.

53. Ibid., pp. 345–346.

54. Ibid., pp. 350, 351.

55. Ibid., pp. 359, 358.

56. Robert G. Hickman and Carol A. Meier, eds., *17th Asilomar Conference on Fire and Blast Effects of Nuclear Weapons,* May 30–June 3, 1983, Asilomar Conference Center, Pacific Grove, Calif., sponsored by the Federal Emergency Management Agency [FEMA] (Livermore, Calif.: Lawrence Livermore Laboratory, University of California, July 1983), p. 2.

57. I am grateful to Stan Martin for providing me with many of the proceedings of the Asilomar conferences.

58. Berl, *International Symposium on the Use of Models,* "Participants," pp. 306–317; Kerr and Gibbons, *5th Annual OCD Fire Research Contractors Meeting,* app. I, List of Participants; Irwin Fieldhouse, phone conversation with author, March 29, 1999; Debra Kerr Fassnacht, *IITRI: A Fifty Year Portrait, 1936–1986* (Chicago: IITRI, 1986), pp. 5–6, 17, 9–10, 22, 30. See also Weldon B. Gibson, *SRI,* vol. 2, *The Take-Off Days* (Los Altos, Calif.: Publishing Services Center, 1986), pp. vii, xv–xvi; "The Sister Institutes," pp. 17–24.

59. James W. Kerr and John F. Christian, *Research Report No. 13, Civil Defense Fire Research, Cumulative Summary of Fire Research and Reports FY 1962–FY 1967* (OCD, Office of the Secretary of the Army, Department of the Army, n.d. [1967]), pp. 7, 8, 16, 29.

60. Clive M. Countryman, *Mass Fires and Fire Behavior,* U.S. Forest Service Research Paper PSW-19 (Berkeley, Calif.: Pacific Southwest Forest and Range Experiment Station, Forest Service, U.S. Department of Agriculture, 1964); Clive M. Countryman, *Project Flambeau . . . An Investigation of Mass Fire (1964–1967), Final Report,* vol. 1, prepared for OCD, Office of the Secretary of the Army, and Defense Atomic Support Agency (Berkeley, Calif.: Pacific Southwest Forest and Range Experiment Station, Forest Service, U.S. Department of Agriculture, 1969).

61. Countryman, *Project Flambeau, Final Report,* p. 1.

62. Countryman, *Mass Fires and Fire Behavior,* unnumbered front matter.

63. Thomas Y. Palmer, "Project Flambeau Experimental Fire Measurements," in Hickman and Meier, *17th Asilomar Conference on Fire and Blast Effects,* p. 66.

64. Countryman, *Mass Fires and Fire Behavior,* p. 5.

65. On the Coal Pier fire, see the front-page story, no byline, "Jersey Fire Engulfs a Mile of Piers and Barges along the Hudson," *New York Times,* August 19, 1961; Craig C. Chandler, "A Study of Mass Fires and Conflagrations," U.S. Forest Service Research Note (Berkeley, Calif.: Pacific Southwest Forest and Range Experiment Station, Forest Service, U.S. Department of Agriculture, PSW-N22, 1963), p. 2; emphasis in original.

66. Countryman, *Mass Fires and Fire Behavior,* foreword.

67. *Annual Report, Fiscal Year 1962–63, National Academy of Sciences–National Research Council* (Washington, D.C.: GPO, referred to the Committee on Labor and Public Welfare on October 6, 1966), p. 71.

68. The playing area of a football field, 300 feet by 160 feet, or 48,000 square feet, is about 1.1 acres. I thank Aaron Clark-Ginsberg for his research.

69. Countryman, *Mass Fires and Fire Behavior,* pp. 15, 18; Countryman, *Project Flambeau, Final Report,* p. 1; Stanley Martin, interview with author, Redwood City, Calif., June 29, 1998.

70. Countryman, *Mass Fires and Fire Behavior,* pp. 18, 15.

71. Ibid., p. 48.

72. Ibid., p. 15.

73. Stanley B. Martin, *The Role of Fire in Nuclear Warfare: An Interpretive Review of the Current Technology for Evaluating the Incendiary Consequences of the Strategic and Tactical Uses of Nuclear Weapons,* DNA 2692F, final report, prepared for Director, Defense Nuclear Agency (San Mateo, Calif.: URS Research Co., 23 August 1974), p. 3-102. The review was written in 1969 but not published until 1974; Martin, interview, June 29, 1998.

74. Countryman, *Mass Fires and Fire Behavior,* pp. 12, 15.

75. Pyne, *Fire in America,* p. 485.

76. Martin, interview, June 29, 1998.

77. Kerr and Gibbons, *5th Annual OCD Fire Research Contractors Meeting,* p. 29.

78. Committee on Fire Research, Division of Engineering, National Research Council, *Directory of Fire Research in the United States 1965–67,* 4th ed. (Washington, D.C.: National Academy of Sciences, 1968), pp. 158, 176–177, 180–182.

79. Countryman, *Project Flambeau, Final Report,* p. 1.

80. Ibid., p. 10.

81. Ibid., p. 12.

82. Ibid., p. 15.

83. Martin, interview, June 29, 1998.

84. Martin, *Role of Fire in Nuclear Warfare,* pp. 3-102–3-103.

85. Brode, interview, September 7, 1989.

86. For example, Martin, *Role of Fire in Nuclear Warfare,* pp. 3-102–3-103; Thomas Y. Palmer, "Project Flambeau Experimental Fire Measurements," in Hickman and Meier, *17th Asilomar Conference on Fire and Blast Effects,* pp. 66–70.

87. Stanley B. Martin and Raymond S. Alger, eds., *Blast/Fire Interactions, Asilomar Conference, April 1981, Proceedings,* prepared for FEMA, Washington, D.C. (Menlo Park, Calif.: SRI International, August 1981), app. B, "Models for Damage and Vulnerability Assessment," p. B-2; Jerry Strope, phone conversation with author, May 24, 1999; Martin, interview, June 29, 1998.

88. Martin, interview, June 29, 1998.

89. Stanley Martin, interview with author, Redwood City, Calif., September 15, 1998.

90. Martin, interview, June 29, 1998.

91. S. Martin, R. Ramstad, and C. Colvin, *Development and Application of an Interim Fire-Behavior Model,* final report for OCD, Office of the Secretary of the Army through U.S. Naval Radiological Defense Laboratory (Burlingame, Calif.: URS Research Co., April 1968), p. 5-2.

92. Martin, interview, June 29, 1998.

93. Strope, phone conversation, May 24, 1999.

94. Martin, interview, September 15, 1998.

95. Martin, interview, June 29, 1998.

96. Martin, Ramstad, and Colvin, *Interim Fire-Behavior Model,* p. 2-1.

97. Harold Brode, letter to author, September 22, 1998, p. 11; Brode, interview, September 7, 1989.

98. Brode, interview, September 7, 1989.

99. Martin, Ramstad, and Colvin, *Interim Fire-Behavior Model,* app. C, "Fire Damage to San Jose in the Five-City Attack," p. C-4.

100. Brode, interview, September 7, 1989.

101. T. E. Waterman and A. N. Takata, IIT Research Institute, "Modeling Urban Fire Growth," in Hickman and Meier, *17th Asilomar Conference on Fire and Blast Effects,* p. 176.

102. On setting fires to buildings and scale models, see Committee on Fire Research, *Directory of Fire Research*, 4th ed., pp. 169–170, 175; Fassnacht, *IITRI: A Fifty Year Portrait*, p. 34. Quote from Eugene Sevin, phone conversation with author, February 4, 2000.

103. ITT Research Institute, "Prediction of Fire Damage to Urban Areas," in Committee on Fire Research, Division of Engineering and Industrial Research, *Directory of Fire Research in the United States*, rev. 1963 (Washington, D.C.: National Academy of Sciences–National Research Council, 1964), p. 97.

104. Keith Miller, Dikewood Corp., "Evaluation of Ignition and Fire Spread Models," in Henry G. Dorsett, OCD, ed., *Research Report No. 15, Technical Summary, 8th Annual OCD Fire Research Contractors Meeting, Asilomar, California,* April 20–24, 1970 (OCD, Office of the Secretary of the Army, Department of Defense, June 1, 1970), p. 31.

105. Good discussions of these studies are Miller, "Evaluation of Ignition and Fire Spread Models," pp. 31–32; and Waterman and Takata, "Modeling Urban Fire Growth," pp. 176–182; see also the summary of OCD fire research from 1962 to 1975 in Robert G. Hahl, *Research Report No. 24, DCPA Fire Research Bibliography* (DCPA [Defense Civil Preparedness Agency], January 1976).

106. Waterman and Takata, "Modeling Urban Fire Growth," p. 177.

107. Martin, Ramstad, and Colvin, *Interim Fire Behavior Model,* app. C, p. C-25.

108. Ibid., p. 2.

109. Martin, *Role of Fire in Nuclear Warfare,* p. 3-102.

110. Martin, Ramstad, and Colvin, *Interim Fire-Behavior Model,* p. 4-32.

111. Committee on Fire Research, *Directory of Fire Research*, 4th ed., p. 177, referring to A. N. Takata and F. Salzberg, *Development and Application of a Complete Fire-Spread Model,* vol. 1, *Development Phase* (Chicago: IIT Research Institute, June 1968).

112. Bond, interview, October 21, 1989.

113. Martin, *Role of Fire in Nuclear Warfare,* p. 3-98.

114. Martin, Ramstad, and Colvin, *Interim Fire-Behavior Model,* p. 4-59.

115. [Stanley B. Martin], *Five City Study Work Plan, Phases III and IV, Analysis Procedures and Presentation of Results,* URS Project 674, prepared for U.S. Naval Radiological Defense Laboratory, San Francisco (Burlingame, Calif.: URS Corp., July 1967), p. 15.

116. Martin, Ramstad, and Colvin, *Interim Fire-Behavior Model,* p. 5-40.

117. Ibid., pp. 4-60–4-61.

118. Ibid., pp. 4-60–4-65.

119. Martin, *Role of Fire in Nuclear Warfare,* p. 3-100.

120. Harold Brode, e-mail to author, September 28, 2000.

121. Martin, Ramstad, and Colvin, *Interim Fire-Behavior Model,* p. 4-66.

122. Ibid., p. 4-68.

123. Summary of Research, in Dorsett, *8th Annual OCD Fire Research Contractors Meeting,* p. 17.

124. Miller, "Evaluation of Ignition and Fire Spread Models," in Dorsett, *8th Annual OCD Fire Research Contractors Meeting,* p. 31.

125. Martin, Ramstad, and Colvin, *Interim Fire-Behavior Model,* p. 2.

126. Stanley B. Martin and Raymond S. Alger, *Blast/Fire Interactions, Program Formulation,* final report on conference at Asilomar, California, May 21–24, 1978, prepared for DCPA, Washington, D.C. (Menlo Park, Calif.: SRI International, October 1978), p. 2.

127. S. B. Martin, *Code for Early Time Fire Phenomenology, Nuclear Weapon Fire Start Code (NWFS),* draft, prepared for Director, Defense Nuclear Agency (Redwood City, Calif.:

Stan Martin & Associates, August 1987), p. 2-3; Martin and Alger, *Blast/Fire Interactions, Asilomar Conference, April 1981,* app. C, "Fire in an Airblast Environment," pp. C-9, C-11.

128. Stanley B. Martin and John R. Rempel (Redwood City, Calif.: Stan Martin & Associates), "Impact of Structural Damage on Mass Fires," paper given at Conference on Large Scale Fire Phenomenology, held at National Bureau of Standards, Gaithersburg, Md. (September 10–13, 1984), p. 12; Martin, *Code for Early Time Fire Phenomenology* (draft), p. 2-4.

129. S. B. Martin, R. W. Ramstad, T. Goodale, and C. A. Start, *Effects of Air Blast on Urban Fire Response,* final report for OCD, Secretary of the Army (Burlingame, Calif.: URS Research Co., May 1969), pp. 2-3 and 6-1.

130. Thomas E. Waterman and Andrew Longinow, "Blast/Fire and Structural-Response/Fire Interactions," in James W. Kerr, DCPA, ed., *Research Report 21, Technical Summary, 11th Annual DCPA Fire Research Contractors' Meeting, Asilomar, California,* April 8–12, 1973 (DCPA, Department of Defense, August 15, 1973), p. 51; Martin and Alger, *Blast/Fire Interactions, Program Formulation* (1978), p. 12. The study to which these reports refer is T. Goodale, "Effects of Air Blast on Urban Fires," final report (San Mateo, Calif.: URS Research Co., December 1970).

131. Stanley B. Martin, SRI, "Blast Perturbations in Fire-Damage Assessments," in Henry G. Dorsett, DCPA, ed., *Research Report No. 19, Technical Summary, 10th Annual DCPA (formerly OCD) Fire Research Contractors Meeting, Asilomar, California,* April 23–27, 1972 (DCPA, Department of Defense, June 1, 1972), p. 29.

132. Martin and Alger, *Blast/Fire Interactions, Program Formulation* (1978), p. 13; Raymond S. Alger and Stanley B. Martin, eds., *Blast/Fire Interactions, Asilomar Conference, May 1980, Proceedings of the Conference,* prepared for FEMA (Menlo Park, Calif.: SRI International, February 1981), p. 6-16.

133. Waterman and Longinow, "Blast/Fire and Structural-Response/Fire Interactions," p. 51.

134. S. J. Wiersma and S. B. Martin, *Evaluation of the Nuclear Fire Threat to Urban Areas* (Menlo Park, Calif.: SRI, September 1973), pp. 40, 43–44.

135. Martin and Alger, *Blast/Fire Interactions, Asilomar Conference, April 1981,* p. C-17.

136. Alger and Martin, *Blast/Fire Interactions, Asilomar Conference, May 1980,* pp. 6-15–6-17.

137. Martin, Ramstad, and Colvin, *Interim Fire-Behavior Model,* p. 5-38.

138. Martin, interview, September 15, 1998.

139. Stanley B. Martin and Robert G. McKee, Jr., "Enclosure Fire Dynamics in Conditions of High Energy-Deposition Rates," paper presented to 2d Joint ASME-JSME Thermal Engineering Conference, Honolulu, Hawaii, March 1987, p. 2.

140. Martin, interview, September 15, 1998; see also James Kerr, "Civil Preparedness Research," in Kerr, DCPA, ed., *Research Report 22, Technical Summary, DCPA All-Effects Research Contractors Meeting Pacific Grove [Asilomar], California,* April 21–25, 1974 (DCPA, Department of Defense, October 1, 1974), p. 17.

141. Brode, interview, September 7, 1989.

142. Martin and Alger, *Blast/Fire Interactions, Asilomar Conference, April 1981,* p. B-1.

143. Not for attribution, interview with author, Washington, D.C., July 10, 1989; not for attribution, interview with author, Washington, D.C., July 22, 1991.

144. Henry G. Dorsett, OCD, ed., *Research Report No. 18, Technical Summary, 9th Annual OCD Fire Research Contractors Meeting, Asilomar, California,* March 28–April 1, 1971 (OCD, Office of the Secretary of the Army, Department of Defense, May 1, 1971), p. 17.

145. James W. Kerr, DCPA, "Civil Preparedness and Emergency Operations," in Kerr, *11th Annual DCPA Fire Research Contractors's Meeting* (1973), pp. 27, 29.

146. Kerr, *DCPA All-Effects Research Contractors Meeting* (1974), p. 17.

CHAPTER 9. THE PHYSICS AND POLITICS OF MASS FIRE

1. Levitt and March argue similarly when they say that "change in operational routines" can occur "without affecting organizational mythology." Barbara Levitt and James G. March, "Organizational Learning," *Annual Review of Sociology* 14 (1988): 324.

2. Stephen Peter Rosen, "New Ways of War: Understanding Military Innovation," *International Security* 13, no. 1 (1988): 134.

3. Robert C. Toth, "U.S. Scratches Nuclear Targets in Soviet Bloc," *Los Angeles Times,* April 19, 1991; R. Jeffrey Smith, "U.S. Trims List of Targets in Soviet Union," *Washington Post,* July 21, 1991.

4. R. P. Turco, O. B. Toon, T. P. Ackerman, J. B. Pollack, and Carl Sagan, "Nuclear Winter: Global Consequences of Multiple Nuclear Explosions," *Science* 222, no. 4630 (December 22, 1983): 1283–1292.

5. David Alan Rosenberg, "The Origins of Overkill: Nuclear Weapons and American Strategy, 1945–1960," *International Security* 7, no. 4 (1983): 4–5, 50ff.

6. Not for attribution, interview with author, Washington, D.C., October 3, 1991.

7. Maj. Gen. Jerome F. O'Malley, "JSTPS: The Link between Strategy and Execution," *Air University Review* (May-June 1977): 39–46; Rosenberg, "Origins of Overkill," pp. 3–71; David A. Rosenberg, "Reality and Responsibility: Power and Process in the Making of United States Nuclear Strategy, 1945–68," *Journal of Strategic Studies* 9, no. 1 (1986): 35–52; Scott D. Sagan, *Moving Targets: Nuclear Strategy and National Security* (Princeton: Princeton University Press, 1989), pp. 10–57.

8. Harold L. Brode, resume [1999], enclosed in Harold Brode, letter to author, June 10, 1999; Harold Brode, interview with author, Los Angeles, September 7, 1989.

9. Harold L. Brode and Robert Bjork, *Cratering from a Megaton Surface Burst,* RM-2600 (Santa Monica: RAND, June 30, 1961).

10. Brode, resume.

11. Harold Brode, letter to author, September 22, 1998.

12. Eugene Sevin, phone conversation with author, February 4, 2000.

13. Harold Brode, e-mail to author, February 8, 2000.

14. Brode, interview, September 7, 1989; Brode, letter, September 22, 1998.

15. Brode, interview, September 7, 1989.

16. Harold Brode, e-mail to author, March 1, 2001.

17. Brode, interview, September 7, 1989; Brode, letter, September 22, 1998.

18. Harold Brode, e-mail to author, February 14, 2000.

19. Harold Brode, e-mail to author, February 27, 2001.

20. R. D. Small and H. L. Brode, *Physics of Large Urban Fires,* PSR Report 1010, final report prepared for Federal Emergency Management Agency [FEMA] (Santa Monica, Calif.: Pacific-Sierra Research Corp. [PSR], March 1980), pp. iii, 22, 16.

21. Small and Brode, *Physics of Large Urban Fires,* pp. 17, v.

22. Raymond S. Alger and Stanley B. Martin, eds., *Blast/Fire Interactions, 1980 Asilomar Conference, May 1980, Proceedings of the Conference,* prepared for FEMA, Washington, D.C. (Menlo Park, Calif.: SRI International, February 1981), "Report of a Workshop on Fire Spread and Threat," p. VI-49. Small was a member of this workshop; the wording clearly reflects Small and Brode, *Physics of Large Urban Fires,* pp. iiiff.

23. Small and Brode, *Physics of Large Urban Fires,* pp. 22–26, iii.

24. Ibid., pp. 22, iii.

25. Harold L. Brode, *Large-Scale Urban Fires,* PSR Note 348, prepared for the Defense Nuclear Agency [DNA] (Santa Monica, Calif.: PSR, December 1980), p. 3.

26. Brode, letter, September 22, 1998, p. 11. See Donald MacKenzie's excellent, more technical discussion of the computer modeling of such "time-dependent fluid flows" in "Nuclear Weapons Labs and Supercomputing," in MacKenzie, *Knowing Machines: Essays on Technical Change* (Cambridge: MIT Press, 1996), p. 110.

27. Brode, letter, June 10, 1999.

28. Ibid.

29. Brode, letter, June 10, 1999.

30. Brode, e-mail, March 1, 2001.

31. Sevin, phone conversation, February 4, 2000.

32. Not for attribution, phone conversation with author, February 8, 2000.

33. R. D. Small and H. L. Brode, "Fire Program Plan Presentation, March 11–12, 1980," prepared for DNA. Copy of slides in author's possession. Brode and his colleagues finished their major work on the fire environment in a two-volume report for FEMA: D. A. Larson and R. D. Small, *Analysis of the Large Urban Fire Environment,* PSR Report 1210 (Los Angeles: PSR, July and November 1982).

34. Brode, letter, September 22, 1998.

35. Small and Brode, "Fire Program Plan Presentation, March 11–12, 1980," p. 8.

36. Stanley B. Martin and Raymond S. Alger, eds., *Fire and the Related Effects of Nuclear Explosions, 1982 Asilomar Conference,* [25 April–29 April, 1982], *Proceedings of the Conference,* prepared for FEMA (Menlo Park, Calif.: SRI International, November 1982), "DNA Fire Program [Fiscal years 82–86]," p. V-2.

37. Martin and Alger, *Fire and the Related Effects of Nuclear Explosions, 1982 Asilomar Conference,* pp. V-3–V-10.

38. H. L. Brode, "Fire from Nuclear Bursts in Urban Areas," briefing for DNA (April 1982). Copy of slides in author's possession.

39. Brode, "Fire from Nuclear Bursts in Urban Areas"; Harold L. Brode and Richard D. Small, *Fire Damage and Strategic Targeting,* PSR Note 567, sponsored by DNA, Washington, D.C. (Los Angeles: PSR, June 1983), preface.

40. The briefing was Brode, "Fire from Nuclear Bursts in Urban Areas."

41. Brode and Small, *Fire Damage and Strategic Targeting,* pp. 16, 20.

42. Ibid.

43. Harold Brode, enclosure, e-mail to author, May 30, 2001.

44. Brode and Small, *Fire Damage and Strategic Targeting,* pp. 16–21. Brode was a student of very large urban fires: Harold L. Brode, *Large-Scale Urban Fires,* PSR Note 348, prepared for DNA (Santa Monica, Calif.: PSR, December 1980).

45. Brode and Small, *Fire Damage and Strategic Targeting,* pp. 11–12.

46. Brode, "Fire from Nuclear Bursts in Urban Areas." This is for a 50 percent probability of damage. See also Brode and Small, *Fire Damage and Strategic Targeting,* p. 12.

47. Samuel Glasstone and Philip J. Dolan, eds., *The Effects of Nuclear Weapons,* 3d ed. (Washington, D.C.: GPO, 1977), p. 285.

48. Brode and Small, *Fire Damage and Strategic Targeting,* pp. 16–18.

49. Brode, "Fire from Nuclear Bursts in Urban Areas."

50. Brode and Small, *Fire Damage and Strategic Targeting,* p. 20.

51. Brode, "Fire from Nuclear Bursts in Urban Areas."

52. Brode and Small, *Fire Damage and Strategic Targeting*, pp. 32–33.

53. Ibid., pp. 32, 33.

54. Turco et al., "Nuclear Winter," pp. 1283, 1290.

55. The information in this paragraph is drawn from Carl Sagan and Richard Turco's defensive but useful *A Path Where No Man Thought: Nuclear Winter and the End of the Arms Race* (New York: Random House, 1990); esp. pp. 455–467.

56. Paul J. Crutzen and John W. Birks, "After a Nuclear War: Twilight at Noon," *Ambio* 11, nos. 2–3 (1982): 114–125.

57. Deputy Under Secretary of Defense T. K. Jones, fall 1981, quoted in Robert Scheer, *With Enough Shovels: Reagan, Bush, and Nuclear War* (New York: Vintage Books, 1983), p. 18.

58. A good brief overview is Frances FitzGerald, *Way Out There in the Blue: Reagan, Star Wars, and the End of the Cold War* (New York: Simon and Schuster, 2000), pp. 179–181. On policy prescriptions in this period, see Lynn Eden, "Introduction: Contours of the Nuclear Controversy," in Lynn Eden and Steven E. Miller, eds., *Nuclear Arguments: Understanding the Strategic Nuclear Arms and Arms Control Debates* (Ithaca: Cornell University Press, 1989), pp. 1–44.

59. William Poundstone, *Carl Sagan: A Life in the Cosmos* (New York: Henry Holt, 1999), pp. 292–349; Joel Achenbach, *Captured by Aliens: The Search for Life and Truth in a Very Large Universe* (New York: Simon and Schuster, 1999), an insightful portrayal of Sagan.

60. Carl Sagan, "Nuclear War and Climatic Catastrophe: Some Policy Implication," *Foreign Affairs* 62, no. 2 (1983/84): 257–292.

61. Ibid., p. 264.

62. Turco et al., "Nuclear Winter," pp. 1283, 1290; Sagan, "Nuclear War and Climatic Catastrophe," pp. 259, 292. A persuasive scientific critique of the threshold concept is Starley L. Thompson and Stephen H. Schneider, "Nuclear Winter Reappraised," *Foreign Affairs* 64, no. 5 (1986): 981–1005.

63. On "inside" and "outside" games, see James M. Lindsay, *Congress and Nuclear Weapons* (Baltimore: Johns Hopkins University Press, 1991).

64. Harold Brode, e-mail to author, May 18, 2000.

65. Turco et al., "Nuclear Winter," p. 1285; Brode's summary of his findings in Brode, e-mail, May 18, 2000.

66. Brode, e-mail, May 18, 2000.

67. Ibid.; Brode, e-mail, February 27, 2001.

68. Brode, interview, September 7, 1989.

69. Bruce Fellman, "'Nuclear Winter' Comes In from the Cold," *The Scientist*, May 1, 1989.

70. [H. L. Brode], "Fire Program Briefing [to DNA]—January 1984." Copy of slides in author's possession.

71. Brode, interview, September 7, 1989.

72. R. D. Small and B. W. Bush, "Smoke Production from Multiple Nuclear Explosions in Nonurban Areas," *Science* 229, no. 4712 (1985): 465–469; B. W. Bush, M. A. Dore, G. H. Anno, and R. D. Small, *Nuclear Winter Source-Term Studies*, vol. 6, *Smoke Produced by a Nuclear Attack on the United States*, Report 1628 (Los Angeles: PSR, 1988); Richard D. Small, "Atmospheric Smoke Loading from a Nuclear Attack on the United States," *Ambio* 18, no. 7 (1989): 377–383.

73. For example, L. M. Ransohoff et al., *Topics in Nuclear Winter Source-Term Research*, vol. 1. *Composition of Residential Structures in the United States*, Report 1761 (Los Angeles: PSR, 1987); G. H. Anno et al., *Nuclear Winter Source-Term Studies*, vol. 4, *Fuel Loads in U.S. Cities*, Report 1628 (Los Angeles: PSR, 1987).

74. Harold L. Brode, "Commercial and Residential Fires from Nuclear Attack," draft, 4 October 1985, PSR Note 664 (Los Angeles: PSR), summary (p. i), table 7 (p. 19), p. 42.

75. Brode, "Commercial and Residential Fires," table 22 (p. 38). I have given the distances in statute miles, not nautical miles as given in the table.

76. Ibid., summary (p. i).

77. Brode, interview, September 7, 1989.

78. H. L. Brode et al., *Fire Damage to Urban/Industrial Targets,* vol. 2, *Technical Report,* PSR Report 1936, prepared for Headquarters, DNA (Los Angeles: PSR, 25 July 1989, Unclassified Pages Only), p. iii.

79. Harold Brode, phone conversation with author, August 11, 1989.

80. H. L. Brode et al., *Fire Damage to Urban/Industrial Targets,* vol. 1, *Executive Summary,* PSR Report 1936, prepared for Headquarters, DNA (Los Angeles: PSR, 25 July 1989, Unclassified), p. 1.

81. Brode, e-mail, February 14, 2000.

82. Eugene Sevin, e-mail to author, February 16, 2000.

83. Brode, e-mail, February 27, 2001.

84. Brode et al., *Fire Damage to Urban/Industrial Targets,* vol. 1, p. 1.

85. Harold L. Brode, *Fire Targeting Methodology, Improvements and Automation, Technical Report,* DNA-TR-94-101 (Alexandria, Va.: Defense Special Weapons Agency, April 1998), p. iii.

86. Brode et al., *Fire Damage to Urban/Industrial Targets,* vol. 1; Brode et al., *Fire Damage to Urban/Industrial Targets,* vol. 2.

87. Not for attribution, interview with author, Alexandria, Va., November 8, 1993.

88. Brode et al., *Fire Damage to Urban/Industrial Targets,* vol. 1, p. 3; Brode et al., *Fire Damage to Urban/Industrial Targets,* vol. 2, pp. 151–153.

89. Brode et al., *Fire Damage to Urban/Industrial Targets,* vol. 1, p. 4.

90. Brode, interview, September 7, 1989.

91. Harold Brode, phone conversation with Ted Postol and author, February 1, 1991; Brode et al., *Fire Damage to Urban/Industrial Targets,* vol. 1, pp. 4–12.

92. Brode et al., *Fire Damage to Urban/Industrial Targets,* vol. 1, p. 4.

93. Ibid., pp. 4–12.

94. Ibid., p. 7.

95. Gilbert Binninger, Roger Craver, and Suzanne Wright, *Staff Officers' Guide for Targeting Uncertainties,* DNA-TR-89-115, prepared for Director, DNA, Washington, D.C. (n.p., January 1990), p. ix. This 123-page document by analysts at Science Applications International Corporation (SAIC) is an exceptionally clear discussion of the VNTK system.

96. Brode et al., *Fire Damage to Urban/Industrial Targets,* vol. 1, p. 8; Brode et al., *Fire Damage to Urban/Industrial Targets,* vol. 2, p. 46.

97. Brode et al., *Fire Damage to Urban/Industrial Targets,* vols. 1 and 2, does not provide figures for specific yield and burst height. In this and the following paragraph, Alex Montgomery and I have used Ted Postol's formulas relating VN, yield, height of burst, range, psi, and thermal fluence to translate Brode's fire-blast VNs into overpressure and thermal fluence at various ranges for a 300-kiloton weapon burst at 1,500 ft.

98. Brode et al., *Fire Damage to Urban/Industrial Targets,* vol. 1, pp. 7–12.

99. Randy Rohr, DNA, briefing, "Fire Damage Methodology, presented to the JSTPS," January 1989. Copy of slides in author's possession.

100. Not for attribution, phone conversation with author, October 29, 1993.

101. Not for attribution, interview, November 8, 1993.

102. Ibid.

103. Marvin C. Atkins, Deputy Director, DNA, to Rear Admiral R. M. Eytchison, USN, Vice Director JSTPS, letter enclosing "an Executive Summary describing a *Fire Targeting Methodology*," 30 March 1989. Document in author's possession.

104. Among other sources, Brode, *Fire Targeting Methodology, Improvements and Automation*, p. 2.

105. Not for attribution, phone conversation, October 29, 1993.

106. Brode, *Fire Targeting Methodology, Improvements and Automation*, p. 71.

107. Ibid., p. 72; see also p. 1.

108. Not for attribution, phone conversation with author, October 28, 1993; not for attribution, phone conversation, October 29, 1993; not for attribution, phone conversation with author, April 16, 1992.

109. Not for attribution, interview, November 8, 1993; not for attribution, phone conversation with author, September 25, 1991; not for attribution, interview with author, October 3, 1991; not for attribution, phone conversation, October 29, 1993.

110. Not for attribution, phone conversation, October 29, 1993.

111. Not for attribution, interview, November 8, 1993.

112. Brode, phone conversation, February 1, 1991; Brode, letter, September 22, 1998.

113. Binninger, Craver, Wright, *Staff Officers' Guide for Targeting Uncertainties*, p. vii.

114. Not for attribution, interview, November 8, 1993.

115. Ibid.; Brode, *Fire Targeting Methodology, Improvements and Automation*, p. 71.

116. Not for attribution, phone conversation, October 29, 1993.

117. Not for attribution, interview, November 8, 1993.

118. See www.dtic.mil.jcs/ and search for operations deputies.

119. Brode, phone conversation, February 1, 1991.

120. Not for attribution, interview, November 8, 1993.

CHAPTER 10. ENCORE AND AFTER

1. The epigraph is from the pilot of a video produced for Lawrence Livermore National Laboratory (Stanford Research Institute International, September 1982).

2. Not for attribution, interview with author.

3. Stanley B. Martin and Raymond S. Alger, *Blast/Fire Interactions, Program Formulation*, final report on conference at Asilomar, California, May 21–24, 1978, prepared for Defense Civil Preparedness Agency, Washington, D.C. (Menlo Park, Calif.: SRI International, October 1978), pp. 21–22.

4. Not for attribution, phone conversation with author, July 3, 1990; not for attribution, interview with author, Washington, D.C., July 27, 1991.

5. Not for attribution, interview with author.

6. Martin and Alger, *Blast/Fire Interactions, Program Formulation* (1978), pp. iv, 1.

7. Ibid., p. v. A more detailed discussion of these models is in Stanley B. Martin and Raymond S. Alger, eds., *Blast/Fire Interactions, Asilomar Conference, April 1981, Proceedings*, prepared for Federal Emergency Management Agency (Menlo Park, Calif.: SRI International, August 1981), app. B, "Models for Damage and Vulnerability Assessment," p. B-1.

8. Martin and Alger, *Blast/Fire Interactions, Program Formulation* (1978), p. v.

9. Stanley Martin, interview with author, Redwood City, Calif., September 15, 1998.

10. Stanley Martin, interview with author, Redwood City, Calif., June 29, 1998.

11. H. D. Bruce, U.S. Dept. of Agriculture, Forest Service, Forest Products Laboratory (Madison, Wisc.), *Operation UPSHOT–KNOTHOLE, March–June 1953, Project 8.11a, Incendiary Effects on Building and Interior Kindling Fuels,* report to the Test Director, WT-774 (Sandia Base, Albuquerque, N.Mex.: Headquarters Field Command, AFSWP, December 1953), p. 22.

12. J. Backovsky, *Early Time Fire Phenomenology,* vol. 2, *ENCORE Phenomenon,* DNA-TR-85-146-V2, prepared for Director, Defense Nuclear Agency [DNA] (Menlo Park, Calif.: SRI International, 14 June 1985), p. iv; Martin, interview, June 29, 1998.

13. Martin, interview, June 29, 1998; Martin, interview, September 15, 1998; Los Alamos Technical Associates, Inc., "Unclassified Review of ENCORE Project 8.11a Data" (June 1983), app. to Backovsky, *ENCORE Phenomenon,* p. 36.

14. Martin and Alger, *Blast/Fire Interactions, Asilomar Conference, April 1981,* p. C-9.

15. Stanley B. Martin and Robert G. McKee, Jr., "Enclosure Fire Dynamics in Conditions of High Energy-Deposition Rates," paper presented to 2d Joint ASME-JSME Thermal Engineering Conference, Honolulu, Hawaii, March 1987, p. 2.

16. Backovsky, *ENCORE Phenomenon,* abstract and pp. 11–14; Martin, interview, June 29, 1998; Martin and McKee, Jr., "Enclosure Fire Dynamics," pp. 5–6.

17. Jana Backovsky, phone conversation with author, August 3, 2000.

18. Backovsky, *ENCORE Phenomenon,* p. iv.

19. Ibid., abstract, p. ii.

20. Backovsky, phone conversation, August 3, 2000.

21. Backovsky, *ENCORE Phenomenon,* p. 18; see also p. 22.

22. Ibid., p. 2.

23. Stanley B. Martin and John R. Rempel, "Impact of Structural Damage on Mass Fires" (Redwood City, Calif.: Stan Martin & Associates), paper given at Conference on Large Scale Fire Phenomenology, held at National Bureau of Standards, Gaithersburg, Md., September 10–13, 1984, p. 12.

24. Martin and McKee, "Enclosure Fire Dynamics," pp. 2, 1.

25. R. H. Craver, S. B. Martin, D. P. Bacon, G. R. Doenges, and W. G. Samuels, Science Applications International Corporation [SAIC] and Stan Martin & Associates, *Nuclear Weapon Induced Urban Fires and Smoke Injection,* technical report, prepared for Director, Defense Supply Service [sponsored by Strategic Forces Policy Office and Office of Net Assessment, Department of Defense] (Bellevue, Nebr.: SAIC, 31 July 1987), p. 75. A copy of this report is in the author's possession.

26. Ibid., p. 1.

27. Franklin C. Miller, then deputy assistant secretary of defense for nuclear forces and arms control policy, headed the Strategic Forces Policy Office. In the mid-1980s Miller became immersed in and deeply knowledgeable about nuclear war planning; see Janne E. Nolan's excellent *Guardians of the Arsenal: The Politics of Nuclear Strategy* (New York: Basic Books, 1989), pp. 248–256.

28. Craver et al., *Nuclear Weapon Induced Urban Fires,* p. 3.

29. In scaled feet, the height of burst (HOB) above the White House and Andrews Air Force Base was 300; calculated for a yield of 500 kilotons, the HOB was 2,381 feet. Craver et al., *Nuclear Weapon Induced Urban Fires,* p. 105.

30. Ibid., p. xii.

31. Not for attribution, interview with author, Washington, D.C., July 22, 1991.

32. Craver et al., *Nuclear Weapon Induced Urban Fires,* p. 75.

33. Ibid., pp. 21–22. The model from the mid-1960s referred to is S. Martin, R. Ramstad, and C. Colvin, *Development and Application of an Interim Fire Behavior Model,* final report

for Office of Civil Defense, Office of the Secretary of the Army through U.S. Naval Radiological Defense Laboratory (Burlingame, Calif.: URS Research Co., April 1968); see chapter 8 for discussion. This model was transformed into what became known as the SRI Blastfire Code, or the URS/SRI Blastfire Code (p. 21).

34. Craver et al., *Nuclear Weapon Induced Urban Fires*, pp. 75–76.

35. Ibid., fig. 13, Power Density (GW/Sq Mi), p. 64, and discussion, p. 68.

36. Ibid., fig. 14, Power Density (GW/Sq Mi), p. 65.

37. Ibid., pp. xviii; see also p. 68.

38. Stanley B. Martin, *The Role of Fire in Nuclear Warfare* (San Mateo, Calif.: URS Research Co., 23 August 1974), p. 3-100, citing T. E. Lommasson, and J. A. Keller, *Fire Mortality Model* [report for OCD] (Albuquerque, N.Mex.: Dikewood Corp., December 1966). The Lommasson and Keller study used a criterion of 500 million Btu per square mile per second, or 500×10^6 Btu/mi^2/sec for a firestorm, which is approximately 200 kW/m^2. They calculated that the firestorm at Hiroshima had a power density of only a tenth that figure. I am grateful to Alex Montgomery for help with calculations.

39. H. L. Brode and R. D. Small, "A Review of the Physics of Large Urban Fires," in Fredric Solomon and Robert Q. Marston, eds., *The Medical Implications of Nuclear War* (Washington, D.C.: National Academy Press, 1986), p. 91.

40. Craver et al., *Nuclear Weapon Induced Urban Fires*, pp. xvii–xviii.

41. The authors used three kinds of measures to predict fire damage: *power density* (i.e., rates of heat release measured in kilowatts per square meter, or gigawatts per square mile), *fire density* measured in fires per square mile, and *percentage of buildings burned out*; power density was the measure used to discern mass fire. Craver et al., *Nuclear Weapon Induced Urban Fires*, pp. xiv, xvii.

42. Ibid., fig. 11, p. 62. Three miles from the White House corresponded to peak overpressure of 4 psi (app. D, p. 105).

43. Ibid., p. 75.

44. Letter, Gary P. Betourne, Strategic Forces Policy, Office of the Assistant Secretary of Defense for International Security Policy, U.S. Department of Defense, to Mr. Roger H. Craver, SAIC, 24 February 1988, in possession of author.

45. Briefing slides, apparently dated August 1987, informally appended to Craver et al., *Nuclear Weapon Induced Urban Fires*, in author's possession.

46. Stanley B. Martin, *Code for Early Time Fire Phenomenology, Nuclear Weapon Fire Start Code*, draft, prepared for Director, DNA (Redwood City, Calif.: Stan Martin & Associates, August 1987), p. i. The established model was Martin, Ramstad, and Colvin, *Interim Fire Behavior Model* (1968). The recent secondary fire start model was J. Backovsky, R. S. Alger, and S. B. Martin, *Early Time Fire Phenomenology*, vol. 1, *Secondary Fires*, DNA-TR-85-146-V1, prepared for Director, DNA (Menlo Park, Calif.: SRI International, 1985).

47. Stanley B. Martin, Roger H. Craver, Thomas C. Goodale, Thomas Y. Palmer, and James V. Zaccor, *Model Development for Nuclear Weapon Induced Large Urban Fires (NWFIRES)*, technical report, prepared for Director, DNA (Redwood City, Calif.: Stan Martin & Associates, March 1990), p. 8.

48. Martin et al., *NWFIRES* (1990), p. 22.

49. Martin, *Nuclear Weapon Fire Start Code*, p. i.

50. Ibid., p. 4-5; see also app. B, pp. B-1–B-9.

51. Ibid., p. 5-3.

52. Martin et al., *NWFIRES* (1990), pp. 32–33.

53. Stanley B. Martin, Roger H. Craver, Thomas C. Goodale, Thomas Y. Palmer, and

James V. Zaccor, Stan Martin & Associates, *Model Development for Nuclear Weapon Induced Large Urban Fires (NWFIRES)*, technical report (Alexandria, Va.: DNA, May 1991), abstract on report documentation page.

54. Martin et al., *NWFIRES* (1990), p. 22: "The Defense Mapping Agency's Digital Feature Analysis Data (DFAD) component of the Digital Landmass System (DLMS) is an unclassified, worldwide-coverage source of map-feature data in digital form, derived from satelite [*sic*] imagery."

55. Martin et al., *NWFIRES* (1991), preface (p. viii).

56. Stan Martin's associates included some who been active in fire research since the early 1950s: Craig Chandler, Clive Countryman, Tom Goodale, Lew Miller, Tom Palmer, and Art Takata. Stan Martin & Associates also subcontracted to consultants Bud Willoughby and Jim Zaccor, at Scientific Services, Inc., and Roger Craver and Bob Doenges, at Science Applications International Corporation. Willoughby and Zaccor had also long been active in the fire research community. See Martin et al., *NWFIRES* (1991), preface (p. viii).

57. Martin et al., *NWFIRES* (1991), p. iv.

58. Martin et al., *NWFIRES* (1990), pp. 33ff.

59. Ibid., p. 32, and "Appendix C, Letter Report from Clive Countryman" to Stan Martin, August 5, 1988, commenting on a memo from Tom Goodale, p. C-9.

60. Ibid., p. 30.

61. Ibid., pp. 13–14.

62. Martin et al., *NWFIRES* (1991), abstract.

63. Martin et al., *NWFIRES* (1990), p. 26.

64. Ibid., p. 20.

65. Ibid., p. 21.

66. Ibid., p. 66.

67. Arthur N. Takata, Stan Martin and Associates, *Mechanistic Urban Fire-Spread Code (FISAT)*, technical report, DNA-TR-90-85 (Alexandria, Va.: DNA, May 1991), p. 13.

68. Martin et al., *NWFIRES* (1991), executive summary.

69. Martin et al., *NWFIRES* (1990), pp. 66–67.

70. Martin et al., *NWFIRES* (1991), pp. vi–vii.

71. Not for attribution, interview with author, Washington, D.C., October 3, 1991.

72. Not for attribution, interview with author, Washington, D.C., September 25, 1990.

73. Not for attribution, interview, July 22, 1991.

74. Not for attribution, interview, October 3, 1991.

75. Not for attribution, interview with author, Washington, D.C., July 24, 1991; Maj. Gen. Frank (Barry) Horton III (USAF), interview with author, Stanford, Calif., December 20, 1991; not for attribution, interview with author, Alexandria, Va., November 8, 1993.

76. Vice Adm. Michael Colley, interview with author, Washington, D.C., November 8, 1993.

77. Not for attribution, phone conversation with author, April 16, 1992.

78. Ibid.

79. Vice Adm. Michael Colley, letter to author, July 8, 1994.

80. This, and other memos, were described in not for attribution, phone conversation with author, November 12, 1993.

81. Colley, interview, November 8, 1993.

82. Not for attribution, phone conversation, November 12, 1993. My interlocutor slowly read the unclassified memo and I took verbatim notes.

83. Not for attribution, phone conversation, November 12, 1993.

84. Unclassified memo by Vice Director of the Joint Staff, Maj. Gen. Rudolph Ostovich III, 11 February 1992, in possession of author.

85. Colley, interview, November 8, 1993.

86. Gen. Lee Butler, conversation with author, Stanford, Calif., October 29, 1998.

87. Unless otherwise noted, quotations are from Colley, interview, November 8, 1993.

88. Gen. Lee Butler, conversation with author, Stanford, Calif., December 3, 1990; R. Jeffrey Smith, "The Dissenter," *Washington Post,* December 7, 1997.

89. R. Jeffrey Smith, "U.S. Trims List of Targets in Soviet Union," *Washington Post,* July 21, 1991.

90. The term is from Colley, interview, November 8, 1993.

91. Ann Devroy and R. Jeffrey Smith, "President Orders Sweeping Reductions in Strategic and Tactical Nuclear Arms," *Washington Post,* September 28, 1991.

92. Maj. Gen. Frank (Barry) Horton III (USAF), interview with author, Bellevue, Nebr., March 26 1992; Maj. Gen. Robert Linhard (USAF), phone conversation with author, November 24, 1992; Smith, "The Dissenter," *Washington Post,* December 7, 1997; not for attribution, interview with author, on flight from Offutt Air Force Base, Nebr. to Palmdale, Calif., March 26, 1992; also Smith, "The Dissenter," *Washington Post,* December 7, 1997.

93. Maj. Gen. Robert Linhard (USAF), phone conversation with author, November 27, 1992.

94. Colley, interview, November 8, 1993.

95. Smith, "The Dissenter," *Washington Post,* December 7, 1997.

96. Colley, interview, November 8, 1993.

97. Colley, letter, July 8, 1994.

98. Colley, telephone conversation with author, June 27, 1994.

99. In other words, Have you fulfilled your organizational target for damage to targets? Levitt and March write "organizations are oriented to targets. . . . Their behavior depends on the relation between the outcomes they observe and the aspirations they have for those outcomes. Sharper distinctions are made between success and failure than among gradations of either." Barbara Levitt and James G. March, "Organizational Learning," *Annual Review of Sociology* 14 (1988): 320.

100. Colley, interview, November 8, 1993.

101. Ibid.

102. Colley, letter, July 8, 1994.

103. Vice Adm. Michael Colley, phone conversation with author, August 16, 1994.

104. Colley, interview, November 8, 1993.

105. For example, there was a flap over a measure Brode devised, a negative K factor; it took some time for him to convince analysts that the measure was kosher. Not for attribution, interview with author, Alexandria, Va., September 27, 1990; not for attribution, interview, July 22, 1991.

106. Not for attribution, interview with author, Bellevue, Nebr., October 21, 1993.

107. Linhard, phone conversation, November 27, 1992.

108. Harold L. Brode, *Fire Targeting Methodology, Improvements and Automation, Technical Report,* DNA-TR-94-101 (Alexandria, Va.: Defense Special Weapons Agency, April 1998), p. i.

109. Harold Brode, letter to author, September 22, 1998.

110. Not for attribution, interview, Bellevue, Nebr., October 21, 1993; [a second] not for attribution, interview with author, Bellevue, Nebr., October 21, 1993.

111. Not for attribution, interview with author, March 12, 1999, New York; not for at-

tribution, interview with author, Stanford, Calif., October 28, 1999; biographical information on Hardebeck at www.stratcom.af.mil/bios; not for attribution, interview, October 21, 1993.

112. Not for attribution, interview, October 28, 1999; not for attribution, phone conversation with author, January 4, 2000; not for attribution, phone conversation with author, February 8, 2000.

113. Not for attribution, interview, October 28, 1999.

114. Ibid.

115. Not for attribution, phone conversation, January 4, 2000; not for attribution, phone conversation, February 8, 2000.

116. See John Baylis, "Exchanging Nuclear Secrets: Laying the Foundations of the Anglo-American Nuclear Relationship," *Diplomatic History* 25, no. 1 (2001): 33–61.

117. Baylis "Exchanging Nuclear Secrets," pp. 33, 54; Lorna Arnold with Katherine Pyne, *Britain and the H-Bomb* (Houndmills, U.K.: Palgrave, 2001), p. 215.

118. Arnold with Pyne, *Britain and the H-Bomb,* p. 215.

119. Not for attribution, phone conversation, February 8, 2000.

120. Not for attribution, interview with author, Washington, D.C., September 25, 1990.

121. Not for attribution, phone conversation with author, December 28, 1999.

122. Not for attribution, phone conversation, January 4, 2000.

123. Not for attribution, phone conversation with author, August 26, 1998; Brode, *Fire Targeting Methodology,* enclosed floppy disk, "Readme" file.

124. Gilbert Binninger, phone conversation with author, January 4, 2000.

125. Brode, *Fire Targeting Methodology.*

126. Not for attribution, phone conversation, August 26, 1998; not for attribution, interview, October 28, 1999.

127. Not for attribution, phone conversation, February 8, 2000; not for attribution, phone conversation, January 4, 2000.

128. Not for attribution, phone conversation, December 28, 1999.

129. Not for attribution, phone conversation, January 4, 2000.

130. Unclassified electronic job posting at Strategic Command, 10/26/2000; job "duration not specified."

131. Not for attribution, phone conversation with author, March 12, 2003.

CONCLUSION

1. Richard Grassy, quoted in chapter 4.

2. Lee Clarke, *Mission Improbable* (Chicago: University of Chicago Press, 1999), p. 12.

3. On self-fulfilling prophecy, technology, and organizations, see Donald MacKenzie, *Inventing Accuracy* (Cambridge: MIT Press, 1990), pp. 387–391.

4. On lock-in, see W. Brian Arthur, *Increasing Returns and Path Dependence in the Economy* (Ann Arbor: University of Michigan Press, 1994), pp. 13–32; on QWERTY, see Paul A. David, "Clio and the Economics of QWERTY," *American Economic Review* 75, no. 2 (1985): 332–337; on VHS and Betamax, see Arthur, *Increasing Returns and Path Dependence,* pp. 2, 25; Diane Vaughan, *The Challenger Launch Decision* (Chicago: University of Chicago Press, 1996), p. 399. See also the devastating treatment of David's historical claims in S. J. Liebowitz and Stephen E. Margolis, "The Fable of the Keys," *Journal of Law and Economics* 33 (April 1990): 1–25; they also throw into doubt the understanding of the VHS/Beta account: S. J. Liebowitz and Stephen E. Margolis, "Path Dependence, Lock-In, and History," *Journal of Law, Economics, and Organization* 1, no. 1 (1995): 205–226. Scott D. Sagan questions the in-

evitability of the *Challenger* launch decision in his review of Vaughan's book in *Administrative Science Quarterly* 42, no. 2 (1997): 404–405.

5. I draw on Wiebe E. Bijker's discussion of innovation across multiple frames in the invention of Bakelite (*Of Bicycles, Bakelites, and Bulbs* [Cambridge: MIT Press, 1995]).

6. Arthur, *Increasing Returns and Path Dependence*, pp. 8, 107.

7. Jack A. Goldstone, "Initial Conditions, General Laws, Path Dependence, and Explanation in Historical Sociology," *American Journal of Sociology* 104, no. 3 (1998): 834; see also James Mahoney, "Path Dependence in Historical Sociology," *Theory and Society* 29, no. 4 (2000): 507–508.

8. William H. Sewell, Jr., "Three Temporalities: Toward an Eventful Sociology," in Terrence J. McDonald, ed., *The Historic Turn in the Human Sciences* (Ann Arbor: University of Michigan Press, 1996), pp. 262–263; a thoughtful critique is Paul Pierson, "Increasing Returns, Path Dependence, and the Study of Politics," *American Political Science Review* 94, no. 2 (2000): 252.

9. Mahoney, "Path Dependence in Historical Sociology," pp. 507, 511.

10. Kathleen Thelen, "Historical Institutionalism in Comparative Politics," *Annual Review of Political Science* 2 (1999): 385.

11. Pierson, "Increasing Returns, Path Dependence, and the Study of Politics," p. 265.

12. Not for attribution, interview with author, Bellevue, Nebr., October 21, 1993.

13. Richard Grassy, interview with author, Lac du Flambeau, Wisc., May 21, 1995.

14. I have drawn some of this from Elaine Scarry, *The Body in Pain: The Making and Unmaking of the World* (New York: Oxford University Press, 1985), pp. 64–70; I am grateful to Suzana Sawyer for her ideas on the social construction of the environment and to Tarak Barkawi for the turn of phrase.

15. Hans Morgenthau, "The Fallacy of Thinking Conventionally about Nuclear Weapons," in David Carlton and Carlo Schaerf, eds., *Arms Control and Technological Innovation* (New York: Wiley, 1976), pp. 256–264; discussed and elaborated in Robert Jervis, *The Illogic of American Nuclear Strategy* (Ithaca: Cornell University Press, 1984), pp. 56–57; see also Steven Kull, *Minds at War: Nuclear Reality and the Inner Conflicts of Defense Policymakers* (New York: Basic Books, 1988), pp. 23–27.

16. Judith Cummings, "Questions and Answers about the Grumman Buses," *New York Times*, December 17, 1980, and other citations in introduction.

17. On corporate wrong-doing, see Robert Jackall, *Moral Mazes: The World of Corporate Managers* (New York: Oxford University Press, 1988); Diane Vaughan, "The Dark Side of Organizations: Mistake, Misconduct, and Disaster," *Annual Review of Sociology* 25 (1999): 271–305; and the discussion of power, interest, and production pressures in Charles Perrow, *Normal Accidents: Living with High-Risk Technologies*, with a new afterword (Princeton: Princeton University Press, 1999). The editorial is quoted in Suzanne Daley, "Mad Cow Disease Panicking Europe as Incidents Rise," *New York Times*, December 1, 2000.

18. Office of Human Research Protections (OHRP), U.S. Department of Health and Human Services, letter to Johns Hopkins University School of Medicine suspending all of the school's human subjects research, July 19, 2001; I thank Roz Leiser for a copy of this widely circulated e-mail message; see also James Glanz, "Clues of Asthma Study Risks May Have Been Overlooked," *New York Times*, July 27, 2001.

19. Barry T. Hill, General Accounting Office, Testimony before the Subcommittee on Forest and Forest Health, Committee on Resources, House of Representatives, "Fire Management: Lessons Learned from the Cerro Grande (Los Alamos) Fire and Actions Needed to Reduce Fire Risks," released August 14, 2000, GAO/T-RCED-00-273, pp. 1, 34. This and the

other two reports cited below on the fire are available at www.fire.nps.gov/fireinfo/cerrogrande/reports/.

20. Report by a panel of the National Academy of Public Administration for the U.S. Department of Interior, *Study of the Implementation of the Federal Wildland Fire Policy,* Phase I Report: *Perspectives on Cerro Grande and Recommended Issues for Further Study* (n.p., December 2000), pp. 14–15.

21. [National Park Service] Board of Inquiry, Final Report, *Cerro Grande Prescribed Fire* (n.p., National Park Service, February 26, 2001), p. i.

22. Board of Inquiry, *Cerro Grande Prescribed Fire,* p. 33; Hill, "Fire Management," p. 11.

23. Hill, "Fire Management," p. 5.

24. Board of Inquiry, *Cerro Grande Prescribed Fire,* pp. 14–22; Hill, "Fire Management," pp. 4, 6.

25. Vaughan, *Challenger Launch Decision,* pp. 119–195; Diane Vaughan, quoted in John Schwartz with Matthew L. Wald, "Echoes of *Challenger,*" *New York Times,* April 13, 2003. See *Columbia Accident Investigation Board Report,* vol. 1 (Washington, D.C.: NASA/GPO, August 2003), www.caib.us/news/report/default.html.

26. On the Precautionary Principle, see "[European] Commission adopts Communication on Precautionary Principle," February 2, 2000, http://europa.eu.int/.

27. The definitive account is Irvine Loudon, *The Tragedy of Childbed Fever* (Oxford: Oxford University Press, 2000); quote on p. 15. I thank Ron Hassner for telling me about this case.

28. Loudon, *Tragedy,* p. 22.

29. Ibid., pp. 18–19, 21, 79–82.

30. Ibid., p. 89.

31. Ibid., pp. 95, 130 ff.

32. This paragraph is drawn from *James Cameron's "Titanic" Explorer* (Fox Interactive CD-ROM, 1997); and Katherine Felkins, H. P. Leighly, Jr., and A. Jankovic, "The Royal Mail Ship *Titanic:* Did a Metallurgical Failure Cause a Night to Remember?" *JOM* [formerly *Journal of Metals*] 50, no. 1 (1998): 12–18, available at www.tms.org/pubs/journals/JOM. I am grateful to my niece, Alia Karter, for lending me her copy of the Cameron CD.

33. Felkins, Leighly, and Jankovic, "The Royal Mail Ship *Titanic.*"

34. Matthys Levy and Mario Salvadori, *Why Buildings Fall Down: How Structures Fail* (New York: Norton, 1992), pp. 109–119; Henry Petroski, *Design Paradigms: Case Histories of Error and Judgment in Engineering* (Cambridge: Cambridge University Press, 1994), pp. 144–165; Henry Petroski, *Engineers of Dreams: Great Bridge Builders and the Spanning of America* (New York: Vintage, 1995), pp. 294–308.

35. Petroski, *Design Paradigms,* pp. 151, 155.

36. The algorithm, based on "deflection theory," is explained in Petroski, *Design Paradigms,* pp. 158–159; and Petroski, *Engineers of Dreams,* pp. 293, 298–303. The lift and drag on the Tacoma Narrows Bridge is most clearly explained in Levy and Salvadori, *Why Buildings Fall Down,* pp. 118–119.

37. Petroski, *Engineers of Dreams,* p. 302, and quoting Glenn Woodruff, an associate of Moisseiff's, p. 305.

38. The account in this and the following paragraphs is drawn from Joe Morgenstern's "The Fifty-Nine-Story Crisis," *New Yorker,* May 29, 1995, pp. 45–53.

39. Robert Campbell, in an article that won a Pulitzer Prize, "Builder Faced Bigger Crisis Than Falling Windows," *Boston Globe,* March 3, 1995; see also Levy and Salvadori, *Why Buildings Fall Down,* pp. 197–205.

40. Rice, quoted in David Johnson and James Risen, "Traces of Terrorism: The Intelligence Reports; Series of Warnings," *New York Times,* May 17, 2002.

41. Abolhassan Astaneh-Asl, interviewed by Terry Gross, *Fresh Air,* National Public Radio, October 16, 2001 (transcript available at www.npr.org).

42. Ibid.

43. Robertson quoted in John Seabrook, "The Tower Builder," *New Yorker,* November 19, 2001, p. 68.

44. Frederick Lighthall, "Launching the Space Shuttle *Challenger:* Disciplinary Deficiencies in the Analysis of Engineering Data," *IEEE Transactions on Engineering Management* 39 (February 1991): 63–74; Edward R. Tufte, *Visual Explanations: Images and Quantities, Evidence and Narrative* (Cheshire, Conn.: Graphics Press, 1997), pp. 38–53.

45. On learning from failure, see Petroski, *Design Paradigms;* on learning from near failure, see James G. March, Lee S. Sproull, and Michal Tamuz, "Learning from Samples of One or Fewer," *Organization Science* 2 (1991): 1–13.

46. Vaughan, *Challenger Launch Decision,* pp. 119–195.

47. Stephen Engelberg and Adam Bryant, "Warnings Unheeded—A Special Report: F.A.A.'s Fatal Fumbles on Commuter Plane's Safety," *New York Times,* February 26, 1995; Peter T. Kilborn, "Ambitious Effort to Cut Mistakes in U.S. Hospitals," *New York Times,* December 26, 1999.

48. See Vaughan, *Challenger Launch Decision,* p. 39. On the demonstration itself, see Tufte, *Visual Explanations,* pp. 50–53.

49. Faina A. Abramova et al., *Proceedings of the National Academy of Sciences, USA* 90 (March 1993): 2291–2294; Matthew Meselson et al., "The Sverdlovsk Anthrax Outbreak of 1979," *Science* 266, no. 5188 (1994): 1202–1208; also Jeanne Guillemin, *Anthrax: The Investigation of a Deadly Outbreak* (Berkeley: University of California Press, 1999).

50. R. Jeffrey Smith, "U.S. Trims List of Targets in Soviet Union," *Washington Post,* July 21, 1991; R. Jeffrey Smith, "Retired Nuclear Warrior Sounds Alarm on Weapons: Ex-SAC Commander Calls Policy 'Irrational,'" *Washington Post,* December 4, 1996; R. Jeffrey Smith, "The Dissenter," *Washington Post,* December 7, 1997; H. L. Brode and R. D. Small, "A Review of the Physics of Large Urban Fires," in Fredric Solomon and Robert Q. Marston, eds., *The Medical Implications of Nuclear War* (Washington, D.C.: National Academy Press, 1986); Theodore A. Postol, "Possible Fatalities from Superfires following Nuclear Attacks in or near Urban Areas," in Solomon and Marston, *Medical Implications of Nuclear War;* William Daugherty, Barbara Levi, and Frank von Hippel, "The Consequences of 'Limited' Nuclear Attacks on the United States," *International Security* 10, no. 4 (1986): 3–45; also, Barbara G. Levi, Frank N. von Hippel, and William H. Daugherty, "Civilian Casualties from 'Limited' Nuclear Attacks on the USSR," *International Security* 12, no. 3 (1987–88): 168–189; Lachlan Forrow et al., "Accidental Nuclear War—A Post–Cold War Assessment," *New England Journal of Medicine* 338, no. 18 (1998): 1326–1331; on fire and other neglected effects see Stansfield Turner, *Caging the Nuclear Genie: An American Challenge for Global Security* (Boulder, Colo.: Westview, 1997), pp. 29–33, 127–133.

51. On secrecy and nuclear weapons, see Hugh Gusterson, *Nuclear Rites: A Weapons Laboratory at the End of the Cold War* (Berkeley: University of California Press, 1996), pp. 68–100; on the implications of government secrecy for democracy, see Daniel Ellsberg, *Secrets: A Memoir of Vietnam and the Pentagon Papers* (New York: Viking, 2002); on the usefulness to technologists of maintaining separate "technical" and "political" spheres, see MacKenzie, *Inventing Accuracy,* pp. 409–417.

52. Levy and Salvadori, *Why Buildings Fall Down,* p. 205.

53. "Excerpts from Senate Judiciary Committee's Counterterrorism Hearing," *New York Times,* June 7, 2002.

Index

357